GOD ISN'T HERE

GOD ISN'T HERE

A YOUNG AMERICAN'S ENTRY INTO WORLD WAR II AND
HIS PARTICIPATION IN THE BATTLE FOR IWO JIMA.

BY RICHARD E. OVERTON

Dedicated to Joanie

Copyright © 2008 By Richard E. Overton

GOD ISN'T HERE: A YOUNG MAN'S ENTRY INTO WORLD WAR II AND HIS PARTICI-
PATION IN THE BATTLE FOR IWO JIMA, 3RD EDITION

Library of Congress Cataloging-in-Publication Data
Overton, Richard E., 1925-
God isn't here : a young man's entry into World War II and his participation in the battle for Iwo Jima / by Richard E. Overton. -- 3rd rev. ed.
p. cm.
Includes index
ISBN 978-0-9796896-0-4 (trade paper)
1. Overton, Richard E., 1925- 2. Iwo Jima, Battle of, Japan, 1945--Personal narratives, American. 3. United States. Marine Corps. Regiment, 26th. Battalion, 2nd 4. United States. Marine Corps--Biography. 5. United States. Navy--Biography. 6. Male nurses--United States--Biography. I. Title.
D767.99.I9O93 2008
940.54'2528--dc22
2007030333

ISBN-10: 0-9796896-0-0
ISBN-13: 978-0-9796896-0-4

Visit us at www.americanlegacymedia.com
info@americanlegacymedia.com

Printed in the United States of America

1 3 5 7 9 8 6 4 2

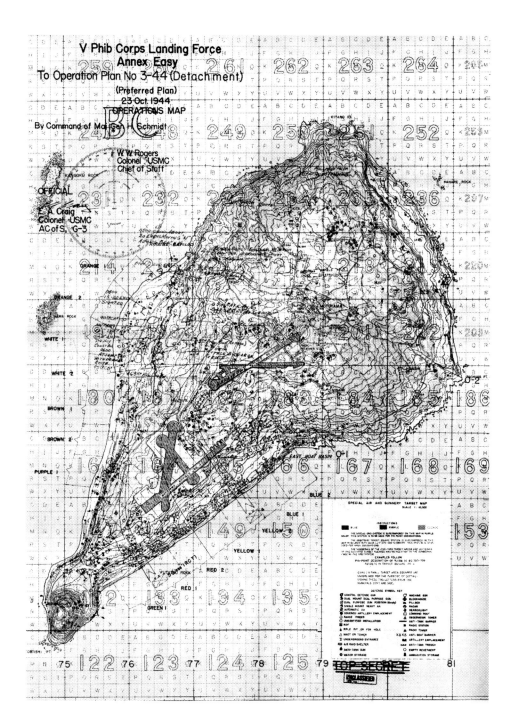

V Phib Corps Landing Force
Annex Easy
To Operation Plan No 3-44 (Detachment)
(Preferred Plan)
23 Oct. 1944
OPERATIONS MAP

By Command of Maj. Gen. H. Schmidt

W. W. Rogers
Colonel USMC
Chief of Staff

OFFICIAL

E. A. Craig
Colonel USMC
AC of S. G-3

Contents

Preface

THIS IS AN account dealing with that time I spent in the U. S. Naval military service during World War II. The events began in June 1943, and ended on April 10, 1946, and are based upon what I observed, heard, smelled or felt. Nothing that I have written is based upon hearsay information unless it is identified as such.

In order to refresh my memory, I relied upon written material I had gathered during those war years. It exists in the form of military pamphlets, directives, newsletters, memoranda, and photographs.

Fortunately, while in Japan just after hostilities ceased, in an attempt to better understand what I had endured, I made hand written notes, which I still have today.

Although I have read published accounts by others concerning the battle for Iwo Jima, I refrained from using their recollections as reference material because of some "difference of impression." Those differences are no doubt due to the confusion and messiness of war. In this account I have intentionally avoided using the twenty-four hour system of expressing time as the military does to make it more easily understood by the average reader

I do not intend this to be a novel. It is meant to record, and to convey to the reader, the experiences an American youth encountered during the Second World War. I hope that the reader may understand in some way that what I experienced.

Richard Eugene Overton

Foreword

On December 7, 1941, the day that President Franklin D. Roosevelt termed "The Day of Infamy," the United States was forcibly propelled into World War II. One week later Richard E. Overton celebrated his sixteenth birthday. He had been raised during the great depression and had experienced the hard time as did most farm boys. The war to them was not frightening, but exciting. Movies of the day showed the glories and heroism of the fight but little of the reality of war. It was their chance to do something great. Many underage boys tried to enlist. Richard was one of them but his mother refused to lie about his age and he returned home to finish high school.

After graduation in July 1943 he was eager to help his country to defeat the Japanese. The story of his experiences in the military from 1943 to war's end in 1945 is the story of many men (boys really) who learned lifelong hard lessons. In Navy boot camp he learned about the world and diverse people in it. While serving in the Navy as a hospital corpsman assigned to a rifle platoon, he learned about authority, loyalty, responsibility and self-esteem. During the battle for Iwo Jima, one of the deadliest military engagements the United States was ever involved in, he learned about the harsh realism of death and powerlessness. Even after all these years his descriptions of the training and the battle are clear and traumatic.

The author served his country during World War II as a United States Navy hospital corpsman assigned to the 2nd battalion, 26th Marine Regiment, 5th Marine Division as a first aid man. He landed with D Company on Red Beach during the initial landing on February 19, 1945.

On September 22, 1945 he accompanied the 26th Marine Regiment in occupying the Japanese Naval Base at Sasebo, on the island of Kyushu, Japan.

In the past several years a number of men who were at Iwo Jima in 1945 read this manuscript, which was written 1981-1986. The hell they went through had not been forgotten and was vividly bought to life again. Men who had not been able to express their own personal experiences concerning the horrors of war were at last able to talk about it with their families making it easier for those families to understand their loved ones even better. Some wrote or telephoned to say, "We know now what Dad saw and experienced in combat."

When the war was over and Richard had finished his military service, he was 20 years old. His youth was over and gone forever.

Joan Steele Overton

Richard E. Overton, 1945

CHAPTER ONE
The Patriot

THE HIGH SCHOOL exercises at the Live Oak Union High School in Morgan Hill, California, in June 1943 ended my twelve years of public school education. It also ended my seventeen and a half years of dependence upon my parents and now I was free to make my own decisions in determining what my future would be.

My future would be influenced by the war that had engulfed the world since September, 1939. Since the Japanese attack on Pearl Harbor, December 7, 1941, all young male Americans could expect to be inducted into the armed forces of the United States. Upon graduating from high school some would be drafted, others could volunteer and be able to choose the branch of service they would enter. I chose to volunteer.

When I was sixteen years old, the year before graduation, I went with several of my high school buddies to San Jose to see the movie, "Wake Island." This picture portrayed the U.S. Marines defending Wake Island, a small speck of land located in the Pacific Ocean, from Japanese attack and in doing so dying to the last man! The story was exciting and full of action and it certainly swelled the sense of patriotism already in our breasts.

When the film ended we passed through the lobby on our way out and discovered that during the film the U.S. Marine Corps had moved a recruiting detail into the area. The Marines, some two dozen or so, were dressed in their beautiful blue dress uniforms. All about the lobby American flags were displayed. Large photographs of our ships being bombed at Pearl Harbor hung from the walls of the room, along with posters depicting "Uncle Sam" pointing his finger at us over the big bold caption of "I WANT YOU!"

Lines of young men formed quickly and I would estimate there were two hundred young men standing there eagerly waiting to be interviewed. I was one of them. I told the recruiting sergeant that I was eighteen years old. He told me to report to a certain office at the San Jose Post Office at a specific time and date. When I kept the appointment the next day, it took the sergeant about five minutes to determine that I was lying about my age. He told me to "Come back next year!" From then until graduation day in June of 1943 I constantly badgered my parents to allow me to join the Marine Corps. They refused to move from their position that I must remain in high school and graduate, and only then could I enter the Navy and not the Marine Corps! They had seen too many news photographs and read too many accounts of the vicious fighting that took place on islands of the South Pacific. Pictures of Marine dead washing about in the surf along the beaches of the Solomon Islands only served to support their argument.

On July 8, 1943, I was sworn into the Navy at the U.S. Federal Building in San Francisco, California. It was a warm sunny morning and a large group of enlistees stood on the steps before the main entrance facing a smaller crowd of parents, relatives and girl friends. The officer in charge was a middle aged Navy commander who appeared resplendent in his dress uniform. He spoke of patriotism and of duty and he commended all enlistees and their parents who supported the fight against world oppression.

At the close of the ceremony the commander allowed a short period of time for those loved ones present to say good-bye to their soon-to-be sailor sons, sweethearts and brothers. After that the civilians were ushered out of the area and the enlistees courteously guided into an inner courtyard, the commander then excused himself after turning authority over to a U.S. Navy chief petty officer.

This U.S. Navy chief petty officer, so beautiful in his dress blues and wearing an unbelievable number of gold service "Hash-marks" on his left sleeve, was to be the first "mean son-of-bitch" that I was to come across in the service of this country. He wasn't the last one though. Before my military service was over I'm sure that this CPO would have been elected to the position of Chaplain by the rest of his kind had they an organization of their own.

The chief told us to stand at attention and listen, and listen well, to what he was to tell us. Almost a hundred of us stood there in a ragged formation, feeling unsure of ourselves and I'm sure with all the appearance of a gang of miscreants the police had just rounded up in some raid. Among us were tall men, short men, fat men and skinny men. Some men were wearing suits and others wore work clothes. Some stood straight, imitating war heroes in the movies, and others just slouched hoping to be among those least noticed.

The chief said loudly with a suggestion of intimidation in his voice, "You are now in the United States Navy and now are governed by military law."

He went on to say that if one of us decided to leave without authorization horrible things would befall us and we would be charged with desertion and be at the mercy of the F.B.I., the Navy Shore Patrol, and the Navy's Intelligence Corps. He went on to produce a loose leaf volume of printed material that he identified as the U.S. Navy's "Rocks and Shoals." He read from it and described terrible punishments for a long list of infractions of the rules, none of which most of us never knew existed. As he spoke my thoughts went back to the comments made by the pleasant speaking commander who had just sworn us in. I wondered if he knew that this chief petty officer was speaking to us in such an offensive manner.

As he spoke I lowered my eyes, feeling dejected. I didn't want to face that horrible, contemptible, petty person who stood before us yelling as though he were a just cut, bull calf. My eyes settled on the brown oxford shoes that I was wearing. They were inexpensive shoes, well worn and scuffed, but the best I had. My brown slacks were wrinkled and stretched out of shape after two days of travel; my light weight sports shirt was rumpled and lightly soiled. The Navy had installed some of us in the local Y. M.C.A. for a few days while awaiting the "swearing in" ceremony, so I had to wear these clothes during the two days wait. I certainly did not feel very comfortable or confident

I felt alone and abandoned as the CPO continued to yell and intimidate. When he finished, we took a walk. We were led onto Market Street and east toward the Ferry Building, which was located of course, at the waterfront. I carried only a small toilet kit. Some of the recruits had suitcases and others carried coats and clothing in their arms. The people we met along the way were very pleasant, supportive and receptive. They applauded us and said words of encouragement. All that made me feel a little better. One old man came alongside of me and said, "Go, get 'em,' Son, I wish I could go with you." He said he was a sailor in the last war and then asked me for two-bits as he was hungry. I only had a dollar, but I gave him a quarter of that.

Once we got to the San Francisco-Oakland Ferry I began to feel better. A fresh breeze and hot cup of coffee lifted my morale. It quickly began to deteriorate again though by that same CPO who herded us off the ferry at the Oakland Train Terminal and urged us onto a dirty gray passenger train that was pointed north toward the Farragut Naval Training Station at Farragut, Idaho.

The train trip to Farragut was rather uneventful, although we did learn to close the windows before the train entered one of the many tunnels along the way. The oil burning engine smoke blackened our faces as if we had deliberately rubbed soot over ourselves. Several other farm boys and I were made fun of for our appearance. My shirt became so soiled I knew that it could never be cleaned.

My last seventy-five cents was spent on sandwiches and a cup of coffee that night. It wasn't until morning that many of us discovered that the food was furnished by the Navy and that the porters had taken advantage of us. They claimed they thought that the money we gave them was a tip. Otherwise, except for a hot-foot someone gave me, while I slept during the second night the long ride was very boring.

We arrived at the Farragut Naval Station at 0230 and I was pretty well chilled through and through. I still think it was extreme and inhuman treatment to take a seventeen-year-old boy off a train at that time in the morning, especially when he doesn't know where he was or what was happening to him next.

After being yelled at some more and being directed into an unheated two story barrack's building we were issued one blanket and told to find an empty bunk to sleep on. To our discomfort all the bunks had been stripped of mattresses and we had to lie upon the cold hard coil springs with our one blanket wrapped around us. Revelry was at 0430. To my dismay, I discovered the Navy had developed a procedure where a recruit would be awakened by someone beating on a steel garbage can while dragging it along between the rows of bunks!

The first meal the Navy gave us new sailors at the Farragut Naval Station consisted of a piece of corn bread and a large spoon of hot white beans which were placed on a cold metal mess tray. They did provide a second cup of coffee, although I thought it best not to ask for cream to go with it. It appeared to me that they waited for me to ask a question just so they could bring scorn and shame down on me.

A short while after we finished breakfast we were herded into four columns, each one had to enter a different doorway of a huge building. We were not told why we were there but when I got near the door I heard a rumor that we were to get our hair cut. When I entered, a barber inside motioned me to a barber type chair. No neck cloth was thought necessary apparently, as none was provided,

"And how would you like your hair cut, sir" the barber asked with a smirk on his face?

"Oh," I answered, "cut it short, I guess!"

He then turned and yelled out to his fellow barbers. "Hey you guys, here is one that wants his hair cut short!" Evidently they thought that was humorous because they all guffawed. You see, this was a time in my life before I found out about the sense of humor of most barbers. Well, anyway my hair was clipped right off to my scalp, just like the rest of the men. When the barber was through he admonished me not to worry about the hair clippings that were hanging all over me and down my neck. Then he directed me to walk through the doorway, which was directly behind the chair.

Once I was through the door a sailor wearing stripes on his blouse sleeves ordered us to undress. We put all of our clothing in a paper bag that was provided and were told to leave it in the room. Another door provided access to a shower room and after we finished with the shower there was still another room for drying off. There was no going back, I found out. All door knobs had been removed preventing us returning to a room we had exited. To this day I have not seen the clothes I left in that paper bag.

After drying ourselves we were issued new Navy clothing, and we were required to dressed quickly. Never before had I ever seen so much good clothing at one time... and all of it new! Boy was I impressed! Our names were stenciled on the clothing just before we dressed. On the way out of the building we were photographed individually and a serial number was assigned to each one of us. My number was #378-40-88 USNR, which I proudly remember to this day.

There was one thing I remember learning after going through this kind of treatment. Certain equality was felt by all the men, as there was no distinction between rich or poor, smart or dumb. We all looked the same, about one hundred of us ridiculous looking wretches. The only consolation experienced in a military "Boot Camp," is that all persons are reduced to zero status, for a short time anyway. The new dungarees and shoes and the stiff hats covering shaved heads all created an image of equality in these lowly recruits. Then slowly there emerged the characteristics of the individual, based upon whatever experience or education he possessed.

Reveille was a brassy, loud, irritating noise that came every morning at 0400. We were required to make our bunks immediately and in proper military manner. Our personal hygiene requirements were strictly enforced and soon these activities became rules of behavior that we would all come to accept.

Up Farragut!

Up, Farragut, your mountains and pines
Are signs of the times - Up, Farragut,
The men of the fleet are all on their feet hitting hard,
In blizzards or heat, in dust or sleet,
There's work to be done ere victory's won.
By Lake Pend d'Oreille we'll call it a day
When it's… Up Farragut.

We honor the man we're proud to claim---
Into the battle he went with one intent, to win or die,
"Damn The Torpedoes," full speed ahead.
(The Official Station Song)

I SUPPOSE HUMILITY plays an important part in the making of a warrior. Maybe it should be pronounced humiliation instead. There is that thing in some men who, when given authority, tend to confuse leading and teaching with intimidation and fear in their search for obedience.

So it was in July of 1943, in Company #519, at Camp Bennion, in the United States Naval Training Base at Farragut, Idaho. I should explain about the U.S. Navy Training Center at Farragut. The Japanese had attacked Pearl Harbor, in the Hawaiian Islands, on December 7, 1941, and immediately the U.S. Government went onto war status. It was determined that military camps would be established across the country to train young men and women to defend their country.

Our government selected one such site on the southwest end of Lake Pend d'Oreille (Pond-er-ray). Why the site was selected, I could never find out. I suspect now it had to do with politics only. It was located about forty-five miles north east of Spokane, Washington, twenty miles north of Coeur d'Alene, Idaho, and about thirty miles south of Sand Point, Idaho. Both the latter towns were small villages in Kootenai County.

The camp was named after the Civil War hero, Admiral David Glasgow

Farragut (1801-1870) who won the battles at Mobile Bay and New Orleans. He is accredited with the phrase, "Damn the Torpedoes, Full Speed Ahead!"

The training center consisted of six individual stations, each designed to accommodate and train five thousand men at one time. These camps were laid out in the shape of a large oval with the parade ground or "grinder" in the center. Along one side was a gigantic drill hall, which contained six basketball courts and a seventy-five foot square swimming pool.

Each camp had its own mess hall, twenty-two double barracks, two medical dispensaries, recreation hall, ship's stores, indoor rifle range, and chief petty officer's quarters. There was an administration building as each camp with their personnel was considered one regiment. In the fifteen months of operation, from September 15, 1942 until late in 1944, about 293,381 sailors trained at the camp.

The six camps within Farragut were named after service men who gave their lives in the defense of their country during the early days of the war and who were posthumously awarded the Congressional Medal of Honor. Construction began on April 10, 1942 and the camps were completed as follows:

CAMP BENNION - Sept. 15, 1942. Named after Capt. M.S. Bennion who died during the Pearl Harbor attack on December 7, 1941 while commanding the battleship, West Virginia.

CAMP WARD - Oct. 1, 1942. Named after Seaman 1/c James Ward who died in the Pearl Harbor attack.

CAMP WALDRON - Nov. 8, 1942. Named after Lt. Commander Waldron, killed at the Battle of Midway in June of 1942.

CAMP HILL - Dec. 2, 1942. Named after Chief Boatswain Mate Edwin Hill, who died during the Pearl Harbor attack.

CAMP SCOTT - December 19, 1942. Named after Rear Admiral Norman Scott, who died at the Battle of Savo Island, May 1942.

CAMP PETERSON - March 25, 1943, named after Oscar V. Peterson, Chief Water Tender, who died at the Battle of the Coral Sea, in May, 1942.

There was a seventh partially constructed camp that was never put into use because it wasn't needed. It was named Camp Gilmore. Who Gilmore was, I don't know. Combined, the camps held 30,000 recruits. With the 36,000 ship's company stationed there, the camp became an instant city with a population of 66,000 people. The social and economic impact on the area must have been phenomenal.

The commanding non-commissioned officer in charge of Company #519 was Athletic Specialist, Chief Petty Officer F.J. Madrigan. Mr. Madrigan, as he was called, the 'Mister,' apparently used instead of the usual Navy designation of "Chief," was a likable sort of an individual. He was often referred to as a "Slick Arm Chief" as he did not have one four-year service stripe on his sleeve. In wartime there was an immediate need for men who were experienced in training young men to follow orders and to work together. These CPO's were drawn in large numbers from the coaching staffs of athletic departments of high schools and colleges throughout the nation. The term, "Slick Arm" was meant to be slightly derogatory as the regular Navy CPO's with years of service felt inclined to look upon this new breed of CPO with some disdain.

The duty of a CPO was to form the one hundred and thirty men assigned to him into one organized corps needed in specific working areas of the Navy. The majority of recruits had just been graduated from high school. There were others though, men in their thirties who had been drafted or who had volunteered. Our company included a man who had served eight years as an enlisted man and who now volunteered to serve again at the age of thirty-five. He was appointed executive NCO of the company. Two draftees, both teachers in private life, were appointed as his assistants. So the short-lived equality status was to disappear and disparity arrived on the scene.

I believed at first the Navy thought discipline should be maintained by fear of punishment only. Somewhere in all those training manuals there must have been directives concerning the training of men. "Punish each poor soul at least one time during each day!" And, so it was in Mr. Madrigan's company. To emphasize personal cleanliness an inspection would be made of all hands. Of course five or more sad rookies would be selected at random and found guilty of having soiled hands or dirty fingernails. These men were made to stand out in front of their comrades, much to their mortification. Sentence would be pronounced, "Wash hands and clean fingernails every thirty minutes until taps," Once the order was carried out the culprits would be required to show their hands for inspection to one of the NCOs in attendance.

Some wise soul once lamented, "Whoever said the world has to be fair?" That question was certainly true in a military 'boot camp.' Once while the company stood at parade rest on the "grinder," an inspection was made of the recruit's bunks and personal belongings. A trio of chief petty officers entered our barracks and emerged with arms full of mattress covers taken from some of the recruits' bunks. Six names were called out and the owners of the covers were presented to the rest of the company as having erred in having soiled linen on their bunks. The mattress covers were laid out upon the 'grinder' pavement and the company was then ordered to march over the linen. Afterward, the owners were told to wash their belongings until all signs of dirt were gone. As the 'grinder' was covered with tarmac this directive was difficult to fulfill.

There are always losers in groups of men, and I was one in those days. I was unfortunate to have as a characteristic weakness, a grin that appeared whenever I was tense and nervous. Mr. Madrigan noticed the grin and asked me what was so amusing? Of course, I thought that nothing was. He asked me if my mattress cover and pillowcase were present among those on the tarmac. After replying in the negative, I was directed to go inside the barracks and return with those items and place them on the ground with the others. Of course I did so while suffering much humiliation. That night after observing the other victims of the day's episode fail in their attempt to wash their sheets clean, I said "To hell with this," and dumped my dirty linen into the nearest garbage can. It was my first rebellious act against authority. I had begun to learn.

There were a few delightful days in 'boot camp' though. One day the company marched in close order drill while its members carried wooden make-believe rifles copied after the famous 1903 Springfield Rifle. An officer stood on a wooden platform out in the middle of the "grinder" and directed a constant barrage of comments toward the chief petty officers drilling their respective companies. Much to our delight, he "dressed down" here and there an errant chief for sloppiness of drill. Using his megaphone the officer would say, "Perhaps we should send you back to boot camp, Mr. Madrigan!" And he might add," Mr. Madrigan, you have a "turd bird" in your outfit."

Remarks made by the Officer and directed at Mr. Madrigan brought to the faces of one hundred and thirty recruits a grin as though on command. Of course there was always the necessary retaliation where the person thought responsible for the chief's embarrassment was ordered to do ten laps around the "grinder" while holding the rifle above his head with both hands.

Other punishments were constant. Hands observed in trousers pockets caused them to be filled with pebbles and to be kept sewn up for several days, much to the mortification of the wearer. Referring to one's rifle as a "gun" could cause the recruit to run a number of laps around the field holding his crotch in one hand and his rifle in the other while yelling loudly, "This is my gun, and this is my rifle".

Probably the lowest job in the Navy is doing scullery work, which is cleaning the galley after the meal is over. It seemed to me that I was detailed to do that chore often. The first time I visited the cleaning gear locker, I asked the CPO, Mr. Madrigan, who was positioned in front of it, for a " mop to mop the floor."

Mr. Madrigan answered, "Swab!"

Not understanding his manner I said, "No, I want a mop,"

He said with a very loud commanding voice, "Swab, you want a swab!"

Well, I knew what I wanted, so I said, "No, I want a mop."

Mr. Madrigan lost control of his emotions and began screaming out repeatedly, "Swab, 'dammit'. You want a swab to swab the deck, not a mop and floor." Before it was all over his face was livid and his eyes bulging and glaring and he told me to work an extra hour. I suppose it was only youthful naiveté that caused me to blurt out, "Oh shit!" in response.

Mr. Madrigan seemed to enter a state of shock. He gasped and struggling for words he finally uttered, "You can't say that to me! You're not supposed to say that to me. You cannot say that to me when I give you an order. You're supposed to respond, "Yes Sir." Do you understand me?"

"Yeah, OK!"

"No..., no..., not Yeah, OK.... It's 'Yes Sir', do you understand?"

"Yeah..., Sir!

Well, I got my swab and went off to clean the mess hall floor. Looking back I could see Mr. Madrigan leaning with his back up against the gear locker door. His shoulders were slumped and he looked as though he was studying the deck for some reason. He looked very, very tired. I supposed that a chief petty officer had a very hard job in the Navy.

It is universally agreed that military basic training is a most hateful experience. Though, one might have to admit that the experience and the information gained may be useful later in life. Recruits are taught such subjects as first aid, life saving techniques, personal hygiene and use of firearms. The training is taken for granted until one day when one is called upon to use some of these skills; he finds to his surprise that he has considerable knowledge and ability.

A certain pride develops when one accomplishes a successful swim across the swimming pool with ease and ahead of his classmates. This type of accomplishment is the beginning of the development of pride and the building of confidence.

Apparently not only positive factors go into character building, but those of a negative nature too. After the horrible mattress cover experience, another was soon to follow. The pay process involving the recruit followed a routine procedure. The recruit would present himself before a table behind which a U.S. naval officer was sitting. On the table were huge stacks of U.S. currency and a roster of personnel to be paid. On either side of the officer stood two armed enlisted men wearing Shore Patrol brassards and side arms.

The recruit would stand before the officer, state his name, rank, and serial number, all the while holding his identification card showing his picture and serial number, in such a way the officer could see it clearly. This was really easy to accomplish, but when I did it the officer straightened up and said to the two-armed men, "Arrest that man!"

I could hardly believe he meant me, but I soon found out he did. They took me to a back room where I found myself being questioned by three officers about my identity. Finally after thirty minutes or so, I was released from custody with the admonishment that I had the wrong serial number on my identification card. When I attempted to explain that I didn't print my identification card or issue myself the number I was greeted with cold threatening stares and told to be quiet and to return to the end of the line. Of course, when I did return to my comrades in line I was met with raised eyebrows, grins and comments like, "What did they catch you doing? Did you grab some money? - What a dumb thing to do," and others accompanied with smirks, grins and more words such as, "I know."

One of the better aspects of 'boot life' was to know there were a few poor souls who were worse off than you, and to feel a least a little superior because of their shortcomings. One poor creature was named Dorsa. He insisted that he could not write a letter although he had graduated from high school in 1942.

Not being able to write home was a problem for him, especially since he had a girl friend back home who might find pleasurable interests elsewhere while he was absent from the scene. He cultivated my friendship so I would write his love letters for him. This was mainly because I too was from the San Jose, area and he thought there should be a bond between us.

Really, after hearing Dorsa speak of his rather personal adventures with the young lady in question I would have gladly paid him to write the letters as the return correspondence was well worth any effort that I put into the endeavor.

The result of this experience was interesting, and soon I was caught up in a series of writings expressing love, passion and fond remembrance between my fellow recruit and his fiancé. He permitted me to read his girl friend's letters as they arrived, probably because there were some words that he couldn't understand as he read them. I also convinced him that in order to write a letter to her I'd have to know what she had written him.

He constantly reminded the girl of their past passions including a number of sexual adventures that took place in the back seat of an automobile while being driven to San Francisco and apparently that was repeated on several different occasions. It became obvious she never knew that her lover was not writing the letters she received, but instead they came from a third party she didn't know. Dorsa and I parted at graduation from "boot camp." I did not see him again, but I wondered how he resolved his problem of communication later on. I don't believe I'll ever seek him out to find out though as I think it wise if I don't ever meet his wife.

Another interesting situation developed with a young recruit who was often seen weeping after being in camp for about two weeks. An investigation revealed that the lad was only fourteen years old and that he had enough of a recruit's life. He was quickly discharged, but not before he was given many slaps across his shoulders and called a "good guy" by the other recruits. He was happy to leave and return to the home he had run away from two months before.

How can one know happiness unless he has experienced sadness? That could be the description of one's feelings at the approach of graduation from 'boot camp.'

This event however was marred somewhat by an incident two days prior to graduation. While showering myself a fellow recruit asked me what the red spots on my chest was? Looking down I found that I had spots all over my body. While I was dressing and contemplating the trip to the dispensary, a discussion regarding my case of measles was held by some of my fellow recruits. It was their opinion that if I turned myself in to sick bay, I probably would not be allowed to graduate and would be forced to repeat 'boot camp' all over again. This thought was enough for me to conceal my affliction until after graduation and the commencement of our thirty-day 'boot' leave.

It later occurred to me that if my disease had been discovered the entire company might have been quarantined much to the chagrin of the other recruits. There would have been some unhappy days ahead for them and me if I were to stay with them until the incubation period was over. No doubt some of my fellow recruits had already thought of this possibility and that had motivated them into encouraging me to conceal my illness from the authorities.

The happy day of 'boot' graduation came and with that event came forth the new Mr. Madrigan, who shook the hands of each of us before our departure. The transformation of his personality from a tyrant to a "good fellow" was astounding to those of us with limited experience in the social behavior of man.

CHAPTER THREE

Boot Graduation and Leave

G RADUATION DAY FOR company #519 was held during the last week of August 1943. We were allowed to leave the Farragut Training Center to go home and enjoy our thirty-day "Boot Leave" due all graduates. I boarded the train for Oakland, California, and to reach there we passed through the cities of Spokane and Seattle, Washington. I didn't get to see Seattle even though we spent several hours just parked in the terminal, as the fog was so thick it was resting on the ground. I wasn't feeling very good either, as my head was shaved and I was wearing a new stiff hat that irritated my scalp. I felt conspicuous because of my ill-fitting white uniform and shiny black shoes that hurt my feet. My body was still covered with red spots from the measles and I had developed a sore throat with laryngitis to the point where I could not speak. I had to depend on a friend, Roland Passarino to order tickets and food for me.

I was very disappointed upon arriving home where I would spend my thirty-day leave. I thought I looked funny in my new sailor's uniform and was embarrassed that the top of my head was covered with fuzz while I waited for the hair to grow. If I had expected people back home would make a big thing about my enlistment, I was sure mistaken. Many of my old acquaintances didn't even know I had enlisted in the Navy. To most people of the community I was just another local boy, one of many who had enlisted in the military service to serve in time of war.

While I was in boot camp my dog 'Socks' had died, and I missed him terribly. Along with that, my parents had sold my motorcycle without discussing it with me first, and after I had worked for a full year to pay for it too. I was miserable being home again. It wasn't what I had expected. All I could think about was returning to the Farragut Training Center and see what my next experience would be. I was happy to board the train in Oakland and return to camp.

CHAPTER FOUR

Hospital Corps School

UPON ARRIVING BACK at the Farragut Training, I discovered that the camp was very crowded and that many of us were assigned to sleep in the interior of a large empty swimming pool at Camp Scott. This camp was being used to collect and hold men after boot camp training that were awaiting assignment to duty at various Navy stations. There must have been eighty of us who slept there on canvas type Army cots.

On the second day there we were ordered outside of the building to stand roll call. After that done we spent the entire day carrying sides of beef from a line of refrigerator train cars and placing them into cold storage lockers that served the personnel of Camp Farragut.

The next morning, I awoke to find a swollen area under my left jaw. "Mumps," was the diagnosis of my fellow sailors. This meant that if I turned into sickbay, I would be rescheduled and delayed in my departure from Farragut, and that I couldn't accept. The best I could do was to hide the fact that I was ill. I pulled up the collar on my pea jacket the next morning to hide evidence of my swollen face.

After roll call, we were ordered to march to the train and storage yards to work. Several of us decided to drop out of the marching order on the way to the work area and disappear into the forest nearby to spend the day. My comrades also decided it would be best for me to get some rest instead of working, as the mumps might produce other medical complications. This, I agreed, should not be allowed to happen. Therefore, a run into the woods each morning after roll call was the most prudent thing to do.

Five days later the swelling subsided on my left jaw. The day after that, swelling developed on my right jaw. Another week was spent hiding in the forest during the daylight working hours.

Several weeks before 'boot' graduation, I had filled out at form indicating my choice for the type of duty I'd like. I had written down that I wanted to be a gunner's mate to serve with the Merchant Marine as a member of a Navy gun crew. After all, why not knock off a few German 'U' boats while on the "Road to Mermansk? "Mermansk, Russia was the destination of many of our ships that carried war supplies to allies. The German submarines were responsible for sinking hundreds of our ships once they entered the North Atlantic Ocean during 1942 and 1943. My second choice was to be a radar technician, because then radar was a new development and I thought the skill could be adapted to civilian use after the war. I had no third choice: it really wasn't much of a concern to me. I was certainly going to be a gunner's mate or a radar technician for sure. At the insistence of one of the Personnel Yeomen though, I wrote down, "Hospital Corps." I had no idea what a Hospital Corpsman did, but since the technician insisted, I did allow that to be written. I would learn about doing such things!

The swelling under my jaw was still evident when I found my name posted on a draft order directing me to report to the U.S. Navy Hospital at Camp Farragut. I was to be trained as a Hospital Corpsman. For hours I wandered about camp wondering what I was to do. I didn't join the Navy to carry bedpans and make beds. This just couldn't be allowed to happen.

During my wanderings about the grounds while feeling sorry for myself I happened to run across my cousin, Byron Wiley Housenecht. "Ike" was my age and had enlisted in the Navy also after graduating from high school in Oakland, California. Although our meeting was joyous I was further dismayed to find that he had been selected to attend the U.S. Navy's aviation radioman-gunner's school. I was envious as there he was looking forward to combat and for sure being given the opportunity to shoot down a lot of America's enemy war planes while I would be spending my time swabbing floors and other things that I would detest doing in some hospital.

With some luck, first thought, I met a yeoman petty officer that attended high school with me back in Morgan Hill. He was assigned to type up lists of men drafted for various jobs. He casually explained to me that I had no problem, that upon his return to his office he would erase my name from the Hospital Corps draft and place it on a list of men going to gunnery school. I told him that I was grateful to him and that it was nice to have a friend like him, he would have a friend for life in me, and that if anytime in the future he needed help I would be at his beck and call. The next morning I was called to board a bus. The bus took me and others to the Hospital Corps School located at the Farragut Navy Hospital. I never saw my friend, the yeoman, again.

I hardly think that anyone else could have felt worse than I that morning when the bus left me off at the Hospital Corps School. I was further disappointed when I discovered that the school was only across the street that separated it from Camp Bennion, the 'boot camp' I had just left after finishing a long eight tedious weeks of training.

Mare Island Naval Hospital

While attending the Hospital Corps School, I was assigned to class 5-44. The class of 350 men was divided into seven companies of 50 men each. The commander of class 5-44 was Pharmacists Mate First Class R. E. Thomas, and he made it difficult for me to find time in which to feel sorry for myself. Once classes began, I found it necessary to keep running just to keep up with the rest of my classmates. The subjects that were being taught us were strange to me but I found interesting. We studied nursing, materia medica, anatomy and physiology, first aid, minor surgery, the effects of gas in warfare and record keeping. But, the thought was always with me, how was I going to explain to my friends at home what was I doing to help with the war effort?

I immediately found that discipline and regimentation play an important part in military learning. Classes began at 8:30 a.m. sharp. A student dare not be late or he was placed on report, and that meant two hours extra duty. This usually involved scrubbing down the head (lavatory) while the rest of the students were off on weekend liberty.

At 4:30 P.M. recall sounded and the time between then and 7:00 P.M. was to be used for personal needs, such as washing clothing and eating dinner. At 7:00 P.M., we could all be found sitting on our bunks studying our lessons. We were not supposed to speak to one another. If we felt we had to, we first had to call out to a proctor who patrolled the barracks room to get permission. We were required to concentrate on studying and if these rules seem childish or ridiculous at least something came from them. For the first time in my life, I began to study seriously.

During my high school days, I had been a C and D level student. I thought that was the best I could do, and I was under the impression my teachers thought so also. But now, I was one person among fifty, in a classroom studying rather complex subject matter. At least twenty-five percent of my classmates had some college experience. Most were older than I and had some type of job before military induction. I was being required to compete with these other students, and I was afraid of the consequences if I didn't measure up. Weeks later I graduated in the top twenty-five per-cent of the class, a feat that amazed me and elevated my own self image considerably.

As I was in the top portion of my class scholastically, I was allowed to select my next duty station where I would take further training. The Navy had a hospital at the Mare Island Naval Base at Vallejo, California. I elected to go there, thinking that it was the nearest to my home. I did so after ignoring warnings from some of the training personnel at the school that the Mare Island Hospital was a "sweatshop" and that it was a place to stay away from because the corpsmen there were made to work fifteen hours a day. Well, I could hardly believe that!

At Mare Island Naval Hospital, I worked fifteen hours a day for six days a week. Upon arrival there I was directed to a beautiful building of Spanish design in which I would be quartered. Each room had two bunks, two comfortable chairs, and reading lamps. Another corpsman shared the room with me.

In the four weeks I was there I never met my roommate, although I did see him asleep on several occasions. I supposed that he too was working a fifteen-hour day somewhere. I was assigned to an amputation ward. Many of the injured were Marines and sailors being brought in from the South Pacific battle areas.

This would be my first contact with injured or sick servicemen just ar-riving from a combat area. I was required to remove bandages that had been placed on an injury while in a combat zone and I saw dirt and leaves and unidentifiable items fall from the dressings as I took them off. I learned quickly about giving out medicines, giving injections, making up beds, and swabbing decks. These were daily chores. One relief for me was that I never handled a bedpan the entire time I was there.

The most unpleasant task that I faced there was when I was told to report to a "Quiet Room" in order to care for a horribly disabled sailor. I was totally unprepared for what I found. He was suspended above the bed by leather straps fastened to his arms, legs, and body. He had been severely burned at the Pearl Harbor attack two years before and remained in a hor-rible condition.

His situation was hopeless, as he was a terminal case. Some of his leg, arm, and facial bones were exposed to the outside air. He was fairly rational in his thinking, although he displayed much anger and hostility and directed a constant torrent of verbal abuse at me the entire time I was there. He told me what my duties were and how to do them. I was to place sterile gauze pads soaked in sterile boric acid solution over his exposed bones, tendons, and muscle tissue to keep them moist and to prevent them from drying out. The odor from his body was dreadful; his attitude was abominable and he continually cursed me the entire fifteen hours that I spent there. I was glad to be relieved at the end of my shift. I was physically exhausted and emotionally shaken; I never went back

I was beginning to change my thinking of the war. At first there was all that glory and glamour at the very thought of going into combat. Now, I found the stark realism of it all was staring me in the face.

One day after finishing my lunch and with a few moments to spend relaxing, I walked down the decline to a nearby concrete wharf where workers were refitting two destroyers that obviously had been damaged. To my interest I found that both had just returned from the South Pacific where they had experienced battle damage near the Solomon Islands. I watched as a worker applied an acetylene cutting torch to the starboard side near the bow of one of the destroyers. Apparently, he was removing a large steel plate that had been welded there in an emergency, in order to make temporary repair. An older man, a "salty' looking Navy chief petty officer wearing well worn overalls approached me from the direction of the dock. In a kindly voice he asked what it was that interested me so.

I told him that I was just curious as to what the workman was doing. The chief stood along side of me for a few moments before speaking again. "You know," he said, not really looking at me, "I don't think you would want to be here when that guy cuts that plate loose."

I turned and looked at him wondering about his statement. "You see..., the ship was struck by a Jap shell and there were several of our boys in there at the time. To save the ship the Captain ordered the compartment sealed. Their bodies are still in there..., it might get a little 'smelly' in a moment!"

I gulped, thanked him and walked back to the hospital without looking back.

Those days at Mare Island were agonizing ones for me. Long, laborious hours were spent constantly being corrected by nurses, patients, and masters-at-arms. Medical officers, when in my presence ignored me as if I didn't exist.

Sometimes I did appreciate that though, as the commanding officer of the hospital upset me when I was near him. On Saturday mornings, he and his entourage came through the wards on an inspection tour. He was followed by doctors, nurses, and last, but not least, the master-at-arms who carried his notebook ready to record any comment that the C.O. might make. Of course, any remark that the C.O. would make would be of a derogatory nature. I never heard him make any other kind.

This officious appearing Navy Captain gave us ward corpsmen the impression that he was to be regarded as a god. His white gloves glided and danced along tabletops and cabinets as they searched for evidence of dust. He scrutinized this object or that overhead with some semblance of a frown. Every so often he would pause long enough to examine his white gloves for signs of dust. Not once did I ever see him nod his head in approval of what he saw. There was often a 'shaking' of his head as if in disapproval or in disgust of what he found. The master-at-arm's pencil would leap into action upon him hearing the comments made by the commanding officer. Its possessor's eyes would glance about the room showing condemnation as they settled momentarily on the faces of ward personnel. By 1300 hours on Saturday there were written comments placed on the ward's office door describing the shortcomings of the nurses and corpsmen in the discharge of their duties.

At first I was concerned about the constant threat of disciplinary action. But, as an older and more experienced corpsman told me, "Since we were already working fifteen hours a day, how could we be assigned any extra duty?"

The Mare Island experience was a low point of my Navy career. Its only highlight came about late one night while I was busy in the linen closet of the ward. A twenty-two year old nurse came into the room behind me and shut the door. She proceeded to get cute with me, but just how far can things go when the door might open from the outside at any moment?

My duties at Mare Island came to a sudden end one morning at 0600. After working my usual shift, I headed toward my bunk and found in my room a chief petty office wearing a worried frown on his face. He acted disturbed. He demanded to know where I had been for the last day and didn't I know that he had been looking for me during that time? He had stayed up most of the night waiting to catch me when I came back to my bunk! He asked me if I had taken unauthorized liberty, as my name was not on the liberty roster.

I was attempting to explain to him that I had been on duty in ward #15 since 2:30 P.M. the day before and had just been relieved, but with a wave of his hand he dismissed all that by saying, "Well, O.K. then," as if he had forgiven my transgressions. He told me a bus was standing outside in front of the barracks and that he would give me five minutes to be on board it with my sea bag and that I had "Better be on it!"

I was being transferred to the U.S. Navy Base at Treasure Island that was located in San Francisco Bay. From there I would go on board the U.S. Navy's hospital ship, the U.S.S. Bountiful. As the chief parted his last comment was, "Guess you'll just have to go without breakfast!"

Treasure Island

T HE BUS TRIP to Treasure Island seemed tiring and boring. I was weary, unshaven, sleepy, and very uncomfortable. However, the other personnel on board looked just as miserable and glum as I felt, and that was some consolation to me. The two-hour ride began by taking us through the small town of Vallejo with its many saloons that catered to the sailors stationed at Mare Island. It was foggy and the streets were damp and dirty. I watched the early morning workers as they swept the litter from the sidewalks and into the gutter that had been deposited there during last night's revelry. But, they could never do away the foul smell of spilled stale beer. We passed over the Carquinez Straits Bridge and through the even more evil smelling Richmond area where the many oil storage and gasoline processing stations were located.

The streets of Oakland and Berkeley were clean and pretty in those days. The solidly built and beautiful San Francisco-Oakland Bay Bridge rose majestically over the waters of San Francisco Bay. In the background view, a few skyscrapers stood tall in back of the San Francisco Ferry building, which is located at the foot of Market Street. To the right in the far distance stretched across the entrance of the Bay, hung the Golden Gate suspension bridge. The base of each one of the pylons was hidden by fog giving them a mystical look. It seemed that the entire bridge structure was floating in the sky while resting on a large sea of cotton.

Treasure Island is a man made island. It is connected to Yerba Buena Island that is located half way between San Francisco and Oakland. The bridge touches down on the island briefly and runs through a five hundred foot tunnel before going on to the opposite shore.

My last visit to Treasure Island had been in 1940, and three of the buildings constructed at that time were still being used by the Navy for various purposes. I had fond memories of the island as I had attended the Exposition several times. A favored recollection was when I went on board the two battleships, the Nevada and California, which were berthed there for public viewing. The year after the exposition ended, both of these ships were resting in the mud on the bottom of Pearl Harbor, after being torpedoed and bombed by the Japanese Navy.

One of the island's buildings billeted the corpsmen assigned to the medical dispensary and was a pleasant place to be lodged. It had comfortable two-bunk bedrooms, a lounge, and a kitchen. During the seven days and nights I only had time to use the bunk and the head facilities. I shared my room with another corpsman, but I never saw him awake, let alone speak to him. It was similar to the same situation I had experienced at Mare Island.

My duties at the dispensary involved dispensing medicines and drugs and giving hypodermic injections to the patients. I've sometimes shuddered since then when I thought of some of the medication errors I may have made. I had to read the doctor's medical instructions and follow them. I seldom found any one around on whom I could depend to give me advice. Since I reported to work at 1800 hours and got off work at 0600, I saw very few medical officers about the premises that I could ask questions of.

One part of my duties was to assist in the emergency clinic when needed. I'd never done anything like that before. On the first night at the base, I was contacted by a pharmacist mate whom I'd never seen before. He instructed me to stand by in the clinic. I asked him what my duties were and he replied, "If someone comes in and they need medical attention, call the doctor. "He's in his office there!" He then pointed to a door at the rear of the clinic. I sat in the room for about three hours without seeing anyone. There was not even a magazine to read. I kept an anxious eye on both the front door and the doctor's office door. Suddenly the front door of the building burst opened and in came two Navy Shore Patrolmen, dragging a very intoxicated sailor between them. One of the patrolmen blurted out, "This bastard is drunk! He has a cut on his leg!" The drunken sailor did have a large jagged cut on his left shinbone caused by broken glass. I motioned for them to place the man on the examination table. After that, they hurriedly left the room. I never saw them again.

The sailor was certainly drunk, but not enough to just lie there and be quiet; I had to hold him down on the table. This made him angry and he wanted to fight me. After a while of pushing him down on the table and knocking his head against the surface, he finally lay still. I went to the doctor's office door and knocked on it, then again and again. After waiting a respectful length of time, I opened the door and found the room empty. There was no one in the room so I concluded that it had been empty the entire time I sat outside the door. I was frustrated and angry for being misinformed.

Somewhat bewildered and because the cut on the sailors leg was bleeding and nasty looking, I went looking for a doctor or anyone for help. I went along the hallway knocking on doors, opening them without finding anyone until I came to one where I could hear voices on the other side. I knocked first and then opened it to find an officer standing before a washbasin washing his hands while conversing with a nurse. He seemed to be reprimanding her for some reason. Startled at my intrusion he glared at me and demanded, "What do you want?" I told him of the injured sailor and that I thought he needed stitches to close the cut.

The doctor, if the officer was one, looked exasperated and shouted at the nurse, "Christ, do I have to do everything around here!" Then looking at me he said, "Goddamn it, if he needs suturing, stitch him up!" I'm sure that the doctor did not know of my capabilities, as he had never seen me before. I retreated quickly and shut the door and went back to the emergency clinic to find the sailor there where I had left him. I think that perhaps I was hoping he had run away by then. But he was still there, sleeping like the drunk he was. Thinking that if I stalled a little while perhaps the pharmacist's mate who had assigned me there would come by and help, I got busy cleaning the wound, which was jagged, and about three inches long. From a cabinet I got a suture kit and stood there perhaps fifteen minutes waiting anxiously for someone to come by. The anxiety of waiting and the uncertainly got to me, so I said to myself "to hell" with it and began to do the job myself. In hospital school we did not practice suturing, but one of the older corpsmen demonstrated the procedure one day by using cloth material instead of real skin. I'm glad I was there to learn. After washing my hands, I began suturing. I put in six stitches and closed the wound. I didn't use a local anesthetic as I was afraid I'd be sent to Portsmouth Naval Prison if something went wrong and the patient became sick or died.

The sailor struggled and groaned from time to time, but I finally finished. After dusting the wound with sulfanilamide powder I covered it with a sterile dressing. When I finished I felt proud of what I had done, but there was no one to show it off to. I waited patently, wishing for a doctor to come by to inspect my work. After an hour had passed the sailor became alert enough to talk to. I helped him clean up at the washbasin and we talked about his injury. I told him to check into a medical station in about five days time to have the sutures removed unless an infection appeared first, and then he should find a doctor for immediate treatment. He left the room a very sorry looking sailor.

Later I realized that I had not recorded the sailor's name in the emergency log as required. And later still, I decided that it was for the best not to have a record of what I had done. I sat in that room until 0600 and did not see another person until I was relieved from duty by another corpsman who made it clear to me he wasn't interested in hearing anything about what I had done. I went directly to my room for some much needed sleep.

I found a chief Petty officer there pacing the floor and wearing a worried look on his face. He asked me my name and when I told him he demanded to know where I'd been, "On liberty?" That astounded me, as it was a repeat of what happened to me at Mare Island. I told him angrily, "No, I've been working all night."

He said, "Oh, you didn't have to work last night. Get your gear together and be ready to board the bus at 0700 hours. You are being shipped out!"

I asked, "Where am I going, on board the hospital ship, the Bountiful?"

"Hell no," he answered. Your records got lost so you are being sent to the Fleet Marine Force at San Diego this morning.

Fleet Marine Force, San Diego

S O FAR, MY five months experiences in the Navy had taught me to be prepared for the unexpected, but I was really surprised by this sudden change of course in my military career. Before enlisting in the Navy, I had tried to join the U.S. Marines. That attempt was frustrated because of my parent's refusal to let me join. Now, it seemed that I was to have my way after all, even though it seemed that I was entering the "Corps" through a back door. I didn't even know until then that the Marines did not have their own medical department, but instead they relied upon the Navy for medical services. So here I was, seventeen years old, a hospital apprentice having my wish come true, that of serving with the U.S. Marines

The direction of the train ride from San Francisco to San Diego was south following the California coastline. About midnight, the train passed within three hundred yards of my parent's home, which was located in the Coyote Valley just south of San Jose. My comrades on the train looked at me oddly when they observed me pressing my nose against the window of the compartment. It was my vain attempt to see the house where my family lived and the countryside in which I grew up. I didn't know any of my traveling companions very well therefore; I did not offer any explanation as to my odd behavior.

Sitting on the train during those long miles I found it difficult to sleep. My mind kept wandering back to the discussions I had with my mother about joining the Marines and the happiness she had displayed when she found out that I was to become a hospital corpsman. She could imagine me safe in some Navy hospital somewhere, probably never to see combat. She was about to find out differently.

At the railroad depot in San Diego we were loaded onto Marine Corps trucks and driven away during a fierce rainstorm. The date was December 7, 1943. About eighty of us that had gathered there were taken to the U.S. Marine Corps Training Station at Camp Elliot. It was located next to the El Toro Marine Corps Air Base, somewhere east of San Diego. We were told to unload in front of a two story barracks. On one side was the camp brig, or stockade, on the other side was a barracks, which housed the women, enlisted Marines of the camp.

While standing formation before our barracks and still in the rain, we were subjected to the always present heckling of one military service by another. We could only stand and take the verbal abuse the Marines hurled at us from windows, doorways, and company streets, "hey, 'swabbie,' where's your boat?" or "hey, ya lost?" Upon entering the barracks I felt suddenly calm. The deck was of wood and it had been swabbed down with stove oil. There was a broken windowpane on the first landing. The glass had been temporarily repaired by someone shoving into an old undershirt into the opening to stop the flow of air. Grinning to myself, I thought that if this was the way they did things here, I was going to like it just fine. What a difference it would be after working in the aseptic atmosphere of a U.S. Navy Hospital.

First Class Pharmacist's Mate Cherry was assigned as our company commander. He first instructed us to get rid of our Navy uniforms, as we weren't going to need them again. We would be issued Marine Corps clothing immediately, he said. The next day we were. We were given new khaki clothing. Handed to us were khaki shirts, trousers, hats, ties, emblems, a steel helmet, Webb belts, and two pairs of those sturdy, rough outside leather combat boots that the Marines referred to as "Boondockers."

Weapons given us were a sheath knife, a 30-caliber carbine and a heavy short machete. In the days to come we were issued two Marine Corps green woolen uniforms with a barracks cap. Then came the entrenching tools, either a pick or shovel, followed by a camouflaged poncho and one half of a small tent referred to as a "shelter half." Last, but certainly not least, came the two medical kits and their contents that I was to become so familiar with over the next two years. In Marine Corps nomenclature, they would be called, Unit #3's.

Before long, our reason for being assigned to Camp Elliot was explained. We were to be trained at the field medical school to be military first aid men and after eight weeks of training we would be assigned to various units of the newly formed 5th Marine Division that was presently being formed at Camp Lejune, North Carolina and soon to arrive at Camp Pendleton, near Oceanside, California which was located about thirty-five miles north of San Diego.

We corpsmen began our education by doing more close order drill and study Machine gun, mortar, flame throwers and other small weapons usage. It was like being in boot camp all over except that this time we had Marine Corps instructors at first. Since we corpsmen were to be integrated into Marine units, we had much catching up to do to learn the necessary Marine Corps nomenclature and training procedures. Soon though, the Navy petty officers and physicians took over and continued the training by replacing the Marine instructors. The inspection of mess halls and eating conditions was to be our responsibility as was the inspection of the sanitary conditions of latrines.

Military first-aid probably received most of our attention as a full eight weeks was spent studying injuries of the nature of those received from bullets, grenade and shell fragments, burns and explosives. Map reading and topography classes were of much interest to me also. I found the Marine Corps brig next door very interesting, but appalling. We could observe it from our upper barracks room window. Its presence always reminded us that it was best not to stray from those rules and regulations we were told to follow

Pershing Square, a city park in Los Angeles in the year 1943 was often crowded with young civilian males wearing weird looking clothing called "zoot suits'. Large brimmed hats, peg leg trousers with large pleats of cloth around the hips seemed to be the most popular apparel to wear. Always a long metal chain that hung from the belt and clear down to the knees then back up again to disappear into the pant's pocket. A brightly colored bow tie seemed to be the focal part of the garb. Apparently some Marine A.W.O.L.'s (absent without leave) were drawn to wearing this style of clothing and many of them had been apprehended and were confined to the brig at the camp.

We were in a position to observe these "unfortunates" during their detention. I don't believe the guards at the brig appreciated the presence of the 'zoot suiters' much as those prisoners were not relieved of their strange garments, as the other prisoners were theirs. The others were given prison dungarees to wear. The 'zoot zooters' were told to keep wearing their odd clothing, though the belt and hat were taken away from them. The long hair of the "zoot suiter" was shaved from the scalp. A large black letter "P" was painted in black on the back of the long coat, and on the trouser knees, both front and back. The "P" was painted also on the unfortunate's forehead and on the back of his skull.

At dawn each day the prisoners were called to formation and to stand on the street in front of the main door. There they would answer roll call. As they exited from the door, which was only four and half feet high or so, they were required to bend forward at the waist as they ran. Outside the door, guards armed with shotguns and rubber hoses awaited them. As each prisoner emerged he was struck across the back by a rubber truncheon wielded by a guard who yelled, "go" at the man.

The prisoners wearing "zoot suits" seemed to attract special attention from the guards who attempted to issue multiple blows to them before the poor soul could reach his designated position in the formation. The prisoners were required to stand in formation once they arrived on the street. Their arms were to be folded high across their chests while their eyes were kept looking straight ahead. A prisoner's overheard comment or a wayward look would bring down the wrath of a guard who would give the offender a blow across the head or shoulders using the rubber truncheon. Once the formation was in order, the detail of prisoners was marched to a mess hall several street blocks away. The column was halted and every third man was ordered to fall out of line and run into the mess, where he was handed a loaf of bread. After that he immediately returned to the formation to stand in his former position. The prisoners then marched back to the brig.

It was our understanding from some of the men incarcerated there, that these prisoners were to exist only on bread and water for two days. Then on the third they would receive full meals, after which they would return to the bread and water diet again for another two days. This diet, in the jargon of the Marine Corps, was called, "piss and punk." During the eight weeks of field medical training at Camp Elliott, prison related scenes did have an effect on our company of corpsmen as far as our behavior was concerned.

Only one corpsman managed to ignore the message that most of us received. He went A.W.O.L. while on liberty in Los Angeles one weekend. He had the misfortune of being apprehended while intoxicated after being several days' overdue back at camp. It would have been better had he surrendered himself. This sad soul was observed by all of us from across the street. For seven days he was seen falling out for roll call each morning and then going through the degrading experience that I have just described. At the end of his period of confinement he returned to our barracks and absolutely refused to answer questions about or discuss his punishment. Until the end of our training period he kept to himself and spoke very little to the rest of his classmates. He became a very lonesome and silent figure around the barracks.

The Field Medical School was to become the basis for the formation of interesting personal relationships among those of us in attendance. It was there I met Edward Monjaras of Cheyenne, Wyoming, Amon Dillard of Georgia, Eugene R. Olson of Minnesota; and the likable, but always mischievous, Ivan Munns of Walla Walla, Washington. Munns and Monjaras were to die on Iwo Jima a year later, but before then, we were to become very close friends.

Another character appeared on the scene at this time. This person cannot be overlooked in retrospect. He definitely would not be called a friend by the rest of us although we were required to tolerate his presence. He was trouble from the beginning and he was trouble for anyone who happened to become involved with him in any manner. His name was William Marshall and he was from the Midwest somewhere. He was a well-built, tall athletic fellow of about twenty-two. His speech and behavior immediately revealed that he had grown up on the streets of a large city where he had learned that if he wanted something, he should just take it.

In contrast, Munns was an easygoing type of guy. He was full of humor, mischievous thoughts, and acts. He often made me angry at his tricks, but he was so likable that it was difficult to stay that way with him. He was also very loyal to his friends. When called upon for it, he was very dependable. He would die for that trait, as you will read later. Munns, often borrowed money from me to finance his liberty escapades and he often forgot to pay me back until I reminded him. Once when arriving back at camp late at night he found that he lacked funds with which to pay the cab fare. He awakened me and while I was still half asleep obtained the cab fare money from me. In the morning I didn't remember the incident much to Munn's delight. I have no way of knowing how many times I paid for his cab fare after that. I suspect many. I could describe Munns as a person who could fall into a den of rattlesnakes and have the serpents all friends with him in a very short time. It was Munns who could handle the hostile and belligerent Marshall best and prevent him from committing violence on the other members of the group. We did not invite Marshall's friendship, nor did we want him to become involved with us.

Since his bunk was next to ours, it was difficult to exclude him. He was prone to express himself with his fists at any opportunity. Because of Munn's good nature, Marshall attached himself more closely to him. The two would often go on liberty together. Usually the rest of us made excuses when they were leaving as to why we couldn't go with them. Then as soon as they left, we would all dress and follow at a safe distance out through the gate of the camp. We all were of the opinion that Munns sacrificed his freedom somewhat, so that we could be free of the tyrannical Marshall. Because of his relationship with Marshall, Munns was to find himself experiencing a series of situations, some of which could have been very disastrous to him.

It was about the end of the fourth week of training that I was awakened at 0200 by voices near my bunk. Apparently some disaster had befallen Marshall and Munns as far as I could ascertain by listening to their conversation. They awakened Dillard and the trio went into the head. My curiosity aroused, I left my bunk and entered that room. I found Marshall sitting on a stool; he had his right trouser leg rolled up to the knee. Munns and Dillard were examining a neat looking bluish tinted hole in the calf of Marshall's leg. The stocking below the wound was soaked with blood that ranged in color from dark brown to bright red. Munns and Dillard were discussing how to treat such an injury while the latter fumbled with the contents of a light basic medical kit. Both seemed hesitant and unsure in their actions.

In a most naive way, I asked Marshall how he got shot. This question brought a quick response, both verbal and physical from him. "Get the hell out of here or I'll cut you," he yelled at me. A switchblade knife suddenly appeared in his right hand and the blade flicked out at me. I decided to leave there and go back to my bunk. The next day Marshall was up and on his feet at reveille. He got out of bed and to my surprise walked to the mess hall with us. He limped a little and I overheard him tell others that he had sprained his ankle. Later in the day, I learned from Munns how Marshall had been injured.

The two men, while on liberty in the small town of Oceanside, ran out of money after spending all they had with them in the many bars there. Marshall, because of his early street training in a Kansas City, decided that there was an easy way to get money right there in Oceanside. Munns encouraged him, but then Marshall insisted that Munns would assist him. The two went to a downtown grocery store that had been closed for the day. Munns stayed outside and stood guard while Marshall kicked in the front door. Marshall went inside and ransacked the cash drawers for money. They were in this position when a merchant patrolman arrived to make his hourly check of the premises. Munns, seeing him appear took the easiest way out of the predicament by running through the parking lot at the side of the building and climbing over the six foot high wooden fence at the rear of the property. As he threw himself over it he heard the patrolman shout, "Stop!"

Inside the store, Marshall heard the shouted command. Through the window he observed his accomplice run alongside the building and head for the fence. Realizing that his safety was in jeopardy, he ran out through the smashed doorway and nearly collided with the patrolman. Ignoring the security man's commands to halt, Marshall ran at the high fence and taking a giant leap he gained the top boards and threw himself over it. As he described it later to Munns, he heard two shots fired and saw one slug tear through the top of a fence board after passing through his leg. He paid the wound no heed and he ran to catch up with Munns. They escaped the town by hitch hiking the distance back to Camp Elliott, thirty miles away.

It was interesting and entertaining to listen to Munn's attempts to explain to Marshall's satisfaction why he didn't call Marshall's attention to the arrival of the merchant patrolman. Over and over again, Munns told the same story. "Didn't you hear me yell at you that a cop was coming? "Didn't you? I did yell, you know. We are good buddies aren't we?" Eventually Munns convinced Marshall of his sincerity and so the latter let the matter drop. Because of Munn's persuasive monologue, I almost believed him myself after a while. Except that, I was learning the meaning of a certain smile that would develop on Munn's face whenever he told an untruth, or he was up to some mischief. The left side of his face would curl up a little. To the surprise and disappointment of my comrades and me, Marshall's leg continued to heal. After six weeks he had only a slight limp and a very fresh looking reddish scar to show of his injury. The wound had no discernible effect on his behavior. It was amazing to us how he managed to complete all the long hikes and field exercises in his condition. He was certainly in good physical shape.

During Marshall's absence our little group often talked about how to gain his speedy and permanent departure. Of course, when he was present, we carefully avoided any discussion or any action that might lead to a hostile confrontation with him.

A pleasant part of our stay at Camp Elliot was the presence of the women Marines next door. They could be counted upon to be a cheery group to be near and were responsible for reminding us of things other than discipline. The ladies carried with them, the somewhat derogatory designation of "B.A.M." an acronym of "Broad Assed Marines." Whether or not the girls became offended at the use of this term depended on how the phrase was used and the obvious intention of the user. The BAMs appreciated the corpsmen's presence too, I believe.

In our company there was a corpsman that was from New York City. He knew many different songs and always busied himself in organizing some of the class members into groups that he could lead in singing songs much to the delight of the women Marines. I believe he must have taught us sixteen verses of one song, one of which goes like this:

> *My girl's a cor-er-ker,*
> *She's a New Yor-er-ker,*
> *I buy her everything—-to keep her in style,*
> *She has a pair of legs,*
> *Just like two whiskey kegs,*
> *That boys, is where my money goe-oh-ohs.*

The woman Marines would appear on their porch and listen each time the singing began on our porch. Usually they would join in when the time was appropriate. We also had other entertainment at Camp Elliot. Several movie personalities appeared much to our delight. Coast Guard Lt. Commander Rudy Valley appeared with a band. He was well received by the personnel.

1st Class Pharmacists Mate Cherry, the man in charge of our class would awaken us with the same act every day except on Sundays. He would hold an empty garbage can in his left hand while he beat on it with a wooden club held in his right. While he did this he walked up and down between our bunks. He would yell out, "Wake up, wake up! You may have been the 'Belle of the Ball' last night, but this morning you're just another poor son-of-a-bitch!"

No one really seemed to take offense at his act, in reality he was a pretty good sort of a guy I considered this field medical school a fun period in my military career. I also learned a lot because of proper discipline and teaching methods. Again I attained a position in the top twenty five-percent of the class scholastically and was promoted to Hospital Apprentice 1/c. It was also a time during which I was learning loyalty to my comrades, my country, my military unit and most of all, confidence in myself.

I also learned that a sense of humor was necessary to get along with others around me. It was hard to grin and laugh sometimes when a joke was played on me. Getting into bed late at night after coming in off liberty and finding the bed short sheeted, or awakening in the middle of the night in a pool of water caused by a ruptured water filled condom that some prankster had placed under the sheet was easier to take if you had a sense of humor. On February 12, 1944, our class graduated and was sent to the U.S. Marine Training Center at Camp Pendleton, where we were assigned to duty with the newly formed 5th Marine Division. Fortunately my closest buddies and I remained together as we were assigned to the 2nd battalion, 26th Marine Regiment, 5th Marine Division.

Camp Pendleton

The Camp Pendleton Marine Corps base, located at Oceanside, California was not a very busy place when I arrived there February 12, 1944. Normally the camp held a full division of seventeen or eighteen thousand men. But, that February only a few could be seen strolling about the streets or lolling around the barracks as though they had nothing else to do. We unloaded ourselves and our gear from trucks at an empty barracks building and told to stay there until we received further instructions. We waited for about thirty days doing nothing constructive the entire time. We attended mess and went on liberty every other night if we wished.

I didn't speak to an officer during that period either. A Pharmacist Mate 2/c, James Vanere, was in charge and issued us liberty cards to use when we were off duty. I rarely used mine after a few visits to the nearby town of Oceanside. There wasn't much there for me to do. The only diversion was to visit a barroom, and since I was just eighteen years old, bartenders kept challenging me for proper identification. The embarrassment of being ordered out of the barroom each time caused me to decide that a milk shake at the camp's Post Exchange was more to my liking anyway. It was at this time that Eugene Olson and Edward Monjaras and I became close friends. Monjaras and I had met once before when we were classmates at the hospital corps school at Farragut, Idaho.

In March, James Vanere assigned me, Gene Olson, Ivan Munns, Amon Dillard, and (much to our dismay) Marshall, to occupy an empty barracks. We were told that it would eventually house Company D, 2nd Battalion, 26th Marine Regiment. Still, we did little but watch each day as individual Marines straggled into camp after being transferred from other stations. Most were young and bewildered about their new assignment and found no enlightenment from us as to what awaited them. They, too, settled down on a bunk to wait the appearance of some authority.

We noticed immediately the varied backgrounds and experience of these Marines. Apparently about sixty percent were just out of boot camp. The rest were veterans of some recent campaign in the South Pacific or from some guard unit.

A large number of men were from the recently disbanded First and Second Raider Battalions and the First and Second Paratroop Battalions. General Alexander A. Vandergrift, the Marine Commandant in Washington, D.C., had decided to do away with such specialized units and to concentrate instead on the development of one compact, well trained, combat organization. He also decided to add another division, the 5th Division

We could learn from these men because of their experiences. Most received promotions in the early training days at Camp Pendleton and many received citations for their brave deeds done in recent campaigns, primarily in the Solomon Islands area of the South Pacific.

The forming of the 5th Marine Division was very interesting to me. The newly arrived men began to familiarize themselves with each other and friendships were formed. Recently appointed corporals and sergeants began to accustom themselves to their new responsibilities.

Much to our surprise we Navy corpsmen were well accepted into the company of Marines. We received a small amount of harassment from some of the newer Marines because of the age-old story of bickering that springs up between the various service branches. Soon we learned why we were mostly accepted. The Marine combat veterans, who had recently returned to the States from places like Guadalcanal, Tulagi, New Britain, and Tarawa, had learned to respect and rely upon the medical services of the corpsmen who served with them.

Many said that they owed their lives to the corpsmen's courage and medical skills. What harassment there was really came from the young Marines who had just graduated from boot camp and who felt their actions were justified because of the long standing inter-service rivalry. We corpsmen learned to remain quiet. If we did, the offender would be chastised by a Marine combat veteran who would warn the novice, "When the time comes, you could be sorry you shot your mouth off!"

The battalion "Slop Chute," as the beer hall was called, was opened after the companies formed. One day Olson, Monjaras and I decided to investigate that place which was located near the Post Exchange. The single story building was constructed of rough-cut lumber. The barroom was a rectangular shaped room about twenty by thirty feet in size. The only furniture consisted of four long wood tables with benches. These ran from the front to the back of the room where a wood plank bar was stretched from one sidewall to the other. Behind the bar stood a stocky marine buck sergeant who greeted us with a nod of his head and an unsmiling face. He had his arms folded across his chest and was certainly unimpressed by our presence. My two comrades selected me to get a pitcher of beer.

"Can I get a pitcher of beer?" I asked the sergeant.

"Why not?" he answered

"Well, I thought you may think I'm too young,"

"Hell, you're old enough to stand there ain't you?" he growled back.

So after handing over fifty cents, I received a pitcher of cold beer and three drinking mugs. My comrades and I found empty benches at a table at the middle of the room to sit. It wasn't very long before we noticed that the room was filling up with Marines most of whom wore dungarees. They were a noisy lot. Each tried to out shout the others as they poured beer from their mugs to their mouths. The sergeant behind the bar was kept busy refilling the large glass pitchers from kegs of beer stacked behind him. He'd shove the glass containers out and across the bar to whoever had fifty cents to hand him.

On the right side of the room we observed Marines gathering who were all wearing boots of a similar style. The boots were high topped, probably eight inches higher than the toe, and the men seemed proud to wear them as they folded the cuffs of their trousers unusually high to expose the footwear to other's view. We came to the conclusion that these were the men from the recently disbanded Marine paratroop battalions who had fought in the Solomon Islands.

On the left side of the room men was a gathering who wore a Marine Corps cap, equipped with a bill, same as ours, but their sun-visor was crimped down the middle in a certain way apparently to distinguish themselves from everyone else. The caps were all worn the same way, the visor pulled down on the forehead to a point just above their eyes. These were the men of the renowned Raider battalions, also just disbanded and who were veterans of the Solomon Island battles too. We watched the developing scene in awe and concern as the laughter and curses became louder.

Undoubtedly, there was friction between the two groups. The paratroopers began to sing some of their old favorite songs, and the Raiders sang theirs. One memorable Raider song referred to Lt. Col. Merritt A Edson, one of the battalion's commanders, and went like this:

Edson's Raiders: (melody - McNamara's Band)

Oh, we are the Edson's Raiders,
We're the members of a band,
Although, we're few in numbers,
We're the finest in the land,
We played on all the islands,
And had a lot of fun,
But, what a day we'll enjoy,
When the war is won.

Chorus:

Oh, the M1's bang, the mortars clang,
The machine guns blaze away.
On and on we fought
Until the break of day.
There's A and B and C and D,
But, no more company E.
A finer band of real Marines,
There never has been seen

We landed on Tulagi,
And the islands we soon had.
We moved on to "Old Canal,"
It really wasn't bad.
We held our lines on Luna Ridge,

And never gave and inch.
The first and second Matanikaw,
They really were a cinch.

Chorus:

Right now we are rehearsing,
For another big affair.
We'll take another island,
And the Japs will all be there.
And when they see us streaming in,
They'll say, "Old pal, 'flum' Guadalcanal,
You didn't come here for fun!"

Chorus:

We wear a suit of dungarees,
It's camouflaged in green.
"A tougher bunch of looking men,"
There never has been seen.
There's Tom and Jack and Sam and Jake,
You'll see no stranger sight,
All dressed up in their battle togs,
All ready for a fight.

Chorus:

This Raider song was heard for the duration of World War II, wherever and whenever Marines gathered for a drink of beer. But, during this particular session at the Slop Chute', the song was obviously sung to infuriate the 'Paramarines' and the troopers were irritated even more when the Raiders sang one of the Paratrooper's own songs. One was the "Chutists" song, sung in what was meant to be in an derogatory manner.

"The Paratrooper's Lament! Melody - Battle Hymn of the Republic)

There was blood upon the risers,
There was blood upon the chute,
There was blood that came a trickling,
Down the Paratrooper's boot.
He lay there rolling round,
In all the welter of his gore,
He ain't gonna jump no more.

Chorus:

Gory, Gory parachutist,
Gory, gory parachutist,
Gory, Gory what a hell of a way to die,
He ain't gonna jump no more!

The Raiders sang, the beer flowed and the noise was becoming unbearable. Hostile glances increased between the two opposing factions. Suddenly, one of the booted paratroopers jumped up from his table behind us and exclaimed, "I've had enough of this bullshit! I'm not going to sit here and take it anymore!"

With that, he pushed his nearest comrades away from him, picked up the bench they had been sitting on and threw it over our heads at the Raiders sitting at the next table. The Raiders tumbled to the floor in an attempt to escape the airborne wood bench. Fortunately, two of them managed to catch the missile preventing it from doing serious damage.

My two buddies and I left our seats quickly with the intention of leaving that place fast. Obviously there was going to be a violent clash between the two factions. Unfortunately, we had been sitting in the center of the room and it took us some time to make our way to the nearest wall and slip along it to the only door out of there. We escaped there receiving only some buffeting about by the 'Slop Chute' warriors.

The three of us crossed the street and stood on the other side as the fight fully erupted inside the beer hall. Tables, glass pitchers, mugs, benches, fists and boots became weapons as the two groups went at it.

Quickly, the military police arrived. Their presence did nothing to quell the violence, but seemed to add to it as the fighters regarded them as adversaries too and ignored the MP Officer's order to desist.

When the police unit arrived, the officer in charge ordered my two buddies and me to leave the area. Eddie Monjaras spoke up "Sir, we are corpsmen and perhaps we could be of some help before this fight ends!"

The Lieutenant paused to look us over, and replied, "Yes, OK..., stay!"

The officer formed up his men and sent them into the fray, he stayed outside the door. It was quite a scene. White helmets of the MP's came flying out of door and bounced into the street. One M.P. was thrown bodily out the door where he landed on his back on the ground and right at the officer's feet. He picked himself up and dashed back inside.

It wasn't the presence of the MP's that caused the cessation of the hostilities after a while, it was the fact that the combatants just wore themselves out. Soon men were leaving the room holding their hands to their heads, face or some other part of their body as they drifted away from the area. The military policemen made no attempt to stop them or make an arrest. We watched as the police helped men to their feet and sent them on their way. "Shove off, or face the consequences," they ordered. Finally peace returned to the area.

The Paratroopers, as evidenced by their parting remarks, were satisfied that they had avenged any insult to the paratrooper battalion's honor. Now, everyone could go on his way again.

The military police, seeing the two groups separate, gathered together with their commanding officer. Straightening their clothing and gear and helping each other to do the same, they set about convincing themselves that it was their involvement that brought about the cessation of hostilities and returned peace to the area.

We corpsmen stood there listening to their remarks and thinking some were making amusing assumptions, and we made the mistake of grinning. The officer saw the looks on our faces and glared at us. He didn't have to verbalize his thoughts; we understood well enough and got the 'hell out of there!'

As far as the military police were concerned, it was obvious they didn't want to try to take one of the Marines into custody for fear that both factions would join together in order to fight a common enemy. We found that the disturbance was not just a one-night affair as the contests continued for several weeks until the adversaries themselves became friends as they were assigned to the same platoons and companies. It wasn't long before the Raiders and Paratroopers were welded together in a tight, well-disciplined fighting organization. Of course, until the war's end there were good-natured jests and remarks made by both groups, and I don't remember any more disturbances between the two groups.

The troops at Camp Pendleton had other forms of entertainment. Each regiment had a Post Exchange and movie theater that showed the latest films from Hollywood. Camp shows were arranged and many of the celebrities appeared and performed.

Judy Garland came and walked among us once. To me, she appeared pale, shy and perhaps afraid. I think all those Marines gathered about her dressed in combat clothing and helmets frightened her. She made small talk and shook hands. I happened to be standing near when she said hello and she offered her hand for me to shake. I was really awed by her presence and stumbled about trying to say hello. I believe she was nineteen years old at the time, a year older than me. She looked very thin and wore a black dress that emphasized the whiteness of her skin.

Training during the spring became very strenuous, but interesting to me. I was eager to learn this type of warfare. Not once did I wish that I was back with the Navy. I was assigned to duty with the 2nd platoon of "D" company along with forty-two enlisted men and one officer. Although my primary duty was that of a combat medic, I trained along with the Marines to become familiar with the use of firearms and other weapons. I liked to fire the machine gun, mortars and bazooka, and also use explosives. We attended many classes on the use and the handling of various types of explosives and learned to make up charges of TNT and shape charges using old bottles.

Probably, the weapon I liked most was the 60 mm mortar. I never missed an opportunity to go along with the mortar section when they went into the field to practice. The mortar can be devastating when used against an enemy. We find that out on Iwo Jima, as the Japanese were very good with that weapon. We expended a considerable number of hand grenades while learning how to throw them correctly and to overcome the fear of handling dangerous explosives like that.

We spent several days each month on the firing ranges of Camp Pendleton until firing the rifle and handgun became second nature to us. Bayonet practice was a constant exercise, as it seemed there was a natural reluctance on the part of our men to use it to stab another human being with the long knife. This had to be overcome with practice. With the advent of the automatic rifle the use of the bayonet became a less important skill for the riflemen. Using it as a defensive weapon was a different matter though, as it was still quite effective when used for that purpose. During the coming battle on Iwo Jima I became very well acquainted with holding one in my hand each and every night, considering it more useful than a rifle.

Captain Thomas M. Fields became the company commander. Actually, he was the second. The first was an older man, a reservist Captain who seemed to become slightly confused at times. He repeatedly appeared before us forgetting to wear his helmet forcing the executive officer Lt. Jack R. Jones to whisper, "Captain..., Captain..., your helmet, you forgot your helmet!" This incident was repeated several times, then one day Captain Fields took his place. This older man was not seen again. I suppose that the older man had been placed in command only to form up the company before turning it over to a younger more energetic officer.

Captain Fields brought with him combat experience that he gained from fighting on the Solomon Islands. He enjoyed a very good reputation and high respect of the men and other officers. To my surprise he was very friendly and kind to his men. He was always at the head of the company and in full authority. He seemed to possess great physical ability and demonstrated it during field exercises. It was difficult to complain about the physical demands that were required of us, especially when the commander did as much or more.

The Top Sergeant of the company was First Sergeant Robert L. Neef. He was about forty years old, tall, lean, and hard as a piece of oak wood. He was what was known as a "China Marine." A China Marine being one who served in China during the Japanese occupation, and the trying days in the late 1930s. He was straight talking, and commanded the respect and attention of all the officers and men alike. His thoughts and speech were easily understood, and I would listen in awe of the man when he admonished us as a unit or individually. His language, though not the tea room variety served to communicate his message to others with power and clarity.

When the object of his concern was a young fledgling marine, his opening remarks were almost fatherly. "Son," he would start out, "what is your problem! What do you use for brains? Do you have sawdust for brains? Do you have shit for brains? Do you understand where your course of action is going to lead you? In battle that kind of behavior can cost you your life, worse yet it can cost the lives of a lot of your buddies, and just because you screwed up. I'm sure you don't want that to happen, so straighten up and do it right this time!"

Likely as not, the young marine would stand there, after such an admonishment, feeling all alone while suffering the wrath of the other men in the company. As for me I would rather be yelled at and threatened than be subjected to one of his lectures. I was never talked to by him in that manner but there were a few times the "Top" called us corpsmen together and explained to us how we could improve our behavior. Each time afterward, I felt as though I had let my buddies in the company down and I would be more determined to improve.

There were times when the "Top" found it necessary to call a second Lieutenant to task for his shortcomings. He would continue to talk to the officer as if he was an errant son, speaking to him in a firm, but understanding voice. I often thought it odd that the enlisted men overhearing such an incident would not take the opportunity to enjoy an officer being dressed down, but instead most of us felt sympathy for the officer. Somehow it made us feel closer and more respectful of the officer as well as the First Sergeant.

A favorite supervisor of mine, one I respected very much, was First Lieutenant Charles F. Horvath who was from Elmwood, Connecticut. He was appointed as the officer in charge of the second platoon. He was a man of good physical ability and appearance, and I believe at the time he was in his late twenties. He had a dark complexion especially when he was exposed to the sun. He was a quiet man, not likely to be flustered when confronted by stressful situations, at least in training anyway. Horvath was respected for his ability to perform his Marine Corps duties as an officer. He believed in training and he respected his supervisors as well as the men he commanded.

The Lieutenant was an avid baseball player and a fan of the game. He participated in any game at the camp, and he often helped organize them. I observed that this deep interest and involvement created some tension and anxiety as far as Captain Fields was concerned, especially when that officer was attempting to carry out a scheduled field exercise. Several times the Lieutenant would say to the Captain, "Sir, I have to be excused now as I have to report for baseball practice!"

Needless to say the Captain would be slightly upset. I suspect there must have been a colonel or major somewhere that liked baseball too, and was making arrangements for a camp game.

Lt. Horvath learned (as we did) and suffered humiliation (as we did) when he also committed an error or infraction of a rule. He later proved himself in battle as a brave and competent officer while under fire, considering that all men have their breaking point. He constantly encouraged men under the most trying circumstances.

In February 1944 the battalion executive officer was Major Daniel Pollock, a stocky figure and one tough marine. He wore jump boots and tucked his pants legs inside the leather. He was frightening to me at that time because he looked and acted so aggressive. We newer enlisted men avoided face-to-face confrontation with him at all cost.

Once, the entire division was out for a three-day field exercise. We bivouacked the first night beside a barbed wire fence inland from Highway #1 near San Clemente Beach. At dawn we were to cross the fence, load our weapons and proceed inland while maintaining our skirmish line, then advance on "enemy positions." We were to fire at cardboard silhouettes of

Japanese soldiers. These cardboard figures were partially concealed among brush and rocks.

After an initial bombardment of the area in front of us by the 13th Marines who were our artillery support, we advanced. But, first we had to cross the barbed wire, and then load our weapons. Being a farm boy, I found the wire easy to cross, but others didn't do find it as easy. PFC James L. Oberg, who against orders had already loaded his weapon, put one foot and leg through the wires which I held apart for him. He let his rifle fall butt first to the ground in order to steady himself. When the butt hit the ground the slide assembly went down and then forward, picked up a live round from the clip and pushed it into the breech and somehow caused the rifle to fire.

The entire division exercise was brought to a halt by the sound of the shot fired. We were ordered to stand fast and not move a foot until further orders. We stood there for about fifteen minutes before listening and watching as two jeeps came dashing, bouncing and clawing their way up the hill toward us. The first jeep contained the huge figure of Major Pollock who stood upright in the front of the vehicle hanging onto the windshield for support. A sergeant was driving the vehicle, and it was being followed by a second jeep carrying two military police sergeants.

"Did one of your men fire their weapon?" The Lieutenant was quick to answer, "Yes sir. That man did, sir," pointing at Oberg who I now figured was standing uncomfortably close to me.

"Did you tell him not to load his weapon before crossing the fence?"

"Yes, Sir, I did!"

Major Pollock leaped from his jeep and taking long quick strides, crossed the open ground separating him from PFC Oberg.

"Did you fire that shot?" He demanded.

"Yes, Sir," Oberg responded, unhesitatingly.

The Major lashed out at Oberg with his fist and struck him on the point of his chin. Oberg fell to the ground and lay there completely unconscious.

Startled, I reacted by turning, intending to kneel beside the fallen man to assist him. But then, I saw the look in the Major's eyes and I changed my mind immediately and stood at attention.

"Arrest that man and take him to the brig" ordered the Major of the two M.P. sergeants. The two did as they were directed and picked up Oberg and dumped him unceremoniously into the back of their jeep. They drove away and all I could see of Oberg was his arms and legs bouncing up and down as the jeep lunged down the hill, over the rough terrain and at last disappeared into the screen of heavy brush and trees. The Major watched as the jeep sped away and then turned toward the Lieutenant and growled,

"OK, let's get on with our business!"

"Yes sir!" replied Lt. Horvath.

We saw nothing of Oberg for over thirty days. When he returned to the company we could see that his head had been shaved after his arrest and the scalp showed indications of bruises and abrasions that he reported had occurred while in the brig. He said that he had received thirty days punishment in the brig after facing a summary court martial, and only because he had failed to follow orders. He described to us how he was beaten almost daily while in the brig, usually over some trivial matter. After hearing his story, I was more determined than ever not to do anything that would cause me to be confined there.

The PFC made some verbal threats against the major because of what had been done to him. We, his buddies, sympathized with him, but eventually convinced him to stop talking that way and just accept what had happened. Besides, we explained to him, if we had been in actual combat that day and infiltrating enemy territory, his actions would have given us away and might have gotten us killed.

Major Pollock was soon promoted to Lt. Colonel and assigned to the 1st battalion to command. Both he and Oberg were seriously wounded on Iwo Jima. I can attest to the fact that Oberg accredited himself very well while in battle.

I did meet Major Pollock once again. This time it was while Company D was on the rifle range. During a pause in the shooting the Marines were given a lecture regarding their personal involvement with the Corps. We corpsmen took advantage of the situation to disappear from sight in a grassy field where we could "goof off." Evidently we were spotted by the Major, who walked up on us. I was lying on my back, eyes shut against the glare of the sun while Munns and Dillard argued about some liberty time they had. I didn't take much notice when they ceased talking suddenly and I remained lying on the ground. I felt someone kick the bottom of my foot. I didn't respond until I felt another kick and heard a strange commanding voice say, "What is your mission in life, son?"

I opened my eyes and looked up at the huge standing figure of Major Pollock who looked as menacing as he did on the day he knocked Oberg unconscious. He was looking down at me. He stood there massive as ever at my feet with his hands on his hips and his feet spread wide apart. He looked mean. I actually began to salute him while lying there on my back, but stopped before I went too far. I jumped up and stood before him at attention. Then I stammered out, "Sir, we are corpsmen attached to D Company. We have been on the firing range and are finished shooting. Right now we are now hiding, trying to keep out of the way of the officers, Sir!"

A slight smile broke out at the corners of his mouth. Apparently, he was caught off guard with my frankness and thought my simple honesty had some humor to it. He actually made small talk with us for a while before walking away saying, "Well, carry on men!"

All the while I was stammering out my explanation to the Major I could see Munns standing behind him making faces at me and wearing that impish grin of his. I was angry that he and Dillard had seen the Major approach and they had let me lie there without warning me just so I'd get caught in that embarrassing position. Munn, mimicked me saying, "Oh, major sir, we are hiding from the officers so they can't see us 'goofing' off!"

All I could think of to say was "Well, go to hell, I'm not going to lie to an officer!"

CHAPTER NINE

Marshall, Munns and Dillard

T HE EARLY DAYS at Camp Pendleton could have been boring except for hospital corpsmen Munns and Marshall helped us to avoid that. During the second week at Camp Pendleton Marshall had gone on liberty wearing his custom-made Navy blue dress uniform. Since we had been told to dispose of our Navy dress uniform and to wear only Marine Corps issue, he was in violation of the camp dress code. Not only did he wear his Navy uniform, he insisted on wearing a shiny black leather jacket with it. This jacket served as "waiving a red flag" at the Navy shore patrolmen on duty in town, as that garb was considered improper dress for enlisted personnel. Two of the patrolmen stopped Marshall for an identification check immediately once they saw him. Marshall's own stupidity led to a shoving and pushing confrontation between him and the Shore Patrolmen. Munns and Dillard, who were with him at the time, faded into the background of the evening scene and Marshall was hauled off to the brig for an overnight stay. He was remanded into the custody of the newly arrived battalion surgeon the next day. The doctor served as our immediate Navy superior officer and he restricted Marshall to camp for the following two weeks. Marshall was ordered not to leave camp for that period of time.

The doctor was not often on station during those early days. To me, he didn't seem to be very concerned about his duties and appeared even less interested in speaking to those who served under his command. In fact, I didn't even see him for six weeks after he reported for duty the battalion aid station.

Marshall took advantage of the doctor's absence and, at the urging of Munns and Dillard, went to the doctor's desk, removed his liberty card, and went off to town. This might have worked well for Marshall; however he so liked wearing his black shiny jacket with his Navy uniform. Munns was right there urging him on, saying there was no need to get caught if he, Marshall, didn't cause a problem while on liberty that would attract the attention of the shore patrol. Munns had a facial expression that seemed to appear when he was intent on playing a joke on someone. The left side of his mouth would turn up and it was present this time as he urged Marshall to go on liberty without official permission. The two of them, Marshall wearing his Navy blues and black jacket, and Munns, properly dressed in his Marine green uniform, went off on liberty to Oceanside. Munns told the rest of us what happened that night in town after he returned alone. He said that he and Marshall had made the rounds of most of the bars in Oceanside and soon found out that they had run out of money. He said that they had drunk considerably but even so, didn't want to return early to camp.

Munns said that he had encouraged Marshall to attempt to persuade some passing "Gyrenes" to loan them money. Marshall failed in his attempt by using some gentle persuasive methods and resorted to a more aggressive way by grabbing a passing Marine and twisting the man's arm around behind his back. This caused the Marine to call out for help as he was suffering pain and terror. All this commotion attracted the attention of two Marine military policemen who came to the man's aid, grabbed Marshall and Munns and arrested them for being drunk and disorderly. Marshall was told that he was going to be charged for being out of uniform along with the other complaints against him. The two corpsmen were shoved into a military police bus and held there to await transportation back to the camp. Munns, always the more alert, found that he could open a bus window, and being of slender build he quietly and easily slipped through it, dropped to the ground and began to run away. When he turned to look back, he saw that Marshall was trying to follow was halfway through the window of the bus, but was being pounded on by the MP's who were using their night sticks with 'delirious abandon'.

After sitting up that night and discussing the incident for two hours, we all turned in to our bunks, looking forward to what the next day would bring. When the MP's had apprehended Munns in town, they had neglected to confiscate his identity and liberty card. It was possible that his name would never be known by the authorities, but just the same he spent a miserable night while waiting to find out. Marshall was sentenced to seven days in the camp brig and later restricted to camp for a specified time. Munns escaped punishment as Marshall refused to give his name to the MP's that night and the next day.

Marshall made our daily existence very uncomfortable. The only time he was pleasant to us was when he wanted something, like help assisting with a medical problem. After receiving our help he'd be grateful for only a short while. The next day however, he would return to his old ways. As for Munns, we should have been more grateful to him, as he kept Marshall busy, and more important, away from us. I think that at times Munns feared for his own safety if he did not agree to go along the Marshall on one of his questionable activities. The stories of their escapades did furnish us with some comic relief at times, although most of the recounts were of a sordid nature.

On several occasions Marshall had returned to camp from liberty with wallets that he claimed to have removed from the pockets of "Queers" (homosexuals) whom he had encountered while on liberty in Los Angeles. It was his story that Munns would attract the attention of these unfortunate "misfits," as they were called at the time, and then lead them to a place where Marshall lay in wait.

We were shown a dozen or more wallets that had been collected and we heard of many more that we never saw. Perhaps we weren't shown more because we displayed obvious disgust at the booty and the stories that accompanied them. We warned Marshall that the wallets he held could be damning evidence against him if they were ever found in his possession.

We were certain that there was some insanity in Marshall. Whenever he took up a knife and held it in his hand his eyes would develop a certain gleam. That look, accompanied by a certain facial expression, aggressive attitude and other actions caused us to fear and suspect him. This guy, according to his statements had been brought up on the streets of Kansas City and lived by a peculiar set of rules that were unfamiliar to the rest of us.

He once pulled a fancy Italian bayonet from PFC Anthony Trocano's belt scabbard. When the Marine objected, saying his father carried that bayonet in the last war, Marshall slashed at Trocano's stomach with it. The point of the blade ran down the row of buttons on the Marine's blouse making a clicking noise as it touched each one in passing. The Marine froze in fear. I think that Marshall would have attacked again if we all had not objected and threatened to intervene forcible if he did so. Even so, he considered fighting us all at one time.

Munns certainly wasn't in accord with all of Marshall's activities while they were on liberty together. He often did not know how to separate himself from his errant partner at times when it was necessary to do so. He described another incident that showed this clearly. He and Marshall went to Los Angeles. A week before, Marshall, in keeping with his love affair with a Navy dress uniform, had ordered a tailor made one of high quality from a tailor shop in the city. As Marshall described it to us, "I'm getting it from this Jew tailor on Main Street!"

Accompanied by Munns, Marshall arrived at the tailor shop and tried the suit on that he had ordered. Standing before a full-length mirror Marshall told he tailor that the suit fit very well and that he would take it. The tailor replied, "That's good, that will be eighty five dollars please."

Marshall picked up his old uniform, tucked it under his arm and said to the tailor, "Screw you," and ran from the store, out onto the street heading south on Main. The tailor recovering from his surprise chased the sailor out on the street where he soon realized he could not catch Marshall so he returned to his shop to telephone the police. Munns who had been caught by surprise sitting down when Marshall ran was told to stay and wait for the police to come. Munns recovered his senses quickly though and ran out the door and down the street.

Why Munns allowed Marshall to drag him along during these escapades, was something the rest of us couldn't understand. Perhaps it was just fear of Marshall or perhaps Munns found it exciting. With the end of our training period approaching we thought that for sure their relationship would end, especially after another incident occurred.

The two of them went to San Diego on liberty. Late at night they approached a young woman, who apparently made it part of her livelihood to stand on street corners at night. A discussion began between the three of them with Marshall becoming less verbal and more physical. Munns described to us what happened after he returned to camp the next day.

Marshall had the woman pushed up against the door of a store. He'd pulled her dress up around her waist and was pinning her body against the door with his own. She began to scream and beat her fists against Marshall's face in a vain attempt to get away from him. Munns became alarmed that the noise would attract the attention of passersby and probably the military police as well. Two shore patrolmen came into view running toward them all the while blowing whistles. Munns went on to recount the incident saying he ran the opposite way and when he looked back saw the shore patrolmen beating on Marshall's head with their nightsticks. Munns said he ran from the area and returned to camp.

The next morning Munns was up early and he appeared to be very upset... and he was not his usually cheery self. He didn't share his Saturday night experience with us. Instead he remained very quiet throughout the day offering no explanation for his early return to camp or why Marshall had not come with him. On Monday, after recall, Marshall still wasn't on duty. That evening we heard that he was in the camp brig again, this time charged with attempted rape, resisting arrest and assaulting shore patrolmen when they attempted to arrest him. We had looked to Munns for an explanation which he gave reluctantly after receiving our promise not to repeat it.

We had no communication with Marshall for the next thirty days and received very little information concerning his predicament. Munns continued to keep silent about, fearing he would surely end up in the brig too. It was doubtful that Marshall would reveal Munn's identity, but it was possible that the woman victim might be called to examine pictures of all of Marshall's known acquaintances in an attempt to identify the second person involved.

Marshall's trial was held in the battalion headquarters offices about thirty days after the incident. A battalion platoon leader, a Lt. Green was appointed to defend Marshall by the battalion commander, Lt. Col. Sayers. We corpsmen placed ourselves in a position to see Marshall as he was brought to the trial place. He was brought there in handcuffs and wearing a clean khaki uniform by two serious looking MP's walking on either side of him. Marshall's head was shaved of all hair and his scalp showed the pink color of freshly healed wounds. There were also a few fresh wounds indicating the brig management's taste for discipline. One of us called out, "How's it going Marshall?

"OK," he answered, "The bastards don't have me yet!"

An MP's baton was jabbed into his back to hurry him along. Whatever he meant by his statement, I wasn't sure at the time, but he was partially right. The woman accuser did not show up for the trial to testify and it was rumored that she had left the state and was living in Las Vegas, Nevada.

Lt. Green asked the court to dismiss the charges on the basis that a crime of rape could not be proven. As for the charge of resisting arrest and assault against the MP's, the defense insisted that since there was no crime, the shore patrol had no right to arrest him; therefore Marshall had the right to defend himself.

It was told later that upon hearing this argument, Lt. Col. Sayers became enraged, as it was he who had ordered Marshall to stand trial. He had to face the facts though, in the face of have no evidence of a crime he reluctantly dismissed all charges and ordered Marshall turned loose the next day. It was also said that he later turned his wrath on all present and especially targeted Lt. Green, who in front of witnesses frustrated the colonel's attempt at obtaining a speedy conviction.

Marshall was released the next day and he returned to duty along side of us, his shaved head still showing scars caused by the wood batons of guards while incarcerated.

We spoke to Lt. Green after the trial. In civilian life he was an attorney. He asked for and received a transfer to another unit, away from our Col. Sayers soon after the incident.

The incident wasn't mentioned much afterward, especially when Marshall was present. He brought the matter up a few times himself though. He would ask Munns to repeat why he, Munns didn't stay and help fight off the shore patrolmen. When he asked that, the rest of us would gather quickly around trying not to smile, but waiting for Munns to come up with a plausible excuse. Munns had come up with several and I must say they got better each time.

Marshall, on occasion, had gone to the senior petty officer of the battalion medical section and had requested transfer back to the Navy. The senior corpsman had always given Marshall a negative answer. Marshall hated his duties as a medical corpsman. He said that he was a trained carpenter in civilian life and that is what he wanted to do in the Navy.

We other corpsmen continually encouraged him to keep trying for the transfer from the 5th Marine Division. I think that Munns led the way in this encouragement now. It was Munns who came up with an idea for Marshall to pretend to be crazy in an attempt to show the battalion surgeon how desperate he was to transfer. Marshall began toying with the idea.

One Saturday he presented a plan to Dillard and me as we sat on our bunks talking. His idea was simple. Dillard and I were to drag him scuffling and resisting, across the camp street and into the dispensary. There could be many witnesses to this act and once we were in the surgeons' office, Dillard and I would tell the officer that Marshall had attempted to commit suicide by hanging himself in our barracks.

Dillard and I didn't think that that was such a good idea and told Marshall so. The main reason was that the doctor wouldn't believe such a shallow attempt at deception and we would all be in trouble. Of course, Dillard and I really didn't want to be involved in such a scheme. Marshall became insistent in his attempt to persuade us to help him. Once, while arguing with him and trying to get him to abandon his plan I happened to glance at Dillard who was looking at me in a very strange way. A thought flashed into my mind and I wondered if he, Dillard, was thinking the same thoughts I was.

It was Marshall's idea to hang him self, by placing a Webb belt around his neck. He would twist it firmly enough to cause abrasions on his skin. Dillard or I would cut the belt in two and then we'd drag Marshall off to the sick bay taking along the Webb belting to show the doctor. Dillard opposed this plan saying the doctor may want to see what the object was that Marshall hanged him self from. It was decided that we should use two belts, fastened together, with a loop at one end that would encircle Marshall's neck. Dillard and I were of the same mind now. If the guy wanted to hang himself, OK, Let him!

Dillard and I were in agreed to let Marshall hang, even though the two of us had not discussed that part of it. If Marshall accidentally hanged himself, good riddance, we would be rid of him once and for all. Marshall, Dillard and I fastened two Webb belts together and went outside to find an overhead projection suitable to conduct the hanging from. It wasn't a very easy task. We went up on the hill to the mess hall, which was the largest building in the immediate area, but didn't find any thing there to tie the belt to that suited us. Back at the barracks we discovered a basketball hoop set up about eight feet off the ground from which we could tie the belt. We decided that this was the place to do the deed!

Marshall placed the belt loop around his neck, the other end he held in has hand. I was thinking that the whole scheme was ridiculous and was trying to keep from laughing. It was hard to keep a straight face. Marshall found that he couldn't reach high enough to tie the loose end of the belt to the basketball backboard bracing. From a nearby trash container Dillard produced a cardboard box. Marshall thought that by standing on the corners it would be strong enough to hold his weight long enough for him to tie the belt to the bracket and for us to cut through the belt with a knife.

Marshall stood there looking at Dillard and me, he said, "OK, now as soon as I get it tied to the brace I'll let my weight down easily until it cuts into my neck a little then you cut the belt, OK?"

No sooner than he uttered those words that the back door of the barracks opened and PFC Melvin Lynch, a member of the machine gun platoon came out on his way to the trash bin. His eyes opened wide in amazement when he saw us standing there and Marshall, with a belt fastened around his neck.

"What the hell are you guys up to?" He blurted out.

"Just fooling around!" I answered.

Marshall spoke up harshly, "Get the hell out of here!" directing his remark at Lynch.

Lynch did just that and disappeared around the corner of the barracks building. As soon as Lynch was gone Marshall turned on Dillard and me saying, "I know what you bastards are up to. You're going to stand there and let me hang!" He was quite right in his summation of the situation, except for one point. We were not going to just stand there watching him hang, we were going to run like hell! Dillard and I denied the allegation, saying trite things like, "How can you say that, we are buddies? Don't be silly, we were trying to help you." All the while I was trying hard to keep a straight face.

Still, Marshall pulled out his switchblade knife while he listened to our protestations of innocence. We eventually got him out of his suspicion that we were going to let him hang. Then we went to work convincing him that we couldn't go through with his plan because Lynch might inform the top sergeant of what he had seen. It really took quite a while before Marshall let go of the entire subject. Lynch, Dillard and I served together for eighteen months after this and not once did Lynch ever bring the subject up again, which suited me just fine.

Marshall never did let up exhibiting his antisocial behavior. He was constantly harassing others, like getting into some one else's footlocker looking for candy or cigarettes. He smuggled liquor onto the base by intimidating taxi drivers into hiding bottles under the engines hood or inside hubcaps of the vehicles. All the while he did these things he acted the part of a physical fitness fanatic. He insisted on eating good food and doing physical fitness exercises every day.

He was a frequent visitor to a camp outdoor gymnasium, which was equipped with a boxing ring. He'd skip rope, shadow box and punch the bag for hours when off duty. God help a physical fitness counterpart who, thinking that he possessed some boxing skill accepted Marshall's invitation to go a few rounds of sparing in the ring. The poor guy would find quickly that he was involved in a bloody free for all fight that would give justice to the heavyweight boxing matches of the world. These events would always end the same way, with Marshall the victor, his opponent lying on the canvas, smeared with his own blood. I never saw any one accept Marshall's invitation to box. As time passed there were less and less Marines for Marshall to spar with. There were some very good boxers in the Marine Corps, but it appeared that few ever wanted to fight Marshall. The guy had the killer instinct, one that other men recognized. It was probably the very characteristic needed to be a champion fighter.

During the last week in May 1944, an incident took place that brought about the closing chapter to Marshall's relationship with the Fifth Marine Division. Well, almost, anyway! One Saturday evening, while I was doing some extra duty at the battalion aid station, accompanied by another corpsman, Donald Green, Marshall and Munns came in looking rather distressed. They complained that they had no money with which to go on liberty. They wanted to borrow some from Green and me. I was quick to point out that we didn't have any or we would be on liberty ourselves instead of volunteering to stand duty for someone else. The two corpsmen believed us, but Marshall became aggressive and hostile. He began to rummage about in the office desk's drawers and came up with the keys to the aid station's jeep. He turned to Munns and said, "Let's go somewhere and find something to drink."

Munns was quick to pick up on the suggestion, "Why don't you go up the officer's quarters and see the officer in charge of your platoon. "He'll probably give you some liquor, if you ask." I could see the corner of Munn's mouth turn up in that suggestion of mischief.

Marshall said, "Yeah, good and I'll pay him back later. "Green and I protested Marshall and Munns taking the jeep but Marshall's hand darted to his pocket where I knew he kept his knife. He said, while giving me a certain look I knew meant danger, "Do you guys want to stop me?" Green and I said no, but we sure wanted to talk him out of taking the jeep or we could end up in a lot of trouble ourselves. Munns was at his best in egging Marshall on by saying, "Who cares? All we're going to do is, go to officer's country on the hill where Marshall will find his Lieutenant and ask him politely for a bottle of whiskey."

Marshall went outside and climbed into the jeep and was trying to start it. Munns stood at the building doorway, wearing his impish grin, saying over and over, "I think the crazy bastard is going to try it!" At Marshall's command, Munns climbed into the jeep. When Marshall put the vehicle into gear, Green and I ran out and climbed into the back of the jeep in an attempt to talk Marshall out of driving away. Instead, we found ourselves being driven away over a camp road and up the hill towards Officers' Country.

Munns was very vocal in his attempt to encourage Marshall on. Green and I still joined in attempting to persuade Marshall to turn the jeep around and to go back to the aid station, but to no avail. When we reached the officers' barracks, Marshall drove around the structure two times at a high rate of speed and in a very careless manner. He then stopped next to the base of a raised verandah. Munns kept at it. "Just climb up there," pointing to the veranda, "and go inside. You'll find the Lieutenant's room as he'll probably have his name on the outside of the door."

Marshall, the idiot, did just as Munns suggested and disappeared somewhere into the darkness of the veranda, taking the keys to the jeep with him. Munns sat there on the front seat of the jeep and laughed and laughed while Green and I jumped out and attempted to push the vehicle down the hill and away from the building. Then, Marshall came bursting out of a door onto the veranda at a run. With a leap he landed on the ground to the rear of the jeep and climbed into the driver's seat. Behind him, on the veranda, came several men, one yelling, "Stop! Who was it?"

These men, I assumed were officers, appeared to be very alarmed and confused about what was going on. They stood at the edge of the veranda and peered down at us the darkness. Marshall got the jeep motor started and drove off with Munns, who was still sitting there laughing. Green and I ran after the jeep, grabbed hold of the back of it and was dragged along a short way until we were able to pull ourselves up into it. Marshall said, "Some son-of-a-bitch stopped and asked me what I was doing there and who I was. I pushed him away and took off."

It wasn't long before I noticed another jeep was following and then it began to chase us as Marshall increased the speed of our jeep. The chase turned into a 'Keystone Cops' act in a way. Green and I were pleading with Marshall to stop the jeep; Munns was laughing and encouraging him on. I was sure the jeep behind us contained the military police or members of the camp guard. Marshall would be driving one way on a street and the pursuing jeep was being driven on the next street over in the opposite direction in an attempt to close the distance between us. Up and down we went, this way and that, skidding around corners and cutting across fields. I was only thinking now of the camp brig and how soon it would be before I would have scars on my head as I had seen on Marshall's and Oberg's in the past.

The chase ended when Marshall drove the jeep down a dead end street, and was forced to stop. Munns was out of the jeep and running as soon as the wheels stopped turning. Marshall jumped out also and ran in the opposite direction. I said to Green, "Let's not run. Let's face the music. We haven't really done anything wrong!" The pursuing jeep was right there in back of us and someone was yelling, "Stand fast there!"

The jeep contained the camp duty officer and the duty sergeant. The officer ordered us to stand fast as he and the duty sergeant arrived. Green and I did what we were told. We found ourselves explaining that two Marines had just stolen the jeep and we were only involved because we were trying to recover it. And that the two who were responsible had run off into the darkness just as the Lieutenant and sergeant drove up. Green and I were fortunate that the Lieutenant and sergeant were of D Company. The officer was 1st Lt. John Noe Jr., and the sergeant was Charles T. Frazier, both of the mortar platoon. Both of whom knew Green and me.

Lt. Noe ordered us to return the jeep to the aid station and to park it there. Whether the Lieutenant believed our story, I never knew, I doubt it though. When Green and I got back to our barracks that night, Munns and Marshall were waiting for us. I told them that the duty officer was Lt. Noe and that he thought he had recognized the two men who had run away from the jeep as he approached it. This little lie was to cause both Munns and Marshall the loss of several nights sleep, much to my satisfaction.

The day after the incident, Munns sat around the barracks nervously waiting to be called into the Captain's office at any moment. Marshall acted as though he didn't give a damn and wandered off unconcerned. I was very worried about Marshall pushing the officer during the incident and knew that it was a serious offense. I walked over to the battalion aid station and reported the entire incident to the senior pharmacist mate, Allen L. Spence. I named both Marshall and Munns and declared that I had enough of Marshall's antics.

As far as I knew, neither Marshall nor Munns were called to task for their deeds that night. However, within a few days, Marshall was called to Spence's office at sickbay. When he returned, he seemed elated He said,

"Christ, I can't believe it. I'm being transferred back to the Navy. The doctor says he found some good duty for me!"

That night, we corpsmen celebrated Marshall's good fortune by taking him to the slop chute and all getting drunk. We were going to be free of him at last, once and for all…, weren't we? The next morning we said our good-byes to Marshall, as he carried his sea bag out of the barracks to a waiting jeep. Neither he nor we had the slightest notion of his destination, but as we waved to him, we all gave an exasperated sigh of relief.

Equipment and Field Training

IN THE SPRING of 1944 as the division was still being formed, assignments were being made, men were being transferred about until things settled down, and evolved into routine training sessions. Promotions were given, and most of my buddies and I were given an advance in rank. I was promoted to pharmacists mate third class (Ph M 3/c). It didn't mean more responsibility for me. I already had enough of that, or so I thought. My petty officer third class status put me on par with the three stripe sergeants.

During the months of March, April, May, and June we were worked hard on the training field. We mustered outside our barracks at 0600 and then went to breakfast. After that we fell into formation at 0800 and the company commander made an inspection. Following that we went into our scheduled activities for the day.

Usually we began by doing close order drill for the first hour, followed by a rifle inspection by the platoon leader after that. We always hiked a few miles somewhere after that. We hiked, rain or shine, and it was obvious that we were required to become accustomed to physical stress and discomfort. We spent many hours in the classrooms listening to lectures, by officers or noncommissioned officers, on subjects in which they were specialists. Once we sat through a two-hour lecture given by Col. James Roosevelt, the president's son who had combat experience in the South Pacific when serving with Col. Carlson's Raiders. Out back in the hills of Camp Pendleton we spent time working on the problems of how to attack enemy positions, including concrete bunkers, tanks, and buildings on city streets. We practiced establishing a defensive line for both day and night fighting. The Lieutenants took time to inspect our clothing, packs, harness, and whatever specialized equipment we carried. Items were adjusted, replaced, or added to when thought necessary.

Our uniforms were just that, uniform. From the commanding general to the lowest private, each man wore the same style of dungarees, helmets, shoes, and all us wore the regular issue underwear.

The G.I. steel helmet and its inside liner had an adjustable headband to fit each man's head size. We were issued a camouflage cloth cover for the helmet. They were colored various shades of green and brown. The green combat dungarees were made of a heavy cotton drill material. Both blouse and trousers were loose fitting and baggy, hanging about the body to allow for maximum movement. They weren't meant to be stylish and never intended to be pressed. The blouses had two breast pockets and two large pockets on either side near the waist. The latter pockets would be used to carry hand grenades during combat. On the left breast pocket was the inked impression of the Marine Corps symbol, the globe and anchor. The letters USMC were imprinted on the cloth above that.

Early in the war, the Japanese proved they had no qualms of shooting at Navy and Army medics, despite the bright Red Cross brassard on the left arm. Realizing the futility of trying to protect the corpsman with a red cross arm band, the Marines ordered corpsmen and doctors to remove the brassard, and instead issued them weapons. These were the same rifles issued to all Marines, and we were trained extensively in their use.

A company member was issued leather ankle high shoes that were manufactured with the rough side on the outside. We were issued two pairs of these boots nicknamed "Boondockers." The recommended method for breaking in a new pair of these shoes was for the wearer to stand in warm water for a half hour while wearing them and then to wear them until they dried. This caused the leather to conform to the wearer's foot. Woe to the man who put on a brand new pair of these boots and then went on a long hike! Blistered feet could stop a foot soldier just as well as an enemy bullet would. All the men wore canvas leggings except those who wore the "jump boots" issued to the paratroopers some time earlier. These "leggins," as they were called, would protect our ankles as they came into contact with rocks and brush. The trousers legs were then pulled down over the leggings to just above the ankle.

The packs we carried on our backs were of two parts. The upper part was a combat pack; (haversack) the lower, of the same size was called a transport pack. The transport pack was only worn with the combat pack because it hung from its bottom by straps. The transport pack was worn only while we were being moved from camp to camp and we needed extra room for personal belongings. The combat pack would be used to carry one pair of field shoes, dungarees, underwear, toilet articles and a few other personal items. When in a combat zone, we would carry extra ammunition in there along with rations.

Each man wore a Webb belt. The riflemen wore a heavy one about his waist that had attached to it bullet pouches, bayonet scabbard, water canteen, first aid kit, and any other specialized equipment necessary for the wearer to do his job. Each of us was issued a heavy cord suspenders with which to hold our belts up, if we thought it necessary to use them.

We carried a camouflage poncho that was folded up and hung over our Webb belt in the small of our back. This canvas was waterproofed and had a hole in the center for our heads to go through. The poncho was large enough to cover a man's pack while being worn and also did a good job of protecting the man's body from the rain.

A shelter half was also carried by each man. It was wrapped around our only blanket, which in turn was rolled up in a four-foot length and strapped to the top of our combat pack. The sides were bent down on each side of the pack and fastened by straps. This waterproof material, when spread out, was about seven feet long and five feet wide. When snapped together with another man's shelter half, it provided a tent that two men could sleep inside of comfortably. Each man also carried a few wood stakes and tent poles which, when used properly, would hold the tent up.

Every man wore, attached to the top of his pack, an entrenching tool. It was either a small shovel or hand pick. These tools, besides being used to dig into the earth, would double as a fighting weapon once its possessor was in hand to hand combat.

The riflemen were equipped with a Garand rifle (M-l) or a Browning automatic rifle (BAR). A smaller carbine, a .30 caliber, was issued to officers, medical corpsmen, machine gunners, mortar men etc. Officers and NCO's were furnished with .45 caliber automatic hand guns if they wished to carry them. This weapon was considered efficient only in a defensive situation and then only when in very close combat. Some specialized troops carried a Thompson submachine gun, but these weapons had a tendency to jam easily. A pump action shotgun that fired double '0' buckshot was carried by members of our assault squad who would use them in very close quarters.

The average medical corpsman didn't carry a bayonet, but a machete. It was useful as a utility tool, as well as for fighting. Instead of one canteen, we carried two. The medic was equipped with two medical bags, which were about the size of the combat pack when opened to full size. These bags, called Unit Threes, were jammed full of battle dressings, serum albumin,

*At day's end a Marine rifle platoon is coming in from the field,
weary, dirty, proud and confident*

morphine Syrettes, rolls of gauze and other dressings, adhesive tape, iodine,
aspirin, Benzedrine tablets, and a kit containing a scalpel, several types of
forceps, tweezers, bandage shears and hemostats.

Every man was issued a gas mask. Its container was slung by a strap
from the neck of its wearer. Besides the mask, the bag usually contained
other essential items of food and cigarettes. These latter items were actually forbidden to be carried in with the gas mask, but I never saw any one
disciplined for doing so.

The "work mules" of the company were the BAR men who had to
carry that heavy weapon and its twenty round ammunition clips. Those
machines used up the ammunition very fast and so the bearer had to carry
extra clips on his belt.

The machine gunners carried their small carbine and the heavy .30
caliber machine guns too. However, some of the men preferred to carry

the Garand instead of the carbine. The machine gun squad consisted of three men. One carried the tripod, the second one the gun and the third the ammunition that was belted and stored in boxes.

The three man mortar teams, the 60 mm. variety were burdened also. One man carried the heavy butt plate, the second the tube and bipod, and the third all the ammunition he could. These men were equipped with carbines generally The heavy water cooled machine guns and the heavy 88 mm. mortars were hauled along on small carts that were constructed by using bicycle wheels.

Each company was assigned an 'assault squad,' a group of men who used specialized weapons or equipment. This unit was made up of men that had been highly trained in the use of flamethrowers and explosives. Special care had to be exercised in the care and storage of such equipment. It was dangerous stuff to be near at any time.

Hand grenades were heavy cumbersome objects. They were carried in blouse pockets or bags during combat and were issued just prior to going in. They were not often carried, as some motion picture heroes often portrayed, by fastening them to the shoulder straps of the combat pack. Though, I have seen a few high ranking officers pose for photographs with the grenades attached to suspender straps. Any experienced foot soldier knew that the grenade could be pulled loose as he crawled along on the ground on his stomach. This could release the firing pin, which would ignite the fuse leading to the powder charge.

Amphibious Exercises

The men of the division were becoming restless because of constant repetitive training. Boredom was setting in. There were more infractions of the rules than usual. To counter this, the commanders seemed to increase the physical aspects of the training. Long day and night marches were scheduled and carried out. Some of them were quite exhausting, apparently done in an attempt to test our physical endurance. Some of the grueling hikes were in excess of twenty miles. Some were on a forced basis where there was no stopping for rest. I noticed that some of the Marines couldn't keep up with the pace of training. I also noted that most of these men were soon transferred out of the line companies into units that were less demanding physically and emotionally. Most went to support groups like transportation, mail, and supply units.

I liked all phases of the training, especially when I understood why it was necessary to learn to do a thing a certain way. Sometimes things got to be pretty perplexing until that understanding came through.

We once took a long hike up a steep road on Murphy's Mountain, which was located in Camp Pendleton. We carried combat packs, rifles, and were other wise fully combat prepared. Everyone displayed his good nature at first, as the battalion was loaded into trucks and taken to the base of the mountain, where we began our hike. I had never heard of getting a ride to where a hike would begin?

At the proper location the men were off loaded and were soon all in marching formation. It was a nice warm clear day. At the beginning there was much talking and laughing and the usual good natured jests men make to each other. We all stepped briskly and confidently along the steep, rough mountain road.

After about five miles of continuous walking, the column had settled down fairly well with each man just plodding along in silence thinking his own thoughts and following the man ahead of him. The incline of the road became more extreme and the sun became brighter and warmer. The hikers began perspiring, and their faces became flushed. There were many red faces among the men as they struggled to suck fresh air into their lungs. Even the complaining stopped, well almost all of it anyway. Most began pulling out their water canteens to take a drink. The officers among us were quick to remark that the men should go easy as the water in their canteens was all that they would get that day.

At about the midway point of the hike, I saw that a few of the men from the marching units up ahead us had fallen out of their formations and were sitting on the edge of the road holding their feet and grimacing some, looking as if they would appreciate a little sympathy. I'm afraid that not many of us had much to give just then. But, it was the corpsman's duty to give aid when needed. By then most of us were a little suspicious of what our commanders might have in store for us.

We corpsman treated blisters so that the man might hobble on. Some complained of twisted ankles or stretched muscle pain. Some complaints were factual, some were imagined, and others fabricated. Most alarming were the men lying along the road unconscious, suffering from heat stroke and heat exhaustion. All this became rather difficult for the corpsmen to handle, as if we stopped to help, we would be left behind by our own platoon. We had been instructed not to become separated from our own unit. To catch up with our platoon, we had to run after each time we stopped to give someone aid.

I noticed that when the men first began to falter and fall out, the officers seemed not to notice or care. Heck, most did not even look back to inspect what was going on behind them. Whenever I reported to them that one of their men had fallen out they would just reply, "Thanks, keep up with your unit!"

About two thirds of the way up the mountain, I came across Ph. M. 3/c Eddie Monjaras, one of my close buddies, kneeling over the prostrated form of Lt. John Noe who was his platoon commander. The Lieutenant was unconscious, red faced and was lying on his back right in the middle of the road. All the following Marines were stepping over or around him to get by. I thought that was deplorable and shouldn't be the case.

Eddie was trying to shade the Lieutenant's face from the hot sun and at the same time trying to get him to drink some water. I stopped to help, and we were bringing the officer around to consciousness when I heard a motor noise in back of me and then a gruff, loud voice order, "You men! Get up and get going! Clear the road!"

Ed and I turned toward the voice and found a jeep had stopped a few feet in back of us. Lt. Col. Joseph P. Sayers, the battalion commander, was standing up in the front compartment of the vehicle. Beside him there was a sergeant who was his driver. The Colonel was glaring at Ed and me, his jaw was firm and set.

"Colonel, this is Lt. Noe. " Eddie said, "He is suffering from heat exhaustion and we .... "`

The Colonel roared out "God damn it! Do you hear me? Get going! Drag that man out of our way and get back to your platoons. "

Ed and I didn't think it proper to treat an officer like Lt. Noe that way, but we did as we were told. We dragged the Lieutenant off to one side and left him hanging over the low berm at the side of the road. We turned to face the Colonel who motioned us to start walking up the road just ahead of the jeep. We were two confused young corpsmen and angry, too, as we glanced back at the colonel riding in his jeep. We hesitated, turned to protest when the colonel growled again, "Get going!" After a quarter of a mile the jeep driver sounded his horn. Looking back, we saw the driver motion us aside. The jeep passed us and the Colonel ignored us as if he had never seen us before.

When we reached the top of the hill, at the end of the nineteen mile hike, I found that possibly ten percent of the men of the battalion had fallen out of the formation and were still unaccounted for. I didn't know it then, but four wheel drive vehicles and Medics had been assigned to follow us up the mountain road and pick up these "casualties". This rescue work happened some time after the conclusion of the hike. We didn't see our fallen comrades again until we returned to the camp hours later.

I felt it necessary to complain to Lieutenant Horvath about the treatment of the men who had fallen by the roadside. As a corpsman I felt it was improper to go off and leave ill men like that unattended. He said, "Do you remember when we started this hike down below, that I told you not to fall behind the platoon regardless of what happened during the hike, that I wanted you to reach the top of hill with us?"

I replied, "Yes, Sir, I do. "

The Lieutenant said, "Well, I meant it. "

He then dismissed me by turning his face away from me. I never brought the subject up again although I spent months after that trying to understand what that was all about.

Seven months later I found out. The incident came to mind again as my platoon prepared to charge up the east slope of Iwo Jima. Lt. Horvath came up beside me while I was crouched in a shell hole and he said, "No matter what happens, do not get left behind. Do not stop to help anyone who has fallen until we get to the top of the island. That's where you'll be needed most. Do you understand?"

I replied, "Yes, Sir, I do. "

The hike that day taught the men of the battalion a number of things, among them were that, when moving forward, military victory is achieved by those men reaching their goal. Victory is not won by those sitting or falling along a roadside.

One task on the lighter side of training was to learn how to dig a rifle pit (fox hole) properly. This tedious assignment was made easier if one could find some humor in doing it. Lieutenant Horvath contributed to that end. A '1-2-6' rifle pit meant that a trench was dug, one foot deep, two feet wide, and six feet in length. A rifleman would be able to lie in that depression, below the level of the ground's surface and escape surveillance or a bullet sent at him from the enemy. In digging the hole, the dirt was removed and placed onto a poncho, then carried to a place some distance from the excavation and concealed from enemy view. After the completion of the exercise, the dirt would be returned and the hole filled up.

The Lieutenant gave relief from the misery involved in digging these holes. One of his duties was to check the holes to see that they were done properly. He would produce a measuring tape and use it to measure the dimensions and comment on whether they were a quarter of an inch too small or too large. With him acting in the roll of a "fussy old school teacher," we always ended up this most disliked assignment by sitting on the ground and laughing our anxiety away.

Today, when its raining and I see a depression the size of a "foxhole," I often think of those 1-2-6 foxholes that we had to dig—and even lie in— as they filled with water. Once, while on a three day bivouac and field problem, we dug rifle pits on a defensive line situated on a ridge. We were ordered to lie in them at dusk and stay in them until dawn. The problem was to simulate a night assault being made upon us by the enemy. The order was easy to comply with until rain began to fall heavily. I lay in my foxhole and heard others calling out to the sergeant: "Hey, what do we do about the rain? It's filling up my foxhole with water. "

The word was passed to remain quiet and to maintain our position until relieved. I lay on my back, in my hole, while it filled with water that was running from higher ground, until only my head and rifle were above the water. After a while I thought the whole scene was ridiculous and I began to laugh. Soon other members of the platoon began to laugh out loud. It wasn't very long before the "Top" came up to us and told us to "Shut up!"

I had my woolen blanket wrapped around me and of course it was soaking wet. I learned that night that a woolen blanket can keep a person warm even though it is completely wet and even while submerged. My comrades and I were made to lie there throughout the night until 0600 the next morning. Our night problem had been canceled because of the rain. We found that we had been able to get some sleep though, in spite of the conditions under which we spent the night.

A somewhat similar incident occurred a week later while assuming a defensive position on San Clemente Beach. The company dug in on the sand beach much too close to the water. When the tide came in that night, we found ourselves floundering about in our sea water filled foxholes. We spent a miserable cold night soaking wet and the early dawn dampness and fog that blanketed the coast only added to our discomfort.

Lying below the level of the ground in a foxhole often provided an escape from cold chilling winds. The pleasure was often offset by unwanted guests that roamed about seeking the same shelter. Tarantula spiders, large as a man's hand, would crawl out of the cracks in the earth that were enlarged by our digging into the soil. During the dark hours they would climb on a man's body or worse, walk across his face as he lay sleeping. The sleeping man would awaken in a fit of terror as he clawed at the spider to knock it away.

Some of us handled that problem by mixing dirt and water together in order to make a heavy paste with which to fill in the cracks in the earth inside the hole, before darkness came. There were scorpions that were far more dangerous than tarantulas. Their venom usually meant the removal of the victim stung by them to the aid station. These scorpions were large and would roam about during their nocturnal quest for food. At the first sign of daylight, they would seek shelter from the light by entering a sleeping man's clothing or blankets. As the sleeping man awakened and moved, the scorpions would become alarmed and strike out with their venomous tail stingers inflicting a very painful wound.

We spent much time in the spring learning about amphibious landings. Who would ever think it necessary to spend time learning about how to get on and off a boat? We learned to enter the landing craft, turn around in squad formation, face forward, kneel on command, rise, and then run forward, leaping from the front ramp as it dropped to the beach. We had to learn to leap from the ramp as far forward as we could in order to escape the lethal steel front edge that could possibly sever a man's legs if it pinned them to the sand beach. The wave action and surge would move the boat and its ramp forward as he struggled toward the dry sand while in the surf.

The craft we used to make these amphibious landings was named a Higgins Boat. It was approximately thirty-six feet long and named after the manufacturer, Andrew Higgins. It carried the designation of LCVP which was an abbreviation for Landing Craft, Vehicle, Personnel. This boat's specifications closely followed one designed by the British in the early days of World War II. It was designed to be rammed ashore onto a hostile beach to get men ashore quickly.

About one hundred feet away from the beach, a kedge anchor would be dropped to engage the sand or rock bottom, and the anchor cable would be let run as the craft continued on to the beach. Moments before the craft touched the beach, Marines the in the bow, upon a signal from the boat-swain, would unhook the bow ramp. The boatswain would then release the winch cable and allow the ramp to fall forward and rest upon the sand. Marines would depart the craft by running forward and leaping from the lowered ramp and then charging up onto the beach. After that, the ramp would be pulled back into its upward position. The anchor cable winch would pull the craft back off the beach if necessary, by pulling against the seaward kedge anchor.

The equipment carried by the average Marine has been described previously. It could vary in weight, according to the man's duties. It could weigh as much as one hundred pounds, and this would make it very difficult for a man to jump very far from the edge of the boat's ramp.

Another part of amphibious training was to teach a man to climb over the edge of a ship's side and descend a rope cargo net to the small landing craft waiting in the water below. This may appear to the casual observer to be easily done, but in reality it is a difficult task to complete without mishap. One moment the net would be lying against the ship's steel side as the ship rolled away from the boat below, the next moment the net would pull away from the ship's side as the ship rolled back toward the smaller craft. This would leave the descending Marines swinging out in midair and hanging on for dear life.

The Marine's heavy equipment included his weapon, back pack, cartridge belt, with all the hanging accessories, made going down the net quite hazardous. Upon hearing the command to go, the Marine would throw his right leg over the ship's rail and with a slight jumping movement would straddle the rail, hesitating just long enough to gain his balance and to find a foot rest on the lateral strands of the rope cargo net hanging below. Then, swinging the other leg over to follow, he descended to the landing craft below. His hands would grasp the vertical strands as he descended to avoid being stepped on by the man above. It was necessary for the descending man to keep looking up at the men above him, and at the same time try and keep a watch below so that he wouldn't step on someone.

The slung rifle, at some time during the descent, would swing and flap about, banging into another man along side. The steel helmet was an awkward thing to be wearing. It hindered one's ability to look around him. The pack on a man's back would rise up as he reached up with his arms and hands, this would cause the top of the pack to push the back of the helmet up and tip the front visor down so that it covered his eyes, temporarily obscuring his view.

Falling equipment and even men's bodies presented a great threat to those men below. One Marine would fall onto another who was clinging to the net below and at times dislodge him also. The Marines, if they saw a man falling toward them, he would cling to the net bracing himself before being hit. The bodies fell, in an awkward fashion, legs and arms flailing about in an attempt to catch onto some object to halt the fall. The unfortunate, falling Marine, would either tumble into the sea between the ship and boat, or glance off the net and crash down into the landing craft below, often landing on some crew member there. If the person landed on the hard surface of the boat, he would always be hauled off to the hospital. When a company of Marines went over the side, there would be as many as a dozen of them clinging to the nets. As hands were smashed between equipment and helmets fell onto those men below, the air would be punctuated with such expletives as, "Watch it, damn it!...," "Sorry!..." "watch out!,..." and many others.

I once dropped my helmet as I went over the side. It bounced off two or three men before one of the sailors caught it in the boat below. I heard all those nasty remarks being made by the Marines after they had been struck by the helmet. It was a good thing that they didn't dare look up to see where the missile came from! In the early days of training, we were told not to fasten the chin strap of the helmet because if we fell into the water from the height of the ship's deck the sudden force of water against its lower edge might break our necks. Finally, some courageous Marine Captain tested this suspected danger by jumping a dozen times or so off the deck of a ship, wearing the helmet strapped. It didn't cause him any damage. After that, we wore the chin strap fastened.

I recall vividly our first landing on a real beach. We journeyed to the Silver Strand Beach area on Balboa Island near San Diego. The entire Second Battalion entered Higgins boats for about a two hour ride on a cold, clammy, foggy morning. We were to simulate a combat landing on one of the isolated beaches. Many of the men became seasick, the rest of us just "bitched" most of the way because we were so uncomfortable.

As we approached our beach landing site and the sun came through the fog, we began to feel better. The Lieutenant waved us into a kneeling position. Soon we felt the front of the boat gently touch the soft sand under the water near the beach. The ramp went forward and down and I saw the Lieutenant and platoon sergeant rise to their feet, turn, run forward, and then leap from the ramp. The entire platoon rose and moved forward in unison to follow. As the Marine in front of me leaped from the ramp, I heard him cry out, "Oh Christ!" As I left the ramp, I could understand his alarm. We were not jumping into the shallow surf as we expected, but instead, into deep water. The boat's bow had hit an underwater sand bar and had stopped some fifty or sixty feet from dry land.

The water between us and the beach was over our heads in depth. Most of the platoon's members up in front of me had disappeared into the surf and were now floundering their way toward the beach. Some of them were swimming and others were being pulled along by their comrades. When I submerged, I felt my feet strike one of the Marines who had gone ahead of me. I never admitted it later though. My helmet, pack, rifle, and medical kits all contributed to my staying under water a little longer than I normally would have.

I crawled out of the water on my hands and knees dragging my rifle behind me and gasping for breath in the cold, damp air. I crawled on past the prostrate forms of my marine comrades. I heard someone yelling and when I looked up for the source I found myself staring into the lens of a large movie camera. The camera was one of those large old fashioned types that had a hand crank. One man turned the crank while another aimed the machine at me and my comrades. A third member of the crew stood off to one side and was yelling at me to "Pretend you're dead, fall flat onto the sand and remain quiet!"

I was still gasping for breath and spitting out sand so I could hardly lie still. My mouth opened and shut involuntarily and my chest heaved as I sought the precious air. After a moment I sat up and watched the camera crew pick up and carry off their camera. I could hear remarks of disgust coming from them. They couldn't understand the poor cooperation they received from us. I never did learn what movie they were making that day. Even today when an old time World War II movie depicts Marines landing on a beach somewhere, I look for a young warrior crawling along on hands and knees while coughing beach sand and sea water from his lungs.

Immediately after the movie episode the 'Gunny Sergeant,' came walking along the beach toward our platoon, yelling, "All right, 'youse' guys...which one of you lost your weapons, you better start diving for them, because if you don't find them, you're gonna' pay for them!"

We spent a few days practicing with landing craft mockups. These were simulated crafts that were just sitting out on a training field. We practiced over and over entering them, turning around, kneeling, raising and running out on command. Once we 'landed' we would form up into our skirmish line and begin our advance on the enemy.

At first, I thought it was ridiculous to spend time on such an elementary maneuver. In the beginning when we tried this maneuver, we became entangled with each other and each other's gear. Then we began to see the reasoning behind the drill. For instance, there were noises that drowned out the verbal commands of the leaders, so it was necessary for us to rely on hand signals.

We tripped and fell over each others' rifles and machine guns that somehow got mixed up with our legs. This in turn would cause a delay in leaving the craft and would give enemy gunners waiting on shore time to zero in on us. If we didn't leave the landing craft properly, we would become mixed up with other units landing along side of us, and the loss of our unit's integrity would occur. This would cause a certain amount of embarrassment to the platoon leader, especially when it happened while high ranking officers watched the proceedings.

A rifle platoon consisted of about forty-three men. Three rifle platoons made up one company, three rifle companies made up one battalion, three battalions made one regiment, and three regiments made one division. With proper planning and training, an entire division could be put ashore in one smooth quick operation. It was very essential that our assault teams could be put ashore on a hostile beach and succeed in overwhelming the enemy quickly with minimum casualties to our side.

One morning in July the battalion was advised to prepare to make a landing on one of the nearby beaches. This landing exercise was to be conducted from assault troop ships. We were loaded onto trucks and taken to the Port of San Diego. We boarded a transport ship that was tied along side of a concrete pier. Once on deck we filed below to our assigned compartments. This turned out to be no easy feat. We struggled along through the passageways, each man crowding the man walking in front of him. We went down ladders (stairways), along narrow aisles between bunks and often were stopped momentarily when our equipment got caught on some obstruction. It would be up to the man in back of us to free us as we couldn't turn to do it ourselves.

As we reached the next empty bunk in line, we stopped and faced the task of removing packs, rifles, helmets, belts, and other equipment and placing them on our bunks. This was not easy. The bunks were stacked six high on either side of the aisle and the aisle was no more than two feet wide. If you try to visualize that, you would realize that twelve Marines would be standing on a floor space of twelve square feet between the bunks, while trying to remove their gear. It cannot be done if all the Marines tried to do it at the same time. Eleven of the men had to stand still while the twelfth removed his gear first. Then another removed his, and then another. As each Marine removed his gear he would then crawl into his bunk so that the others could do the same.

The loading of the troop ship in this fashion created a lot of confusion and noise. Once the troops were moving along the decks and passageways and down ladders, there were heard the constant cries of "Keep moving", "Don't stop", "Get along", of supervisory personnel. It seemed to me that I couldn't have stopped if I wanted to. There must have been a giant of a man, who was following at the back of the line pushing with all his might at the man in front of him to keep the line moving. There was constant body contact between us and that wasn't very comfortable, as rifle barrels, picks, and shovels kept gouging at our face and bodies.

Also, there was the problem of going through those small water tight doors or hatches. In order to go through, a man would have to step over an eighteen inch high bottom sill and at the same time bend over enough to clear his helmeted head so that it wouldn't bang on the overhead. If the Marine was successful in avoiding banging his helmet, his rifle or pack would certainly catch on some bulkhead projection.

For those young warriors who had promised their mothers to refrain from swearing once they were away from home, the time had come to break that vow. The ship's passageways were filled with some rather vile comments as the men struggled against the obstacles that barred their way. When I first stepped through the hatchway into the interior of the ship, I knew that I didn't want any part of this ship or way of life. The warm air mixed with body, galley and fuel odors combined to make a nauseating feeling much to my discomfort.

The bunks were uncomfortable to me. They were constructed of tubular steel, rather oval shaped and about six feet in length. Their width was about two feet. A piece of canvas was stretched across the interior and fastened to the metal rim with cord lacing. These bunks were head to toe to each other and the rims at the ends were separated by one or two inches. Those figures don't add up to very much comfort when there are people like me who are over six feet tall. Somewhere I had to conceal three inches of my length as I lay there or my feet would extend to the head of the man who lay in the bunk nearest my feet. That situation would not be conducive to the development of good comradeship. Also, lying flat in the bunk, I noticed that once the Marine in the bunk above me got in there, he sagged down until he touched my chest. This made turning over in my bunk virtually impossible.

To make it worse yet, the bunks were suspended side by side and hung between stanchions, or vertical posts that fastened to the ceiling and extended to the deck below. The bunks were side by side with other bunks that were reached by the next aisle over. There was an arrangement of chains that held the bunks suspended from the stanchions. When the bunks were not in use, they could be lifted up on the aisle side, out of the way a little.

There was a problem of what to do with our equipment, helmet, rifle, and pack along with all the gear we carried on our belts. All those items were supposed to be suspended from the inside edge of the bunk which was above ours. Since the two bunks that were arranged side by side were only separated by four inches of empty space, the two men's equipment jammed in between left only about eighteen inches of bunk to lie on.

The thought of retiring for the night under these conditions was disheartening. If I removed my outer clothing, were would I store it? Some men put their clothing under their heads for a pillow. Shoes were a problem, especially for a tall man. If he were to leave his shoes on, they would certainly come into contact with the man at his feet. If he removed the shoes, he had better have washed his feet before retiring and then put on a clean pair of stockings too!

The Marines prided themselves in being rugged creatures and being able to exist in the most trying of environments. They were most disdainful of the U. S. Army's soldiers who, it was rumored, were transported about overseas on a large and luxurious passenger liner, the soldiers being waited upon by room stewards while lounging about in their private staterooms or loafing around one of several swimming pools on board.

So there we were, on board ship, the ship's mooring lines were cast off and the craft headed out toward the open sea, away from the safety of the harbor. Our destination was San Clemente Island which stood dozens of miles off the California coast.

Once at sea we began disembarkation drills. Our compartment's public address system would blare out, "All troops lay up to your disembarkation stations." We troops standing below decks by our bunks would then file up the ladders to our predestinated stations along the ship's rail until dismissed. At first we began by not carrying our rifles and packs. Later when we had perfected our movements, we donned our gear and practiced that way.

This procedure also doubled for a fire drill or abandon ship drill, which is quite necessary during wartime. When the ship arrived off the island of San Clemente the next morning, we climbed down into the landing crafts below while they kept pace with our slow moving attack transport. That part of the exercise passed without incident. We patiently waited in the boats while Navy boat crews practiced their maneuvers.

These small craft would circle after receiving their complement of Marines, until all the other boats were filled with men. Then upon another signal, the boats would break from the circle and go toward the beach in single file. Upon reaching a previously determined point some hundreds of yards from the beach, the boats would be signaled into a line formation before approaching the beach.

These wave formations were complex in their planning. The troops had to be put ashore so that the integrity of each unit was maintained. If that were lost, a disorganized military operation could develop into a disaster. We were old hands at landing on a beach now and we made this one easily. While waiting to be recalled on board ship, we came upon an interesting thing. We found an area where Army troops had bivouacked apparently some time before. Upon leaving, they had abandoned a large amount of supplies. There was clothing and rain gear that seemed to be of new issue. As a result of this find, we members of the Second Platoon, fared very well in equipping ourselves with new woolen stockings, shirts, sweaters, and rain coats. We never did learn the reason for that kind of military carelessness. The small boats picked us up and returned us to the ship where we clambered aboard by way of boarding nets. The ship's crew then got the craft under way again.

The next morning we were standing off Aliso Beach, a few miles north of Oceanside. We began the process of disembarking over the side again and into the small boats. This procedure went very smoothly again and we were developing a cocky attitude about our ability to do so well. The LCVPs headed for the landing area on the beach. When we were about two miles off the beach, a heavy coastal fog enveloped us along with the entire landing force. The boat crews were ordered to reduce speed and to circle tightly to avoid the possibility of a collision. They were to follow this procedure until the fog lifted. The Marines on board the crafts settled down to wait patiently.

The fog covered ocean was calm, except for a small swell that ran in at an angle toward the beach. We, in our craft, all sat on the deck to wait. Some of the men became drowsy, some slept, while others smoked and talked. I sat down and leaned against the side of the boat feeling sort of drowsy and a little odd. We had been in this position for about an hour when Sgt. Charles Goodling looked at me curiously. Then grinning, he said aloud so all could hear, "What's the matter, Doc? You look green. "With that I jumped up and hung myself over the side of the boat and vomited my breakfast into the sea. Goodling was roaring with laughter now. "Look at Doc, You Guys. He's the only "swabbie" with us and he's the only one seasick!"

After the first convulsions left me and before the second series began, I raised my head and looked about me. I saw that all the other men in the boat had gone to the rail and were vomiting in the sea. The Lieutenant and even Sgt. Goodling were there. Goodling's face was pale and he looked very solemn as he found room between two of his squad's members. I looked at the boat's crew. One was lying face down on the motor cowling, heaving over the side. The other two were sitting very quietly and were wearing that silly little grin most people get as motion sickness begins to come upon them. There were no more remarks made about seasickness that day. Later on though, I couldn't resist just smiling at Goodling every time I caught his eye.

When the fog did lift, we continued on to finish our exercise and landed on the beach. The cockiness that had begun the journey with us had all disappeared. After the landing we moved inland to state Highway #1, and crossed that. This highway runs parallel with the coast line at that point. We had our attention called toward a point of land that projected out toward the sea just to the south of us. Up on a high rise of land we could see a large group of people gathered along with military and civilian type vehicles. We saw people clustered about a large black convertible vehicle that had its canvas top down. "Some 'big wig' from Washington!" one of the sergeants commented.

The next day we were informed that President Roosevelt had watched our landing exercise on Aliso Beach from that bluff's viewpoint and in company with the 5th Division's commanding officer, Major General Keller E Rockey and staff who were there to oversee the landing. It was officially reported to us that they were highly satisfied with the conduct of the division's personnel in carrying out the maneuvers.

Training Hell

They called for the Army to come to Tulagi
But Douglas Mac Arthur said, "No!"
He said there's no reason, It's not the season,
Besides there is no USO.

Chorus:

Bless 'em all, bless 'em' all,
The long and the short and the tall.
Bless all the 'Pelicans' and 'Dogfaces' too,
Bless all the Generals and, above all, bless you.
So we're saying goodbye to them all,
As back to our foxholes we crawl,
There's no promotion on Mac Arthur's blue ocean,
So cheer up my lads bless 'em' all.
* Pelicans - Sailors
* Dogfaces - Soldiers

WHILE VISITING THE area of the battalion sick bay one day, the senior corpsman asked me if I had a California driver's license. I said that I did. He said, "Well, you just volunteered to be a jeep driver." I was told to report to the Regimental Transportation Office and apply for a military driver's license. I thought that having one of those couldn't hurt me so I was soon driving a jeep around the camp streets demonstrating to a Marine sergeant my driving skills. He advised me afterwards that I did well and that I could expect to receive the license soon. I was told to report to a certain office, in one week, and I would be given my license. Who would ever think that a simple task like picking up a driver's license would result in a horrible, embarrassing and humiliating experience? It did!

The next Saturday afternoon at 1300 hours, while my buddies were leaving the base on liberty, I, the 'volunteer,' walked a mile to the transportation office. It was in a small wooden frame building that was located in the middle of a field. The structure was raised and sitting on concrete blocks. The number of the building was painted above the doorway and the door was wide open when I got there.

I walked up to the doorway and stood outside of it. Looking inside I saw a desk at the back of the room. Sitting behind the desk was a Marine Sergeant-Major. He was a big man. I could hardly see his features at first because of the shadows within the room, which were in contrast to the full bright sunlight in which I was standing. Looking at the sergeant, I got the impression that he was kind of ugly, in fact, it struck me that he had similar features to those of the Marine Corps mascot, the bull dog. A noticeable difference was that this sergeant's features were larger and coarser than the mascot's. I was slightly bothered at this point because I had come there expecting to see that nice young marine sergeant who had given me my driving test.

I hesitated before going into the room. I had reason to, I thought, as it was a commonly accepted fact that some of these older and longtime professional Marines relished in intimidating young fledgling Marines. I had the impression that an eighteen year old hospital corpsman like me was not going to escape that fate either. Because I was a little upset, I forgot all the military protocol that I'd ever been taught.

I entered the door in a hesitant manner and forced myself to approach the sergeant. I stood there in front of his desk and looked at him. God, did he look mean! He had six stripes on each sleeve of his tailor made faded khaki shirt. I thought, "This is one very 'salty' Marine. The sergeant was looking down at some papers when I approached and did not look up at me when I stopped before him. After a moment, though it seemed much longer, I mumbled something like, "I'm, mm, I'm here to pick up my license." Then that large bulldog head slowly began to rise up to where its eyes focused on me.

"What?" he barked.

I replied, "I'm here,' umm... umm', for my license."

He sat there looking at me for a moment. There was no expression on his face whatsoever to give me a clue to what he was thinking. Then he said to me very pointedly. "Go outside and wait a moment and then come back in to my desk and do it right!" As I turned to walk out of the room and into the sunshine of the outdoors I could feel my legs shaking and I could hardly restrain myself from breaking into a run.

Once outside, in the warm fresh air, I stepped off to one side so that the sergeant couldn't see me. I thought that perhaps I should give this whole thing up and just go back to the barracks without the license. After all, the sergeant didn't know my name. I really considered it for a while before discarding the thought. I realized the sergeant had my license on his desk somewhere and he would soon track me down.

I finally got up my courage and decided to go back in to face him again. I walked into the office for the second time, hesitated by the doorway and then cautiously walked to the desk. The sergeant was looking down at papers on his desk, just like before. Then he slowly raised his head and looked at me unsmilingly. Then slowly a trace of a smile appeared on his face but it sure as 'hell' didn't look like a friendly one to me. I said, "I'm here to pick up my drivers license!"

The Sergeant-Major jumped to his feet, knocking his chair away from him as he did. He leaned forward over his desk toward me and placed his huge hands on either edge so as to brace himself. I could now see the full size of this Marine. He was well over six feet in height and was well built like Joe Louis, the heavyweight champ of the world at the time. The sergeant must have weighed over two hundred pounds. "Turn around and walk out that door!" he commanded. "Stay out there where I can see you and when I call you, come back in here and tell me what it is you want. Do you understand?"

My wobbly knees turned me around as I stammered out, "Yes Sir."

He yelled out, "And 'Goddammit… don't call me Sir… I'm not an officer!" I don't think I answered that last directive as I was already going out the door, banging into the door jam on the way out. I stood in the yard again, about seventy-five feet out in front of the doorway and in a position so that the sergeant could see me. I contemplated running for it again. I gave that up because I noticed that there was a jeep parked alongside the building that no doubt belonged to the sergeant. He could easily overtake me in that vehicle. Then suddenly the frustration of it all wore off and I settled down a little and thought that the best way out of this situation was to think more about what it was the sergeant wanted of me.

I stood there in the hot sun for a long time. I was really beginning to sweat because of all the heat. My mouth and throat were dry and I wanted a drink of water. After about twenty minutes had passed the sergeant called out to me, "All right, try again!"

I marched into the room again and up to the sergeant's desk and stood there. He raised his unsmiling face and said, "Yes?" this time in a slightly pleasant way I thought.

I answered, "I'm Pharmacist Mate 3rd Class, Richard E. Overton, D Company corpsman, and I'm here to pick up my drivers license. I took the test last week!"

A semblance of a smile formed on his face, then he said, very politely, "Oh yes, I think I have it here on my desk. Why, here it is, right in front of me, waiting for you." He tenderly picked up the license and gave me a very pleasant smile, both motions slightly exaggerated I thought.

I stammered out, "Thank you, err... sergeant."

He replied in a very cheerful tone, "That's all right. Glad to help you."

I turned and walked out through the door and to freedom. The hot sun never felt so good before. I never looked back, but I knew the Sergeant-Major was watching me as I walked away and I'm sure he was grinning.

The drivers' license that I obtained was used for a specific purpose. Company D was chosen to represent the 5th Marine Division in 'defending' San Onofre Beach against an 'invasion' by a U.S. Army division. This Army division was en route to the Pacific from the East Coast of the United States and was pausing on the West Coast long enough to practice an amphibious operation before going on to the South Pacific and to a Japanese held island.

On the day of the landing, I drove the battalion aide station jeep to the proposed landing site. Captain Fields directed me to an area where he wanted the aid station to be established. There my two assistants and I set up our equipment inland about two hundred yards from the surf line.

At midmorning, the invading landing force appeared offshore. It came in through a curtain of fog that hung out there over the water. The Army division looked as our division would look as it approached a hostile shore. Nothing seemed improper until the 'invader's' landing craft touched our beach. Then it appeared that the Army's landing units were in total disorganization. The soldiers left the ramps in a hesitating and awkward manner, some men actually turned their backs to us as they tried to step backward and down that into the surf and in front of the boat's ramp. It was easily apparent that they had never practiced this type of landing before. Many of the soldiers would jump and fall flat into the surf. Some rolled about in the water as they tried to regain their footing. Their LSTs (Landing Ship Tanks) were beached and their ramps lowered. General Sherman tanks rumbled ashore followed by other vehicles, mostly jeeps. Once the tanks got ashore they all stopped suddenly and their crew's disembarked and began to mill about in apparent confusion. They evidently didn't know what was expected of them next.

There was more confusion when Lt. Jack Jones, our company executive officer, approached one of the tanks coming ashore and threw a quarter pound block of TNT up on one of the machine's flat areas. As he ran for safety, the charge exploded. The tank stopped and after a couple of moments its turret cover was thrown open and an angry tank commander emerged. He held his head with both hands and was he angry? He was screaming mad! Once he identified the Marine responsible, he cursed and cursed the Lieutenant. Lt. Jones stood in front of the tank, with his hands on his hips, and laughed at the Army tank commander's predicament. "Why, we heard you wanted realism. You did, didn't you? Well, you got it!"

By our assessment of the situation, the whole training and landing operation was a fiasco. In talking with some of the Army's medics later, we found they had sustained a large number of casualties. One man's leg was smashed by a landing craft's ramp and another was killed when he was crushed between two pieces of equipment and drowned in the surf. These medics said that their Division was en route to combat somewhere in the Pacific, they didn't know where. They added that they had never practiced making an amphibious landing before. This was their first attempt!

Weeks later, we found that this Army division, I believe named the "Wildcat Division," landed with the First Marine Division on Peleliu Island in the Palau Group. This battle was one of the bloodiest of the Pacific battles that year, and the Army's reported casualties were very high. It was the opinion of most of us there that day during that practice landing, that this Army unit was ill prepared to enter a battle of that consequence. We had to feel sorry for those soldiers involved. It made me feel more determined to be better trained.

Periodically we trained with tanks. We learned to work with them under combat conditions. Once, a Marine Corps major stood before our company and told us how much the tank crews depended upon us for protection and support. I really thought it was the other way around until then.

He stood there dressed in his 'tanker' jacket, dungarees that had the pants legs tucked into the top of his 'jump boots,' and wearing his 'tanker's' leather helmet and dark eyeglasses. He apparently was trying to impress us that he was one 'mean son-of-a-bitch.' He faced us with his feet spread wide apart and hands on his hips. He stood before a General Sherman tank, its

75mm. gun barrel just over his head was pointing at us. "We're tough, we're mean, and we'll knock out anything before us, if given a chance. However, we're blind and we need your help to do our job." He growled it all out, in one breath.

While sitting there before him on the ground, I began to think about the crew inside that iron monster who were protected from bullets by three or four inches of solid steel, while we, on the outside, had only our cloth dungarees to protect us. I began to wonder who was the toughest, a tanker or an infantryman?

The major and his crew instructed us on how we could help them assault various types of enemy positions. The tank would move toward its goal and a crewman inside would fire the turret's machine guns at the target. When the bullets of the machine guns were hitting the proper place, the gunner would fire the cannon. The cannon, which was synchronized with the machine guns, would send a shell directly to the same place the machine gun's bullets were hitting, hopefully destroying the target.

The infantrymen on the outside of the tank would either be directly behind the tank or spread out on either side of it in a skirmish line. It would be the job of the infantrymen to protect the tank from the enemy soldiers who would try to disable it with explosives. Also, the foot soldiers would have a clear view of the immediate battle area and could relay to the crew inside pertinent information regarding possible targets or dangers. This communication was accomplished by the use of a field telephone that was attached to the rear of the tank. While the major and his men talked, I could hear men who were sitting about me whispering and muttering, "Who the hell is going to protect us when the Japs begin to shell the tank!" None of us had the nerve to ask that question of the major though, as we thought he considered himself a tough, mean "Gung ho" type Marine and might resent our question's implication.

One part of the tank training concerned how to assist the crew of a disabled tank to abandon the machine safely in the presence of enemy soldiers. The crew would open a trap door which was in the floor of the machine beside the driver. One crewman would exit the tank through this door then another would pass down and out to him a .30 cal. light machine gun and ammunition. He would then follow it out. The third man would follow in turn. Once outside the tank, the three crewmen would join us infantrymen in defensive positions around the machine to protect it from the enemy. The whole procedure seemed reasonable and well thought out to me.

To increase our enthusiasm for tank warfare the major said, "You're lucky. We are going to let you all ride inside the tanks. You can sit in the tank commander's seat! In that way you'll know how he feels when he is there." When it was my turn, I climbed up onto the turret, entered the hatch and sat down in a small bucket type seat, where the commander would normally sit. A crewman instructed me on how to fasten my seat belt and how to close the hatch cover over my head. The hatch cover had, on its underside, a sponge rubber cup designed to fit over the top portion of a tanker's helmet. My regular steel helmet seemed too large for this cup and besides I was probably taller than most tankers, as when the hatch cover was closed, it pressed my head down onto my neck and shoulders in an awkward and uncomfortable way. I found that I couldn't turn my head to the left or right, but I could barely see through the periscope that was immediately in front of me.

Before I had time to inform the crewman who was sitting down below and directly in front of me about my uncomfortable position, the engine roared to life and the machine lurched off across the terrain at a fast speed. My body began to bounce up and down, back and forth, all except for my head that is. It stayed jammed into the rubber cup that held tight to my steel helmet. My neck was really hurting. Then I saw through the periscope that we were approaching a small dry water course while still traveling at a good speed. I attempted to hang on tight as I felt the front of the tank dip and then a resounding crash occurred as the heavy machine bottomed out in the wash. I saw colored lights flashing before my eyes that I'd never seen before and I felt sharp pains at the back of my neck and the base of my skull.

I don't remember much of the ride after that. I do recall a tanker urging me to get out of the seat and leave the turret. Then the two of them helped me down off the tank to the ground. As I stumbled away I heard one say, "What's the matter with that guy?"

The other replied, "I don't know. Maybe he went to sleep in there!"

I came to the conclusion that day that most tank commanders are smaller men than I, and that they wear those small leather helmets instead of the steel ones for a good reason. I also decided I did not want ever to be a 'Tanker!"

Orders For Guam

Bless 'Em All
Bless 'em all, Bless 'em all,
The long and the short and the tall.
Bless all the corporals who we must obey,
Bless all the sergeants who drill us all day,
We're saying good-bye to them all,
The long and the short and the tall.
No ice cream and cookies,
For flat footed rookies,
So cheer up my lads, Bless em all.

TWELVE JULY, 1944: You are restricted to the confines of the barrack area of Camp Pendleton until further notice!" The 'Top' Sergeant had spoken to us as usual that morning after muster. He was reading something, "From: The Commanding General, 5th Marine Division. To: The Personnel of the 26th Marine Regiment!"

These memoranda were getting to be old stuff to us. But, this time there was something different, perhaps a different tone in his voice. I noticed that the men around me straightened up and listened too.

Top Sergeant Robert Neef went on to read aloud, "The division is now on alert status. All leave is canceled. All personnel will be prepared to depart the United States within three days. All personnel are urged to put their personal affairs in order!" Around me the younger men appeared excited and were smiling. The married ones and those who had children at home were not. I began to feel sad for them, as I knew that they were thinking of their families.

All further training was suspended. The next day the restrictions regarding leave were relaxed. Those men who had relatives or families in the area were given special leave to visit them. Across the nation, girl friends, wives, mothers and fathers, and other relatives were hurrying to catch a train or bus or were beginning an auto trip with their destination Oceanside, where they hoped to see a loved one before he departed the country.

PFC Paul L. Pugh, the youngest Marine in the battalion was called before company commander Captain Tom Fields and informed that it was known that he was only sixteen years old and was subject to discharge from the military. The Captain asked him, "Do you want out I can get you a discharge, or do you want to go on with us?"

Without hesitating Pugh replied, "I want to go on with my buddies!"

The fiancé of PFC Rex T. Hull arrived from far away to meet with him to get married. The two were married upon her arrival and the two spent one night together; he left with us the next day.

We were not told of our eventual destination or even why we were leaving at this time. Later it was revealed that the 26th Marine Regiment was assigned to support the 3rd Marine Division which had landed with Army units on the island of Guam in an attempt to wrest the island back from the Japanese who had taken it from us in 1942.

On 21 July, the order came through to ready our combat packs. Other equipment and personal property was to be placed in our sea bags or to be sent to our homes. All of the sea bags were to be stacked in the barracks to await storage in one of the many warehouses in Camp Pendleton. They would wait there for our return.

The next morning the regiment and its support units were loaded onto trucks and driven to the Port of San Diego. The 27th and 28th Marine Regiments were to follow on August 12. Our regiment was to be unloaded on the dock at the foot of Broadway Street in the city. Upon entering the city of San Diego, our caravan of trucks rolled south along the Great Pacific Highway. We passed the huge aircraft manufacturing plants that were on the seaward side of the road. The buildings were camouflaged by huge brown, green, and gray nets that had been strung over them. From the netting hung a multitude of ribbons and of various dull colors.

I wondered if I would ever see this sight again, or would I die in some strange and foreign place? Most of the men were strangely quiet too. Usually when we were transported in trucks, there would be conversation and jokes being made about each other in a good natured way. Even the usually jovial Sgt. Goodling was quiet and appeared to be deep in thought. I suppose that most of us were thinking about the loved ones that we were leaving behind.

Our thoughts were interrupted and returned to our present situation when a Marine, who seemed proud of his nick name, "Rebel" was printed on the back of his shirt, yelled out to a civilian standing on the side walk and waving to us, "Hey, 4-F!" he cried out. The civilian dropped his arm, abandoned his smile and turned away from us as his shoulders slumped. Sgt. Russell Renner, the platoon guidon looked at the "Rebel" with obvious contempt and said, "What the hell...!"

I added, "Jerk!"

The designation, "Four F" was, at the time, a designation given to someone who couldn't serve in the military. Just prior to World War II, the U.S. Congress passed the Selective Service Act into law. The act meant that all male civilians were to register for the military draft and all were subject to compulsory military training. Once registered, the men were divided into several categories. Those who were physically and mentally fit and had no dependents were placed into 1-A. Those who were at the other end of the scale and were the least expected to be called were placed in the "4-F" category. It was doubtful that this category would ever be called upon to serve. Many a good American man who wanted to fight for his country was placed in the "4-F" category, due to no fault of his own. The majority of my comrades, as well as I, thought that the "Rebel" was out of line by publicly humiliating the civilian who stood on the street. Because of the Rebel's remark, we were embarrassed and we told him so.

The ship that our battalion was assigned to board was moored with the bow pointing outward away from the land and toward the channel leading to the open sea. The stern was pointed toward the city street that ran along the waterfront. The dock and ship were protected from the street by a ten foot high wire hurricane fence. There was a gate through which personnel made their way to and from the ship. This gate was guarded by shore patrolmen and marine military police. Across the street from the ship were the huge office buildings of the U.S. Navy's 4th Naval District Headquarters.

Once we men of the 2nd battalion were on board the ship, we stored our gear below in our assigned compartments. We were advised by orders coming over the ship's public address systems that we were permitted to roam about the ship's deck and the concrete dock. But that we could not leave the fenced in area. Taking advantage of this concession, Dillard, Munns, and I left the ship and took up a position along the fence near the city street. As we talked and speculated about our possible destination, we heard a loud shouting coming from the direction of the street. A voice yelled, "Munns! Hey, Munns!" The name calling was repeated several times before we could locate the owner who was in the crowd of people who stood on the outside of the fence. Through the mesh of the wire fence we could see the outline of a rather large man who was wearing a Navy enlisted man's white uniform. With rising interest we recognized our old acquaintance, Bill Marshall.

His words and mood indicated his great affection for Munns, Dillard, and me. He told us how much he missed us and how he wished he were back with us in his old outfit having fun again. We couldn't believe this guy! He did all that he could to get out of the FMF and back to the Navy and now he wanted to come back again and go overseas with us. I stood silent as Munns and Dillard sympathized with him as he told how the battalion surgeon had sent him to a relocation center at the naval station in San Diego. Instead of duty as a carpenter he was assigned to a special unit containing men who, it appeared, had all been in a lot of trouble at one time or another. He added that, because of the harsh way they were being treated and the heavy manual labor they were performing, he suspected they were on some sort of a "shit" detail. He thought that this might be the Navy's way of punishing them.

I saw Munn's face break out in that all so familiar grin of his, the one where he is beginning to think of mischief. I thought to myself that Marshall had better watch out! Munns told Marshall that it was a shame that he was being treated the way he was. He said we all missed him and even the Marines in the company had asked about him and wondered where he was stationed. All that was a 'damn' lie of course, but it got Marshall going strong. I saw him rise to the bait. Marshall began saying things like, "Do you think the doctor would take me back into the battalion now?" Munns was right there with, "Why don't you ask him? He would probably like to see you." Then Munns would turn and grin and Dillard and me. I was thinking, "Oh Christ, here we go again!"

Marshall was asking, "How do I get in there?" Munns replied that all he had to do was to go the gate and ask the guards to let him in as he wanted to talk to the battalion surgeon on board the ship for a moment. Marshall said, "OK," then turned and walked away from us toward the gate. The three of us stood there a few moments waiting for Marshall to return to his former spot outside of the fence after being shooed away by the gate guards. Then suddenly we heard his voice from behind us. We turned to face him and Munns blurted out, "How did you do that!" Marshall replied that he went up to a guard and told him that his brother was sailing on the ship tonight and he only wanted to visit with him for five minutes before saying good-bye.

Dillard and I waited patiently while Marshall tried to convince Munns to take him before the battalion surgeon. He wanted Munns to help him convince the doctor that he, Marshall, should rejoin his old battalion. Of course the doctor had no authority to do that, even if he wanted to. Munns knew that very well. Before many minutes passed, Munns has turned the conversation around and now it was, "It would be better if you came on board and stowed away. After we are at sea you can turn yourself in to the doctor. After all what can they do? They can't put you ashore, can they?" Munns went on to explain that the doctor would let him stay and even think well of him for trying to get back to the old outfit so that he could go into combat with his old friends. Marshall began to buy that plan and Munns began to laugh joyously. Dillard and I were both thinking that this is a good time to separate ourselves from the other two when the ship's public address system blared out, "All troops and crew still on the dock will now board ship immediately."

I said that I was going on board. Dillard said he was too. Marshall said, "What am I going to do?" Munns was still at it as he said to Marshall, "Come on board. Once we're at sea they won't kick you off. They will have keep you. You will be treated like a hero for going AWOL trying to return to your old outfit so you can get into battle!" Then Munns laughed that certain laugh of his. "Just walk up the gangway and follow us down to our compartment and you'll be safe there!"

Well, Dillard and I knew that since Marshall was dressed in Navy whites, he was not going to get past the ship's deck officer and the master- at-arms, who stood watch at the head of the gangway. They would challenge him as soon as he stepped on deck from the gangway. The officer of the deck and master-at-arms stood there watching all who came up the gangway. I fell in line first; Dillard was behind me, then Munns who was followed by Marshall. As I stepped onto the deck, a blue clad sailor approached the officer of the deck and said, "Sir!" and handed him a paper. This distracted the officer long enough for me, Dillard, Munns and then Marshall to step onto the deck of the ship and walk away and down a ladder leading to our compartment. On the way down I could hear Munns laughing the entire way.

Once in our compartment, we stood by our bunks in the passageway. Dillard and I were wishing that we were somewhere else. Munns was trying to laugh it all away as Marshall was saying, "If I get caught, I'm going to tell them you hid me," directing his words at Munns.

We were standing there when suddenly the top sergeant stepped through the compartment hatchway and shouted out, "Stand by for Captain's inspection!" Marshall began looking about wildly in an attempt to find a hiding place. Munns interrupted that by saying to him, "Now calm down. Captain Fields won't even take notice of you being here. What's it to him if a sailor is visiting here and talking to us?"

The ranking officer who stepped through the hatchway was not Captain Fields, but a full Navy commander who was the ship's Captain and who was intent upon inspecting his ship before sailing. He was followed by a Navy Lieutenant, then a Marine Corps major, then a Navy Ensign and the always present, master-at-Arms, who was equipped with the usual pencil and note pad. The Captain paused to stare at Marshall a moment, then turning his head, said to the Lieutenant who stood in back of him, "What's that sailor doing here? You know my policy on ship's personnel being in troop quarters." The Lieutenant replied, "I don't know, Sir!"

He then turned to the Ensign, "What the...?" The Ensign cut him short with, "I don't know sir, "and he turned to look at the master-at-Arms, who was already stepping forward and grabbing at Marshall's right arm.

"You follow me!" he demanded. Marshall followed him from the compartment, only turning his head once to glance back at us. I looked at Munns. He was looking straight ahead now, his eyes were wide open and the left side of his mouth turned up a little as he tried to hold back laughter that was building inside of him.

The inspection was over very quickly in our compartment and we were released to go up on deck again. Munns, Dillard and I ran for the ship's rail that stood above the concrete dock to a place where we could stand and watch for Marshall as he left the ship. For a few moments we thought that perhaps he had already left after being reprimanded and ordered off. We wondered if he was still in custody though.

We didn't wait very long to find out as three enlisted men wearing white uniforms approached the ship's gangway and walked down it single file from the ship toward the dock below. The tall sailor in the middle was easily identified. It was Marshall and his hands were handcuffed together in front of him. He never looked back as he walked through the gate and got into the rear compartment of a Navy shore patrol wagon which was parked at the curb. The door was slammed shut and the van driven away.

I turned and looked at Munns; he wasn't laughing or even smiling now. He appeared miserable. Dillard looked at Munns for a moment, then he said, "You're a dirty bastard, Munns!"

"Yeah!" I added.

CHAPTER FOURTEEN

Farewell to the States

Bless 'em all, bless 'em all,
The long and the short and the tall,
Bless all the blondes and all the brunettes,
Bless every man who takes what he gets
So we're saying good-bye to them all,
The long and the short and the tall,
Maude, Maggie or Susie,
You can't be too choosy,
So cheer up my lads, bless 'em all.

ON JULY 22, 1944, as the sun began to settle down beyond the horizon to the west, the mooring lines that held our ship fast to the wharf were cast loose. "Let go the forward lines," then "Let go the after lines," came the loud order from the bridge over the loudspeaker. The command caused men on the wharf to scurry here and there in their efforts to free the huge hawsers that held the ship fast to the dock.

Our ship, along with four others containing elements of the 26th Regiment, worked its way through the port channel which was crowded with all types of Navy and Merchant Marine vessels. Two aircraft carriers lay at anchor near the North Island Naval Air Base, and several destroyers lolled about placidly in the channel not hindered by the restraints of an anchor chain. As we approached the channel entrance our attention was drawn away from the many rows of airplanes parked on North Island on our port side, to a row of ugly squat gray submarines berthed alongside a 'mother' ship off to our starboard. A sailor, standing near me, identified the large ship as a submarine tender.

Our small convoy of ships continued out through the harbor's mouth and passed the large land projection, known as "Land's End," that was on our starboard side. The convoy's ships were in single file. Ours was first in line. In front of us a submarine net tender's propeller churned the blue water into a frothy white spray, as it tugged on the heavy chain netting to pull it clear of the entrance, allowing our passage to the open sea.

Once through the entrance, a destroyer fell in front of our ship and preceded us toward the western horizon. Far out in front of it, two more destroyers were busy cruising in wide circles. As we got within a mile or so they separated to spread apart, heading west also. The destroyer in front of us then began a zigzag course. The little ship would heel this way and that as it made its turns at fast speed. Those of us watching on the deck of our larger transport wondered how the destroyer's crew could possibly maintain their footing as the little craft bucked and rolled along through the choppy water.

Our attention was drawn from the destroyers to a large number of porpoises off on our starboard bow that raced alongside and kept pace with our ship. We were delighted with the little animals' antics as they splashed through the water. Up and down they went, in and out of the water. It looked like fun. Some of the men around me, waved and shouted encouragement to the 'performers'! I wondered if the porpoises were responding to that applause!

The sky was darkening. Looking back I could see the California coastline becoming very dim in the distance. It looked cold and barren from where I stood. Of course, I couldn't see the city of San Diego. It was wartime and no lights were permitted to be shown outdoors after dusk. The wind was increasing and cold sprays of water were being whipped up over the sides of the ship's bow. The vessel began to buck and roll more often as we encountered the full forces of the coastal ocean current.

In front of us there appeared a dark, thick, ominous looking fog bank. We were soon enveloped by it and the deck we stood upon became wet and sticky with its moisture. When a Marine commented that we wouldn't be able to see much soon because of the darkness, a nearby sailor answered, "Neither will the Jap submariners!" Then suddenly, it was dark, and most of us filed below to our compartments.

As the ships in the convoy left the harbor entrance that evening, my mother and a friend were standing at the dock gate entrance. Unknown to me, they had driven from San Jose the day previously. The friend, who had relatives in Carlsbad, California, decided to visit them and invited my mother to accompany her on the drive, Mom went along with no time to alert me that she was coming. The two of them had gone to Camp Pendleton and were informed by an officer at the main gate that the 26th Regiment had just departed for the dock area in San Diego. The two women hurriedly drove to the dock only to be informed by guards at the gate, "You're too late. There they go now!" and pointed to the four ships leaving the harbor entrance. I hadn't seen my mother for nine months; I was not to see her until the war was ended, some eighteen months later.

I awakened the next morning at the sound of "General Quarters" being called over the ship's public address system. At first, I could hear the sounds made by the crew as they ran to their duty stations. It was that one half hour before dawn in which ship travel is so dangerous. This was the opportune time for the crews of those enemy submarines, who had been patiently waiting, to dispatch their torpedoes at a helpless passing enemy ship.

For a moment I lay very still in my bunk as I had a funny feeling in my stomach. The compartment was full of stale, damp, heavy air and strange odors. I could smell body sweat, smelly stockings, and oil fumes that hung about in the air. All this contributed to the nausea that was beginning to develop in my stomach. I rolled out of my bunk and quickly slipped my shoes on. I was thankful I hadn't taken my clothing off the night before. I felt ill and knew I had to vomit and I felt distressed knowing that I was two levels below the weather deck. I ran to the ladder and ran up the two flights to the top deck. I leaped through the hatchway leading to the outside deck and ran for the nearest portion of the ship's rail.

On deck, there were seven sailors standing muster before a Navy Ensign. As I ran past them, one called out in alarm, "Don't!" But it was too late. I fell to my knees at the deck's edge and vomited up everything I had in my stomach. To my further dismay, the vomit didn't fall over the side of the ship and into the water as I expected, but was whipped back over my right shoulder by the wind. It sprayed the mustering sailors and their supervising officer. I had made a grievous mistake, one that no experienced sailor would make. Never try to discharge liquid overboard on the windward side of a ship at sea. Once a person does it, they will never to it again. I didn't have to turn around to tell what happened to the sailors. I could hear their curses and rude remarks.

I wiped my face with a sleeve of my dungaree blouse and turned around to face the crewmen and said, "Sorry fellows." When they saw the pale color of my face and the sorry state I was in, they relaxed a little and some even smiled sympathetically.

I stumbled over to the nearest large cargo hatch cover and threw myself down on it. I suffered from seasickness as I never had before. For the rest of the day, that night, the next day and night and then part of the next day,

I lay on that hatch cover in agony. At intervals I would attempt to vomit but that only brought about dry heaves. I would stagger over to the deck scuttle and drink some water and then return to the hatch cover and lie down again.

The fact that there were other passengers who were seasick also held no consolation for me, whatsoever. On the third day at sea, one of my Marine comrades brought me a piece of corn bread, which I forced myself to eat. I immediately felt better. I walked forward to near the number one cargo hatch and observed a card game in progress. The players were sitting in a circle on the deck. Another eight or so Marines stood on their feet and appeared to be grossly interested in the poker game. Moving closer I could see that the whole thing was a sham and the men standing were in fact shielding the men on the deck from the ship's personnel on the bridge. The Marines had opened an inspection hatch, crawled into it and removed a five gallon can of pineapple. I got a huge slice, and gosh, it was great. I continued eating until the can was empty. I have never tasted better pineapple since. At noon, I went down to the troop's mess and ate two slices of bread and drank some

Why no, he's not sea-sick... he just likes to feed the fish!

hot coffee. I then found, much to my elation, that I was no longer sick but feeling much better as each moment passed.

On the fourth day at sea, the troops were advised that the battle for the island of Guam was well in control by our military forces there, and that we wouldn't be needed to reinforce the 3rd Marine Division after all. Our immediate destination was changed to the island of Hawaii, the largest of the Hawaiian Islands which was located some twenty two hundred miles southwest of the California coast. So after five terrible days at sea for me, the ship arrived at the beautiful small port of Hilo on the eastern side of the "Big Island."

Camp Tarawa

Hawaii was exciting for most of us at first. There was the sweet odor of flower blossoms to greet us. On the day our ship docked, we disembarked and then were marched to the town of Hilo, a distance of about one mile. Because, there were no trucks available to carry us to our camp sixty-five miles away, we bivouacked that night on the beautiful green lawn of the city park. We were told to erect our shelter halves because of the possibility of rain, even though the sky was clear and the day was warm. After establishing our camp, we were allowed to wander about the immediate area and get some exercise. This felt good after being cooped up on that stuffy, crowded troop ship we had just left. At 1730 we were served peanut butter and jelly sandwiches, coffee, and punch for our dinner. About 2100, we turned in to get some sleep. Sometime around 2200 it began to rain, and it rained hard!

The water level raised inside of the tents as well as on the outside. It rose around our bodies as we attempted to sleep. My tent partner and I were lying on our backs. I had suspended my rifle from the ridge pole of the tent in an attempt to keep it dry. The young PFC who lay along side of me was attempting to sleep while holding his rifle balanced on his stomach. He covered himself and the weapon with his poncho to keep out the cool night air. As the water rose to about two inches up and around our bodies, the young marine asked, "What are we going to do, Doc.?"

I could only answer, "We're already wet so moving won't help us now. I'm going to lie on my back and try to stay warm." It was the only thing to do. The rain was coming down in torrents and if we did leave the tent, we would get soaked. Anyway, there was no place to go for shelter from the rain, even if we did get up.

We lay there listening to the noises of rain drops falling on our little tent. The other members in their shelters were making some interesting comments about the Marine Corps, the war, and of Hawaii. I began to laugh, a little at first and then out loud. My tent partner, who at first, didn't see any humor in the situation began to giggle a little, then he burst out in laughter. I heard a marine near us, who seemed irate, remark, "What are those idiots out there doing laughing?" Another responded," They must be cracking up!" In a little while, other men were beginning to laugh, their anger and frustration was being replaced by the resignation of knowing that they had to face the inevitable. Soon, men were calling out to each other with humorous comments.

All this commotion subsided suddenly, when above the noise, we heard the strong commanding voice of the Top Sergeant. "You men, knock it off and try to get some sleep!"

The men's voices quieted down. The last of the comments that I heard was from two wags nearby, "Burt, please hand me the soap!"

"Well, OK, but you'll have to hand me my towel."

Quiet settled down over the temporary camp. For the rest of the night, I could hear only the steady light drumming of the rain on the tent material over my head.

When reveille sounded at dawn the next morning, there wasn't a cloud in the sky. Instead there was only sunshine and warmth about us. As the sun rose higher in the east, clouds of steam rose from the drying clothing and blankets hung on tree limbs and bushes about the camp.

The Top Sergeant made his rounds, bidding the company good morning and inquiring after a man's health here and there. He stopped at our shelter as I was crawling out of it and made small talk about last night's rain fall. My tent mate crawled out after me, carrying his rifle. He held it up for us to see. He was very dismayed as the rifle was completely covered with a fine covering of rust. The "Top" looked at the weapon and his face turned red. "How," he demanded, "did that happen?"

"I held it on my stomach all night and kept it covered with my poncho to keep the rain off it," wailed the Marine.

"Son, you got shit for brains, do you? Don't you know that metal sweats under a waterproof cover like a poncho, and that causes rust? God Damn it, Son, don't you?" The 'Top's' words caused me to stand there in awe of him, with my mouth hanging open, as I listened.

The kid was still on his knees; his clothes were pretty well soaked through with rain water. He was staring at his rusty rifle and I thought he was about to cry as tears were forming in the corners of his eyes. The 'Top' must have seen what I saw, as his tone softened suddenly. He said, in a much quieter and milder tone, "Well OK, son. You get your cleaning gear and you take that rifle over there in the sunshine and you start working on it. When we get to camp, we'll see about you turning that M-1 in and getting another to replace it." While the Top spoke, I could see perhaps another half dozen Marines who were standing in back of him, grab their rifles and inspect them. A few of them hurriedly took their rifle out of the sergeant's view.

The sixty-five mile ride to Camp Tarawa, wasn't pleasant. We sat on hard board bench seats, in the back of the trucks, and bounced about quite a bit as the vehicles rumbled over a rough dirt and gravel road. The road was referred to as the 'hump,' as it ascended the eastern slope of the island, crossed over its middle between two live volcanoes, then turned to the north where the little town of Kamuela and Camp Tarawa lay. We only made one stop on the entire trip that took about three hours to complete. On the top of the island we stopped on a fresh lava flow while some of the men dismounted from the trucks so that they could wet down the volcanic ash a little.

When we approached the tent camp at Tarawa, we were anything but joyous. We were downright appalled at what we saw. The tents were all dirty looking and sagging something awful. On the ground around them and on the streets, the grass grew high and ragged. In answer to some of the bitching concerning the condition of the camp, one sergeant said, "And guess who is going to clean this place up!" How right he was!

The camp was first established to house the 2nd Marine Division while it was being reorganized after its terrible battle ordeal at Betio Island in the Tarawa Group of the Gilbert Islands in November of 1943. The camp was established, just at the southern edge of Kamuela, much to the shock of the little town's inhabitants when one day they looked up and found seventeen thousand or so Marines moving in on them. The 2nd Division, had departed several months prior, and now was a brand new division to take its place. Of course our presence meant a lot to the war time economy of Kamuela, Hawaii.

When Will It End?

Oh, we have a doctor,
His name is McLarney,
Instead of the treatment,
He shoots you the blarney.

Oh, we go to sick bay,
When we are in pain,
And old Doc Skinner,
Says he has the same.

IT WAS WITHIN A two week period that the remainder of the division came into camp, having arrived from San Diego without incident. The 28th Regiment arrived with their mascot, a male lion cub. Whenever on parade, the lion took his place sitting on a red U.S. Marine Corps banner which was draped over the hood of a jeep. The lion grew surprisingly fast and before the division left for combat the animal was shipped back to the States to the San Diego Zoo, a full sized male lion.

During the war years, Hawaii was still a territory. The United States proper was referred to as the "mainland" or "stateside." The 27th and 28th Regiments, the 13th Marines which was the artillery regiment, the 5th Medical Battalion and other support units all settled down with our 26th Regiment to help clean up the camp and to start a training program.

It was generally agreed upon that we all had enough training, and now it was time to take some more islands from the Japanese. We were not allowed to sit around and complain about it though. Discipline was maintained at a high level.

Each morning a bulletin was posted announcing the training events for the day following. A day's training scheduled might read like this:

0800 - 0900 - calisthenics and running
0900 - 1000 - nomenclature 60 mm. mortar
1000 - 1100 - nomenclature 30 cal. light. machine gun
1100 - 1200 - gas warfare, Lt. Brown
1200 - 1300 - lunch - field rations
1300 - 1500 - lecture - tank tactics
1500 - 1630 - field tactics - skirmish line formation
1630   - recall

The next day's training schedule was posted early I suppose to alert us as to what equipment was necessary for that specific training period and to keep our interest up. One day I stopped by the bulletin board and read the following day's schedule. I was horrified to read that at 1500 hours the next day I was to give a lecture on first aid to the entire company. I just knew that someone had made a mistake, so I immediately went seeking the senior pharmacist mate who was in charge of the D company corpsmen. When I found Cecil Thrower, I told him that there was an error and that I couldn't possibly give a lecture, that I was just eighteen years old and couldn't stand up before a group of one hundred and eighty Marines which included seven officers. Many of those men were combat veterans and knew more about first aid than I. How could I describe wounds and treatment that I had never seen and they had?

The senior corpsman wasn't sympathetic at all. He said that he had to give many talks, and there always a was first time for everyone. He added that I had better come up with something to say or there would be trouble for me. He didn't give me any encouragement or even offer to help me prepare for the fifty minute talk.

That night I lay awake on my bunk thinking about the lecture the following day. I wondered about all the possibilities of escaping the affair. I thought of my high school days when I stood before my classmates and stuttered and stammered out an oral recitation. Why some days I had even skipped school or played sick so I wouldn't have to recite.

The appointed time came the next day and I stood before the company not knowing what I was saying or doing. It was horrible. The officers forced themselves to look at me, but would not allow their facial expressions to reveal their thoughts. My fellow corpsmen either hid their faces by holding their hands over their eyes or they just looked down and avoided eye contact with me as I stammered. Some of the older combat veterans just looked at me in wonder and showed no other expression on their faces. Sgt. Charles Goodling sat on the ground near me making faces and he grinned at me the entire length of time I stood there. He was apparently getting quite a kick out seeing me so miserable. When the lecture ended I stood off to one side feeling humiliated, embarrassed, and washed out, I waited for someone to say something to me. I didn't get many comments, but some Marines took the time to pause just long enough to ask me what it was I was talking about. I looked to Sgt. Goodling for support. He grinned, wrinkled up his nose, shook his head and said, "Goddamn Corpsman!"

I learned that I was to give more talks, on various medical problems that might occur in the field. No other company corpsman was asked to do the same. I could never find out why it was always me. Thrower wouldn't give an answer even though I told him I was by far the youngest man of the group. He wouldn't give me any assistance in preparing myself for the talks either. I finally resigned myself to the fact that I was going to have to give the lectures.

I went to my friend Nyle Weiler, a Pharmacist Mate 2/c, who was assigned to the sick bay to assist the battalion surgeon. He was in his middle twenties, had a college background and in civilian life was a mortician. He seemed knowledgeable and appeared to have things well organized. Under his guidance I restricted my talks to specific areas of the medical problems that would face us in the field. Under his tutelage I studied those problems and prepared outlines that I could follow while I spoke. The next time I stood before the company, I felt much more confident.

I spoke on the effects of shock and how a man looked, felt and acted when suffering from it. Then I gave a demonstration on how to combat it. I finished my talk a little early and that was just as well as many of the Marines had a lot of questions to ask. Some of the veterans told of their experiences concerning shock during battle and this helped me put my points across very well. After the lecture I felt much better than I did the previous time. Several of the officers found the time to approach me and to make favorable comments about my presentation. Even my corpsman buddies found a few nice remarks to say about how well I had done, though most of them agreed that they, "didn't know I was that bright!"

Nyle Weiler continued to coach and assist me in organizing my lectures, and I continued to give them. I gained self confidence, the confidence of my Marine comrades, and was better prepared to do my job as a medical corpsman.

A: THOUGH CAMP TARAWA was established on the very edge of Kamuela, it was also on the property owned by the huge Parker Cattle Ranch. This ranch consisted of thousands of acres and had been leased to the United States government until the war's end. The terrain and vegetation there were quite similar to that of many of the islands in the Pacific Ocean. Our troops made simulated battle landings on various beaches, then moved inland to do mock battle with a supposed enemy.

The ground on the western slope between camp and the sea was not easy to maneuver on. It was covered with old decaying rough chunks of lava from an eruption hundreds of years old. In among the large pieces of lava rock, opuntia cactus grew, sometimes as high as fifteen feet high. For a person to walk through the area he would have to climb up on a chunk of lava, jump down while avoiding the cactus, climb the next chunk of lava and so on. The process of moving across the land was very slow for troops doing maneuvers. This area had been heavily fortified during the early days of the war for fear of an invasion by the Japanese from the sea. The Army had built hundreds of gun emplacements in that rough country of broken lava. No doubt many are still in existence today.

A note is warranted concerning the cactus. It is not a native of Hawaii. It was reportedly brought to the island during the early exploration and settlement days from Mexico. It had been transported by ship in cattle food when the animals were introduced into the islands during the middle 1880s. Some twenty years after the war ended in 1945, I returned to this area and to my surprise the cactus was all but gone from the land. The U.S. government had imported some insect that was an enemy to the cactus and it had generally been eradicated. The plant was becoming a serious nuisance as it had adapted very well to the soil and climate of Hawaii.

There was a beautiful bathing beach located on the Parker Ranch about twelve miles from Kamuela. It too, was leased by our government and served as a battalion beach camp for us. We used it for recreational purposes as well as for amphibious training purposes. There was some difficulty in getting to the site as the road stopped two miles from it and that distance had to be walked by foot along a rough footpath.

In getting to the beach from Kamuela one would either walk or ride for about nine miles down to a public beach. From there on it was just a footpath through briars and in and out of gullies and over chunks of lava. Our first visit to Camp Drews, as it was known to us at the time, was when our entire battalion was sent down there to camp, as there was a water shortage in the main camp. Our drinking water was hauled into Camp Drews by boat from the other side of the island. For water to bathe with we had to use the ocean water which left our bodies sticky and itching.

During the month of August, 1944, with combat packs on our backs and carrying our rifles and other gear, we began our hike down the road that led to the seashore. Kamuela, which is located at about eighteen hundred feet in elevation, has nice cool weather. The climate changed considerably as we descended the road. The temperature rose higher and higher, as did the humidity too.

We soon learned that we were on a forced march. That meant that there would be no ten minute break for every hour we walked as was usual. Instead we would continue right on until we reached our destination which was twelve or more miles from Camp Tarawa. Since most of the way was downhill we hikers thought at first that this was to be an easy walk even though there were no rest periods permitted. It was easy; we accepted the challenge and got down to the public beach in fair shape. We turned south, but at the same time began to feel the heat and humidity of the air. Men became noticeably affected by the strain.

With the heat at about the 100 degree Fahrenheit level and the humidity very high, the men began to suffer from heat exhaustion. Some would suddenly stop and collapse to the ground. Others would lie down or just sit on the ground. They all showed the same symptoms, perspiration, and pale looking skin, rolling unfocused eyes and fainting.

This was a tough time again to be a corpsman. Hell! We suffered just as much as anyone else from the heat, yet it was our duty to help our Marine comrades if we could. We dragged the stricken men from the foot path to keep him from blocking it. We would stretch the fallen man out flat on the ground in the shade if possible. We'd loosen his blouse from around his waist, give him water and a salt tablet, and then walk off to catch up with our platoons. This delay in stopping to help a man would put the corpsman far behind his unit. The medic would have to run through the heat in order to catch up.

Along this mile or so stretch of hot, dusty path, close to fifty men lay prostrate on the ground, while the main portion of the column reached Camp Drews. For a couple of hours afterward, a mixture of officers and enlisted men straggled into camp. Most of the downed men recovered on their own and walked in. Some of the corpsmen who were assigned to the aid station rode the first nine or so miles in the jeep ambulance. Being fresher, they were to follow the column and help some of the stricken men. The last two miles of the road, well it couldn't be called a road actually because the jeep couldn't traverse it under its own power. Four of the corpsmen walked along side of it and either lifted it over the rough spots or pushed it through.

The high temperature at Drews Beach that summer was such that it prevented us from training during the day. We would commence our training sessions at 1630 hours and work until 0100. During that time we would walk into the surrounding brush and uneven hill terrain to practice maintaining night defensive lines or making simulated assaults on an enemy position. Most of that training was hazardous.

We incurred many minor injuries at night. There were many twisted ankles and scraped legs and arms to treat with sulfa, iodine, and bandages. I pulled many a cactus spine out of tender skin after getting back to camp in the early hours of the morning. Aside from the injuries, some of us kept getting lost during the exercise, and when we did, we just sat down until we were found.

Once we were back at Drews Beach, we were allowed to go swimming. I would spend the entire time allowed in the water which was warm and about perfect at that time of the morning. Afterward, we'd lie around on the beautiful sand beach until ordered to bed at two o'clock in the morning.

The days were nicely spent. We were up at dawn and swam before and after breakfast and lunch. We did a little sack time in our tents in the afternoon and were fit to go to work at 1600 hours.

That is a nice beach; however, there are rip tides present there. PFC Rex Hull and I swam to a rocky point and got caught in a rip tide and couldn't escape it so we just paddled around and floated trying to figure how to free ourselves.

Colonel Sayers, sitting in front of his tent watched us for a while with his binoculars and sent Lt. Horvath down to order us out of the water. The Lieutenant stood on the rocks and said, "Get out of there, the Colonel is watching and he is raising hell about you in such a dangerous place!"

I yelled up at him and said, "We can't Lieutenant, we are caught in a rip tide here and can't escape it!"

"Well, get out anyway, the Colonel is 'madder'n all hell' and he's taking it out on me!"

Rex and I swam away from the rocks, out toward sea for a short way and then curved around and came back to the beach to safety. We left the Lieutenant standing on the rocks yelling at us and demanding that we get out immediately. I don't know what explanation he offered the colonel, but we stayed away from the platoon leader for a while.

The Colonel had a reason for his action. We were told that several weeks before one of the units training there in small rubber boats suffered a disaster. Five men and a Lieutenant were in a rubber boat when the wind caught it and swept it to sea. Two miles out one of them who had been a life guard at one time in civilian life convinced the officer that he could swim the distance and seek help. The young Marine drowned in the attempt.

Years later, long after the war had ended, I visited that location. It was, of course, no longer a military camp but the site of a multimillion dollar hotel, the Moana Kea. The guests then were paying $150.00 a day for the average room and swimming on the beach that I was once paid to swim on. There was a very modern paved road between Kamuela and the beach. A new beautiful green golf course stretched over the rugged terrain where we once struggled through the nights, over prickly cactus, thorn brush, and broken chunks of lava rock.

Although Camp Drews was nice as far as swimming went it was rather uncomfortable away from the water's edge. Even the water was somewhat of a hazard. A few Marines reported into sick bay after they had stepped on spine bearing fish or shells. Several men swam over the top of the Portuguese Man o' War as it lay on the water's surface. Its sting was very painful and it was common to see a man's chest and stomach area covered with a red rash caused by the venom. An injection of adrenaline would help clear it up, and an application of Novocaine ointment over the affected parts would help also to lessen the pain a little.

We welcomed our return to Camp Tarawa and the cool soothing weather around Kamuela. But, it seemed that the rain clouds still came dashing over the camp each day about the same time. It rained a lot over a high mountain to the northwest of the camp. Because of a steady wind that blew from that direction, rain drops were often falling even though the sun shone brightly.

The constant field problems we carried out in the plains and hills near camp got to be quite wearisome. We would usually march the six or seven miles to begin a problem. Then after spreading out in a skirmish line across the broken terrain, we would simulate an attack on the enemy positions which were usually a row of bunkers or a line of rifle pits.

The wind was constantly blowing out on the plains to the east of camp. The air was full of the light volcanic ash or sand as some called it. That stuff got into our eyes, ears, and mouths and worked through our clothing and even lodged in our skins. It was in our rifle mechanisms, our bedding, packs and when we filled our coffee cups it floated about on the surface of the coffee. For lunch out there we mostly got peanut butter and jelly sandwiches to eat. Of course they were sprinkled liberally with volcanic ash.

Camp life itself was, at best, sufferable. A large Quonset mess hall was constructed, and the food prepared there was tolerated by the men but still with the usual amount of complaining. Actually the food quality was adequate, but the method in which it was prepared was not very acceptable to the men. No amount of complaining by them seemed to have any effect on the situation. I suppose it was always the expectation that we would move out for battle at any moment that gave an excuse to delay improvement.

We would file through the mess hall with our aluminum mess kits and be served our meal, after which we exited that building, walked across an open space of about one hundred feet, and entered a large tent. There we sat at rough wooden tables to eat. On cool mornings and sometimes when it rained, few of the men would make fun of the procedure by actually turning their mess kits upside down while the food was still inside them.

The gooey powdered eggs and Spam slices would have congealed in the cold air and would stick to the metal mess kit. At least if we carried the food kit upside down, the rain couldn't fall into the food.

Our battalion's sick bay was located in a small Quonset hut. It was manned by a battalion surgeon and his assistant and those two were aided by a pharmacist's mate first class, and about six other corpsmen of various rates.

Each of the rifle platoons in the rifle companies had one corpsman assigned to it. That man trained and lived as a Marine with the platoon's members. The corpsman's immediate supervisors within the platoon were the platoon commander and the platoon Sergeant. However, neither of those men had anything to say about the medical practices of the corpsman.

That was all covered by the US Navy's Bureau of Medicine regulations, and supervised by Navy supervisors.

There were three rifle platoons in each rifle company, accompanied by a mortar and machine gun platoon whose members could be assigned to whichever of the rifle platoons the situation called for. Also assigned to each company was an 'assault squad' whose members were well trained in using explosives and flame-throwers and other special weapons.

The mortar and machine gun platoons each had a corpsman assigned to it. The senior and one extra corpsman stayed with the company headquarters staff, which included the company commander (who was a Captain), the executive officer, master sergeant, his clerks, communication men and message runners.

The extra corpsman was used to fill in for other corpsman during their absence. During the war years that the second platoon was in existence, I was the only corpsman assigned as an aid man.

I was under the impression that a few Navy medical officers became an embarrassment to his command he might be transferred from regular Navy duty to the Fleet Marine Force. The same seemed to apply to a few of the petty officers of higher ratings.

I don't mean to imply in any way that all doctors were in that category, but certainly a lot of them were. I knew many good men who served with the Marines who were there of their own volition. Also young new medical officers who had just come into the service and youngsters like me, just out of high school, were used to fill the need for medics to serve with the fighting battalions.

Certainly not many of the older doctors relished the idea of serving with the Marines, where they were forced to live a rather primitive life. To sleep on the ground, to eat standing up because the mud on the ground offered no place to sit, and all that sort of thing was in sharp contrast to the life they knew before while serving in a clean hospital atmosphere and living quarters.

One night, I was confined to the sick bay because of a high fever induced by an inoculation for yellow fever. Several of my Marine comrades were also afflicted and occupied canvas cots in the same room. At approximately 2200 hours, the only corpsman on duty came into the ward and asked me to answer the telephone if it rang as he wanted to go to the nearby Red

Cross shack for a coffee and doughnuts. "Oh, sure," I said. And there I was, volunteering again!

About 2200 we heard a man's and a woman's voice outside the building. As luck would have it, through the doorway came a doctor, I'll call Dr. X, dragging behind him a red haired Red Cross woman. Both were much intoxicated and their actions rather unsuitable considering their positions.

The doctor was staggering about and falling against the room's furniture while he pulled the woman along between the rows of cots that my buddies and I reclined upon. When the two revelers got to the back of the room, the doctor wrestled the laughing woman onto an empty cot and fell on top of her. They both lay there with their arms and legs flailing about. First, he would be on top and then the woman would take her turn. Then one or the other would fall to the floor and then climb back onto the other lying on the bed. God! Was I embarrassed? There was one of my commanding officers, drunk and trying to have sexual relations with a woman, right there in front of my companions and me.

The Marines and I sat on our bunks as the scene developed. I suffered from a bout of catarrhal fever; I felt terrible and I didn't know what to do. Finally, I couldn't stand it any longer as the doctor and the woman were beginning to discard their clothing onto the floor. I got up and walked over to where the two were undressing. The woman lay on her back and the doctor was straddling her with his knees. I said, "Doctor, you're drunk! Get her out of here!"

I repeated myself and after a moment the doctor realized that he had better see what it was that I wanted. He sat up on the cot, looked at me and said, "whaa...?"

I said, "You're drunk and you ought to pull up your pants and get her out of here!"

He said something about being "God damned" and then the woman said, "Wassa matter, honey?" The doctor stood up and began pulling up his trousers from around his ankles. I returned to my bunk and lay down again. Gee, but I sure felt bad!

The Doctor and the woman became quiet and were whispering back there a while as they straightened up their clothing. She was asking questions in a low voice, "What's the matter? What's wrong? What's up?"

When the two of them were ready to leave, they filed along between the rows of bunks. I was lying on my back and trying to look the doctor straight in the eyes as he passed. He hesitated, then stared at me, he mumbled some phrase with the words, "You, you, I'll fix you!"

One of the Marine patients said, "Wait 'til' I tell the other guys about this!" I lay back on my bunk and I felt sicker than ever.

The next day, the word spread around that the doctor had received a telegram from his home announcing that his wife had a baby. I suppose I ruined the doctor's celebration. Needless to say, the relationship between the physician and me was very strained after this; even though I didn't remember him ever speaking to me. Upon Nyle Weiler's advice, I stayed away from the sick bay after the incident to avoid meeting him face to face.

Ready For Battle

The corpsmen that they give us,
They say they are the best,
But if you go for treatment,
They are always taking a rest,
I don't want anymore of the U. S. Marines.
I just want to go home!

BY SEPTEMBER 1944 the men of the division were becoming restless. They complained about the incessant training and thought it time to go into battle or go home. It appeared that the more they complained the more the training increased. All this work they did was apparently designed to keep the men's minds and bodies busy.

We were involved mostly in field problems lasting three days. We'd hike for miles across the high plateaus of the island to reach the location where we would train. The unit would 'jump off,' at a given point and we would begin simulated assaults on the enemy positions, such as bunkers or infantry that was well dug in.

Working our way through the broken lava and the many clumps of cactus, we would simulate assaulting the enemy's position while at the same time trying to maintain our own unit's integrity. Communications and logistical problems were identified and overcome by this practice, a very important aspect of military training.

Solving those problems put another strain on us front line troops. Often we would just sit and wait, usually not knowing why but, probably because the commanders had gathered to make corrections in their plans or revise some training procedure. Sitting and waiting can be a very tiresome thing and our men would often complain about, it much to the chagrin of the junior officers who waited with us.

When we were out in the field under those conditions, we would often have meals brought from the camp mess. It was probably done to help break the monotony from eating K rations. The lunch menu never varied, it was always peanut butter and jelly sandwiches, and the jelly was always apple flavor. The beverage was delivered in clean thirty-five gallon galvanized garbage cans. At the noon break, men lined up to receive their two sandwiches (a coarsely ground bread), and their choice of beverage, either luke warm coffee or lukewarm lemonade.

Since the wind blew constantly on part of the island, the beverage was covered with that volcanic ash from the Mauna Kea volcano. It floated and swirled through the air and settled on the liquid in the containers. Most of us balked at this sight at first, then got used to and consumed a great deal of volcanic dust When eating in the field like that the enlisted men received their food first, then the officers fell in line after. By the time they got their food the coffee was less than lukewarm, the lemonade warmer and the sandwiches were well covered with volcanic ash.

Correct sanitation procedures in the field were strictly adhered to. The latrine problem was handled by each platoon. Men were assigned to dig a slit trench under the supervision of the corpsman. The trench would be dug to specifications. It would be one foot wide, two feet deep and perhaps

"The beverage was lukewarm coffee or lukewarm lemonade punch that was delivered in clean thirty-five gallon galvanized garbage cans"

twelve to fifteen feet long. The trench would usually be dug downwind from the bivouac area in some out-of-the-way place. Before abandoning the site the trench would be filled in to the ground level and a stick with a note tied to it was pounded into the dirt, indicating when the trench was closed. An empty ration can was placed over the top to protect the memo from the weather. It would have been a problem for another military unit to come that way and set up another campsite there.

The second battalion was called out one day for briefing on a pending three day exercise. The place indicated for the exercise was west of Kamuela, high up on a mountainside, where it appeared to rain perpetually.. The Captain stood before us and detailed the plan. He also told us that previously another battalion had been training there and some of the men took it upon themselves to butcher a Parker Ranch cow, one of thousands grazing there. The culprits were of the 28th Regiment, and were forced to pay two hundred dollars for their ill-gotten meal. The Captain went on to warn us that harsh and swift disciplinary action occur if any such act took place while we were there.

Still, I figured that a hunk of barbecued beef would certainly be worth the two dollars per man it would take to pay for the meat regardless of the disciplinary threat. Other men thought the same thing and I believe it was an indication of the frame of mind we were reaching. They were bored with all this training stuff and wanted to get to the battle. Even being punished would provide some excitement to their lives and many were willing to endure it.

Rain fell the entire three days we spent on that hill wiping out any chance of a training exercise. It was so wet that we could not have built a fire to roast a cow, even if we had killed one.

Gene Olson and I teamed up in the same tent. We cut boughs from trees and stacked them high enough so that the water would run through and under them. This permitted us to lie on top of the brush and stay above the water. We spent a pretty fair first night in the little tent we fashioned with our shelter halves. Others nearby did not fare so well. They erected their tents in an old artillery emplacement depression and during night the crater filled with water flooding them out. When dawn arrived we found them huddled against tree trunks displaying a sour disposition. After the third night the exercise was called off and we hiked home soaking wet and hungry. Later back at camp it seemed that the men's morale was faltering.

We had been expecting to go into battle when we left California. That was postponed. Now months later we were still just practicing while we heard of other units fighting the war.

Men's attitudes were suffering and this was displayed by more drinking, more arguments and fighting and sometimes by ignoring authority of officers. To counter this, the battalion commander called us together and gave a speech where he said that he, too, was anxious to see battle and all this training was to our benefit. He was looking forward to lead us into battle and that he was sure he would be doing so soon. That kind of talk only helped morale for a brief time and then it began to slip again.

There were incidents though that perked the men up. The division borrowed from the US Army a company of black soldiers to man amphibious vehicles for a training exercise. These vehicles with the designation of DUKWs, and called 'ducks' were used to transport men, equipment and supplies overland and through waterways. These black soldiers were bivouacked at the south end of our camp.

One evening as dusk approached and the usual preparations were being made for the weekly movie to start, the black soldiers appeared at the outdoor battalion movie theater area. They came early and occupied the two front rows of sand bag seating. Some Marines there informed them that as a courtesy and sign of respect the two front rows were reserved for our battalion officers and that these soldiers were welcome to sit with the rest of the men.

The soldiers took immediate offense, and became argumentative and hostile. They said that they were not about to move, and our officers could find somewhere else to sit. That was a very unwise position to take. A racial incident took place. I first knew of the incident when the 'Rebel' came dashing into my tent and very excitedly told us about a 'lot of niggers' out by the theater wanting to fight, He yelled, "I'm going to get a nigger." Then he grabbed my machete from its scabbard and ran from the tent. My other tent buddies and I followed him toward the theater area where we found a large group of men, black and white gathered there amidst a lot of confusion.

A number of black soldiers were backed up against the front of the stage by twice as many Marines who prevented them from leaving. Some of the Marines were hacking and stabbing at the Negroes with trench knives and bayonets. Others had found rocks to throw and many were throwing punches with their fists.

A few Marine officers showed up for the movies and tried to quell the disturbance by moving in between the two factions. The Marines backed off when commanded to do so and the black soldiers were ordered to return to their own area. An announcement was made that the movie was canceled and that all enlisted men must return to their tent area.

The next morning the battalion was called to formation. Battalion commander Lt. Col. Sayers climbed upon the hood of his jeep. He stood there and proceeded to give us all 'hell' for our behavior. His words left no doubt in our minds that the last night's event should never be repeated. After a long time he changed his tone and gave us that same old 'bull' about how he would soon lead us into battle. But, the men weren't buying it anymore. I could feel hostility and resentment in the air.

While we were at Camp Tarawa, a constant movement of personnel was being made. Men were being transferred in and out of the battalion. NCO's were asked to comment on the dependability and physical capabilities of various men under their supervision.

I was instrumental in getting rid of the 'Rebel.' The Captain asked me directly if I would want to go into combat with the Rebel. I quickly replied, "No sir!" That was the end of that, as the 'Rebel' was transferred quickly and reassigned to mail detail. I saw him several months later. He was wearing handcuffs and two Marine MP's were escorting him to prison since he had just had a general court martial, after he had been caught stealing from the mail.

Some men were transferred from the line companies because of their inability to withstand the hard physical demand placed upon them. Others were unable to handle the emotional stress of the discipline under which we operated. Some officers disappeared, obviously because they could not gain the respect of the men they commanded or make clear, understandable decisions in the field. Our platoon received a new platoon sergeant. We had all hoped that our own sergeant Russ Renner would have the job, but an outside man was brought in. Russ was an experienced combat veteran. He had seen combat in the Solomon Islands as a member of the Raider battalion, and it was reported that he had acquitted himself very well. Instead of Russ being appointed we received instead a 'Guard Marine,' as our lead sergeant. The 'Guard Marine' expression came about in describing a Marine who had only the experience of standing guard at some Navy installation or on board a capital ship. This was in contrast with men assigned to serve with the Fleet Marine Force (FMF) and formed up the infantry units designated to go ashore in amphibious assault formations.

Shortly after the new sergeant reported for duty one morning he appeared before the platoon and called it to attention. He introduced himself as Sgt. Nicholas Abromavich and described his previous duties in the Corps. We stood with some amazement as he spoke. He was unsmiling and with a trace of a frown upon his brow. His dungarees, if not new certainly gave the impression of being so. The trousers were pressed and the legs had creases down the front and the back. The sergeant's helmet, obvious newly issued, had been polished with some substance, probably shoe polish. I caught myself staring at his shoes as he had applied brown shoe polish to the rough boondockers in an attempt to make them shine.

As the sergeant spoke on in an officious commentary describing his past duties I could hear Marines about me muttering in whispered tones. "My God, look at his shoes; I'm not going to shine my shoes like that!"

"Hope he doesn't last very long!" and "Does he really expect us to look like that?"

I could not help but look down at my shapeless shoes, all worn and sloppy. My dungarees had been issued nine months before and had long lost their original shape and color. They were stained and baggy and resembled potato sacks with the potatoes still in them. The knees had begun to wear through and I had tried my best to repair them. The thread that I had used showed very well as it was an assortment of various colors. The majority of the platoon member's dungarees appeared no better than mine, except for those newly arrived men fresh from the training bases.

I think that most of us began to feel self conscious about the condition of our clothing. I realized later that a number of real combat Marines in the platoon became angry when they first saw the sergeant. They thought that this spit and polish guard Marine was too big for his britches.

While the sergeant spoke we could see Lt. Horvath approaching from behind us. As was proper procedure the Lieutenant would wait until the platoon sergeant made roll call, then he would approach and receive command of the platoon. For all of the Lieutenant's attributes there was one thing I noticed about him. He always looked unkempt while wearing any type of uniform. Even after recently shaving he looked as though he had a day old beard. His blouse always seemed not to fit him. Perhaps this was because of his athletic build and the close firm fit of a military man's uniform was just not suitable for him.

The Lieutenant approached the sergeant, received the salute and then listened to the sergeant's report. I could see the Lieutenant's face clearly as he stood there, his eyes dropping lower and lower as he examined the sergeants uniform and shoes. After a pause the officer turned and looked at us, standing at attention. He studied our faces and what was revealed I don't know but he turned back to the sergeant.

He welcomed the sergeant to our unit and was quite sure that we would all work together with mutual respect. I could see the sergeant's face reveal a trace of smugness as he listened to the officer speak. Then as the officer was about to conclude his remarks, he paused and said, "Oh yes, there is one more thing I want to comment on. I understand about your guard duty background of the past and the need to keep things tidy and shiny there. But, out here in the fighting units we must be battle prepared and keep our equipment ready also. We don't shine our combat boots or helmets because the enemy can see the reflection off them, see us and shoot. So it's for the best that you take the shine off them so that they will appear more like ours!" With that the Lieutenant raised his right foot and placed his shoe sole on the sergeant's polished shoe toe then he dragged it across leaving a dirty smudge behind. He rubbed it back and forth several times to emphasize his point. "Now, that's a lot better!" The sergeant's face froze in shock at this unexpected turn of events. As the smile disappeared from his face smiles appeared on ours.

The sergeant was to reveal over the ensuing weeks that he was a quiet man, but reluctant to discuss his private life with any one. About a month passed when I saw him produce a photograph from his barracks bag. He propped it up on the little table attached to the tent pole. The other four of us that slept in the tent were sitting on our cots watching him and our attention was drawn to the face in the picture. It was portrait of a handsome young Japanese woman. The sergeant's manner became rather brusque, "That's my wife!" he blurted out after which he looked each one of us straight in the eyes. I was surprised, but I could still figure out what was going on. I said, looking at the photograph, "You know, she looks like a neighbor girl I went to school with in California for ten years. I wonder where she is now. Her brothers and I used to pal around together. They were a good family. We're still good friends."

That seemed to reduce what ever tension there was. He went on to say his wife was a U.S. citizen born in Hawaii, that she was of Japanese descent and that they married while he was stationed at Pearl Harbor. I did not ever hear of another comment on the matter after that.

Sgt. Abromavich, always a fine Marine, developed into a very competent and liked platoon sergeant during the next few months and became highly respected by the men and officers. He was killed on Iwo Jima on February 22, 1945. I was at his side.

How Embarrassing!

Oh, they say we are the Marines,
And we're the very best,
But let them do the fighting,
And we'll go take a rest.
I don't want any more of the U.S. Marines,
Gee, I wanna go home.

"EVEN IN DISASTER there is humor" is an old adage. I think it is so, although the humor may be grim, too. Usually the humor is there, we just have to look for it at times. A young Marine called me from my tent one night. He said that he had a problem he needed to discuss with me. He was about eighteen years old. No doubt he was of a good family background and of good moral character. I knew him to be well liked and respected by the other members of the platoon.

He told me that he had a medical problem and that it was a very embarrassing one as it concerned the condition of his penis. I took him over to sick bay and to the examination room. He took out his penis and showed it to me. It looked awful! The skin was red and swollen and had white blotches all over it. Obviously the young Marine was in a lot of pain. He said, "It must be one of those venereal diseases you told us about, Doc!" I told him that I'd never seen anything like it before and that he should wait there while I went to get a battalion doctor. I walked over to officer's country and found Doctor Fred Popkess, the assistant battalion surgeon, sitting in his tent. I told him of the Marine's plight. The doctor asked me if the problem was a case of the "clapp." I answered that I'd never seen a case of gonorrhea, but from what I had studied, it wasn't and that I'd never heard about this disease. He replied that he, too, had limited experience with venereal disease, but that we would go and find out what it was.

At the sick bay the doctor examined the Marine and said, "Jesus Christ, I've never seen anything like that before!" I thought the young Marine was going to fall down on the floor when he heard that. He did reach out and grab for the back of a nearby chair to steady himself. He appeared very dismayed, and I thought maybe he might begin to cry.

The doctor asked him if he had been exposed recently, meaning of course, of a sexual nature. The Marine said that he had gone to the town of Hilo two days before with a couple of his buddies. After drinking several beers, they said they were going to get him, 'bred.' Upon their continued insistence, he allowed them to drag him off to a whore house. He said that the experience had scared the hell out of him and that the woman stank of body sweat and other odors that he couldn't identify.

Doctor Popkess asked him if he had washed up afterward. The young Marine said that he did that right away and then he used one of those pro-phylactic kits too, just to be sure. Then after he returned to camp he went to the washroom and washed again before going to bed. "Well," the doctor said, "You have a good case of something there, but I don't know what it is!" He went on to say he'd have to research the problem. The physician went on to smear a lot of Novocaine ointment over the red swollen skin of the penis to kill the pain and then wrapped it lightly with gauze bandage. He then wrote up a no duty slip and told the kid to stay off his feet the best he could until he saw him again.

I accompanied the Marine back to his tent. He walked very slowly with his feet spread far apart. He was in constant pain and seemed very depressed. He lamented on his condition and swore that if he ever was cured, he would never "do that" again. After leaving him I went directly to the wash house and scrubbed my hands thoroughly with the strong laundry soap that was kept there, just in case I had gotten some of those strange and vicious germs on me.

The next day after recall, I was notified to report to Dr. Popkess and to bring my patient with me. The doctor asked the Marine to tell him again what had happened after he had intercourse with the woman in Hilo. The PFC told him in detail. Then he was asked if he washed again after he got back to camp. The kid said yes he had, in fact he went to the wash house and scrubbed with that strong laundry soap that he found there before he went to bed and then again in the morning when he got up. He said that he had been washing his penis with that soap twice every day since the incident happened. Dr. Popkess looked at me and began to laugh. I think more from the relief of finding the solution, than the humor of it.

The physician explained to the Marine that he had no venereal disease but that the lye in the laundry soap was the culprit that had caused the irritation. Tears of relief came to the kid's eyes. After two days of using no soap, the inflammation, pain and spots were all but gone.

Another penis incident that occurred involved our good 'buddy,' Amon Dillard, of Georgia. He was a quiet man and a very good natured one too. Often he and I were victims of Munn's jokes. The three of us sat in our tent one night discussing circumcision. Someone suggested that it was wrong not to have had the operation done. Dillard, in his quiet way said, "Well, I never had it done to me!"

Munns never missed an opening like that, he jumped at the opportunity. The left corner of his lip curled up and he had that little grin on his face that appeared whenever he was going to cause mischief. "Oh, oh," he said and looked at me while raising his eyebrows.

Dillard said to Munns, "What's the matter with you?" Quickly Munns came back with, "Well if you don't know, I'm not going to tell you!" But then Munns immediately went into a discourse about the ills and disadvantages of a man not being circumcised. Those of us who sat there and listened quickly gave our support to Munns who went, causing Dillard to feel as though he had been deprived of something as a child.

Soon Dillard was over at one side of the tent. He unbuttoned his pants and pulled his penis out and began examining it for defects. He refused Munns's offer of professional assistance and continued to examine it as Munns asked him questions. "When it's small like that, does the skin come down over the head?"

"Well, yes, but not far!"

"That's not the way it's supposed to be! You can get infection in there and the damn thing will rot off!"

Dillard, worried a little about Munn's comment then asked all the rest of us if we had been circumcised when we were small. We all answered, "Certainly, of course we did!" All of which was a damn lie. A discussion of this nature went on into the late hours of the night. Before we went to bed, Dillard was convinced that he should have been circumcised as a youngster. The rest of us lay there on our bunks in the darkness trying not to make giggling noises.

The next day we failed to convince Dillard that he should go see the doctor about having an operation done on him. He was just too embarrassed to go talk with one of the surgeons. While at the sick bay, during Dillard's absence, Munns asked Dr. Popkess if he had ever done a circumcision operation. The doctor, answered, "No. Why, do want it done to you?"

Munns said with a most sincere look on his face, "Well no, Doctor, but one of the other corpsmen wants it done to him. But he is too shy to ask you to do it."

The doctor came back with, "You tell him to be here in the dispensary on Saturday morning and we will do it!" Of course, when Munns told Dillard about the doctor's agreement to operate, Dillard refused to believe him. Later in the day, when the doctor was busy in the sick bay, Munns dragged Dillard into the room and said in a loud voice to Doctor Popkess, "Doctor, didn't you say you wanted to do that little job on Dillard on Saturday morning?"

The doctor interrupted his work just long enough to raise his head and look at Dillard. "Just be here in the office. I'd like to do that, OK?"

Dillard was startled by the doctor's direct manner and so he immediately answered, "OK". He then turned sort of pale and looked scared; he wasn't smiling. Munns looked at me standing behind Dillard's back and gave me that smile, where his left lip curled up. The rest of us went along with the joke and encouraged Dillard to have the operation done. At times though, I thought he was going to go see Dr. Popkess and beg his way out of the situation.

On Saturday at 0900 several of us accompanied Dillard to the clinic door of the sick bay where the operation was going to take place. Doctor Popkess and pharmacist mate R.L. Halferty were there already getting things ready for the operation. Dillard had to be pushed through the door and into the room. Once inside he turned around and prevented us from entering. He raised his fists and quietly and very seriously said, "Not one of you is going to watch!" Munns and I tried to argue but the doctor intervened and told us that if Dillard didn't want us to watch, we would have to stay outside the room.

Munns and I waited outside for a whole hour. I was beginning to feel bad about my part in this scheme. Dillard was such a nice guy and I had let Munns drag me along in this thing. Munns thought it was funny and kept making jokes about the doctor cutting off too much and things like that. He would tell other battalion corpsmen, as they came and went, they should hang around and watch Dillard come out of the room after his surgery. Of course, he talked loud enough so that Dillard inside the room could hear what he was saying

When the door finally opened, Dillard walked out very slowly, stiff legged and with his feet spread far apart. His pants fly was unbuttoned to allow room for the bandages that covered his sore penis. He didn't smile as he met us. He said that he didn't know why he ever let us talk him into letting the doctor do the operation. The whole thing hurt, especially when the doctor stuck a needle into the foreskin four times in an attempt to deaden the pain.

We escorted Dillard back to our tent and Munns made light of the whole incident. I tried to sympathize with Dillard some because I knew how uncomfortable he was. Dillard was somewhat uncomplimentary about the way that Doctor Popkess handled the operation. "He kept dropping instruments and fumbled around a lot of the time!" he complained.

Munns just couldn't keep his mouth shut. "What the hell did you expect?" he blurted out. "It's the first circumcision he ever did!" "How do you know that?" Dillard demanded,

Munns looked at him, and with that big grin said, "I asked him. Just ask Overton if you don't believe me!"

Poor Dillard got pretty upset, "You dirty 'bastards,' I'll get you for this!" he yelled at us. Munns began to laugh louder and I was beginning to feel pretty bad about the whole affair.

The next day was Sunday and Dillard didn't move off his cot much, just did the necessary things. This routine was repeated on Monday too. Tuesday was going to be different. About 0500 I was awakened by a loud yell that came from Dillard who was sitting up on his bunk, in the darkness across the room. He was holding his bandaged penis with both hands. Once we got a light turned on we could see that the entire bandage was soaked with fresh blood. When Dillard finally calmed down, which took some doing as he was in a lot of pain, he told us what had happened. He said that as he lay on his cot sound asleep, he had a night time erection. As the penis grew larger, the stitches began to tear loose and the blood began to flow.

With our help, Dillard removed the gauze dressings that covered the incision. The sight was terrible to behold. Most of the stitches had pulled loose tearing the skin horribly as they did. Some weren't holding the skin at all, they were just dangling loose. We finally got the mess cleaned up and wrapped it again in a new loose bandage.

Later we contacted Dr. Popkess and he came over to sick bay where Dillard waited. He cleaned up the wound some more and put another dressing on it. He said that he couldn't put more sutures in there because that might invite infection. All the time he worked, Munns kept up chatter only now I didn't think it was so funny. He would say, "Doctor, do you think you'll have to amputate?" and "God, Dillard, wait until' your wife sees that thing for the first time!" For a while there I thought Dillard was going to punch him. Munns went outside of the room and was heard to invite all men in the outer rooms to come in and see the "goddamnest, funniest thing you'll ever see!"

Well, eventually the incision did heal. It took a very long time to do so though. And fortunately no infection set in. The penis took on a very odd shape as the foreskin was all ruffled up and fluted like. For some time after Munns would encourage other men to come in to our tent and have a look see at the oddity, much to the chagrin of Dillard. Finally it was all healed and most of the guys around thought that it wasn't much of a curiosity any more. Dillard had just about gotten around to forgiving Munns and me. He even asked the senior surgeon about the operation one day and was told by him that it wasn't too uncommon for the stitches to pull loose like they did. So Dillard began to forgive Dr. Popkess too. But it wasn't really ended yet. We were sitting on our bunks one day talking about the incident when Munns blurted out, "Well, I'll never have it done to me!"

Dillard looked at Munns and his face turned red. "You told me that you had it done!"

Nope! Then Munns said and after glancing at me produced that mischievous grin of his.

Dillard turned and stared at me, I shook my head to indicate 'no' also. Dillard jumped to his feet yelling, "I'll get even with you, dirty bastards!"

Some Entertainment Please

THE SECOND BATTALION outdoor movie theater was located at the base of a small hill at the rear of our company street. It wasn't very far from the enlisted men's outdoor latrine. Sometimes, the wind blew toward the movie area from the direction of the latrine and caused the men to hold their breath until a change in the direction of the wind brought fresh air. Then long and loud sighs could be heard from among the viewers. The big viewing screen faced the slight incline of the hill upon which rows of dirt filled gunny sacks lay for the men to sit on. About thirty minutes before movie time, men would begin arriving to find a favored seat. Most officers and men dressed the same when attending the movies. They wore dungarees and helmet liners and usually brought along a poncho to sit on and to use later if it began to rain. Each brought his own supply of cigars, cigarettes, candy bars, or whatever else he might think necessary for him to survive the two hour show.

The movie was often preceded by a short 'sing-a-long' film that encouraged the viewers to join in group singing. These films were popular in the 1930s and 1940s. Words to the songs were flashed on the screen and were accompanied by the music. At the same time a bouncing ball appeared on the screen and touched each word, keeping in time with the beat of the music. The songs presented were the older favorites. 'Red Sails in the Sunset' and 'Shine on Harvest Moon' was most often heard.

The movies were mostly recently made and often were comedies. Bing Crosby, Bob Hope, Phil Harris, Jack Carson, and Jack Benny appeared in many of the films. Alice Faye was very popular and the script of her movies seemed to be the same over and over. She met and fell in love with a service man that was then sent overseas and was reported killed in action. Near the end of the story he would show up suffering from wounds, and always a hero. There would be a happy, emotional reunion to the joy of all. Usually, when an emotionally loaded film like that ended, the men would all leave the area and go to their tents walking along quietly in a pensive mood.

Many of the films produced during those war years were designed to have an affect on the civilian population at home. They had patriotic themes and were meant to encourage people to work harder in order to help the war effort. Most films portrayed service men and women, and the actors, ironically, were those left behind in Hollywood and who were unable to join the service themselves for some reason.

Mostly the films showed battle scenes that were very entertaining to the Marines in camp. From the viewers came shouts of encouragement which were directed at the actors who appeared on the screen. The Hollywood heroes received 'whoops' and 'hollers' as they wiped out dozens of the enemy in hand to hand combat. Even most of the officers watching the films had to break down some and lose a little of their composure when a wit in the audience yelled out something clever and humorous.

Once in a while we had USO (United Service Organization) shows also. The USO events were often very good. Many of the Hollywood personalities who came were unknown to most of us. I suppose the actors were offering their talents but along with that they wanted the publicity to advance their careers. I attended one show in the little village in Kamuela. The town's people generously offered the town meeting hall to the Marines whenever the weather appeared inclement. The building wasn't large but it held about two hundred people if they crammed us in.

The production I saw there was earlier announced as a Hawaiian hula girl show and dancing exhibition. Eddie Monjaras, Gene Olson, and I went over there expecting to see some beautiful Hawaiian girls come out on the stage wearing hula skirts. We found the room already crowded when we arrived half an hour early, but did find room to stand along a wall. When the show began, the master of ceremonies came out onto the stage and greeted us. He spoke with a New York accent. He said loudly, "Hello, Everybody!" then began to introduce the show. His accent drew lots of comments from those men around us. Apparently they couldn't associate it with dancing hula girls at all. One Marine was heard to say, "That guy is from 'Yonkers.'" At the time I didn't know where Yonkers was and supposed that it was a foreign country.

Once the curtains were drawn back, the music began. It emanated from a portable record player off to one side of the stage. The record player ran after being wound up by a hand crank. The girls made their entrance from the side of the stage. The Marines watching became bewildered and were disappointed. The girls were not Hawaiian, but instead, from stateside.

They had fair skin and their blonde or light brown colored hair seemed to have been tinted.

Their Hawaiian style costumes looked like nothing we had seen yet in the islands. The girls danced to the music played by the portable phonograph, and the record was changed about every three minutes. The girls reminded me of some women I'd seen in some of the West Coast burlesque theaters while back in the States. Apparently others thought so too, as some of the Marines began to yell and stamp their feet. Others yelled out at the girls rudely. "You're not Hawaiian, Honey!" and "What street do you work?" were some of the things that the girls heard.

I thought the whole thing was embarrassing. It most certainly was to the girls and it began to show on their faces and caused them to miss steps in their routines. Tears began to show on a few faces up there on stage as the girls struggled to continue their dance. It was evident that more and more were missing their steps and each time they left the stage there were one or two who didn't come back out.

After the first few dance numbers, Marines began to leave the theater. This exodus continued throughout the show. Eddie, Gene, and I felt too compassionate for the girls to leave, so we took seats and watched until the spectacle ended. After what seemed a very long time, the curtain closed. The master of ceremonies walked out onto the stage and thanked us for coming. He went through the motions of 'blowing kisses' at us and said something about loving us. Well, about that time there weren't many of us left there to love! Also, he might do and say those things in New York but certainly not to a bunch of combat Marines in the South Pacific. He quickly disappeared after and I don't remember any curtain calls. The few of us still left, got up and walked quietly from the hall.

Most of the Marines; who at first attended the show and had left early, were now across the street watching a baseball game. The teams were the best that the three regiments of the division had and had attracted a lot of attention because of their member's playing ability and competitive spirit. The Marines watching had their spirits up again and were drinking beer and yelling out words of encouragement to their favorite players.

My comrades and I stood watching the ball game. After a while I saw a bus being driven out from behind the town hall. It turned onto the road that ran between the baseball field and the hall. As it passed by us I could clearly see the dancers inside. Very few of them looked toward the Marines busily enjoying themselves. The ones that did were not smiling; some looked like they were weeping, even or at least were very sad.

I supposed that the performers found it difficult to understand, but the Marines, facing the uncertainty of the future and of battle and the possibility of death or dismemberment, turned away from the spectacle they considered superficial and inane. They, the Marines preferred the company, the comradeship, and the solace of their friends as the next best thing to the company of their families back home. Anyway, I don't remember any more USO shows being held at the Kamuela Town Hall after that.

Some of the best entertainment shows which were put on at the camp were organized from the divisions own members. There were a lot of musicians, actors of some talent, and guys who had experience in organizing such things. A Special Services Entertainment Unit was organized and some of these skilled people were enlisted in it. Gerald G. Kohrt, one of the battalion's pharmacist mates, was a very talented guitar player and was quickly recruited as a member. One of the battalion's officers excelled as administrator and master of ceremonies. This unit became so competent that they entertained at other military installations in the Pacific Theater at times, putting on shows that consisted of skits, songs, and musical arrangements.

The popular band leader at the time, Bob Crosby, became a member of the division for a short while. I remember him as a good looking young man, very neat in his 2nd Lieutenant's uniform. He was mild mannered and pleasant and enjoyed carrying on conversations with us enlisted men. He didn't stay with us very long. When we packed up to leave for battle, he disappeared unceremoniously from our group. I don't suppose he was trained as a combat Marine, but as a special unit one instead. He organized some good shows which involved a lot of the better known movie stars of the time. One show I remember favorably was a USO show that had as its main personalities Jack Carson and Betty Hutton.

Those two were at the top of their careers then and were two of the more prominent personalities of their time. The two put on a terrific show for us. Betty Hutton was a beautiful young woman. She wore a tight sweater and black form fitting satin shorts on stage, much to the delight to the men watching. She did song and dance acts, monologues, and skits with certain members of the division which we really enjoyed.

Jack Carson came on stage and utilized his comedy experience and background to tell jokes and sing songs. Some of the Marines down front razzed him some and because of that he lost his temper while on stage, and he threatened to quit. Actually, he was under the wrong impression, as the Marines really liked the guy. He finally came back on stage after regaining his composure and like the good guy he was, he finished the show much to the enjoyment of the audience.

Other than those staged shows in camp, we only had the service of a lone radio in the battalion to entertain us or a portable wind up type record player that some of the men lugged along with them. Our only radio was lodged in a small Quonset hut that contained an old wooden table that the radio rested on and several chairs. Otherwise the room was completely bare except maybe for a few old magazines that lay about. It seemed to me that the radio was constantly playing the same favorites of the time. Several of those that I'll never forget were, 'Don't Fence Me In' by Bing Crosby, 'Rum and Coca Cola' (Working for the Yankee Dollar) by the Andrews Sisters and 'Pistol Packing Momma' by a number of different western singers.

Because of the war restrictions, the war news was very limited and was hardly worth listening to. The best program was one that was beamed to us from the enemy territory of Tokyo, Japan. "Tokyo Rose" would broadcast from there several times a day. Rose's real name was Iva D'Aquino, and was actually a American citizen. Her program came in very clear and we enjoyed listening to the music she played from records. Usually the music was from recordings of Glenn Miller and his orchestra. He was a very popular band leader at the time.

Undoubtedly, Tokyo Rose meant for the program to be demoralizing to the American fighting men. She failed in that mission. She spoke in a very soft and pleasant voice directly to the American service men doing duty in the Pacific. She would comment on how it was "such a shame" that we were all far away in the Pacific while our loved ones waited for us at home. "They must be lonesome back home," and, "wives and girl friends will probably find comfort in other men's attentions while they wait." She would go on describing how she was sympathetic toward us as she knew that many of us would die soon in the war with Japan. She said that we should resist American government authority and demand that the war be halted and that we servicemen should be sent home. With some irony I have to note here that she often mentioned that the 5th Marine Division was stationed at Kamuela, Hawaii. We men of the division were not allowed to write such information in our letters home to the United States.

Our letters were censored of all such reference to our location. At the war's end, Rose was apprehended by American authorities. She was returned to the United States and prosecuted for treason and served a prison sentence of a rather short duration. Years later she was given a pardon by the President of the United States.

During evenings in camp the men usually sat around in their tents just talking, singing songs, playing cards, or writing letters. There was a lot of beer drinking, but not too much in excess. The unit commanders saw to it that the supply was controlled pretty well except for Saturday nights. Then there seemed to be a large supply for the men. Typically, a large refrigerated truck would stop in the battalion area just after noon on Saturday. Cases of beer would be sold to the men who wanted it. The ice supply was limited some, but that didn't cut down on the amount of beer consumed.

While sitting around camp, the men told a lot of stories. The stories were mostly humorous, hardly ever about past battles unless there was an amusing aspect to them. As the beer flowed, the stories by the men became more vivid and were dramatized by gestures and loud voices. The storytellers would compete with each other in their attempts to outdo the others.

Sergeant Charles Goodling, the older and grizzled Marine veteran of several Solomon Island battles, always had stories to tell. He enjoyed trying to embarrass us younger men with tales from his past experiences in the Corps. One story, I heard from him many times over. He had been stationed at the Guantanamo Navy Base in Cuba, just before the war broke out. He and several buddies were in a Havana bar drinking while sitting at a table. For some time he had been buying beer for a lady drinking companion, in an attempt to get her drunk enough to have his way with her.

Goodling said the she was a good looker and neatly dressed. For some time they had been drinking and 'necking' until he just got impatient. He had his hand on her knee and quickly slipped it up her thigh as far as it would go. "Jesus Christ," he said, the lady was a man. He went wild and knocked the 'queer' off the chair, then pushed the table over on top of him and was in the process of kicking hell out of him when the cops arrived and began to assault the Marine.

Goodling described how his buddies helped him to take on the cops and were doing very well too, until enough Navy shore patrolmen came to break up the fight. He was hauled off back to the base and ordered to stand before his company commander. The Captain asked him what was it he had to say about the assault and battery charge that was facing him. Goodling explained how his being misled had prompted the disturbance. The Captain turned to the company sergeant and said, "Hell, why do I have to be bothered by this 'crap' and dismissed the charges. Goodling told this story many times. How well he told it and how well it was received largely depended on how many beers he and his audience had consumed.

Sgt. Goodling had a way with the men. He could relieve tension and raise morale when the platoon leader or platoon sergeant couldn't. He had a favorite saying when things sort of got out of hand or confusing and the men got frustrated. He'd sing out, "That's right, just 'mill' around and bitch!" That comment was usually enough to get the men to smile and relax.

When the beer was issued, the songs would come along spontaneously. Someone in the group would pull out a harmonica and begin to play. The type of song played and sung depended on the singers or player's experience and background. Many of these camp songs were quite clever in their construction. Unfortunately, with time many of them have disappeared. Some of the songs I heard and sang with the Marines in those days have been incorporated into this writing. I hope more were preserved, remembered, or recorded somewhere as they were an interesting aspect of the military camp life of those days.

A Texan, PFC Paul Bush, was a guitar player and carried his instrument and a small hand cranked record player among his belongings. His favorite song was the Australian fighting song at the time, "Waltzing Matilda." Its mourning strains could be heard every night coming from his tent just before taps would sound. He timed it so that the song ended moments before the first bugler would begin to blow taps.

The first bugler to play was often our own Company D Marine Clifford H. Clayburn, who was assigned as one of the 26th Regiment's musicians. He would sound his instrument loud and clear at the head of our camp street. When he finished the next musician who was farther away and assigned to the 27th Regiment would begin to blow his horn. After that the bugler from the 28th Regiment far across the camp would sound off, the notes diminishing in intensity each time because of the distance. By then the electric switch controlling the tent lights would be pulled plunging the camp into darkness. The usual effect was that the weary men lying on their bunks would relax as sleep began to envelope them.

By the time we went into battle and Paul was killed, his favorite record was to become very worn and scratched. We often had told Paul, in a whimsical manner that upon our return from battle we would all chip in and buy him another "Waltzing Matilda" record.

But the men didn't always settle down after taps sounded. Once in a while, usually on a Friday or Saturday night after the men had enjoyed an evening of beer drinking and revelry they did not quiet down. I recall one such incident where First Sergeant Neef failed in his first two attempts to quiet the company area. He sent the camp guards along each row of tents to order all men to fall out into the company street, only wearing their shoes and underwear.

I wasn't too concerned at first as I thought we were in for another one of the sergeant's 'dressing downs' for our misdeeds. But he seemed very calm and ordered us all to lean over and tie our shoe laces, which we did. Then he said that we will go for some exercise. "Follow me," he ordered and turning began to double time along the company street out of camp and onto the state highway where we turned south. We ran for a good quarter mile before he turned us around. I felt foolish running along a dark country road dressed only in my underwear and shoes and was sure the others did too. During the run back to our tent area I noticed that the men had quieted down considerably. The sergeant dismissed us by saying. "Now men, I hope you all get a good night's rest!"

I sat on my bunk and began to laugh. "What the hell is wrong with you?" one of my tent buddies asked.

"Don't you see what happened," I said. "The Top Sergeant punished us by making us run all that distance and in doing so, he did it too, by leading us. How can you not love that guy?"

During the month of November of 1944 rumors of battle became rife about the camp. It was discussed so much it became wearisome to even have to listen to all the scuttlebutt that went on. A small frame building had been erected near the regimental headquarters offices and a high barbed wire fence constructed around it. There was a gate leading through the fence and this was always locked except to let staff officers in and out of the compound. It looked very ominous and was assumed by those interested enough to care, that this building was where all the plans for battle were being made and stored. Inside the compound, there were two armed guards who patrolled the building constantly.

Once after a three day field problem the men in the battalion intelligence section had discovered what Jap held island we were going to attack. They had taken the maps of our last field exercise and by placing them over maps of all the existing islands they discovered that the training maps had fit portions of the Japanese occupied island of Formosa (Taiwan) which is situated close to the eastern coast of China. So the rumors began afresh. Months later it was revealed that the men of the intelligence section were correct in their assumption. There were plans made for our division to invade Formosa, but that plan was canceled as the Navy decided to bypass that island and attack another one closer to mainland Japan instead.

A few days prior to Christmas, 1944, the division was notified to be ready to leave on a day's notice. This information was restricted to the men of the division and our mail was heavily censored accordingly. Within days, Tokyo Rose broadcast that same information from Tokyo. I heard her say that the 5th Division would be leaving Hawaii soon and suggested that our destination was the island of Formosa. She commented that, "It is too bad that the 5th Marine Division will suffer a lot of casualties and American boys will die!"

After a few more field problems, we were told to pack up. We placed our extra and unneeded belongings in our sea bags and stacked them for storage until our return. The rumor mill was busy again now. The intelligence section men said it appeared that the Formosa Island invasion was off and that the training map overlays now indicated that we were to assault a small island named Iwo Jima much closer to Japan. None of us ever heard of a place named Iwo Jima so most of us dismissed it from our minds. My only concern was that we were finally going to go somewhere and do something.

CHAPTER TWENTY

Boarding The Assault Ship

TWO DAYS BEFORE Christmas, 1944, the entire appearance of Camp Tarawa had begun to change. The 26th Marines were about to leave camp. Our extra clothing and gear had all been stored and our combat packs were holding only the minimum of clothing and personal items that we would take with us. We were restricted to our own company tent area and told to be ready to fall out at a moment's notice. That night most of us were found wrapped in our single blanket trying to put aside our thoughts of a long voyage and battle, in order that we might get some sleep. We had to be refreshed for the morning's very demanding activity.

At dawn, when reveille sounded and we fell out into the company street for muster, no one had to tell us that this was the day we were leaving. We could feel the suspense of it all about us. After breakfast the company stood on the drill field and the Top stood before us. "Company personnel will stand by at their respective tents with full battle gear and await further orders!"

The order was short and direct and to the point. We were not expected to ask questions. Within the hour a long line of trucks arrived and we soon were involved helping each other up into them. That little physical activity seemed to trigger the release of tension and anxiety that had obviously been building for the past day. Jokes, bantering, and horseplay began to return.

The regiment was transported by trucks to a railhead about fifteen miles away at the village of Honokaa. There we all climbed onto the flat cars of a narrow gauge railroad. A small wooden platform was all that we had to sit upon. These cars were normally used to haul sugar cane from the fields to the sugar mill located at the north end of Hilo. At the head of the train was a ridiculously small steam engine that huffed and puffed and chugged away as it tugged at the long line of little flat cars as it dragged them along down the hill toward Hilo.

The speed of the train never did get over fifteen miles an hour as it moved along through the lush green foliage on the windward side of the island. The narrow gauge rails were uneven and so the little cars swayed this way and that. The little gaps between the ends of the rails caused bumps each time the car's metal wheels passed over them. These small annoying motions jarred each man just enough so that there was friction between the seat of his pants and the rough wooden boards of the car's bed. Many men began to complain about the splinters they were collecting in their posteriors.

The monotony of the ride was broken at times by the Marines leaping from the cars and running alongside for a while. Some would run off and onto private property where they would grab some fresh fruit from a tree, then run back to their car. This would cause some of the junior officers to be annoyed and they would order some NCO to tell the men to stop the practice. The NCO would yell out to the offender to "knock it off," but the situation would soon be repeated.

This area of the 'Big Island' was particularly beautiful. Along with the lush foliage there were many small cottages surrounded by brilliant flame trees and neat looking flower and vegetable gardens. The people living there came outside and smiled, waiving their hands in greeting high above their heads. A few waved American flags. Many of these people were Americans of Japanese descent and they reminded me of the many Japanese-American families that I knew in the Santa Clara Valley where I was born and grew up.

I also thought of one night barely a month before we left Hawaii. 2nd Battalion was dispatched at 2200 hours and hurriedly loaded onto trucks and were driven up high on the plateaus of Mauna Kea. We were told that a clandestine radio was operating and was sending coded messages presumably to an enemy submarine out at sea. We were formed into a wide skirmish line and told to apprehend any suspicious person found up there and confiscate their equipment. I don't know if anyone was found as we were not informed of the results of our search.

When the train arrived at the sugar mill in Hilo after about six hours, the men eagerly jumped from the cars and a lot of them were rubbing their sore behinds. Using my thumb forceps I pulled a few splinters from men's hands, elbows, and legs, and applied iodine to the perforated skin. The regiment formed up and walked the mile to the dock area. The hike felt good to us. It was more to our liking than riding on flat cars.

As we walked along the waterfront of Hilo, many of the townspeople came out to watch and wave at us. Many had words of encouragement for us and some even threw or handed flowers to us. The battalion walked onto the concrete loading dock, but then we were told to relax and wait before boarding. Two incendiary devices had been found among the cargo already on board. Someone had intended to set the ship on fire once it was loaded and at sea. We waited as the crews searched all the ships for other indications of sabotage.

The 2nd Battalion of the 26th Regiment was assigned to board the U.S.S. Hocking, APA 121, which was an Attack Personnel ship. By late afternoon we had gone on board; the enlisted men filed down into their assigned compartments and officers went to their quarters on the main deck level.

All two hundred and twenty or more of D Company were crammed into the forward bow compartment, located under the forecastle deck. The bunks were stacked eight high, two higher than I'd ever seen them on any other ship. It was impossible for one third of the men to stand in the aisles at one time. After stowing my gear on my bunk, I beat a hasty retreat to the weather deck. I found the decks crowded with men. Instead of the usual one thousand men who made up the battalion, the number had increased by another five hundred men who were added as support units.

The landing crafts for this large number of men were stacked in tiers on deck, reducing the deck space usually reserved for troops. The logistics for an operation such as we faced must have been phenomenal to work out. We didn't know it at the time, but we would be on this ship for forty-seven days. To store supplies to feed and service that many men must have taken much thought and planning.

As usual, our departure from port was made just after sunset to conceal our movements from the enemy. That night I lay on my bunk, which was on the bottom of the stack, and listened to the swishing sounds of rushing sea water which passed by the outside of the one-half-inch thick steel hull.

When one of the men commented on the possibility of danger caused by a collision, exploding mine or torpedo, Sgt. Goodling was there to say, "Don't worry about that. If the hull gives way, you will hardly even know it!"

Some time during the night I awakened. I knew I was sick, but had never felt like this before. My brain wasn't functioning right and I couldn't move my legs and arms very well as they seemed very heavy. I finally rolled out of the bunk and onto the deck. Slowly it came to me that I was suffering from oxygen starvation. I crawled along on my stomach to the bottom of the ladder leading to the weather deck and step by step I went up it on my hands and knees. I had to struggle to get my strength up enough so that I could unlatch the interior hatch leading to the small compartment that lay between it and the outer hatch that led to the weather deck.

Once inside that compartment I attempted to open the hatch leading to the deck and fresh air. To my dismay, I found that hatch locked from the outside. I banged on the steel door with my fists in an attempt to attract attention, but gave that up soon when no one answered and I began to lose strength. I just sat there on the compartment's deck and waited until I heard general quarters sound at dawn.

The door was finally opened by a Navy chief boatswain, who looked down at me curiously. I asked him why the door was locked. He explained, "It's the custom to lock the hatches leading to this bow compartment at night in the event the ship hits a mine or receives a torpedo up front. That would stop the water from rushing through the ship and sinking it." I came back with, "What about all those men sleeping down there, how would they get out?" His answer was rather casual, "Oh, I don't think that they will even know it if it happens."

I went on to tell him that there was no fresh air down there and that I was suffering from lack of oxygen. He said that someone had inadvertently turned off the fresh air blowers. Then he left me saying that he would go turn the blowers on. After a while the men down below began to straggle out of the hold looking dragged out and complaining about not feeling good at all. After a while on deck in fresh air they all recovered. That experience was enough to frighten me. For the rest of the voyage, with the exception of the last night, I slept on the main deck.

The next day found our ship lying off the small Hawaiian island of Kahoolawe. There we practiced a final disembarkation and landing drill. We went ashore and then came back to the ship. The battalion command-ers announced that it had been a perfect drill. They went on to say that the regiment would now go to Pearl Harbor for a few days and we would be allowed liberty in Honolulu. The spirit and morale of the men rose considerably after hearing that.

At one point of the cruise while we were involved in a shipboard drill, all activity was suspended as our ship sailed among a number of large whales. The mammals, which included several youngsters, would submerge and then surface and blow water spray high into the air, much to the delight of those of us who watched. They seemed not at all perturbed by our presence and continued with their play-like activity as the ship's Captain ordered a directional change and we sailed away to avoid any conflict with them.

The ships, carrying the regiment sailed through the channel entrance to Pearl Harbor at a fast speed. The tug boat tending the submarine net timed our entrance perfectly as it pulled the net away from us, and then closed it immediately after the last ship entered. This was the spot a small Japanese submarine was sunk as it attempted to enter the harbor just prior to the Pearl Harbor attack two years before. Our ship anchored just east of Battleship Row and Ford Island. We were to stay for several days while we waited for the rest of the division to load onto ships back in Hilo.

While at Pearl each day one half of the troops were allowed to go ashore on liberty to Honolulu, while the other half was allowed ashore at a small recreational island that was situated within the harbor about one mile from our anchorage. Because we were ready for combat and carried only combat clothing, we were faced with wearing khaki uniforms on liberty. We had one suit of those with us in case we needed to wear them in combat for camouflage purposes. Most of us looked terrible as the shirts and pants were much wrinkled after being stuffed and carried in our combat packs along with our extra shoes and other equipment. Also, the only shoes we had were those rough side out 'boondockers.' All that didn't add to the supposedly glamorous image of a neat looking Marine on liberty. I felt so conspicuous that I stopped at an Army-Navy type clothing store in Honolulu and purchased a new khaki shirt to replace the worn wrinkled one I carried.

Once in Honolulu proper the troops wandered about the streets that were lined with saloons, tattoo parlors, tourist and photography shops that catered mainly to the service men. Many of the men followed and talked to girls walking along the streets. Many of the girls were professional prostitutes; others were locals carrying on their personal business or looking for some excitement. Several of the company's Marines came back to the ship sporting fresh tattoos all of the same design.

The one which caught my eye was a large black panther with red eyes that was depicted in the act of leaping. It looked ferocious! Two of the Marines had it placed on their left arm, between the shoulder and elbow; others had it done on their chests.

Hundreds of men went into the photography shops and had pictures made of themselves or with their buddies. Most of these shops furnished girls dressed in hula or native dress, wearing flowers in their hair who would pose with the servicemen. Pictures appeared to be very popular with the serviceman. For many Marines heading for combat, these photographs were the last that they would ever have taken of themselves.

The little recreational island in the harbor was just a plain flat piece of land and just slightly above water level at high tide. It was about two or three acres in size. What a "god awful" place to spend an entire day! The only structures there were several old outhouses. No trees or shrubs grew on the land and very few blades of grass could be seen. A baseball diamond was laid out in the center of the small atoll.

Several hundred of us chose to go ashore there on the second day. Perhaps fifty cases of beer were hauled along with us in the landing craft which took us there. That was all gone within an hour or so and more was brought out to us. A baseball game was organized and the play began. Several junior Marine officers accompanied us to the island and unwisely decided to play ball with the men. One officer served as the umpire, which was another mistake. As the hours passed and the sun's heat increased, there was very little breeze to cool us. The men consumed beer and more beer; after all it was free to us.

The game play became more intense and arguments began to develop. The language being used was becoming increasingly cruder and often accompanied by some gesture of the hand. Some of the bystanders who had been watching the game now lay on the ground, and were just plain drunk. Some of the wiser men returned to the ship by way of the liberty boat that plied its way back and forth between ship and shore. It wasn't too long before a few punches were thrown between the game's participants. When an officer, the umpire, was cussed out, the rest quit the game and returned to the ship. That was a wise decision. Then some of the Marines began to challenge others to fight and then friends took sides. My buddies and I decided it was time that we returned to the ship.

Several more hours had passed when we, standing at the ship's rail, saw two large landing craft go by our ship heading for the little island. We could see a large number of Marine Corps military policemen in the craft. Perhaps another hour passed before we observed the landing craft approaching our ship, then we could see that the boats were filled with our Marine comrades from the island. The landing craft came alongside the cargo nets which were hung over the side of the ship. The Marines were in a deplorable state. Most were intoxicated and dirty with their clothing in disarray.

Those of us already on board the ship crowded to the rail in order to watch the Marines below us in the small boats. The MP's down there were helping men get to their feet and pushing them toward the bottom rungs of the net. It wasn't an easy climb even when cold sober, let alone when drunk! One Marine lay on the boat's bottom. Two of his buddies tried to get him on his feet and failed. The military policemen didn't succeed either. A call was sent up for a physician.

The other Marines climbing the netting were all having trouble. Some lost their hold on the strands and fell back into the landing craft. Some allowed a foot to slip through the netting causing them to let go the rope strands and that left them hanging upside down. Luckily, the MP's were there to catch them and prevent serious injuries that could have resulted from such a fall. In ascending, the men stepped on each others hands, shoulders and heads. Most, once reaching the deck of the ship, would turn and call down to their struggling comrades and offer them advice and encouragement. "If I can do it, so can you. C'mon, boy, you can make it!"

The unconscious Marine still lay on the small craft's bottom as the more able Marines climbed to the ship's rail. Several of the stricken Marine's buddies remained near their fallen friend to help him and they warned the MP's to "Stay away!" and "Keep your hands off him!" An officer came pushing his way through the crowd at the ship's rail. He was yelling, "Gangway for the ship's surgeon. Let me through!" He was a rotund middle aged man, dressed in khaki's and he displayed a rather officious attitude, considering the circumstances. He climbed the rail and went over the side and down the cargo net with apparent ease into the boat below. The Marines who stood around their fallen comrade gave way in order for the officer to approach.

The doctor attempted to get the prostrated Marine to speak. When this failed, the doctor loudly ordered the man to get up. When the Marine failed to respond to that command, the physician pulled him to a sitting position and slapped him hard across the face. The doctor should never have done that!

Immediately, the Marines lining the ship's rail shouted down in protest. "Stop that!" - "Don't do that again!" - "Throw that old 'son-of-bitch' overboard!" and "If you do that again, we'll come down there and slap you around!" The doctor straightened up when he heard all those remarks directed at him. He looked puzzled. It was obvious he was unprepared for this turn of events and didn't know what to do next.

A quick thinking bos'un's mate appeared among us and yelled down to the small boat's crew that he was lowering a cargo net and to put the unconscious Marine in it. I think that his actions prevented a nasty situation from developing. After all, some of these Marines were thinking of going down there and throwing a ship's officer overboard. That could hardly be passed off as an insignificant incident during time of war.

The unconscious Marine's buddies placed him in the lowered cargo net and he was winched up the side of the ship and dumped onto the aft cargo hatch cover. His arms and legs were sticking through the cargo netting as he came up, and as he was moved he regained some consciousness and began to move his limbs about in a wild and uncontrollable manner. As he was untangled from the netting, he cursed all of us around him who watched. Helping hands reached out and lifted him to his feet. A Marine Lieutenant appeared quickly and said, "Get him below decks quickly fellows, and keep him out of sight!" Those of us on deck could feel the tension leave the crowd of Marines as their hapless comrade was carried below and out of view.

I looked over the side of the ship and down at the ship's doctor in the small craft lying along side. He was still standing there, but looked rather forlorn. The boat was moving toward the ship's gangway up forward. As the surgeon climbed the steps, he avoided looking up at the faces of the Marines lining the rail. He now seemed to be a very humble man as he ascended and disappeared into the superstructure of the ship. I felt sorry for him. He had made a mistake and was now suffering for it. The little drama was over. The U.S. Marines again had "taken care of their own."

Our days at Pearl were just about ended. The men ashore on liberty and in Honolulu came back to the ship as the sun receded into the western sky. The men, fresh from liberty, were all bubbling over with cheerfulness and the excitement of their experiences ashore. I heard stories being told of their adventures and was certain that each time the tale was told it got to be longer and more interesting. One thing all the Marines had agreed upon, they had never seen so many white sailor hats. During those war years there were many thousands of sailors stationed ashore in the islands and on board ships. When only a small percentage went ashore on liberty, the streets of downtown Honolulu were packed with white uniforms. The sidewalks could barely be seen unless one looked down between their own feet at the pavement. As two Marines discussed it one said, "Must have been a million white hats!" the other answered, "Oh..., twice that many!"

One last word, regarding the city of Honolulu; there was some friction between the local Hawaiian people and the stateside servicemen. It was evidenced by signs posted in the civilian buses that traveled from the Pearl Harbor Naval base to downtown Honolulu. These posters would read something like this: "To our stateside servicemen friends. The people of Hawaii are Americans like you and they welcome you as friends. However, it is not conducive to the formulation of good relationships for you to refer to them as 'Gooks' or to ask a young man, 'What is your sister doing tonight?' or 'What does she look like?' or words to that effect!"

Chapter Twenty-One

Aloha and Mahalo

O N January 22, 1945, Ships carrying units of the 5th Marine Division began moving out of Pearl Harbor. When the sun disappeared beyond the western hills of Oahu, anchors were pulled up from the murky waters of the harbor and the mud hosed off. Once the anchors were secured, the ships moved slowly forward and formed a single file passing by Ford Island.

Silence fell among the crowd of Marines standing on deck. They turned as one to face to starboard where the U.S.S. Arizona lay, her keel still embedded in the mud at the harbor bottom. Over a thousand men lay dead within her. The superstructure, deck, derricks, and huge guns were still above water. An American flag, whipping about in the wind, flew from her mast. Our ship sounded its horn in salute as we passed. The Navy officers standing on our ship's deck, as well as those on the bridge, gave a hand salute to the still commissioned Navy battleship. A Marine standing near me said, "We'll get 'em for that, too!" Maybe a little trite perhaps, but it was quite appropriate at the time.

As our ship turned to port and headed for the harbor entrance, we passed many warships of various designs. We saw submarines at berth and many destroyers and cruisers anchored. A ship's officer standing nearby directed our attention to the spot near the inside channel entrance, where the Battleship U.S.S. Nevada was beached during the attack on December 7, 1941. She had been bombed and torpedoed, so one of her officers wisely ran her into the mud to keep her from sinking in the channel and blocking it.

Some of the personnel on nearby ships waved and shouted encouragement to us as we passed by. They gestured while horns of the ships sounded in saluting us. It was as if they knew that we were on our way into battle. We were very much impressed by their concern.

As we entered the channel proper we observed several destroyers in a line preceding us. Our ship increased its speed and I estimated that we were making about twelve knots. We mustn't dally about in the channel as it was no place to get caught in an attack as a sunken ship could easily block the channel passage. We saw the tug pulling the steel submarine net back out of the way of the leading destroyer to allow our passage to the open sea.

We passed the station of the Admiral of the Port, the officer in charge of the channel entrance. The officer in charge of the sailors on our deck ordered them to face that station and stand at attention as he gave a hand salute. This salute is made to acknowledge the rank of the port's commanding officer, who presumably was standing at attention and returning the salute from behind the blue tinted office windows on shore.

One Marine, standing near me said, "Do you really think that there is an Admiral standing there?" Another responded, "Hell no, but if he is, though, he hasn't many brains. He should be up at the officer's club boozing it up like the rest of them!" I've often thought since then, a lot of the Navy officers on those troop ships appeared to be hard of hearing. Marines sometime made ridiculous remarks like that one while on board, and in the presence of a Navy officer, without the officer seeming to take notice.

We cleared the seaside channel entrance at good speed for about a mile before turning suddenly to a westerly zig-zag course and we found ourselves looking toward the fast diminishing light of the sun already fallen beyond the horizon. What was awaiting us out there? I think that question was foremost in our minds.

I could feel a sudden attitude change among the Marines who crowded around me. A silence seemed to fall over us as most gazed back toward the island of Oahu, at Pearl Harbor, and the city of Honolulu. We couldn't see much now, only a light smudge of the island lying on the darkening sea, No lights were showing on the land due to the wartime restrictions mandating blackouts. I felt a small hollow feeling develop in my stomach.

During the passage out of the channel mess call had sounded, and those of us left on deck straggled down below to eat. As I fell in at the end of the chow line and moved slowly along the semi-dark passageways, the stench of foul odors hit me again as if someone had slapped me in the face with a wet towel. The smell of cooked food and the body odors of a thousand or more men standing in the mess compartment and cramped passageways caused a nausea to build in my stomach. Misery gripped me as I contemplated the agony of being seasick for the next few days. I had little appetite when I reached the first food station and picked up my hot metal mess tray. I pushed the tray forward and allowed the attendants behind the counter dump whatever food they offered into it.

The food was pork chops, and I was given two and a helping of those white Navy beans. I got some canned corn and carrots and as many slices of bread that I wanted. Near the end of the line the mess attendant slapped a large spoon full of chocolate pudding into the tray's upper right corner. At the end of the line I picked up a hot mug of coffee and, positioning my feet wide apart to compensate for the roll of the ship, made my way cautiously toward a mess table. The tables were fastened between two stanchions which held them about four and a half feet from the deck. The posts were vertical pipes which had the upper end fastened to the overhead and the lower end to the deck. There were no chairs or stools to sit on, there was only standing room. I eased in between two Marines. I placed my tray on the table and then leaned forward and with my elbows braced myself for support against the roll of the ship. The tray in front of me would start to slide this way and that, so I'd hold it with one hand and try to eat with the other. The coffee cup would begin to slide also, but if I was skillful enough,

"Dining" on a troop transport ship

145

I could hold the corner of the tray with one hand and with that same hand hold the cup in position too..

The coffee pot was held from the overhead by a heavy wire and hook. Even though the ship pitched and rolled, the pot stayed hanging perpendicular, most of the time. However, there were times, because of a rough sea it would begin swinging in a large arc and crash against our heads. The taller men like me were vulnerable to this danger. And it was best to have a friendly dining companion who would hold your mug still while you poured coffee from the pot

Since those days of military service my family and some friends have commented on the fact that I'm a rapid eater. I suspect my eating habits were ingrained in my behavior during those days of military service.

That night the troops all seemed to hit the sack early. I found a spot to sleep under one of the many landing craft that were stacked on the main deck. My friend, Gene Olson, usually accompanied me and slept there too. I really don't know if he wanted to or it was just a show of loyalty toward me. Perhaps it was the story I had told him of what to expect if the ship were struck by a torpedo or mine that helped him to decide. I could describe very vividly what it would be like to be trapped below decks in such an event, as the water flooded in on us.

Other troops slept on deck too. At times ship's officers tried to discourage this practice. It often interfered with the crew's activity especially in the early morning when they had to run to their general quarters post in daily practice. It was then that a running sailor would trip and fall over our prostrate forms in the darkness, a fact to which I could personally attest.

We soon became accustomed to the hardness of the steel deck. Our hipbones, knees, and ankles suffered most because of the lack of padding between bone and skin. We kept our shoes on while we slept as we feared some sailor might kick them overboard either intentionally or otherwise.

When it rained, this sleeping arrangement could be very uncomfortable. We always slept with our clothes on because clothes would be necessary to protect our bodies from sun or cold if we had to abandon ship suddenly. We wore the belt type life preservers which were always fastened around our waists when aboard ship. At night we lay upon our shelter halves and used our one blanket to cover us when it became chilly during the early morning hours.

We got wet when it rained but seldom very cold as the wool in the blanket kept our body heat next to our skin. When the rain fell heavily, the situation became intolerable. The ship's deck would load up with water and when it rolled side to side the water would rush to the lower side and then back again as the ship rolled back the other way. A two or three inch rim at the side of the ship's deck kept the water from going over the side and into the sea directly. Drains on deck drained the water off, but slowly and usually inadequately.

Olson and I had it all figured out. We found a place to sleep under a life boat, which was slung from a davit. In case of the ship beginning to sink we would jump into the life boat and refuse to get out as we waited for it to be lowered into the water. Not even the ship's Captain would be able to get us out of there. Fortunately, the situation never arose where we might try out our plan of survival.

Other than the sleeping quarters and the mess compartment, there was one more place on board these ships that I really detested. That was the heads. The heads, civilians call them bathrooms, were kept very clean and sanitary. Nevertheless they were not a very nice place to visit. The showers contained sea water and salt water soap was provided for us to use. I think a rock would have done as well. The salt water, fresh from the sea did wash dirt from our bodies, but left us feeling sticky and itchy.

The wash basins were provided with salt water also. It was difficult to shave every day but that was the order and we were to do it or be reprimanded. We brushed our teeth in fresh water from the scuttle mostly, but I used sea water now and then after I found it to be clean. I believed that the water from the sea was good for my gums. To use the wash basins we usually had to stand in line.

Urinals were hung on the bulkheads or walls of the ship. They were fashioned in the shape of long metal troughs. The sea water was pumped in at one end which was slightly elevated. The water would flow down the length of the trough and exit at the lower end, entering a pipe which would carry it and other waste into the sea. Along with the urine, the flowing water would carry spent matches, cigar and cigarette butts and candy wrappers and whatever the troops happened to discard there.

The most displeasing thing in the head was the latrine. It too was made of metal and fashioned into the shape of a trough and stretched the length of the compartment. Sea water was pumped in at one end and allowed to flow the length of the trough and exit in the same manner as the urinal. About every three feet on this trough there were two board slats placed ten inches apart to provide a crude sort of toilet seat. I thought it was humiliating to have to sit there and wait for a bowel movement, especially when having to sit alongside another person. Sometimes there would be as many as eight men sitting there side by side. The stench in the compartment was terrible, but unavoidable. There were electric fans that blew the stale air out and some fresh in though, and that helped the situation some.

It was awful to sit there while human waste and toilet paper floated along under us, coming down the trough from those men upstream from us. For this reason, when approaching the latrine, each man would try to get a place to sit nearest the end where the water flowed into the trough. Once the men sat down, they would keep their eyes straight ahead. In doing this they could avoid looking at their neighbor.

Sitting there the men had to be conscious of the pitch and roll of the ship as it plowed through the action of the sea. The water, instead of flowing naturally along the trough would rise at times and flood the receptacle. This was caused by the ship's bow rising or falling as it conformed to the wave action of the sea. When the bow rose and the water in the trough rose, the men sitting there would use their knee action to rise from the slats and then as the water subsided they would let themselves back down into the sitting position. To an observer, it did seem a little humorous to see all eight men rise in unison, pause, and then sit down all together again.

There were times when looking straight ahead had its disadvantages. Sometimes a prankster, sitting at the upper end of the trough, would ball up a huge amount of toilet paper and let it float downstream, where it would touch each man's behind as it passed under, causing him to jump up. Some of the jokers would go a step further than that. They would ignite the paper before letting it float downstream. The fellows who practiced that form of entertainment were usually ones who had finished their mission at the latrine and were intent upon leaving quickly anyway.

CHAPTER TWENTY-TWO

Life On Board a War Ship

DURING THE FIRST three or four days after leaving Pearl Harbor, sea sickness was again a problem for some of the troops. I suffered a lot, but not nearly as much as before and not as severely as some of my Marine buddies. One of them, PFC Paul Pugh, of Salt Lake City, suffered more that anyone I had ever seen. He became so ill, we had to restrain him at times for fear that he would leap overboard. Several of us who knew him best kept a close watch on him for three days and even stood his guard watches until he recovered.

At one time the ship's doctor had seasick pills issued to the troops. They didn't help anyone at all that I knew of. Later I found out that the pills didn't contain anything but powdered sugar. So much for the placebo effect!

General Quarters would sound one half hour before sunrise. It was followed by reveille one half hour later. The mess call came, but not before the chow lines began to form. At one time these lines would have two hundred men standing in them. The line would form at the entrance to the mess serving area and then back up the ladder to the deck where it would weave in and round winches and other deck apparatus. I detested having to queue up like that and wondered why men would stand there that long. Why would the last man stand in a long line like that when all that he had to do was to sit near the hatch leading below and join the end of the line as it passed by? I observed certain Marines who would be at the head of the line at breakfast time, then would be waiting at the same hatchway two hours before the lunch and dinner calls too. It seemed to me that food was all they thought of.

For breakfast, the menu hardly varied. It was fried powdered eggs, two slices of Spam and those white Navy beans. The coffee was always scalding hot and black. I developed a liking for that beverage and still drink it that way today.

After breakfast we troops were required to exercise. Usually it was calisthenics, knee bends, and running in place. Periodically we'd form a circle on the cargo hatches and throw the medicine ball to each other until we worked up a good sweat. We were required to shave, shower, and exercise every day. None of us combat troops were allowed to have facial hair, as it would interfere with the treatment of facial wounds. The hair would get pushed into the wound and encourage infection.

On the 29th of January, D company was ordered topside and directed to gather around our platoon leaders who explained that we were en route to a small island named Iwo Jima. This island was located about six hundred and sixty miles south of Tokyo, Japan.

A rubber relief map of the island was laid out on a canvas covered hatch cover and as we viewed it our military objectives were explained to us. We were to overcome the Japanese defenders there in three days and then come back on board ship and go on to another larger objective.

The next target would be Okinawa, but this wasn't revealed to us then. The entire Iwo Jima operation sounded easy and we didn't seem to be excited about it at first. Iwo Jima, in Japanese, means "Sulfur Island." This island was actually a barren volcanic mountain peak that protruded above the sea. It contained a large number of sulfur deposits and fumaroles that emitted volcanic vapors.

Once while I was below in the troop compartment I heard a loud crashing sound coming from the deck above. At first, some of us thought we were under attack by a Japanese submarine. It wasn't though. It was our ship's crew practicing with the two five inch guns on board. The gun crews were firing at a drone aircraft flying overhead that was serving as a practice target. Evidently they didn't do too well as the gunnery officer on the ship's bridge used a hand-held megaphone and told the gunners so. The gun crews continued to fire some fifty to sixty shells at the aircraft without achieving the desired effect. The men manning the guns suffered considerably from the critiques, comments and suggestion offered by the Marines observing.

Later in the day an airplane pulling a large canvas target came over the ship. He passed over several times while our gunners banged away with their guns. Again they failed to achieve the desired effect and the officer on the bridge became irate and told them so. All this was to the delight of the Marines watching from the deck.

One marine yelled out loudly, "Ya know, I feel kinda helpless out here!"

A ship's officer was standing directly behind the Marine and I could see his ears turn red when he heard the remark. Other than that, he didn't react.

We had periods of weapons training also. We stood at the rail of the ship and fired our rifles outboard. We used white wave caps, flying fish, and the birds which followed the ships as targets. I noticed that the accompanying destroyers moved out of bullet range during these training sessions. This type of exercise helped reduce the tensions and anxiety that was gradually building in the men as we approached battle. Even the cleaning of our rifles, a chore often regarded as a bother, was now done enthusiastically.

Other shipboard training consisted of lectures, not necessarily of a military nature though. The battalion roster contained names of men who had expertise in their fields in civilian life. Lt. Richard Lewis, for instance, talked much on economics; others spoke on politics or history.

We had plenty of time to ourselves. We washed our clothing in the sea water showers, read, if we could find something to read other than the comic books the Red Cross furnished, smoked, and played cards. I never smoked cigarettes but, did try a few cigars. That pastime was cut short though. One day I crawled up on some barrels lashed to the deck, lit up a cigar and sat there puffing away. I thought that I was doing the ship's crew a favor by staying out of their way. A Navy chief petty officer came along and saw me. His face turned red and he began to yell at me. It seemed that the barrels I sat on contained gasoline. As I walked away I said to him, "The least you could do would be to put a danger sign on the barrels!" That just made him angrier and louder. The cigar's smoke combined with my tendency for motion sickness caused me to give the rest of the cigars away and to set aside any desire to smoke again.

Many cigarettes in those days were given free to the servicemen overseas. The cigarettes were donated by the various tobacco companies and were distributed to troops on board by the chaplain's office. I suspect that many young men were induced to smoke in that manner and that many never would have used tobacco otherwise. I resisted the temptation and traded off my share of cigarettes for candy bars.

All ship's life wasn't routine and boring though as one day at dawn a sailor fell overboard from the ship's starboard side. His work mates saw him go over and sounded the alarm. Ships at sea during wartime in a battle zone don't stop to pick up sailors who fall overboard, and so we continued on our zigzag course. A destroyer stationed off our starboard side turned about and headed for the spot where the poor man was last seen. The craft circled the area for a while and then caught up with us to resume its former station. Its crew failed to find the unfortunate sailor.

1,620 men watch guarded mail come across from a destroyer

One incident did provide good entertainment for us passengers. A destroyer came alongside while we were underway and delivered mail to us by way of a breeches buoy. Afterwards, a khaki clad naval officer was transferred in the same manner. The sea was rather rough and the two side-by-side ships had a difficult time maintaining the proper speed and the distance required to stay away from each other. The line stretched between the two ships must be kept taut. As the ships closed together the breeches buoy, holding the officer, would dip into the ocean. When the ships pulled apart, the officer would be pulled from under the water and come shooting up like a missile. The troops standing on deck watching the operation loved it! As the officer being transferred was dunked into the water, the men would cheer. When the officer would come shooting up out of the water, the men would cry out, "Do it again! Do it again!" I'm sure that all this display of exuberance on the part of the men was well meant, but I couldn't help notice that a few ship's officers seemed a little vexed by it all. But what do you do in a case like this when facing over sixteen hundred marine fighting men who are about to enter battle?

CHAPTER TWENTY-THREE

Eniwetok and Beyond

WHEN OUR CONVOY approached near the equator, the weather was very hot and humid, and the skies clear of clouds. The temperature was insufferable with no breezes to give us relief. The men complained about feeling highly uncomfortable, if not ill. The hatch cover over the troop galley was removed so that the below deck heat could escape and the air there could circulate better. The steel weather deck of the ship became so hot from the direct sun at midday we wouldn't dare try to cross over it, but sought out the safer sheltered passages of the below decks.

The sea was so calm it resembled a huge mirror that lay flat on the ground reflecting the blue sky overhead. Huge sea snakes swam slowly away from the bow as it sliced through the tepid brackish water. These were horrible looking creatures some as long as ten feet and were a mixture of brown, orange, yellow and gray in color. The water below the surface appeared to me as brown with bits of sea growth floating and yet motionless. So far on this trip I had felt fear when I thought we may have to abandon ship. Now that feeling intensified. I had not nerve enough to swim in such a sea filled with such serpents as I saw there.

Our ship never crossed the equator as we turned west toward the Marshall Islands. When we were twenty or thirty miles away from Eniwetok Atoll we saw the tops of the masts of ships anchored there. Because of the curvature of the earth we couldn't see the island or ship superstructures at first, only the naked masts of the ships standing up straight as if they were part of some diseased forest where the trees were denuded of limbs, branches and leaves.

Eniwetok was devoid of any foliage including the coconut palms which are found on most of the Pacific Islands. This atoll had recently been taken from the Japanese by members of the 4th Marine Division and the Navy's pre-landing bombardment had eliminated all structures, trees and other vegetation from the entire island. It looked to me that the island rose from the ocean surface not more than twelve to fifteen feet.

We entered the narrow opening into the lagoon at full speed and passed the wreckage of Japanese and American small craft beached near the opening. Once in the lagoon the water appeared to be cobalt blue, very clear, quiet and deep. The ship was stopped, the anchor dropped and an announcement was made over the ship's communication system that all hands were allowed to go overboard for a swim if they wished. Almost immediately there were over a hundred of us diving and jumping from the ship's railing into the water where we swam and splashed about happily like a group of school kids.

While we anchored there that afternoon, many small craft scuttled back and forth between the beach and ships carrying Marine and Navy officers, obviously to attend business meetings ashore. Watching them I could sense

*Marines of the 5th Division en route to Iwo Jima welcomed
an opportunity to go swimming over the side of the ship.*

the enthusiasm and the anxiety that seemed to be building within the invasion force. We spent a very peaceful night in the lagoon, satisfied with dinner, watching a movie, feeling safe without the fear of being torpedoed by an enemy submarine.

The next morning the ship was made ready to depart. The anchor was raised, washed off and secured. The ship's engines began to throb; propellers began to churn up the water, the ship's bow turned slowly to face the coral opening to the sea. The convoy formed into a single file and moved toward the narrow entry of the lagoon. Speed was of the essence here as danger existed in the form of a ship being torpedoed and sunk in the opening, blocking it from further entry or egress of war ships.

The troops proceeded on deck after breakfast to stand at the railings to watch the ship get underway. Comments and suggestions were offered to any of the crew who happened to be stationed within hearing distance, much to their displeasure if not anguish.

After dashing through the opening and safely reaching the open sea only elicited more troop remarks, "pretty good" or "just lucky," or "couldn't have done it any better myself!"

I felt curious that the ship's deck officers could retain that impassive facial expression when overhearing those comments by the passengers. I supposed it must have been part of their training and instructions.

Turning west the ships spread out into a prearranged convoy formation. Suddenly I realized that there were twice as many ships now as there had been before. Where had they come from? "Must have been over the horizon waiting" some one offered.

I counted twenty-two troop and supply ships and half a dozen destroyers out far to the front, sides, and one tagging along to the rear of the convoy. These small ships would dash here and there zig-zagging their way through the convoy at fast speeds, throwing up sprays of white frothy water and turning into and out of the path of our lumbering larger ships. Bouncing, twisting and turning like that reminded me of small young terrier dog playful, full of energy and life.

I noticed changes in ship's procedure. The guns aboard were being manned twenty-four hours a day. The gun crews were on full alert in case enemy ships, aircraft, or submarines intercepted us. I made the acquaintance of the five inch gun crews on the forecastle deck and whenever possible I spent time with them assisting with the lookout. I convinced them I had good eyesight and could see a submarine's periscope a mile away as well as they. I suppose that old urge of mine to be a gunner's mate was still with me.

We troops were occupied every day on deck going over battle plans, learning Japanese language, exercising, and have our equipment examined. We cleaned our weapons, made certain they worked properly and had them examined again by superior NCO's and officers.

I could feel a change in myself. For the first time since I joined the service I realized I was in close contact with the enemy. We had trained for this day and it was here. There was no longer a buffer or sanctuary between us and the enemy's territory. I noticed that others around me were behaving different too. The conversations became more subdued, less interesting and the jokes not as humorous as before. Anxiety became a constant companion, I tried to shake it completely but couldn't. The exercise on deck and lectures helped to dispel it, but not much.

Ammunition was issued. Each rifleman with an MI rifle was issued one hundred rounds which he would carry on his belt in pouches and bandoleers that would hang over his neck and shoulders. Those of us who carried the smaller thirty caliber carbines were issued sixty rounds. The machine gunners stacked boxes of their thirty caliber ammunition on the hatch covers and began loading it into belts later to be folded into boxes to be carried ashore.

We corpsmen were called to a lower deck compartment and told to equip ourselves to whatever medical supplies we thought we might need. We jammed as many battle dressings (compression bandages) as we could manage into our two medical bags that we would carry ashore. I think I managed to get twenty four in there even though could not imagine using that many. We would carry bottles of serum albumin to replace blood loss, boxes of one half grain morphine tartrate Syrettes, iodine, cellophane wrapped packets of sulfanilamide crystals, tourniquets and burn ointment that we had prepared ourselves. The ointment was sterile petroleum jelly mixed with sulfanilamide powder which we packed into sterile metal containers.

I noticed the change in the men again after we finished preparations and were ready at last to go ashore. The troops became quiet and meditative and went off by themselves to stare at the ocean or to write letters home to those they left behind. We had been told that no letters would leave the ship until after the battalion had landed on Iwo Jima. The top sergeant went about the decks talking to the men and encouraging us to write letters home. I didn't know what to write as we were not permitted to say anything about where we had been or where we were going. I don't know what I did write if anything. It would have been some trite thing probably as my thinking was that by the time the letter arrived home I could be dead anyway. The battle plans were complete and they were certain to be implemented in just a few more days.

On February 11, 1945, our convoy of ships arrived at Saipan Island in the Marianas. This island had belonged to the Japanese since the end of the 1st World War and they had built it into a military stronghold. The U.S. Navy, Marines and Army had attacked and invaded it a few months before and secured it after a very bloody battle.

Although we had control of it there were still Japanese soldiers in the hills who refused to surrender but chose to continue fighting. We watched as a U.S. Navy warship that was standing off shore fired at targets on a mountainside said to contain Japanese stragglers who refused to lay down their weapons.

The island was beautiful. It was lush and green covered with jungle growth, and scattered across it at the lower elevation there were fields that at one time had contained crops of sugar cane. The remains of a sugar mill stood near the water's edge on the western side of the island, its huge smoke stack rising from the rubble at its base that at one time had been a building. The smoke stack seemed to me an alien thing as it stood there with all the natural beauty surrounding it.

I could see in the distance another island, this one was flat and huge airplanes were taking off from its airstrip. I did not know it at the time but the air planes taking off from Tinian Island were the famed B29 bombers.

Our group of ships continued on to the northern end of Saipan and there we anchored among the largest collection of ships I had ever seen in one place at one time. There were also ships there that had been sunk during the initial battle for Saipan. U.S. and Japanese wrecked ships had settled to the bottom near to each other, their masts, superstructures, or sides showing above water as a reminder of the terrific struggle for the island.

No sooner than the ship's anchor was let go we were ordered to our disembarkation stations and then into our landing crafts for a last practiced landing exercise before assaulting Iwo Jima. We did very well disembarking from the ship and making the make-believe assault landing on the beach. Once ashore we were ordered back into the boats to return to the ship. Immediately the crew of the landing craft became lost. There were so many ships lying out there they could not distinguish our APA from the dozens of others as they all looked alike. It was four hours later that the boatswain and crew found the APA Hocking. By then were all fairly well sunburned, thirsty, hungry and worse yet our weapons were covered with a fine reddish brown rust caused by the salt water ocean spray that came down upon us. Once on board the mother ship the deck felt good under our feet, but we turned to right away cleaning our weapons before having lunch.

Before dawn, on the morning of February 16, we were at sea again. Saipan was nowhere in sight behind us, nor were many of the ships from our previous day's convoy. We were a smaller convoy again with many destroyers now escorting us. Six battleships, five cruisers, sixteen other destroyers, a dozen aircraft carriers that were to participate in the attack of Iwo Jima had gone on ahead to prepare the island for our landing. Some of these warships left Saipan on February 13 to begin the bombardment.

For the next three days that it took us to arrive at Iwo Jima, we were kept busy improving our disembarkation and ship abandonment skills. Each day we would go fully equipped to our stations only to be told to return to our compartments and prepare to do it all over again. Every time we did it we did the same thing, bang our helmets and rifles against bulkheads and overheads, get our other battle gear caught on each other or some ship's protuberance, then curse and complain (quietly of course). We became so proficient at getting to the disembarkation station quickly I could have done it with my eyes closed.

As we got closer to Iwo Jima I could feel the tension continue to rise throughout my body and I am sure that the other men felt as I did. The constant drills drained some of it away. Perhaps that was some of the purpose of doing them.

On the day before we landed, we were ordered to the weather deck where we formed a long line. We found that we were to be deloused, not that we were infected by body lice, but in case we would contact some once ashore. DDT, (chlorinated hydrochloride) an insecticide, was blown up our pants legs, sleeves, under our blouses, front and back side and the most degrading down our trousers from the waist. This was a new experience to me and I didn't care for it at all.

Later we were called on deck and again we were invited to take more ammunition. I took one hundred more rounds for my carbine and that added up to one hundred seventy-five and figured that if I killed one Jap with every bullet I carried, I would be quite a combat hero.

In the afternoon the ship's Captain permitted its radio receivers to broadcast over the ship intercommunication system some of the battle talk between ships already at Iwo Jima that were bombarding the island. When listening to the talk we wondered if anything was going to be left of the island and its defenders for us to see. The damage that was being done sounded immense and terribly destructive at the same time.

We gathered from the radio talk that the big Japanese guns ashore were not firing back at our ships very often. There was a rumor though, that the U.S.S. Pensacola, a cruiser had been struck by a large Japanese shell that made a direct hit on the bridge killing seventeen men including the executive officer. One hundred and twenty other personnel were reported wounded. Unfortunately, it was confirmed later.

Some men lined the rail to watch the receding sun, each with their own thoughts on what the future may bring.

The troops on board our ship now seemed more calm to me. I don't know if that was because they resigned themselves to go into battle or because of the favorable news about the enemy not fighting back. Most just sat around the deck that day playing cards and writing letters home. Religious services were held on deck and confessions were heard. Catholic services were held on the forward hatch cover and I sat among those attending that service. I wasn't Catholic but I had been sitting on a winch operating console when suddenly the priest and congregation gathered around me and since I couldn't escape without embarrassment I merely sat through it. I must say, I had never seen so many of the battalion's Catholics attend service as I did this day, perhaps they were playing the percentages.

When dusk fell over the ship that night our officers came down to the men's sleeping compartment and made small talk and advised us to pack up and sleep with all our clothes on. They added that we should prepare for all eventualities during the night as we would arrive off the island long before dawn. We were also informed that for breakfast we would have fresh eggs, bacon, ham or steak and all the milk and juice we could want.

The men became very quiet, more so than ever before. The darkened ships of the convoy almost silently glided through the darkness. On deck I found the guns fully manned and the crews huddled together speaking in whispered tones. I was aware of the swishing of the bow wake and I looked over the side to watch it curl over and show its fluorescent glow. I was aware of the dark forms of other men standing at the rail along side of me. There was little conversation as most men seemed to be deep in their own private thoughts, perhaps for the last time.

I dreaded the thought of going below decks to sleep, but it had been announced over the ship's address system that we must; there would be no sleeping on deck this night! For the second time since we boarded the ship forty-six days before, I went below and tried to sleep in my bunk. I was being forced to breathe the foul air of the D Company's troop compartment.

Chapter Twenty-Four

D-day, February 19, 1945

"Where dark tides billow in the ocean,
A wink-shaped isle of mighty fame
Guards the gate to our Empire,
Iwo Jima is its name."

Japanese patriotic song

I WAS AWAKENED at 0530 hours by the shrill sound of the boatswain's whistle blaring out over the ship's public address system. My first conscious thought was that I hadn't slept at all. I could feel the vibration of the engines and thought that they were operating at a much reduced speed. The ship must be barely moving through the water. I could feel the anxiety began to build in my body as I rolled from my bunk and onto the deck, where I struggled momentarily to put on my shoes.

The hatch above leading down to our compartment was already opened and fresh air flowed down into the compartment, I felt exhilaration as the oxygen entered my bloodstream. I joined other men as they climbed the ladder leading to the weather deck. Pushing aside the black canvas curtain that served as a light barrier, we stepped outside onto the chilled and still darkened deck. Several of us stood at the port railing, squinting toward the dim silhouette of a pyramid shaped rock, which rose sharply from the ocean surface about a half mile away. The sun, still far below the eastern horizon, caused a faint orange glow which outlined the rock. At my remark that I couldn't see any gunfire out there, someone responded, "That's not Iwo. It's on the other side of the ship!"

Several Marines and I crossed the deck and found room at the starboard rail among a line of men who stood silently and gazed out across the water at a dark smudge of an island which seemed several miles away. As we watched, the light coming from the rising sun, now at our backs, began to illuminate the distant island. At the same time I became aware of a rumbling sound that emanated from the same direction. I had never heard naval gunfire before that sounded like this. The scene, odors, and sounds of the early dawn seemed ominous to me. I realized that men were dying out there as I stood here in comparative safety. A tight, hard feeling began to grow in my chest and stomach. I looked at the Marines on either side of me. They stood as I, with hands on the rail, gazed out over the water in apparent casualness. But, I knew each had the same gnawing feeling in the pit of his stomach as I did.

The dawn continued to illuminate the island even though there was a high overcast of light clouds in the sky above. Men began to make comments on the five hundred and fifty-five foot mountain the Japanese had named Mt. Suribachi. Its name in Japanese means 'cone shaped.' From our view, the southern side of the mountain rose sharply from the water, leveled off on top, and then descended sharply for about four hundred feet to land that stretched to the north at a gradual incline for approximately five miles. In the increasing light, I could see that the island was covered with a light haze that I assumed was from the U.S. Navy shells exploding there.

One of my comrades pointed to the north of the island and said, "Here come the 'Hellcats'" At first I had to squint before I made out several formations of small planes in the distant sky. As we watched, the planes broke from their formations and one following another went into a shallow dive that culminated with the pilots loosing their bombs and rockets at targets on the northern slope of Mt. Suribachi.

When mess call sounded a few moments later, I reluctantly left my position at the rail and went below to eat breakfast. After waiting a while in line, I reached the food counter. I shoved my food tray outward and the server dumped some gooey cooked powdered eggs and two slices of Spam onto it. It was then I realized that the men in line in front of me were complaining about not getting the fresh fried eggs, bacon, ham, and steak we had been promised. I noticed that no Navy NCO's were present, only the galley workers who served the troops, and could hardly be held responsible for this deceit we thought was perpetrated on us. I went on and picked up my slice of corn bread and mug of hot coffee. It didn't take me long to eat that morning. I don't think that I would have enjoyed the steak, eggs, fruit juice, and milk anyway, as I continued to have a strange and heavy feeling in my stomach.

Back on deck I thought how much different this morning was than I had expected. The men around me seemed calm, not excited. They were speaking in low tones to those around them. The ship's Captain had ordered that radio messages being received concerning the battle be broadcast to all on board. We could hear the voices of Navy and Marine personnel coordinating the efforts of the landing force being prepared for the initial landing. We listened to reports coming in describing damage on enemy targets, caused by our shell fire and bombing attacks.

About 0830 the voice of a Marine Corps officer identifying himself as reporting from the 28th Regiment described his unit's approach to the island while being transported in amphibious tractors. He asked that the naval bombardment be lifted so they could land.

At 0900 that same voice described the landing of the 28th Marine Regiment on the beach, and continuing up the first series of steppes facing them. On they went and moved inland across the low saddle separating Mt. Suribachi from the rest of the island. The speaker came through with a "so far so good" statement and said that the Marines ashore were only meeting with sporadic small arms fire. He added that his men were half way across the island and had yet to meet much resistance.

A few of the Marines around me began to speculate that the naval fire power had just about neutralized the island defenders and that the rest of us "would just walk ashore." The speculation was cut short by an announcement over the ship's public address system, following a shrill bos'un's (Boatswain) whistle, "Now hear this, all troops will lay below to their quarters and prepare to disembark!" That command made me feel good now that I had excitement and tension building in me. Besides, I was getting off this gawd-awful ship at last, and onto the island where I could stand and walk on solid earth again.

This time, even in the crowded compartment, we could put on our gear with little effort. I could feel the eagerness and excitement of the men around me. They were in a good mood and helped each other into battle gear, fastening straps and adjusting packs. It was very crowded down there and we had to assist each other in turning around in order to face the ladder leading to the upper decks. It was these 'hurry up and wait' situations that put an edge on the men's nerves. Right then we were in the 'wait' part. To make more room, we chained up third, fourth and fifth bunks to permit three men to sit side by side on the second bunk. This allowed the men standing and waiting in the aisles more room.

We didn't have to wait long before our next order. Again, we heard the shrill whistle followed by the brisk command, "Now hear this, all troops report to your disembarkation stations!" Rapidly and in practiced formation we filed up the ladder, crossed over the weather deck to the starboard side, and quickly lined up against the rail to our assigned positions. I observed that the heavy cargo nets that we would descend upon, had been hung over the sides of the ship in our absence. There was no talking, no joking, no horseplay, only the deadly seriousness of troops preparing to go over the side. We were professionals and this is what we had trained for.

Marine work crews were stacking supplies near each of the disembarkation stations. These were the supplies of high explosives, hand grenades, bandoleers of ammunition, and boxes of 30 caliber ammunition for the BARs, carbines and the M-1 rifles. I picked up four grenades and placed two in each side pocket of my blouse. On a second thought I picked up another 100 rounds for my carbine, a good decision as it turned out.

We stood at the rail a very long time, or at least it seemed that way to me. The ship's landing craft had already been launched after responding to a command from the bridge of, "Away all boats!" They had all scurried out from both sides of the ship to keep pace with the mother ship as it slowly moved closer toward the island. Then, on an apparent command from the bridge of the Hocking, they formed into two circles on either side of the ship. The small craft in each circle were moving in the opposite direction to those in the other circle, on that same side of the ship, in order to minimize a chance of collision.

The weather was changing. In the far distance, beyond the island, a squall coming directly toward us. A brisk wind had come up and this turned the sea around us very choppy. The small boats to our right were rolling and pitching and throwing up white water spray away from their bows. I could see the crews in them hunching over trying to escape the heavy spray, but to no avail. I wondered if this was an omen of what was to come.

I occupied my mind by watching the boats bounce around amongst the white caps and with the developing scene ashore. The island was now covered with a heavy cloud of smoke and dust from the exploding shells and bombs and the bombardment from our warships off shore. I couldn't really see much, just smoke, dust and those little flashes of glowing orange spots that appeared from one end of the island to the other.

I was aware of the increasing acrid odor of burning gun and shell powder which was being carried to us by the western breeze. There was a frightening aspect to that, a bad feeling was beginning to form in my mind about this island. I did not like it!

Suddenly, the small boats broke from their formation of circles, apparently again on some command from the bridge. They dashed splashing in toward the ship in single file then scattered. Each one going to its assigned position at the lower end of the many cargo nets that hung from the sides of the ship. At the head of the line in front of me I saw the athletic form of Lt. Horvath climb the rail of the ship. He paused, balanced there a moment straddling the horizontal iron pipe rail, and looked down at the small craft then back toward us. He waived his hand toward the sea and shouted, "All right, Second platoon, let's go!" Then he disappeared from my view as he went over the side of the ship.

Quickly, we were all business. We were like a well crafted machine as each Marine helped the one in front of him get over the rail. Each was held by the other until it was certain that he had his hands and feet securely in place on the strands of the net before he was released.

As I went over the railing, I looked down at the boat bouncing and swaying in the choppy water below. This was going to be one of the rougher boarding that I had ever experienced as the squall struck at us full force. As the ship rolled away from the small boat, I was left hanging on the net and was slammed against the steel side of the ship. Then as the ship rolled to starboard and toward the small craft, and I was thrown outward to hang suspended in mid air. All the time the smaller craft below would rise swiftly ten or fifteen feet and then fall away again. I stepped down the net and was horrified to see the small landing craft come rising rapidly toward me.

"Step backward onto the gunwale and then let go the net!" Some one was screaming it at me from below.

To do that I would need to have much confidence in my fellow Marines, but I did it! The small craft fell away from the larger ship and there I was caught balancing and weightless on my right foot with the shoe sole and heel caught up against the gunwale. Fortunately, one of my comrades had grabbed the back of my shoe and held it tightly to the boat. Down I plummeted with the boat until it bottomed out in the ocean trough and my momentum carried me crashing to the deck.

Well, not exactly to the deck, as two of my Marine buddies were crushed under me. I weighed two hundred pounds, and it was figured that I carried another seventy-five in gear and that totaled weight did a certain amount of physical damage along with the bruised dignities to my two comrades. Recovering from the fall I found myself the subject of no small verbal abuse. One Marine, pushing out from under me yelled, "Take my place, dammit, I'm getting out of here!"

I looked upward and realized that the small boat was shooting upward rapidly along side of the ship and that Sgt. Renner, the last man to board was hanging up there by one foot on the cargo net while flailing around with the other trying to meet the rising gunwale. He jammed his foot down as I scrambled to my feet and I reached up and grabbed the heel of his shoe and held it to the gunwale as the small boat began to plummet downward. Down we went with Renner seemingly to float in mid air until the boat bottomed out and the sergeant came crashing down, crushing me onto the deck.

Fortunately, no one was seriously hurt in boarding the landing craft. This was probably because we descended the nets as we were trained to do even when hampered by the heavy loads we carried. We knew that if a man fell into the water between the ship and boat with all the ammunition and gear he carried, he wouldn't surface at all but would go straight to the bottom! If he didn't sink he was sure to be crushed between the side of the larger ship and that of the smaller boat as the two were dashed together by the wave action.

The entire platoon fit snugly into this little craft. Lt. Horvath stood up front on the right side of the ramp. Sgt. Abromovich stood in front on the left side of the ramp, both men facing aft toward the rest of us. The three squads were lined up in their proper order facing forward. I stood in my assigned position which was to the rear of the troop compartment on the left side. PFC Jesse Prunty, stood to my right, and to the right of him was the platoon guide-on, Sgt. Russell Renner.

My back was pressed against the small bulkhead separating the troop compartment from the large Chrysler Marine engine. The heat from the engine felt good against my lower back. I decided not to share my secret with any of those men around me. Standing directly in back of me on a slightly raised deck of the coxswain's cockpit was a Navy Lieutenant who was the assigned 'Wave Officer.' It was his duty to direct and maintain the integrity of the line of boats approaching the shore. He accomplished this mainly by standing up where he could be seen and giving hand signals to the other boats assigned to his command. His craft was distinguished from others in the 'wave' by a red flag placed in the right front corner of the boat where all could see it.

To his right behind the steering wheel was the coxswain, or in nautical lingo, 'cox'un' who maneuvered the boat. Behind him stood a Bo'sun who was in overall charge of operating the craft. At both rear corners of the Higgins boat, tucked into small circular gun pits, were two Marines who grasped the handles of their thirty caliber swing mounted machine guns and peered intently up at the sky watching for enemy aircraft.

As soon as Sgt. Renner, the last man of the platoon to leave the larger ship, let go the net and entered the boat, the cox'un opened the throttles. The engine roared to life and the little boat lunged forward through the white choppy water. The bow dipped slightly and bucked its way into an oncoming wave which sent a sheet of water up and over the bow ramp and drenched us.

I think Lt. Horvath, standing up there with his back to the ramp, caught the bulk of it. It splashed down onto his head and shoulders. I tried, unsuccessfully, to restrain a grin as the Lieutenant wiped the water from his face and eyes with the back of his free hand. The officer shrugged his shoulders, overcame his embarrassment and displayed to us a big, good-natured smile. That seemed to dispel some of our anxiety.

To clear away from the side of the mother ship, the cox'un had turned the boat into the heavy gust of wind and was receiving the rough wave action head on. I was very concerned as it would take only one wave to hit us in a way that would swamp the boat and send us to the bottom. My mind went quickly over the procedure for dropping my gun belt, pack, helmet and rifle and attempt swimming to safety.

We had to endure the rough water for about ten minutes until our craft increased speed and left the larger ship behind. I was aware that the officer who stood elevated behind me was using both hands to give signals to the other boats, now filled with men of the battalion. In order to steady himself and keep his hands free he forced his knees into the back side of my pack. I nodded my assent to his action and he tapped the top of my helmet in acknowledgement. At his direction the other boats began to take their properly assigned positions behind our craft.

We were still three or four miles away from the island, that to me resembled a huge whale lying on the surface of the water, its head to the north and its tail, Mt. Suribachi, to the south. As we closed the distance we watched as the Marine and Navy planes continued their assault on the mountain top and sides. They would come from the north, which was to our right side, like so many busy bees, break formation and one by one, dive at their targets. Some dropped fragmentation bombs, others the concussion type, and still others those horrible frightening napalm canisters that exploded and covered men and gun positions with a flaming gasoline jelly. We appreciated the airmen's efforts, as we realized that there were many gun emplacements up there on Mt. Suribachi and that the Japanese gunnery observers were directing fire on our troops coming ashore. Undoubtedly, the Japanese up there had a clear view of the entire Marine landing force.

Leading the others in our wave, our boat continued on toward shore. The Cox'un handling the wheel was steering directly toward the eastern base of Mt. Suribachi. The only faces I could see in our craft were those of Lt. Horvath and Sgt. Abromovich who still stood at the bow facing the rest of us. All I could see of the other men was the back and top of their wet helmets, packs, and the barrels of their slung rifles. The Lieutenant and the sergeant stood, holding their rifle slings tightly to their chests with their right hands and with their left, grasped that portion of the gunwale nearest them. Their faces appeared impassive to me, I wondered what they were thinking.

En route to the island we passed many small warships, some of which had deck guns firing away at the island. Directly in front of us, about a mile from the base of Mt. Suribachi, stood a battleship, her stern toward us. I identified her later as the *U.S.S. Tennessee*. She was firing broadsides at targets ashore in the area of the beach where we were assigned to land. One of the Marines on my right turned his head in my direction and asked to no one in particular, "How come they're firing at targets where the 28th Marines have already passed?"

He didn't get an answer or expect one, I suppose. He was right though, as we all knew the Marines ahead of us had passed that spot already and yet it was being bombarded as if the enemy were still there. Several of the men were lamenting the fact that the island would be secured before we landed and that we'd miss all the fun. "Those bastards will get the best souvenirs!" one complained.

We approached the stern of the *U.S.S. Tennessee*. The ship lay still in the water. I could not see one sailor on its decks. It looked eerie and I was awed by its huge size. I could not understand how that much steel could float on the water. We passed close to her stern, but keeping safely away from the turbulence of her huge slowly turning propellers. The ship's large guns aft were pointed outward from her starboard side and aimed at a point several hundred yards above the beach on which we were to land.

I was looking at the guns, which were off to my left as we passed by, when I saw three of the guns move. I heard a loud rumbling noise, the gun barrels jumped, smoke, flame, and burning particles came flying out of the muzzles. Out of the smoke and flame came projectiles, which looked like small garbage cans that were being hurled at the island. My eyes could follow the missiles clear to the target.

The exploding shells tore apart a huge concrete bunker that was inland from the beach and which had been partially concealed with a covering of sand. Chunks of concrete, along with dust and sand were thrown high in the air.

I watched as the recoil of the huge guns forced the battleship slowly down into the water. When the pressure of the ship became too great for the surrounding water to bear, the ship was slowly driven upward and back to its former position. When the guns fired, the concussion from the blast smoothed the water in front of them. The white chop that been caused by the fresh breeze disappeared completely. A line appeared in the water forming a quickly expanding semicircle out and away from the battleship. The line raced toward us at a frightful speed, flattening the water as it approached. I heard the Navy officer in back of me mutter, "Oh, Christ!"

When the line in the water reached us, I felt my body rise from the deck, held momentarily in the air and then slapped, as if by the hand of a giant. I felt as though I was hitting the earth after being dropped from a great height. All my buddies too were collapsing to the deck in a heap of bodies and battle gear.

We recovered enough to begin disengaging ourselves from one another and struggle to our feet. We attempted to shake off the effects of the concussion coming from the mouths of those huge guns. I heard the officer in back of me attempting to calm the men, "It's OK! They won't fire again now that we're in the line of fire."

Our landing craft continued on toward the shore. I could look back over my left shoulder and see the battleship. I was very impressed by her size, might, and formidable look. Then I heard that rumbling sound again, saw the guns jump as they belched out smoke, fire, burning debris and projectiles. The projectiles came closer to us this time because of our boat's course through the water. But, I was watching that line that formed in the water and came racing at us from the direction of the battleship. I heard the officer in back of me yell out, "Oh No! Cover your ears!"

As the concussion reached us, it raised us into the air, and again we were violently slammed down onto the deck in a mass of flailing arms and legs. For a few moments, I found it difficult to organize my thoughts as I again struggled to my feet. The wave commander ordered the cox'un to turn the boat away from the battleship's line of fire and to run parallel to the beach for a safer route.

We continued north for several hundred yards before I heard him yell again, to the cox'un. "OK right here cut your engine and point her at the beach!" The sailor steering the boat reduced the throttle and spun the wheel hard to the left. The bow came around quickly and I could see the higher elevation of Mt. Suribachi over the top of the ramp. I turned to look over my shoulder and up at the wave commander. He was standing upright and holding his hands high above his head, and at the same time giving hand signals to the boat crews behind us.

In accordance with his signals some of the boats passed by us to take up positions on our right side. Others did not pass us, but instead took up

Higgins boats circle in preparation for their landing.

positions on our left. These boats were maneuvered until they formed one long horizontal line facing the beach. There they all sat, their motors idling, their propellers turning just enough to maintain headway.

The wave officer dropped his arms to extend horizontally out from his shoulders. He looked right and he looked left several times before being satisfied of the proper wave alignment. Only then was he ready to move us in toward the shore. The thought came to mind that we had better not dally about here very long. Mentally, I was visualizing the Japanese gunners peering through their gun's sights and making elevation and range corrections while waiting for the signal to fire. I felt a sudden surge of anxiety flood through my body. Again, the officer in back of me was signaling. The dozens of assault boats containing the second battalion began to move slowly toward the beach. To the Japanese defenders we must have appeared to be an awesome and frightful sight.

Onlookers watch the invasion unfold. More than 800 vessels were involved in the invasion armada.

Hostile Beach

THE WATER BETWEEN the us and the beach appeared calm except for those little flecks of restless white on top of the small chop caused by the off shore breeze. The clouds, dust, and smoke that came our way from the island were heavy and odoriferous and were drifting out to engulf us. The rays of the sun broke through the high overcast. The ever moving shadows created by the transient clouds revealed a panoramic and constantly changing color schemes that appeared on the restless surface of the ocean. From where we stood in our boats to the distant beach we could see the small white tipped waves form and roll casually along toward the shore. As they approached within one hundred yards of the beach they suddenly grew in size, threw foam into the air and dashed forward until they smashed themselves on the black sand of the island.

The formations of airplanes were still arriving from the north. Each of the warplanes, in beginning their attack, would break from the formation and dive toward an assigned target on the steep sides of Mt. Suribachi. After releasing their bombs, they would bank to the right and be out over the ocean within seconds to return to their carrier to rearm, refuel, or whatever. I estimated that each of these planes was over the island from five to eight seconds during each run. Some of the pilots daringly went close in to the mountain, barely missing the rocky surface before banking. Others pulled up short in a rather conservative show of fighting spirit. The latter pilots caused some of the men around me to yell out, "Chicken...! Chicken!"

Our line of boats was about four hundred yards off the beach when I heard the wave officer in back of me yell out to the boat crew, "Let's go!" The cox'un pushed the throttles wide open and the engines roared, the bow rose in the water and the boat lunged forward. The Marines standing in front of me swayed backward in the sudden movement and I was forced back against the motor cowling and held there momentarily. No one fell down during the movement, as we were all jammed in there so firmly that our bodies were held upright by the others.

The next wave of Higgins Boats line up in preparation for landing

I could hear the wave commander shouting, "Go! Go! Go!" Looking back, I saw him standing above me. He steadied himself with his left hand on the entrenching tool fastened to the top of my pack, his knees flexed with the kneecaps forced against the back of my haversack. With his right hand elevated above his shoulder he repeatedly pointed to the beach in front of us. The image of a Roman gladiator riding his war chariot into battle flashed into my mind. "Go! Go! Go!" the officer commanded. To the crews of the other boats on either side of us, the message was not audible but was being made very clear to them. Their boats surged forward, maneuvering until they were dashing along parallel with us in one straight line. I felt my chest tightening as the adrenalin flowed, and I found myself enjoying the excitement as I succumbed to the scent of the impending battle.

Up front in our boat, Lt. Horvath and Sgt. Abromovich still stood facing us. Up until now, they had been talking to men near them, probably in an attempt to keep morale up and tension down. As the boat surged ahead both men braced themselves, turned serious and I believe each lost a shade or two of color from his face.

The Marine standing directly in front of me was PFC Paul Rush, a big friendly, but serious Texan. He carried a BAR slung over his right shoulder and its barrel kept threatening to strike me in the face each time he shifted his weight or the boat lurched. Paul carried his own personal revolver on his hip. He was proud of that handgun and we had kidded him about being a 'Texas sheriff from the Panhandle.'

The rest of the men stood very quietly, their eyes focusing in on the top of Mt. Suribachi as it began to loom larger in our view over the left upper bow ramp of our boat. I began to watch the battle taking place on the sides of the mountain more intensely. I realized that I could see flame throwers at work and shells exploding at its base. There were puffs of smoke and flashes of light as powder ignited.

Looking to either side of me, I was impressed by the lines of boats racing through the water and splashing white frothy spray upward and outward around their bows. It was really a pretty scene, but no different from any other time when making our practice runs while preparing for this day.

My eyes were drawn to a movement of Lt. Horvath as he raised both outstretched arms forward and upward from his shoulders and brought his hands slowly downward in a command for us to kneel on the deck. Unfortunately, I reacted too quickly. As my right knee touched the deck, Paul Rush lowered his weight onto it, twisting it. Feeling a sharp pain and fearing that my knee muscles might cramp and prevent me from running from the boat, I told Paul about my problem and pushed him forward in order to free myself. Once loose, I stood up to get myself reorganized.

In that instant the entire scene about us changed. There were explosions in the water surrounding our craft. Plumes of water shot upward around the boat and poured back down into it drenching us. The din was painful to my ears. I heard the crew members in back of me yelling, but I couldn't understand their words because of the noise. Lt. Horvath was still on his feet facing us. I think he was trying to calm us, though his face looked paler than before.

Noises like those resembling hammer blows striking wood sounded outside of the left side of the boat near where I stood and that startled me. I stared and assumed that the sound was that of bullets striking the exterior wooden sides of the boat. Apparently they were being deflected some by the craft's interior construction. Then I was aware of the sound of metal hitting metal coming from the front of the craft as bullets struck the outside of the steel ramp close to Lt. Horvath. He turned to stare at the ramp he leaned against, then turned slowly back toward us, shrugged his shoulders and gave us a weak smile.

I looked around us. Our boats were running through a deluge of falling high explosive shells coming from many mortar and artillery pieces high on the island. The missiles were falling at such a rate that I could see a dozen or more bursts in the water at one time. Our boat ran the gamut of explosions without being hit by anything except the waterspouts we ran through which sent heavy sheets of water onto our heads and shoulders.

I looked to our right and saw a shell burst occur in a distant landing craft. The LCVP turned sharply to the left, slowed, then stopped dead in the water as its left side tipped toward the sea. I could see rifles, helmets, packs, and other gear fly out and upward as the explosion tore apart men and their equipment. Instantly I felt a heavy sick feeling grab me in my stomach. I became aware that the Navy Lieutenant, in back of me, had reached forward with his hand and was pushing down on the top of my helmet, forcing me back down to a kneeling position. I could hear his voice, "Down!" he commanded.

I glanced back at him. To my surprise he was still standing up, facing forward, his knees flexed as he braced them against me. His feet were squarely planted on the deck. The coxswain, beside him leaned forward over the steering wheel, his teeth bared in a show of grim determination to take his boat into the shore.

The bos'un, not to be outdone, stood straight behind the cox'un, his right hand resting on his hip, the other holding onto the cox'uns belt for support. I could only guess what was happening now. The Japanese had let the initial wave of Marines come ashore. Now they were trying to destroy us in the water as we approached and would continue to try more intently as we reached the beach. Afterwards they would concentrate their efforts on destroying the initial landing force that were already on shore. We had been told about this Japanese battle tactic during our training sessions. It was a good plan, one that damn well nearly worked!

Kneeling there I could feel the boat buck and rock as it entered the white water backwash near the beach. The Lieutenant and the Sergeant turned simultaneously, apparently on command given by the bos'un in back of me, and released the large metal hooks that secured both sides of the ramp to the boat. I saw them brace themselves against the expected contact between the boat's hull and the sand of the beach. After a moment passed I heard the bos'un cry out, "Stand by!"

When the contact came, I was surprised. It was a softer landing than I had expected. Lt. Horvath and Sgt. Abromovich slammed their shoulders hard against the ramp to force it loose and outward when they saw the bos'un release the cable holding it vertically. The ramp fell outward and down. There, before us, lay the black volcanic sands of Iwo Jima!

This is the point in an amphibious landing where fear rises in the hearts of men landing from an assault boat. It is caused mostly by their knowing that well trained defending troops will turn their weapons on the front of the craft disgorging its occupants. The defending machine gunners will coordinate their fire so that the bullets fired from their guns will intersect and cross immediately in front of the emerging soldiers so that the attackers will run into the crossfire of bullets.

I was very afraid as the men in front of me rose and began to move forward. They were trying desperately to build up momentum so that they could leap forward and away from the sharp forward edge of the ramp. I pushed Paul Rush's pack upward to help him gain his feet more easily and then made a full effort in standing myself. The wave commander reached down, grabbed my pack straps and pulled upward, helping me to my feet, "Good luck Son," he said rather weakly I thought as he slapped the back of my pack." Take care of yourself!" His words were of some comfort to me, but the words of thanks to him somehow caught deep in my throat and didn't come out very well.

PFC Prunty and I were the last ones to leave the boat. We took hold of the five gallon Jerry can (water container) that had been sitting on the deck between us, in order to carry it up on the beach. With it between us we ran toward the end of the ramp and leaped forward. Unexpectedly, because of the extra weight, we jumped only about three feet out in front of the ramp. We were still about thirty feet from shore and both hit the water falling forward onto our knees. The wave action water came from behind and washed over my shoulders before I could regain my footing and stand up.

After establishing a foot hold I felt the terrifying sensation of being struck in the back by the sharp edge of the steel ramp as the craft was lifted and thrust forward by the next wave. I struggled, fighting against the wave back-lash when another wave struck me from behind and pushed me toward the shore.

As I leaped from the ramp and into the water my left knee had struck the shoulder of a Marine lying face down, floating in the surf. The blow sent the body spinning under water, but it quickly bobbed back to the surface face down. Not knowing if were one of our platoon's men or not mattered little at the time. I took hold of the entrenching tool fastened to the top of his pack and pulled him along with me until I stepped from the surf. I left him with his head out of the water for someone else to attend to. I thought he was dead, but if he wasn't I hoped to prevent him from drowning. Prunty and I carried the water can up on to the sand and ran several yards before dropping it. As we did so, a great flash of red and orange light blossomed up directly in front of us, it was obviously a mortar or artillery shell explosion. Together, we were thrown down onto the sand. I felt that I was dying for sure but just hadn't felt the pain yet. I was aware that Prunty was struggling to his feet and crawling away. I could hear him saying above the din of the battle, "I'm getting the hell out of here!" as he crawled off to the right.

The beach was in complete confusion, immersed in an inferno. I don't know how to explain it any other way. It seemed that the entire area was erupting in multiple fiery explosions which ballooned the sand upward into huge mounds of gray black sand which then disintegrated, turning into fountains of gray translucent spray.

The wreckage surrounding us was appalling. Landing crafts at the surf line were turned this way and that, some swamped, some lying on their sides. To further complicate the situation some still had their ramps down and these dug into the sides or ends of other craft in such a way that the crews were having a problem raising them so they could leave the beach and go back seaward.

Men, helmets, rifles and other gear that the men carried were flying about above the surface of the beach only to come back to earth bouncing, skidding or burrowing into the sand. Men were crumpled to the earth, some moving, others not, their clothing smoking or burning because of the hot steel fragments which struck them. The portion of the beach on which the 26th Regiment landed was perhaps four hundred yards wide. As far as I could see, it was completely covered with men and equipment.

To add to the confusion was a burning amphibious tractor landing craft off to our right. Red, orange and black flame swirled upward from its interior and its cargo of exploding shells flew outward, some exploding in mid air, others landing among the men lying on the sand nearby. Only good discipline could make those men to stay there without bolting, I thought.

At least two battalions of the 26th Marine Regiment had been landed, that would be well over two thousand men. According to the battle plan, we should have advanced inland on the heels of the 28th Marine Regiment which had landed at that same spot before us. Now that our advance had been stopped by the enemy there was danger of our men and units becoming mixed up with others while on the beach and that would cause confusion hindering a smooth amphibious landing operation.

The Japanese mortar and artillery fire was taking a heavy toll of our men and equipment and was increasing with every second. The Japanese up high on Mt. Suribachi's slopes had a clear view of our landing and were directing very intense shell fire on us from the north. They didn't have to zero in on individuals, they had only to point in our direction and shoot. To them, we must have looked like a machine gunner's paradise as they couldn't miss hitting someone with each burst. Men were being injured or killed with every shell explosion; there was nowhere to escape. Not a second passed without several explosions taking place right in and among the men of the 2nd battalion.

The Jap mortar men were very good. They were firing from Mt. Suribachi and perhaps somewhere from the higher ground to the north of us. The latter direction I couldn't understand as the 27th Regiment was assigned to capture that ground and by now the Japs that had been there shouldn't have been within mortar range any longer. Regardless of that, those mortar men had to have been dropping the shells into their tubes one after another and as fast as they could.

Despite all that noise I could hear men yelling out, "Corpsman, help!" I began applying battle dressings over wounds, trying to stop bleeding, and injecting morphine into bodies. I was at first confused as I couldn't recognize the wounded as from my battalion. Only later would I realize that most of these casualties were from the 28th Marine Regiment that had preceded us and were now hoping to reach the beach in order to be evacuated.

I used many of the tourniquets that I carried in just the first few minutes on the beach. I was in danger of using all of my two dozen battle dressing's right then. I hadn't ever done this kind of work before. I don't think that many men have ever done it. In training, we had practiced applying bandages under clean and proper conditions with all the time necessary to do a very nice job. Here, the wounds were real and horrible. Huge chunks of flesh were torn from men's bodies and red hot steel fragments tore into flesh taking dirt and clothing with them. Often as I reached a fallen man I would see smoke or steam coming from the wound as the hot steel would ignite the clothing that had been pushed into the wound.

A bullet entering flesh would make a small reddish blue hole but when it exited it tore a chunk out with it and blood would gush freely. This was a common type wound that I treated on the beach, perhaps one dozen, maybe two, I don't recall the number. Besides, who would count anyway? I soon realized that I had used more than half of the two dozen battle dressing I had brought ashore. Each Marine carried one bandage on his belt and I made an attempt to use that one first.

One of the Marines who was down on his knees crawling on the sand suddenly leaped to his feet, dropped his rifle as he did. That movement served to alert me that the man had been struck by a bullet or shell fragment. He turned toward the beach and attempted to run by me, but stumbled and I could see blood pumping out of his right leg from a wound above the knee. I reached out and pulled him to the ground then grabbed for his wounded

As Marines spread out, they seek cover behind wreckage
while taking fire from Mt. Suribachi

leg. I managed to place the heel of my right palm over the spouting blood and stop it, but not before I was spurted in the face, mouth and eyes with his blood blinding me momentarily. I was trying to suppress the blood flow with one hand, while reaching for a compression bandage with the other and at the same time I was partially blinded; it was beyond my capabilities. The injured man franticly struggled to get to his feet in order to run to the water's edge, I struck him in the chest with my open hand and pushed him backward to lay him out flat on the sand. I was yelling for him to lie still so I could put the bandage on the wound to stop the bleeding. He insisted on fighting me off in an attempt to get up and that caused me to react by my cursing and striking him again in the chest with my fist. This time he lay back on the sand and seem to relax allowing me to fix the bandage.

I got a syrette of morphine out of my kit which I injected into his leg above the wound. When I finished, I turned toward his head and lay beside him hoping to escape the flurry of bullets coming from Mt. Suribachi. I yelled at him to start crawling toward the water and get into any boat that was attempting to leave. He didn't respond. It was almost as if he did not care any more. I slapped his helmet with my hand and yelled, "OK, you were in such a damned hurry to leave, goddamit, get the hell out of here!" When he failed to respond again, I grabbed him by his blouse on his shoulder and pulled. His head wobbled loosely and only then did I see blood on the left side of his neck. I reached over him, placed a hand on top of his helmet and pulled his head toward me. There was small round blue hole on the right side of his neck. A bullet had entered there and exited the left side after smashing through his vertebral column. He was dead. Perhaps, if I had not forced him back on the ground, the bullet might not have hit him. Then again, he may have been struck while sitting up too! I don't know.

We corpsmen were trying to perform under almost impossible conditions as we were forced to lie on the sand alongside of the injured while working. While we worked over one casualty, other wounded cried out for help, or stood up and stumbled about dazed and shouting incoherently obviously in shock.

Some of the injured were wounded again and even a third time as they lay on the sand or stumbled about. Many of them were given help by fellow Marines who did their best to assist. While I gave aid to one man, I shouted instructions to nearby Marines on how to stop the bleeding of an injured buddy he was assisting.

Approaching the beach I had some doubts about my ability to do my job correctly. Those doubts left me as I worked over the injured. It seemed that everything that I had ever been taught in hospital corps or field medical school now was laid out before me very clearly and I didn't hesitate to take advantage of that knowledge.

Before this day I had never seen a dead person. Some of the dead which lay about me looked as though they were sleeping men. Others were in horrible shape as their bodies and limbs were twisted in unnatural form or parts were missing. The corpses all looked pale and the more seriously mutilated ones looked almost white, due to the loss of blood from their flesh. Arms, legs, and even heads were torn from bodies by the explosions, and I could see bone fragments and pieces of flesh lying on the beach. The parts appeared colorless and sticking to them was that light volcanic black sand that we would all soon detest. The sand hindered our movements, got into wounds, our mouths, eyes and ears. Worst of all it fouled our weapons so that we couldn't depend on them. Never in my wildest thoughts did I ever think combat could to be anything like this!

The more fortunate of the wounded were carried or dragged aboard the still beached boats by their fellow Marines, corpsmen or members of the boat crews. The boats were strewn every which way in the surf, being washed this way and that way, banging into each other, being struck by artillery and mortar shells and machine gun fire. Many of the LCVPs still had their ramps down and the crews were trying to get them up as they backed away from the beach. This hesitation did allow some of the injured to be placed on board. The Navy and coast guardsmen manning the boats that day were very brave to stand their ground under that heavy fire coming at them. I can't thank them enough!

Much later, after the battle was over, I thought of this time we spent on the beach during that first half hour, or however long it really was, and how the men there responded so well to the immediate challenge. Lesser trained men, I'm sure, could never have accomplished as much that day.

The men who landed there went into an unexpected inferno and when all seemed lost, rose up to meet the challenge and overcame it. I saw many acts of heroism committed, most of which were never recorded in any battle logs.

Those of us on that beach that day knew that we had to leave it soon and that we had to charge inland; though I'm sure there were some of us who would just as soon go back the way we had come. If we stayed on that beach, we would all soon perish from the shell fire and the bullets that descended upon us.

Remembering what the Lieutenant had once told me about staying with the platoon, I broke away from the wounded near the water's edge and crawled to the base of the first cliff leading up the side of the island, where I had seen some of my comrades go.

The men of the 2nd platoon had formed into a skirmish line and all lay on their stomachs and faced the rising ground in front of them. I threw myself down on the sand among them and attempted to get below ground level by crawling into a small mortar shell hole. It wasn't over a foot deep and only about three feet in diameter. Sgt. Charles Goodling fell to the ground on my right side and tried to move into the same hole with me, the only part of our bodies that we got in there was our stomachs. Even under those conditions, he grinned at me. "What do you think of combat now, Doc?" he yelled.

"I don't like it. I'm scared," I replied.

"Who the hell ain't!" he retorted.

"Charley we've got to get the hell off this beach, what's wrong, why don't we?"

Goodling grinned, "We will when the Lieutenant says so, if we're not dead first!"

We both tried to squirm into the shell hole a little further. It was a ridiculous attempt, and we both began to laugh. Goodling said, "Stay near me from now on Doc."

"Why?" I asked, thinking he had some plan to assist me.

"To plug up any holes you see in me, that's why!"

"Is that why you're snuggling up to me this way?"

"Hell yes! Don't you know that most of the bullets are coming from your side?"

He laughed, shook his head and added, "goddamn corpsman!"

It was all crazy, we lying there and laughing and yelling like that while passing bullets made those, "Tzing - tzing - tzing" sounds as they went by us. The bullets that hit near us would make a "splat" sound and the sand where it hit would kick forward in the same direction the bullet was going. It was fascinating in a way to watch it all take place.

The steel fragments from the exploding shells were making another louder sound. The sounds varied depending on the size and shape of the fragment. Some would go "Shuush," others, "Shus - shus - shus" and when they hit the sand a puff of steam or smoke would rise and blow away because of the breeze. The attempt at laughter was rather a weak one, though it did help dispel tension. I was really scared. Every man of us there was scared.

The exploding shells continued landing among the men, bouncing or tossing them into the air. I asked Goodling a rather dumb question.

"How do you know who is dead around here and who is not?"

He simply answered, with a grin, "Oh, Hell! That's easy. The ones that don't get up when it's time to go are dead!"

Lt. Horvath appeared at Goodling's side and fell to the ground with his head near ours. "We've got to get off this beach. Get your men ready to move out!" he yelled out in order that he could be heard above the noise. "Go tell your men!" The sergeant leapfrogged over me and scrambled away in response to the Lieutenant's order. The Lieutenant began to move away from me and then settled back down. He turned to me. "When we move out I want you to keep up with me. Don't stop to help anyone! Do you understand me?" He startled me with that order. The picture of that long, hot, exhausting hike up the side of Murphy's mountain back at Camp Pendleton flashed in my mind, "Yes Sir, I do," I answered, though it was still difficult for me to accept that I had to ignore my fallen comrades as they lay wounded on the ground needing help, as I continued to run by.

The bluff directly in front of us was twenty to thirty feet high. I would guess that it was constructed by sand that had been blown there during storms coming in off the sea. It was a long ridge, running from the base of Mt. Suribachi, along the beach northward for about thirty five hundred yards. The D Company Marines were lying along the base of this bluff or embankment seeking the shelter of its overhang from the steady deluge of bullets coming down onto us from the mountain. I could see some of our officers crawling out in front of the line, positioning themselves so that they could be seen by the rest of us. I knew that we were about to leave this terrible beach to go charging up the side of the island to meet the Japanese. That suited me fine!

CHAPTER TWENTY-SIX

Gaining a Foothold

WE KEPT OUR eyes on him waiting for the signal to rise and run forward. He was kneeling on his left knee, his right supported his elbow, arm and hand that held his carbine. He kept glancing over his right shoulder expectantly, probably watching Captain Fields who would be making a signal to him soon.

A bullet passed by my face and struck the ground just beyond the officer's right knee, kicking up a spray of black sand. He seemed to ignore it. Another bullet struck the sand near the front of his left knee sending up a spray of sand into his face. That one drew his attention; he brushed the sand from his eyes and stared at the pock mark left in the sand.

I thought that something was wrong with him and shouted for him to get down; I could not understand why he ignored me. Was he really that brave or unconcerned of the danger he faced, or was it the stress of battle that was affecting his behavior so?

Regardless of the reason he remained kneeling and looking back over his right shoulder. I stared at him in amazement, expecting him to be struck down by a bullet at any second. Later on I would come to realize that he faced the danger knowing that those of us who depended on him were watching him. By positioning himself like that he assured us that he remained in command and his very actions gave us courage, confidence, and the will to continue on.

Suddenly, he rose to his feet. He apparently received the signal he was waiting for. He stood there with shell fragments and bullets whizzing by on either side of him while he demanded our attention by waving his hands and arms up and down. I didn't think he was going to do that for very long and expected to see him cut down at any moment by a piece of flying jagged steel. He paused near where I lay and yelled out, "Come on! Fix your bayonets, make sure your rifles are loaded, we're going over the top!"

To me this was the first I saw him get excited. He turned his back to us and began running straight up the steep grade in front of us. The men of the 2nd platoon rose from the ground, quickly formed into a skirmish line and charged forward. I intended to run right up to the top of the bluff, but I ran no more than twenty feet before being forced to slow down. The loose, soft sand sucked at my feet and buried them above the ankles. Each step I took seemed to take a lot of my energy.

Looking to my right I saw that all of Company D was on their feet and charging the steep grade. Obviously the Japanese observers saw the move and called for more shelling. It came down too, but most of it went into the ground that we had just left. I thought, "God help those men back there!" The Japs were determined not to let us leave that beach area. They wanted to hold us there until they pounded us into oblivion with their shelling. We were just as determined to escape that fate, and so we charged ahead to meet them on more equal terms.

The bank of sand that confronted us was very steep. Its face showed bodies of some of our fallen comrades, probably from various units of the 28th Regiment. Some had just crumpled onto the sand; others had been struck down and had slid back down the slope to an easier resting place. I fell into line behind members of Sgt. Goodling's squad and stepped in

Despite the hail of bullets, mortars and artillery, Marines who didn't keep moving became stationary targets.

their footsteps. I found that the earth was compacted more there and that made for firmer footing.

Halfway up the incline, the Marine in front of me paused and cautiously put his foot onto the ankle of a dead Marine lying in front of him. He was using the dead man's foot as a firm step, in order to climb higher on the incline as those before him had done. I followed and did the same. My heavier weight drove the dead Marine's foot deeper into the sand. I silently apologized to him and the thought struck me that even in death the marine was helping his comrade's move forward.

The din of the artillery and mortar shells smashing into the beach in back and below us was terrible. During the climb I could see the hot shell fragments tear into the sand on either side of me. I never would have believed that I would get this far without being hit and I can't understand it today. I reached the rim of the steppe by crawling on my hands and knees. I paused at the edge fighting to suck air into my lungs. In front of me lay a wide, flat, clear area that gradually rose to the saddle back of the island. To my left, about four hundred yards away was the northern base of Mount Suribachi.

One of our General Sherman tanks there was firing its cannon point blank at a target. I supposed it was at some type of bunker and that Japs were inside defending it. Up higher on the mountain side I saw artillery and naval shells exploding. Our Navy gunners off shore were blasting gun emplacements up there with their huge bore guns. I saw large chunks of rock smashed and then fall, the pieces sliding down the steep sides of the mountain. I was immensely impressed with the Navy's accurate gun fire.

Another tank, with the number 77 on it, rumbled up to join the first. Once alongside, its cannon pointed in the same general area as the other and then it let go a huge sheet of flame from its gun. The jellied gasoline, or napalm as it was commonly called, blossomed out covering a huge area in front of the tanks. It struck the ground and covered it with flame that continued to burn. As horrible as it must have been for the Jap defenders inside the bunker, I couldn't feel a bit sorry for them.

Our flame throwing tanks all carried the numeral seven incorporated in their numbered designation somewhere to let us know they were so equipped. The machines were frightening to someone standing on the outside watching them work. They rumbled, growled, and hissed and then all that burning gas and jelly shot out of the barrel of the gun barrel. I wondered just how a

Japanese soldier in a bunker would feel as he watched that tank rumble up, its gun pointed at him, and fire that stuff just before he was incinerated.

The slightly ascending plain in front of us was fairly clear of exploding shells. Most of the shells coming into our area were still landing onto the beach in back and below us. Since the noise from the explosions were further distant, I could hear better. Now I was aware of the "tzing - tzing - tzing - tzing" of passing bullets. I could actually count the bullets fired by different gunners up on the mountain. The bursts were in fours and fives and sixes. The slugs tore into the sand around our bodies and kicked up sand in a decorative 'rooster tail' design.

Seeing the feet of a Marine ahead of me I crawled up beside him until my left shoulder touched his right. He was lying there in a prone firing position. He appeared to be aiming his M1 rifle at a target far out in front of us. Thinking the he was one of my platoon comrades; I pushed my rifle out in front of me too and pointed in the same general direction as he. I shouted toward his ear, "What do you see?" He didn't answer nor did he appear to hear me, because of the racket I thought. I struck out with the back of my left hand and struck his right shoulder. He didn't answer or even move his head. I realized he looked as though he were dozing there with his right cheek resting on his rifle stock. I placed my hand on the top of his helmet and pulled it toward me and then I saw the little round hole in its left side. I pushed the helmet back and a gray looking liquid oozed from under the right side of it and down the side of his face. It was the first time I had seen a human's brains.

I was up and running in a second and away as fast as I could. I felt panic for the first time rise in my chest. I ran to catch up with my comrades whom I could see crawling along the ground off to my right. I felt that I had to get away from that dead marine. The ones I had seen on the beach were different than this one to me; they were mutilated badly as they died. This dead Marine looked as though he were sleeping. He died quickly and for some reason that bothered me more, perhaps because the realization that he was dead took me by surprise; I don't know. Once I reached my comrades I threw myself down among them. Then as I fought for breath I realized what a stupid thing I had just done. I had ignored my training and further jeopardized my life giving in to panic like that. I was determined not to do that again!

Part of the 28th Marine Regiment had come this way before us. They had come up somewhere near the place we were now, then swung their battle line to the left in a huge arc and faced Mt. Suribachi to commence assaulting it. Now, that entire regiment was facing the mountain and the backs of those men were to the north and the rest of the island.

The island at this point was approximately one thousand yards across. It was the narrowest part of the island and the immediate goal of our landing force was to cross the island, cutting it in two separating Mt. Suribachi from the high northern land. Units of the 28th Marine Regiment had reached the top of the saddleback by around 1030 hours and could look down onto the western beaches. They reported at that time that they had cut the island in two. Maybe they did, but it was only visually done I believe as I spoke to some of those Marines later in their forward position and they had told me that they had not gone onto the beach itself.

The Marines of the 27th Regiment had landed on the right flank of the 28th Marines. They drove inland and then their left flank curved and swung to the right in a large arc until they faced the northern part of the island with their left flank supposedly touching the western beaches. To the right flank of the 27th was the 4th Marine Division. It had landed at the same time as the 5th Division and formed a line from the beach on which they had landed, inland to a point at about the center of the island to where their left flank was in contact with the 27th's right flank.

The plan was for the 4th Marine Division to be on the right, the 27th Marines on the left and that would form an assault line from beach to beach facing north. At their backs were the 28th Marine Regiment facing south in their assault of Mt. Suribachi. As I saw it there was a corridor between these two units of about three hundred yards. The 26th Marine Regiment, of which I was a member, landed and drove inland along this corridor until we reached the opposite shore. Once we filled the corridor with our troops, we were in a position to reinforce any unit, either north or south of us, involved in a direct assault on the enemy. At least that was the best laid plan!

Once Lt. Horvath had led us to the top of the steppe, we turned slightly to the right where we merged with the rest of D Company and became much too closely involved with the men of the other platoons. There was a lot of confusion for a few moments until the officers finally got us straightened out. When troops are lying face down on the ground to escape bullets and steel splinters, it is difficult to hear or see signals directing them to move one way or another. When men of several units are interspersed, it is almost impossible to separate them quickly.

The men of Company D were now strung out two and three abreast and we moved up a gulch or dry wash, to the north which led to Airfield #1. We crawled along on our hands and knees to escape the constant hail of bullets still coming in at us from Mt. Suribachi in back of us.

I heard loud voices coming from the direction of in front of us. Raising my head from the sand I saw Captain Tom Fields and 1st Lieutenant Jack Jones come back our way from the head of the column. They were scrambling over the sand and on top of any Marines who happened to be lying in their way. Lt. Jones yelled to Lt. Horvath to "take over and lead the company on up the hill," as he and the Captain were going to talk with Col. Sayers, the battalion commander. Lt. Jones then crawled right over me on his knees as he passed by. The two officers continued on back down the wash to the rear of the column while the long line of men began to move slowly on up the draw.

About ten minutes passed. We had only gained about a hundred yards while crawling on our stomachs when I heard Lt. Jones yelling again. He

Marines near the beach poised to attack

came up the line in back of us, "Stop! Stop, Goddamn it stop..., stop! Horvath... you're leading the men into the Jap lines!" Jones went on to scramble over any man who happened to be in his way and that included me again. Those of us who heard his words lay face down in the sand to pause until we were given further orders.

Within a few minutes, Lt. Horvath came back to the platoon. He was red faced, upset and muttering to himself, I believe because he had been cussed out in front of the men. Evidently, he was supposed to have taken us straight up the rise to the center of the island instead of the diagonal route we were on. I thought Lt. Horvath acted correctly as I heard Lt. Jones tell him to lead us up the hill and I presumed that was in the direction we had been going.

It was here that something leaped into my mind. The 27th Regiment was supposed to be, according to the battle plan, now on our right flank. Then what was this about us moving into the Jap lines there now. I began to think that all was not going right and that there was a lot of confusion as to where each unit was to be.

It was amazing to watch Lt. Horvath disengage our platoon from the rest of the company. He did it by standing up in all that confusion and shouting out, "Second platoon, this way..., this way...." Then he ran away off to our left. Those of us nearby picked on the call and repeated his words, "Second platoon, this way..., this way!" Then we all followed him. When I caught up to him the thought crossed my mind to congratulate him for doing such a fine job of separating us from the rest of the men. I quickly changed my mind though, when I saw the look on his face; he seemed to be under a lot of stress and probably would not appreciate hearing any comment from me.

Once Lt. Horvath got the platoon separated from the rest of the company he said that we would go straight up the hill to the saddleback and cut the island in half. The squad leaders took over their men and were encouraging them to move out. We all got up on our feet and scrambled along on hands and knees, 'crab like' across the sand. We floundered in and out of shell holes and crawled from one to another on our knees. The sand was very soft, but we received small cuts on our legs as we crawled over shell fragments buried partly in the sand. Again, the Lieutenant had fallen to the ground beside me and admonished, "Keep up with me, no matter what!" Then he scrambled away. Taking his words literally, I followed him and stayed close by his left side. If one of my Marine comrades fell to the ground with a bullet in him, I would just as soon not know it as I ran forward.

The platoon approached the huge concrete bunker that the *U.S.S. Tennessee's* guns had been firing at. Big chunks of reinforced concrete lay about on the ground and most of the bunker's foundation was reduced to rubble. It was only natural that my comrades gravitated toward the chunks of concrete as it afforded them protection from the enemy fire. The Lieutenant saw what was happening and paused long enough to yell at the men to spread out and not to bunch up or stop. He ran right through the rubble and out the other side. We were about one hundred and fifty feet past the bunker when the officer fell to the ground. He looked back over his shoulder and muttered, "What the hell...!" I looked back and saw two men struggling with each other on the ground. The Lieutenant jumped to his feet and ran back toward them.

I lay flat and buried my face in the sand. In a moment the Lieutenant was back and was urging us up and forward again. It wasn't until much later in the day that I found out that one of the men struggling back there

Marine on alert for snipers, seemingly oblivious
to dead Japanese officer beside him.

was a Japanese soldier who had come out of the broken bunker and had attacked one of our men. The Jap had been killed and later one of our company men, carrying a flame thrower came up and burned out what was left of the bunker. There were Japanese soldiers lying dead in this area. Their bodies were horribly mutilated, apparently by the shell fire from our warships. There were many parts of bodies lying on the ground and covered with black volcanic sand and flies.

Questions kept coming to mind about why the *USS Tennessee* had been shooting here when it was supposed that the 28th Marines had already been this way. I didn't see any sign of Marine Corps equipment here and I thought maybe things weren't going the way they should. The Lieutenant paused long enough to reorganize the skirmish line. The first squad was on the right side and Sgt. Goodling's 2nd squad took the left flank. The third squad would follow in a line spread out in back of the other two as we advanced. In this formation our left flank would be in touch with the men of the 28th Marines, who faced away from us and toward Mt. Suribachi. I moved over to the left flank and took a position there as we moved forward. I heard the Lieutenant shout to the men on either side of him, "When we move out, we are going straight over the top of the island and to the other beach. We'll cut the island in half."

Lying there on the sand waiting to move, I found I was confused about where we were. I couldn't see any Marines up front of us. But on my left, up on the slope I did see some helmets pop up and down as the wearers took a quick glance around. Those helmets belonged to Marines of the 28th Regiment I supposed.

As I rose from the ground with my comrades I could see wounded and dead Marines up on that slope to our left. I crawled over to some wounded and spoke to them. Most had already been attended to by their own company corpsmen. They told me that they had been lying in the sand for several hours now and were waiting for litter bearers to come up and evacuate them. They had yet to see anyone come up to help them back to the beach. Most of the dead and wounded had been struck by bullets that left a neat looking little blue hole tinged with red in their skins.

I put bandages on several of the men and offered some sulfadiazine tablets for them to swallow to prevent as much infection as possible. I probably treated a dozen men in that area, all of whom I identified belonging to the 28th Marine Regiment. I told the injured men that I couldn't get any help for them and that if they could, they should crawl back toward the beach before it got dark. To my surprise one of the men who had a serious flesh wound got to his knees and said, "Oh, the hell with it, I'm going back up and fight." Another younger wounded Marine joined him, they crawled away toward Mt. Suribachi in a valiant attempt rejoin their comrades.

Because I got involved with these men, I had been left behind just as Lt. Horvath said I might. I jumped to my feet, bent over and ran along the hill side to catch up. Running like that I could see more of the sand around me and that felt good. I saw those little spurts of sand and heard the "splat" as the bullets hit the ground. I was getting accustomed to the "tzing - tzing - tzing" of bullets going by. I could run better up here, even crab like where the sand was hard.

The Lieutenant had told us sometime before to drop our gas masks as they were pretty heavy and impeded our movement. Mine contained, besides the mask, several cans of Van Camp pork & beans and a dozen candy bars that I later was sorry I lost.

I watched the 2nd platoon up in front and to the right of me and from slightly higher ground. I saw them as they moved forward from one shell hole to the next. They looked like real combat veterans and I felt a sense of pride in them. They kept the skirmish line straight and used the terrain to their best advantage. I came up abreast of them on their left flank. Then I saw the tops of two Marine Corps helmets show above the rim of a shell crater off to my left. I threw myself onto the ground alongside two Marines who were huddled together in a small crater. I took them by surprise. One pointed his carbine at me and demanded, "Who are you?" I took him to be an officer.

"D Company, 26th Marines," I answered.

"Well, thank God you guys are here, but what the hell are you doing up here?"

"We're going to cut the island in half and go onto the western beach below." I answered.

"You're crazy! You'll never make it! You can't do that. There's only Japs ahead of us. They have stopped us cold right here! We've got a lot of wounded and dead right now!"

"Well, that's what we have been ordered to do," I replied.

"You go find your officer and tell him what I told you..., you understand?"

"Okay," I answered.

Both Marines looked very weary and dejected. They shook their heads, said nothing more and slumped down in their rifle pit.

I left there scrambling along on hands and knees. The 2nd platoon was strung out to my right. I could see only a few at a time as the men would leap from one hole and disappear into another. It was impossible for me to make an accurate count of them; fearfully, I was wondering how many men we had lost so far.

I looked about me to find that I had crawled into an area strewn with what appeared to be smashed building materials; there was a lot of wood and galvanized sheet iron there. On the far side I saw a barbed wire entanglement that had been constructed by the Japanese as a defensive measure facing the western beach. I lay there wondering how I was to continue on with that obstacle facing me when Sgt. Goodling came charging up and threw himself down beside me spraying sand over me. He gave me a big reassuring grin. It sure was good to see him right then.

We lay there side by side in the shallow crater and I told him what the two 28th Regiment Marines had said to me. I told him that I thought that one of Marines was an officer and he ordered me to report to my officer and tell him what he had told me. Goodling retorted, "I don't like the way things are going, something is definitely wrong and we could be right in among Japanese troops now; let's go find the Lieutenant and tell him what you learned!"

We crawled forward slowly, moving through the building material debris and on toward the barbed wire entanglement. An obstacle lying on the ground confronted me. Instead of crawling around it I reached out and took hold of a piece of metal pipe that was about six feet in length and about two inches in diameter, it was heavy and didn't seem hollow to me. I showed Goodling the Jap writing on it and said, "Look, this stupid pipe is plugged up with something!"

He shook his head as in disgust, saying, "That's a bangalore torpedo. If a bullet hits it when you're waving it around like that, it will explode and kill us." I knew what was coming next. "Goddamn Corpsman!" he said. Then he followed it with that big grin of his.

I answered, "How would I know, I can't read Japanese!" trying to make light of the situation.

When Sgt. Goodling had joined me, I had been looking at the barbed wire entanglement confronting me, barring my progress. The wire that lay in loose coils was often called concertina wire because when it was unrolled and stretched out it resembled the movement of that particular musical instrument. It was designed for placement in front of the defender's position to protect them from a frontal assault by enemy infantrymen.

There are several ways to affect a passageway through a wire entanglement. One method is to smash the wire with artillery. Another is to use a bangalore torpedo, a pipe shaped device filled with explosive that can be shoved under the wire and detonated. The bits of steel from the pipe will cut the wire strands. A third way is to cut the wire with wire cutters, but that takes time and allows the soldier to become an inviting target to the defender. One method taught us in training is where one soldier runs forward and throws his body up on top of the wire, smashing it down low enough so that his comrades can run forward and using the prone soldier's body as a bridge, cross over to the other side.

This is an effective, quick way, but one that is very painful to the man acting as the bridge. In all innocence I asked Sgt. Goodling which method we were going to use to get through the wire. He grimaced, shook his head and told me to follow him. I crawled along behind him. He slipped his bayonet and rifle barrel under the wire, turned quickly to lay on his back and lifted up a portion of it high enough so that I could crawl through, then he followed. Once on the other side I did the same for him. It was the first of many lessons I was to learn from this combat veteran.

We crawled forward and found ourselves on top of the saddleback separating Mt. Suribachi from the rest of the island. This was on flat ground. A dirt road, or the remains of it, came down from the highland to the north of us and continued on toward the base of Mt. Suribachi which lay to our left. To the front of us and down the incline lay the western beaches two to three hundred yards away.

Off shore, about one mile or so there was one of our destroyers turning and twisting, throwing up spray. Hundreds of yards beyond, a plume of water shot high in the air. The Japanese gunners were not having an easy time finding that ship as their target.

Far out to sea beyond the destroyer I could make out the silhouettes of larger ships, probably battle ships and cruisers. They only looked like gray smudges to me. There were also small orange glows that appeared periodically indicating broadsides of high explosive shells were being sent on their way. They were reassuring to me.

On the flat area where we lay were several sand revetments fashioned from sand that apparently had been built to protect airplanes from bomb fragments. Smashed pieces of concrete gave evidence that there had been bunkers which faced both the western and eastern beaches. There were no dead Japanese or Marines there and this caused the sergeant who lay beside me to murmur, "I don't like the looks of this at all. I think we're the first Marines to come this way!"

His repeated remark caused a sick feeling to increase in my stomach. I had on my mind what the two 28th Regiment Marines had told me about no one in front of them. I turned on my right side so I could face in that direction. I was very concerned that Japanese soldiers would come out of the rubble and attack us with bayonets. The sergeant and I lay there waiting for the rest of the platoon to come up abreast of us.

Lt. Horvath appeared, scrambling along over the ground toward us. He was urging the rest of the men behind him to hurry up. When he saw the sergeant and me lying there, he brushed off the sergeant's attempt to explain what information we discovered. It bothered me very much that he ignored what information we had. He seemed very excited and yelled at us, "Let's go, all the way, don't stop; cut the island in half!" Then rising to his feet he ran in the direction of the beach.

Goodling rose from the ground, "What the hell, why not?" he said. "Let's go, let's be the first!" I answered. It wasn't bravado that I wanted to be first, just an attempt to expel all the tension I felt building inside me. I knew we had been lucky so far in not meeting head on with the Japanese and that contact had to be made very soon. Sgt. Goodling turned and waived at the members of his squad and directed them forward, "C'mon, lets go!" he yelled. The entire quad rose in unison and charged forward. When I saw that happen, I was sure that we could expect a lot of mortar shells to arrive soon. If they did come, I wasn't aware of them tearing apart the ground as I wasn't there any longer.

The sergeant and I, followed by the squad, bent low to the ground, ran hard and fast. We went down the sharp incline toward the beach picking up momentum. We slid along on our stomachs, ran around and leaped over chunks of broken concrete and twisted reinforcement metal rods from the destroyed bunkers. We leaped from rock to rock on our way down. Fear gripped me, as I knew it did the rest of the men. There must be Japanese soldiers lying in wait among all that wreckage, for an opportunity to shoot at us. As we ran we pointed our rifles this way and that always expecting to fire at a Jap soldier who rose up in front of us. We jumped into shell holes, tripped, fell down, got up, ran on, never pausing long enough to allow an enemy marksman to sight in on us, we hoped. If they were going to shoot us, it would have to be while we were on the run.

Half way down the steep slope I had a good view of the beach that lay before us. It was smooth black sand and casual surf was breaking over it. At any other time it would have appeared pleasant and inviting enough for a person to stroll on. I knew death awaited us there now, the smooth sand hiding hundreds of anti personnel and antitank mines that the Japanese had buried while awaiting our arrival.

Goodling began screaming out, "What the hell has happened to my squad; why aren't they following us, who stopped them!" He stopped suddenly to look back up the cliff where he expected to see the men of his detail.

When he stopped I continued to go on and I passed Goodling running down the steep slope. He and I had come out onto a flat surface just back from the beach itself. In front of me was a Japanese military truck that was tipped over and lying on its right side, its engine toward the ocean. I believe the truck was a 1934 Ford flatbed, with dual rear wheels, and was quite similar to many of those I was accustomed to seeing in the fruit orchards of California. This truck had a metal cab and had wooden stakes fixed to the edge of the bed. To the right of the truck were the remains of a galvanized metal building. The walls had been smashed and had collapsed allowing the roof to settle down onto the wreckage.

Suddenly a hail of machine gun bullets came and scattered around us throwing up a lot of rocks and sand. Evidently we had come into view of Japanese defenders well concealed in bunkers located on the beach.

I heard the gun fire again and could hear the bullets pass by me. I no longer hesitated trying to decide where I was to run to next. I took another three steps and threw myself down on the ground on the south side of the overturned vehicle trying to find protection behind the engine. The surf came up and washed over most of me adding to my misery.

The Jap gunner seemed to know exactly where I was and began to shoot pieces off the hood and motor above my head. I crawled to the rear of the truck and tried to hide behind the protection of the dual wheels on the ground. Sgt. Goodling was there and we both huddled on the hard ground keeping the rear axle, springs, dual wheels and tires between us and the Jap gunner who shifted his fire to that part of the truck. That Japanese gunner seemed very frantic as well as angry as the bullets seemed to come at us in furious bursts and he didn't hesitate until he had at least used up a belt of ammunition. Those bullets hitting the wooden boards of the truck bed sounded as though there were a couple of men on the other side of the bed beating on it with hammers. Bullets were striking the dual tires over our heads and that made a 'whump' sound as they struck the rubber and caused the tires to spin lazily around, stop and go the other way.

Some of the bullets came through the wooden truck bed and tore out chunks of wood and splinters that showered us. Several pieces stuck into the skin on my face. We dared not raise our heads from the ground for fear of getting struck in the face by more of the wood and metal splinters or by the bullets.

We lay there on our stomachs, faces pressed to the surface of the ground, and made a futile attempt to dig away the earth with our hands to form a depression into which we could lower our bodies for better protection. The ground was too hard; we were lying on ground that had been prepared for a road surface. Somehow, we must rise up off the ground far enough to reach back and loosen the entrenching tools that were strapped to the back of our packs. I reached out and began to fumble with the straps holding Goodling's shovel. He yelled out, "No, don't, wait!"

Above the noise of the bullets striking the wood and metal of the truck I could hear someone yelling. The voice was coming from the direction of the incline that we had just descended. I looked and saw Lt. Horvath who was crouched in a dry wash or crevice in the earth about a hundred yards up on the hillside. The rest of the platoon was nowhere in sight. Goodling said, "It's Horvath. I think he wants us to come back up there."

"How the hell are we going to do that? We'll get killed!" I answered.

We lay there for several more minutes realizing that it was just a matter of time before one of those bullets would tear into us or before the Jap would call up a mortar and blow the truck and us into small pieces. The Lieutenant kept yelling at us. I could only raise my head a little and peer out from under the visor of my helmet at him. With my face pressed into the dirt I asked Sgt. Goodling what we were going to do, He did come up with a suggestion. He said with some sarcasm that the machine gunner was on the other side of the wrecked building and why didn't I just throw a grenade at him?

Not thinking that he was joking under these circumstances, I pulled a grenade out of my dungaree pocket, pulled the safety pin and threw the grenade as far as I could out toward the building. Then I pressed my face to the dirt just before the grenade exploded. That didn't slow the machine gunner up one bit, he kept on firing. I raised my head up enough to look at Goodling. Even under these circumstances he was grinning at me and said, "That gunner is probably one hundred or so yards away on the other side of the building, you could never throw that far!"

That remark disturbed me greatly as I realized he was making fun of me. I had already realized that when he fell to the earth along side of me. It was by no accident that he placed his body on the opposite side of me from where the bullets were coming. But, I was angry at myself too for being so ignorant, if not stupid. Regardless of my feelings at the time, I was about to get another lesson of survival from my friend.

Goodling explained that he estimated, from the time the machine gun fired and to when the bullets struck the truck, which perhaps a second to a second and a half passed. He said that as soon as the bullets struck the truck he would jump up, take three steps and dive for a shell hole or cover before bullets came in the next burst. He warned me, "No more than three quick steps you hear!" I nodded at him in agreement, but thinking that it a crazy damn fool idea! The Jap gunner, seeing him run like that would take two to three seconds to change his aim before firing and hopefully this would allow Goodling enough time for those three steps. I thought there was more wishful thinking to the idea than common sense.

But, no sooner than the sergeant spoke did a burst of slugs tear splinters out of the truck's wooden bed just above my head. Goodling was up in an instant and took those three steps. I last saw his body stretched out horizontally as he made a diving lunge forward into a shell hole some ten feet away. As his feet disappeared over the lip of the hole I could see the next burst of machine gun bullets smash into the crater's edge.

I don't believe I thought at all. Later, I thought perhaps I panicked again. To my surprise I was on my feet, and I took those three steps before hurtling my self forward toward the same hole that Goodling had disappeared into. I landed on my head, shoulders and upside down at the bottom and as I twisted around I saw Goodling's feet disappear over the rim closest to the incline on the side of the island. I couldn't believe that I wasn't hit as I tested my arms and legs to see if they would work properly. I was very afraid. I realized that Goodling and I had run onto the beach and out in front of the Japanese bunkers defending the western beach. We had done a foolhardy thing placing ourselves in plain view of the Japanese machine gunners.

Being left alone, I was fighting the panic that was enveloping me. I struggled to retain control. I didn't want to jump up foolishly and be shot. At the same time I had no desire to be left alone down there on that beach that I knew was under the control of the Japs. I didn't get up and run again. I knew the Jap was waiting for me so I dug a trench through to the next hole and I moved across quite a few yards of terrain that way toward the cliff until I believed I was safely out of the view of that Jap gunner. Anyway, he didn't fire at me anymore that I knew of.

When I reached the base of the incline, I crawled into a dry wash leading back up the way we had come. I couldn't see Goodling or the Lieutenant anywhere. I supposed that if they had been wounded or killed I would have seen their bodies somewhere along my route.

I crawled through the rubble on the side of the steep incline. It was slower moving than when I had come down earlier. I pushed my carbine out in front of me with my right hand and pointed it this way and that way, ready to fire at any movement among the broken concrete or crevasses.

While on board ship we had been told that the Japanese had constructed tunnels throughout the island that connected their numerous caves and bunkers to one another. I expected a Jap soldier to appear at any moment from one of those and I wondered what would happen and how I would react. It took me fifteen or twenty minutes to crawl up the island's side and I was feeling very lonely and vulnerable. I figured I was lost and that I should try and join up with a 28th Marine regiment unit when I crawled into one shell hole and to my relief found Lt. Horvath and Sgt. Goodling huddled inside it talking. They stared at me and Goodling said, "Oh, there he is now!"

The sergeant was reporting to the Lieutenant what we had seen down on the beach. I listened, but all I wanted to hear was the Lieutenant's explanation of why had he ordered us to go down to the beach, then as we got there he called us back. We were almost killed! But, I didn't ask..., and he didn't offer an explanation.

Chapter Twenty-Seven

Touching the Enemy

Lt. Horvath told us that we were to 'dig in' and hold the line 'right there' for the night. Goodling's squad along with the remainder of the 2nd platoon of the company were to dig in beginning with a line that extended from us back a short way toward the eastern beach and then curved around to the north. The company would be tied in with the rest of the battalion and the 27th Marines which was on its right flank.

The Lieutenant jumped up suddenly and without explanation, ran off leaving Goodling and me sitting alone in the shell hole. The Sergeant explained to me that we were sitting at an apex of a triangle and that we were to dig a rifle pit right here. He then got to his feet, and told me that he was going to check on the rest of his squad, but he would be right back. He scurried quickly off to the rear somewhere leaving me feeling very lonesome and vulnerable.

When he returned, I had the rifle pit almost dug out and he helped me finish it. We had it figured that we had to face the enemy toward the beach to west and at the same time to the north. The rest of his squad, which was strung out in a line back toward the eastern beach, would face north toward the highland where the 27th Marines were supposedly dug in.

The Lieutenant had informed the sergeant that the men of the 28th Marine Regiment were stretched out in a line beginning with our position to the base of Mt. Suribachi to our south. If there were Marines a short way off in that direction, I couldn't see them as I was not going to risk getting shot by raising my head above the edge of our hole to look for them.

Throwing the sand out of the pit did attract two young Marines of the 28th Regiment though. They came crawling and sliding across the sand to us on their stomachs. They appeared happy to see us and forced themselves into our small foxhole without invitation. They were a sorry looking twosome and described their battalion's position as 'bad'.

They told us that after landing on the beach hours prior, they had forced their way up to this area without much opposition. When they could look down and see the western beach they stopped. Then all hell had broken loose as mortar, artillery and machine gun fire had cut their men down. The two went on to describe how many casualties they had suffered and that only about fifty feet from where we now sat was a large shell or bomb crater that had about fifty or sixty wounded men in it awaiting evacuation back to the invasion beach, but so far no one had come up to help. They and two other riflemen were the only able men to protect both the wounded and their position from an enemy attack. The two agreed that they had not seen an officer for over two hours. They had understood that all of the officers were dead or wounded now and the highest ranking man that they had seen was a corporal. He had come by some time ago and told them to dig in and hold their position; he then went away and never returned.

As they talked my morale was certainly dropping and I guess that Sgt. Goodling heard enough too. He told the two men to return to their rifle pit and to tell the other two men over there to stay put also until otherwise directed by a superior. He reassured them that we were on their right flank and that we would protect them here All they had to be concerned with were the Japanese coming up from the beach, The two 28th Marines looked a little relieved and went scrambling up and out of our hole and back toward their own position. As we watched them go, neither they nor us knew that they would not be alive when dawn came.

Out at sea to the west, I could see an array of warships and coming from several of the larger ones were puffs of billowing smoke and flashes of black and dull orange. These were battleships and cruisers that were firing at targets on the island to the north of us. Even above the noise of the battle going on for Mt. Suribachi to our left, I could hear the rumbling of the ship's heavy guns rolling in across the water. The crash of their exploding shells off to our right made me think hopefully, that the gunners out there could clearly see their target and would not confuse us with the enemy.

Goodling and I were quite concerned. We were on the defensive line just at the point it turned 45 degrees to the left. We felt as though we were abandoned and out on a point where we had little protection on either side of us. Darkness was coming fast and a heavy choking acrid black smoke drifted along the ground coming from the northwest and from the area of the exploding naval shells. The smoke hugged the wet sand and a slight drizzle kept pushing it down so that it couldn't escape. Off to the north we began to see the orange flash of artillery shell fire now that the sun had fallen below the horizon.

The Japanese on Mt. Suribachi kept up an incessant fire in our direction. They might as well shoot everything they had at us, as not many were going to live more than a few more days anyway. Now that there was darkness coming on, we could see the tracer bullets that were interspersed with the regular ball ammunition come down searching for us. I kept thinking as I watched the streams of tracers float out toward us, why don't they shoot at the Marines down at the mountain's base instead of us, after all they are closer! I really supposed it was because the Japanese soldiers couldn't see past the ledges below them in order to get a proper aim. It was obvious that most of the artillery shells exploding among our troops were between our position and the invasion beach down in back of us where we had landed. Marines down there on the beach were unloading ammunition, food, and other supplies in plain view of the Japanese on the mountain and those artillery observers up there were bringing guns to bear on the beach and the vehicles leaving from it. Not only did artillery shells arrive from the

LCVP buffeted by the rough surf as he attempts a landing .

mountainside defender's positions, but many more were being sent from the northern part of the island as well. From the sergeant's and my position, we could not see the beach very well though, due to the curvature of the land between the two points. I did see a few amphibious landing craft that came dashing up to our position stop, back up to a certain spot, and dump out onto the ground many loads of Jerry cans containing fresh water for us. These tracked vehicles would then dash off for the beach amid a hail of cannon and mortar fire as the Japanese gunners sighted in on them.

I knelt there in my foxhole and had an almost unbelievable view of what war was really like. Exploding shells covered the terrain, blowing men and equipment high into the air. Men running across open land were cut down by bullets and appeared as though a scythe had been swung at their legs. Those terrible flame throwing tanks were still at work at the fortifications at the base of the mountain. I wondered again how the Japs might feel as they watched the monsters work closer and closer to them and could imagine how frantic they must appear and act as they fought for their lives. I watched the beautiful and sinister looking tracers float out from the sides of the mountain and arc down into the assaulting troops below.

Some of them hit the five gallon Jerry cans in a dump near our position. I could hear the bullets strike the cans making a "pok, pok, pok," metallic sound and on some cans I could see the little streams of water pouring out. I commented to Sgt. Goodling on how many bullets were coming our way, "Don't worry about it. You'll never hear the one that gets you," was his casual and cynical remark. One LCT unloaded its load of cans and then instead of speeding away back toward the beach, swung around in a backing motion until it was a few feet from our rifle pit. Goodling began screaming as loud as he could, "Get that 'goddamn' thing out of here! You're going to draw fire on us!

One crew member jumped from the vehicle and stooped over along the right side tracks and was peering into the area between the sprockets and the dollies. "It's barbed wire all right, it's all hung up in there," he yelled up toward the vehicle's cockpit. Then he reached into the track area between the track's mechanisms and grabbed at the wire caught there. The driver not aware what he was doing put the vehicle in gear and moved ahead slightly, trapping the Marine's arm in the gears and cutting it almost off just below the elbow. The Marine stood up, stared at his arm began was screaming, "My arm, my arm, its cut off!

I leaped from my foxhole and reached the Marine where I placed a tourniquet near the stump and stopped the bleeding. I injected morphine in the man's upper arm and just then another battalion corpsman appeared on the scene. Ph M. 3/c Billy Sims came up suddenly from nowhere it seemed and helped me bandage the stump of the man's arm using his bayonet scabbard as a splint. Billy said he knew where the battalion aid station was and helped the Marine to his feet and then with his arm around the injured man to assist him the two of them walked slowly across an open space toward the rear of our position. That was an amazing sight to behold. As the men walked slowly, I could see those little puffs of sand spurting up in front, in the rear, and on either side of them as a machine gunner on the mountain in back of me kept firing bursts of bullets at them. I ran to my foxhole and dived into it, then straightened myself out and watched as the two men disappeared from view behind a hummock of sand. Sgt. Goodling watching shook his head side to side and muttered, "Well, I'll be Goddamned!" All I could think was, "How come no bullets hit them?"

All troops entering combat are given passwords to be used, usually at night. Prior to leaving the ship we were given one too. For the four first days the password would be the name of an American president. The password procedure was this: the challenger would call out, "Who's there?" and the person challenged would have to answer back the name of a president. The first Marine would have to come back with the name of yet another president. To forget the password could result in someone being shot by a comrade.

As darkness settled over the island, Goodling and I leaned forward and watched over the edge of the foxhole. We pushed our rifles out in front of us and held them in readiness. We knelt there side by side, our arms and elbows supporting our weight. We peered into the gloom watching for any movement that occurred out in front of our position that seemed suspicious. Goodling concentrated on the ground to the west and toward the beach while I watched the flat ground to the north and the slope that began some fifty yards across it.

Later my knees and leg muscles began to ache because of me leaning forward putting a strain on them. I straightened up a bit, but stayed on my knees and tried to massage the muscles in my legs. There was slight drizzle falling and I foolishly placed my carbine in a waterproof cover that I carried for that purpose, and then I laid the rifle down on the edge of the foxhole at my right side. It was then that I saw a Marine running toward our position from about one hundred feet away. He seemed to have come from my right and from the same direction that I had seen Billy Sims disappear with the injured Marine. My first impression of the lone Marine was that he was a 'runner,' a Marine who carries messages between command posts of the various units in the field. This one's apparent intended route was to run by us on our right along the remnants of the dirt road leading to Mt. Suribachi. Sgt. Goodling called out a challenge, "Halt, who goes there? What's the password?"

The running man turned abruptly toward us and dropped to his right knee at the edge of our hole at my right side. He shoved the muzzle of the carbine he was carrying out until it was inches from my chest. "Never mind the password, 'Bud,' I'm in a hurry to find the regimental CP!"

I was astounded. I could barely see his face in the dim light and his features were similar to those of some of the Navajo Indians we had in the battalion who acted as communication personnel. But, I could recognize a Japanese person when I saw one. Many of my schoolmates throughout the years in California had been of Japanese descent. Still I could hardly believe what confronted me. This guy was dressed in an American Marine uniform. His Marine helmet shaded his face from the dim light and from further scrutiny. He held his right forefinger on the trigger mechanism of the carbine and my eyes focused on the safety button that projected through to the left side of the weapon. The safety button was off and the rifle ready to fire.

In training it is pounded into a Marine's head that he is not to point a weapon at anyone unless he is ready to shoot that person. Here I had an impulse to tell that to this Jap, even though I knew he was one. Goodling challenged the man again, "What's the password? You're supposed to give the password!" The Sergeant's voice sounded strained and sort of choked; I wished that he wouldn't ask for the password again.

The Jap said, "Never mind, I've got to find the regimental CP and the colonel!"

"Why?" asked the sergeant.

"Because I have to send a 'wireless message', Mac, that's why."

His English was perfect. There was no suggestion or hint of a dialect. Even the slang words, 'Bud' and 'Mac', came out perfect..., much too perfect! No Marine I ever knew spoke like that let alone use 'wireless' as a substitute for the word 'radio.' I felt my stomach rise in my chest!

Goodling finally made a comeback and said, "I don't know where the colonel or the CP is." Thank God, he didn't insist on challenging the Jap any further as I was about to get a bullet in my chest if he did and maybe could still yet. Upon hearing Goodling's words I shrugged my shoulders and shook my head, indicating to the Jap that I didn't know the answer either. The Japanese soldier leaped backward for several feet, swung around and facing Mt. Suribachi disappeared out of sight over the brow of a slight rise of sand next to me and into the darkness.

"That's a Jap!" I blurted out

"I know it!" Goodling answered and he knocked me aside with his raised M-1 rifle. And pushed it out toward where we had last seen the Jap. I don't remember whether he fired or not as I huddled in the bottom of the pit. To fire he would have to shoot in the direction of some of his men who were dug in about thirty feet away. I pulled my carbine out of its rain proof cover and began to shake a little all over. I told Goodling that the Jap would have shot me in another second for sure if he were challenged again. Goodling responded to that by saying, "I know that, but I would have gotten him though." I knew that the sergeant was grinning at me; I could see his white teeth in the dim light. We settled down to wait some more. I felt disgust and anger rise in me because of the way I had allowed the Jap to get the advantage on me. I was determined not to have it happen again. I would kill the next man who didn't give the password. Goodling agreed with me and said he would do the same.

We poised ourselves to await the next threat. It was dark and the blackness was interrupted by the amber parachute flares that floated down toward the ground between us and the beach where we had landed hours before. Also, those pretty arcing tracer bullets were still floating out from the side of the mountain trying to find some luckless Marine.

Suddenly there was an explosion up on the little rise to the north west of us. Flame shot out from the hillside and came right at us. It was accompanied by the sound of a shell passing directly above our heads. I felt the breeze from the shell it was so close. Instinctively I fell to the bottom of our rifle pit and lay there. The shell exploded perhaps a hundred feet in back of us sending a sheet of sand over us. I thought it landed near the huge crater that had been described to us earlier by the two 28th Marines that contained the several dozen wounded Marines.

"Sounds like a 75mm. field piece," said the sergeant. "It's hidden up there on the hillside only about one hundred or a hundred and fifty yards away."

I said, "I think I felt the rushing air current as the shell passed shell passed by." It couldn't have been over a couple of feet above us! Another shell was fired, then another. Goodling said that if the barrel of that gun was lowered only fraction of an inch that it would be the end of us!

From behind us came the sounds of men's voices. Some of it was a call for help; others were cursing, moaning and howling. The sergeant and I leaned forward peering into the night toward the area of the gun flashes. We listened for sounds that would betray the Japanese approaching our position. Then very gradually the sounds coming from the men in the area in back of us began to diminish. The area was then lit up again by a series of illuminating flares.

For a moment, Goodling's helmet, shoulders, arms and rifle were easily discernible in the glare. His helmet kept the light off of his face down to his mouth area. At times his mouth and chin were exposed to the flickering light of the flare that swung to and fro while in its descent. The shadowy movement around the sergeant's mouth, nose and chin gave him a ghastly appearance. I didn't like to see him like that. When I realized that he was grinning at me, I felt better.

Once it became very dark on the battlefield the shelling of our positions by the Japanese decreased considerably, undoubtedly due to the fact they couldn't see the results of their fire. Their indiscriminate machine-gun fire continued and the tracer bullets floated down toward us from Mt. Suribachi and from the north. Here and there on the ground about us a sudden flash would appear as a shell or hand grenade exploded.

I knew from our training experiences what the rest of our assault force was doing. They were digging in and preparing to defend the ground that had been taken from the enemy during the daylight hours. I knew what the Japanese were doing also; we had been trained to expect them to begin their counterattacks now that it was dark. They would rush our positions, attempt to disrupt communication lines, take prisoners for interrogation and try to kill our higher ranking officers. We were told to expect those tactics once we were in battle and that's exactly what was happening.

Goodling and I leaned forward, straining our hearing and eyes for movements that would betray the Japanese as they approached. Then I heard running footsteps and it felt as though my stomach jumped up into my chest. I could feel the adrenaline enter my bloodstream. I released the safety on my carbine and I began to squeeze the trigger as I saw a moving form in front of me. Before I could fire, Sgt. Goodling swung his rifle barrel abruptly, picked up my rifle barrel with the end of his bayonet and whispered sharply, "No, hold it!" The form stopped at the edge of our foxhole, sending a spray of sand into our faces.

"It's Horvath!" a whispered voice rasped. The Lieutenant lay there laboring in order to regain his breath. I desperately tried to regain my composure. I had been a split second away from shooting him. After a moment he swung his feet around and forced them into the foxhole between Goodling and me. He then gradually but forcibly lowered his body until the three of us were jammed into the hole shoulder to shoulder.

He told us that Japanese had stripped uniforms and equipment from some of our dead and were now wearing them in order to infiltrate our lines. They were known to be carrying explosives which they intended to use to blow up our ammunition supply dumps. Sgt. Goodling replied, "No kidding!" and proceeded to tell the Lieutenant about the Jap dressed as a Marine who had approached us and who was trying to locate the colonel. He described how the man spoke perfect English.

The Lieutenant said that about two hundred and fifty of the enemy had been moving along the western beach, just where Goodling and I had sought refuge behind the overturned truck. They were seen walking through the surf and also were known to be transporting troops by boat from the north to reinforce their positions on Mt. Suribachi. He added that we had better expect to be attacked and to be prepared for it.

I was thinking, "Oh Christ, and I was all for staying down there on the beach and defending it. Maybe I don't know a hell of a lot about military tactics after all!"

The three of us knelt there for a while in silence and watched the tracer bullets streaming along over the ground, forming all kinds of crisscross patterns. Suddenly, the Japanese field piece fired again and then three more times. Each time the shell went directly over our heads forcing us to cringe lower into the hole. I could again feel the breeze created by each of the passing missiles. The shells exploded in that same area in back of us where the wounded 28th Marines had been reported as being collected. Apparently, the Jap gunners had seen Marines moving about there before darkness fell;

sighted in on them and were now using that area as a known target.

I could hear Sgt. Goodling whisper to the Lieutenant, telling him what the two 28th Marines had told us earlier about the condition their battalion was in when the officer cut him off short and said, "You've been in combat before, sergeant, were those artillery shells or rifle bullets?"

He was referring to the shells that had, just moments before, passed over head. Puzzled by his question, I waited to hear the sergeant's reply. He waited for several seconds before answering, "Field piece..., Lieutenant!"

"Yeah, I thought so!" came back the officer.

The Lieutenant paused a moment before admonishing us again to kill everything above ground. He said, "Don't fire your weapons though as the Japs will locate you by the muzzle flash. Then off he ran. I was relieved that he was gone.

The sergeant and I sat in silence for about three minutes without speaking before the he leaned toward me and whispered, "The Lieutenant's beginning to act funny!" He was referring to the absurd question that the officer had asked about whether the shell had come from a mere rifle or cannon. The officer's behavior in this incident was the first of many abnormal acts I was to hear and observe of men while under the stress of battle, including my own.

Within the next two hours the Lieutenant came back two more times to check on our position and to tell us to be alert and to kill anyone "above ground." Both of the times that he appeared he ignored our demand for a password and caused me to push my rifle barrel out toward him in the dark with one hand, and my knife ready to stab him with the other. The sergeant had a bayonet on the end of his M-1 and it's a wonder he didn't stick him with it. The Lieutenant continued to encourage Goodling and me to kill everything that moved above ground. He sure caused a lot of uncertainly in our mind as to how we were to know who was approaching us the next time, a Jap or him. We hoped he wouldn't come back for the remainder of the night!

Chapter Twenty-Eight

The Infiltrators

We prepared for the worst as we were sure that we were facing Japanese soldiers to the front of us and on both sides. Then, too, we were aware of those who had infiltrated our lines and were in back of us. We took the hand grenades from our pockets and placed them on the edge of the foxhole in front of us and we familiarized ourselves on where they were and how we could reach for them in the darkness. I had a bayonet I had picked up off one of the dead Marines earlier in the day and had been carrying that in my belt. Now I stuck it in the sand beside the grenades. The carbine I carried didn't have a bayonet attachment as did the larger M-1s. I wished that it did. We settled down to wait quietly, even fearfully of whispering for fear of revealing our position.

My mind began to look for and find problems. I did whisper to Goodling after a long wait, "How am I to kill a Jap if I'm not allowed to shoot him and without a bayonet on the end of my rifle to stick him with?" He whispered back, "I wondered how long it would take you to think of that." I knew he was grinning at me in the darkness. We continued to sit there as a slight chilling rain began to fall on us. Often a flare would ignite and illuminate us and we would raise our heads only enough so that we could look quickly around our foxhole for a sign of an enemy. Both the Japanese and the Marines sent up many flares in order to see what the other side might be up to.

An illumination flare was sent up in the same manner as a regular mortar shell. The missile was dropped into the mortar tube where it slid to the bottom. Where there was a stationary firing pin affixed at the bottom of the tube that ignited the missile's propelling charge cap as contact was made. The missile was dropped into the mortar tube where it slid to the bottom, and its propelling charge was ignited by a stationary firing pin, and the flare was propelled out of the tube with a bang. At the very top of its trajectory the flare would ignite and a parachute would be released to float the illuminating and burning material slowly back to the ground. An observer watching at night, could see the shell arc after being launched in the darkness and be

Hoping to reduce enemy infiltration, illuminating shells, fired from supporting warships, light up the dark no-mans land between the Japanese and the front lines.

able to see its progress due to the burning propellant charge that hurtled it through the air. Because of the advance warning it would be possible to lower one's head below ground level before the illuminating flare burst out above in maximum brilliant light.

Once the flare was ignited it was lowered to earth gently as it swung back and forth under the parachute's canopy. An object on the ground that would ordinarily cast a shadow caused by sunlight would cast one here too under these circumstances. However, the flare swinging back and forth like that would cause the shadows on the ground to move and jump about in an eerie way. One's imagination can do interesting things. A rock or tree stump can become an enemy soldier whose intent is to crawl up to you and do you harm. A corpse, lying upon the ground near your foxhole can come alive and began to move.

The Japanese first came at us about 1900 hours. It had been about ten or so minutes since the last flare and Goodling and I had been kneeling there quietly waiting for some time. I heard footsteps on the sand on either side of us and then I could hear metal against metal, groans and curses, thudding sounds and exploding grenades off on our right side. Then someone was in the foxhole with us. I could sense that Goodling was struggling with him and I could hear the groans and grunts of two men battling. I reached out at the dark forms but was kicked backward by either Goodling or the Japanese soldier. Then I could see a dark form scrambling up the back and high side of the foxhole and I pushed my hand held bayonet out at it in a feeble attempt to stab at the moving form. Since it was very dark I couldn't see the sergeant who was crumpled at the bottom of the hole.

I whispered his name, he heard me and answered that he was OK and how was I? I said, "I'm all right." We both crouched there waiting and listening to men in the large crater in back of us. Some were crying for help. One voice was telling others to be quiet! We figured that the Japanese ran into and through our lines and they stumbled and fell into our line of rifle pits and on top of us. How all those injured men in back of us fared we didn't know and there wasn't any way to find out.

We crouched in the darkness while the cold rainwater fell, running from our helmets and down our necks, interfering with our attempt to hear well. Soon another flare lit up the area and we raised our heads just enough to peer over the side of the hole. We crouched in that position for another hour listening in the darkness and peering out whenever flares lit up the area. We strained our eyes watching any objects that appeared to move under the dim light of the flares.

I found it a problem to discipline my mind. It kept telling me that all our buddies were dead and that we were the only ones left alive and alone with the Japanese. I was armed with a carbine, bayonet, knife, and several grenades. How do I defend myself? Do I hold the rifle in my right hand and knife or bayonet in the other? If so, how do I throw a grenade? If I hold the rifle and a grenade, what do I do if a Jap jumps into the hole on top of me? I won't have my knife in my hand with which to stab him. With both hands occupied I couldn't pull the safety pin out anyway if I had to throw the grenade. The fuses on these first grenades were of the seven second duration type. That meant that once the pin was pulled and the handle released allowing the firing pin to strike the cap, there were seven seconds before the grenade would explode. Hell! A man could run a hundred feet easy in seven seconds. If I threw the grenade out in front of me, the Japanese soldier running at me would be in the hole with me when the grenade exploded. All these thoughts came at me and I was trying to organize them into some acceptable form when the Japanese came again.

They came at us at approximately 2000 hours the second time. Again, I heard the sound of padding feet on the sand out in front of us. I pushed my rifle barrel out from me to ward off an expected bayonet. I saw several dark forms running at us and one of those seemed to pick me as his target. I could see the gleam of metal from his rifle barrel and bayonet. He was almost upon me when he sidestepped to my right as he either saw me or sensed that I was there. As he placed his foot on the rim of the hole I ducked my head and quickly leaned to my right striking out with the barrel of my carbine. I held the stock in my left hand and the barrel near the breech with my right and I swung the rifle barrel hard at where I thought his right knee should

Night time infiltration attacks.

be. As the rifle struck bone there was a jolt to my hands and a loud crack and the running form fell to the ground with a thud and uttering a groan. I threw myself up on the edge of the foxhole in that direction and probed for the man's body with the carbine's rifle barrel's end with the intention of shooting. I couldn't feel him anywhere I thought he should be. I think his bayonet passed over my left shoulder as he took a swipe at me.

My attention turned to what was going on behind me as I could feel someone struggling while lying on the back of my legs. I kicked myself loose, twisted over on my back, reached out and grabbed. My left hand grasped the top of a closely shaved skull but lost my grip as the head twisted away. I could smell 'Jap' again. I reached, and this time I grabbed some clothing. My grasp came loose again and the dark form in front of me pulled away and scrambled up the back side of the rifle pit and disappeared in the blackness. There was struggling still going on, I could hear Goodling's curses, grunts, and groans and other thudding sounds associated with men grappling with each other.

Other forms were scrambling up the side of the foxhole sending down an avalanche of sand onto us. Then from the direction the soldiers had disappeared, came the sounds of more fighting, yells and curses. I turned my attention to Goodling who was lying on the bottom of the hole. This time I was sure he was dead. But, he was moving soon and struggling to sit up. I asked how he was and he answered that he supposed he was all right. After a moment he began to give me hell. He said, "Goddamit! There were two of them at least on me. Why didn't you help me? The bastards were trying to kill me!"

I did my best to describe what I had been doing while he had been fighting and that I had hurt one Japanese pretty bad. After a while he calmed down and told me that he thought he had been smashed on the head with a rifle butt. He didn't think he was bleeding or hurt bad though. And he thought he had stuck one of the assailants with his bayonet. We sat there trying to reorganize and prepare ourselves for whatever was to happen next, and I felt desperate. The sounds of fighting in back of us had ended, but now we could hear wounded men talking and asking for help as others told them to "shut up." or the Japs would zero in on them. I could visualize those poor guys lying there wounded and unable to defend themselves and not knowing what was to happen. Goodling and I sat there thinking that we were very lucky to have survived the second attack.

When a flare illuminated us again, Sgt. Goodling took the opportunity to look at his G.I. issue wrist watch; it was then 2050 hours. When darkness returned we poised ourselves and waited the next attack. I felt like I was about to jump from my skin, I was so keyed up. We strained to listen to every little sound that may identify an enemy who was creeping up on us.

I was startled when I heard a voice speak out just in back of us where the Jap intruders had climbed from our hole. The sergeant and I whirled about just as another flare lighted above us. We saw a young marine lying on the sand and peering down at us. He had crawled up to within four or five feet of us without our seeing or hearing him.

Goodling pointed his M-1 at him and demanded, "Who are you? "We could easily see the Marine's face by the light of the flare; he was no Japanese. The Marine said, "Fellows, can I come in. All my buddies are dead back there!" I felt something rise in my throat and I swallowed hard to get it back down. Goodling paused a moment while he looked the Marine over and then he said

"Yeah, sure, come on down!"

The Marine swung his feet around and let them down into our hole and then let himself down, forcing his way in between the sergeant and me. He was about my age and size, perhaps just a little over six feet tall and two hundred pounds in weight. He wore a pair of 'jump boots,' and spoke in a low wavering voice and described how he and five other Marine riflemen had dug their foxholes along the west side of a large crater that held the injured Marines we had heard about earlier.

He said that small groups of Japanese soldiers had come at them from our direction and from the western beach. He described how the Japanese ran at them with their bayonets held out in front of them and hurtled themselves into the marine's foxholes. Even though the Marines had killed many of these Japanese, this one Marine's five buddies were dead now, including the two who had crawled over and had spoken to us earlier. I remembered that those two earlier had said there were four of them in back of us instead of six, but didn't think it necessary to comment on that.

He said that he was the only survivor of the six men who had dug in together on the little knoll in the afternoon. He said that he did not know what state the wounded Marines in the large crater were in, but knew that they had been set upon and some killed or wounded when the Japs went through there before. Now, he said, he was scared and that he couldn't possibly stay back there all by himself.

Sgt. Goodling cut the conversation short by saying, "OK! Let's get ready for the next ones that come. They will come again! Doc, we have bayonets on our rifles, we'll hold them out in front of us. You lean forward and throw the grenades when they come at us."

Because of the Marine rifleman now squeezed into our small rifle pit I had been forced up against the right side of the foxhole. There was no time to make the hole larger. I leaned forward and the rifleman's right arm and shoulder went behind my left shoulder. This movement allowed him and the sergeant more room to maneuver as they held their rifles high. The rifleman in back of me had his right arm and rifle held up at a angle while he waited. Slowly, as the minutes passed his arm tired and he allowed it to settle down until the forearm was resting on my left shoulder. The three of us crouched there, waiting in silence.

We watched and listened. Grenades continued to burst over on our right side indicating to us that the Japanese were still trying to infiltrate there. As yet, I had not learned to distinguish the sound difference between the Japanese grenade and ours as they exploded. The Japanese machine gunners kept up that constant firing from the higher ground and I thought how ironic it would be if they shot their own men as they infiltrated our lines.

The rain fell lightly, the acrid odor of burning cordite powder was strong and heavy in the damp air. The odor bit into our nostrils and burned the back of our throats. I wanted to clear my throat, but was afraid that Japanese soldiers might be within hearing distance and would respond by throwing grenades or rushing at us with those long rifles and terrible bayonets. My back and leg muscles were cramping because I had been in one position for such a long while. The night was young; it would be a long time before morning came. I was scared, cold and miserable and I was sure the same applied to Goodling and the other rifleman as well. Now and then we could hear a wounded man, along the line of defense, cry out in pain or for help. Some of those sounds came from in back of us and some of the cries were cut off short as if muffled by a hand being placed over a mouth.

As I crouched and waited, my mind formed a plan of action. It turned out not to be the best. I unwisely pulled the safety pin on a grenade I was holding. I held it in my right hand and knew that as long as I held the handle tight against the body of the bomb, the cap couldn't fire and ignite the seven second fuse. I held my carbine with my left hand and pointed it out in front of me over the rim of the foxhole. I waited anxiously resting on my knees and leaning forward while resting on my forearms.

After about ten minutes had passed, my right hand, which held the grenade began to pain, I realized too late that I had been gripping it too tightly and strained my arm and hand muscles. I'd made a mistake! I couldn't put the safety pin back into the grenade's firing mechanism in the dark and besides, I had dropped and lost the damn thing anyway. I was stuck with a live grenade in my hand and I didn't dare ask Sgt. Goodling what to do as I knew what kind of an answer I'd get from him. I had just about decided to throw the grenade out in front of our foxhole when I heard running footsteps there. At the same time I felt Goodling's rifle bayonet slap the side of my shoulder and heard him say, "Here they come, throw it!"

I don't remember a thing for a long time after that. I believe I regained

Sgt. C. Goodling at top, unknown Marine from the 28th Marines, in center, dead with a bayonet wound to the chest, and under him is Richard Overton, unconscious because of a blow to the head.

consciousness because of the pain in my head and the back of my neck. I awakened to hearing an odd noise that seemed to be repeated over and over again. The noises soon formed the word "Doc" and only then I realized that someone was calling out for me in a whisper. The sharp strikes of pain kept repeating too and I realized that someone was jerking on the shoulder of my blouse and with each pull the waves of agony came. I recognized Sgt. Goodling's voice.

The sharpest pain was at the back of my skull and upper neck. I lay there feeling the rain water coming onto my face and eyes and thinking that I was hurting too much to be dead. I was on my back, my head elevated slightly up against the wall of the foxhole and it seemed that my legs were doubled back under my body and off to one side, but I couldn't feel any sensation in them. There seemed to be a heavy weight pressing on my body and holding me onto the floor of the hole. Other than some distant popping noises of small arms fire and tracers going by overhead it was quieter than any time since we landed.

I kept telling myself, "Don't move..._! Don't move...! Play dead! I was wondering about how bad I was hurt, if I was alone, and if it was safe for me to move.

Then I heard Goodling's voice, in almost a whisper, "Doc, Doc!" I felt him tug at my dungaree collar, "Doc, you OK?"

"Yeah, guess so, but there's something wrong with my head and neck, they hurt. What happened?"

He said that we had been in one "hellava" fight with a lot of Japs who had come into the hole on top of us and that I had been unconscious for about two hours and twenty minutes as it was now 2330 hours. He assumed that I was dead as I hadn't moved all that while even though my eyes were wide open and my face was covered with blood and rainwater.

I asked the sergeant, "Who's on top of me, a Jap?"

"No, I don't know who he is. He's that 28th [Regiment] Marine who crawled in with us," the Sergeant replied.

"Oh," I replied, however I could not remember any '28th Marine.'

I had a difficult time remembering what it was he was talking about. Perhaps an hour passed before my memory began to return, but very slowly, but even so, I could not recall most of what had happened immediately before the attack.

When I tried to move, I could only see dark red and the pain became even more unbearable, so I just lay there for a while. I felt nauseated and began to vomit and that stuff ran out of my mouth, down over my chin and onto my chest. I didn't have much to vomit since I had neither food nor water since 0600. When I recovered some I pushed on the body of the dead Marine and struggled to an almost sitting position. The dead body was then left sitting on my lap, his right shoulder against the back wall of the foxhole. The back of his helmet was up against the sand bank and when I moved him a lot of sand came cascading down into the hole.

When the next flare ignited overhead Goodling examined me the best he could under the circumstances as he had to lean over the corpse. He said he couldn't see any wounds although I was covered with blood that he assumed came from the dead rifleman.

When the next flare illuminated I turned my head and looked at the dead man. His blouse was ripped open and I could see a large gaping wound that went deep into his chest. The injury was a vertical cut that appeared about six inches long. With the light of the flare coming in over my right shoulder, I could see clearly into the Marine's chest cavity. Sgt. Goodling said, "Well, you can see now what a bayonet can do to you!"

There was no doubt that the Marine was dead. His eyes were partially open and his lower jaw sagged enough so that I could see his teeth and even inside his mouth. His skin was a light yellow color due to the loss of blood and the amber color of the flare reflecting off his skin. The descending swinging flare caused the shadows around his eyes, nose and mouth to move and jump. This caused the corpse to assume the appearance of him mimicking me. I felt an impulse to speak out and tell him to "stop it!"

While he lay on top of me all that time his blood had flowed from the wound and down over my body. It seemed that my lower body was fairly well soaked with his urine too as when death occurred, his muscles had relaxed, allowing that fluid to run from his body.

I removed my helmet and examined my head with my hands, it was painful when I moved, I felt sick to my stomach. I discovered a large dent on top of the helmet, probably caused by a kick of a foot or a rifle butt I supposed. Regardless of how the dent got there, I figured that helmet saved my life.

Goodling said that he was OK. He said that he got kicked and punched a few times but, couldn't find any bleeding. He was under the impression that he did stick one of the Japs with his bayonet as they came in, but he wasn't sure. He said that once the enemy was on top of us his rifle wasn't of much use.

Eventually, he and I agreed that we should try to lift the body of the dead Marine off of me and push it out of the foxhole. We grabbed the corpse by the belt around its waist and by the arms on both sides and began to lift and shove it up the back side of the foxhole. Each time we thought it was near the top and let go, it would slowly slide down and back on top of me. After a few tries at this I was beginning to believe that it didn't want to leave us and was intentionally resisting our efforts. We positioned ourselves for one last try. I finally got my knees up and under me and I was determined to throw the corpse up and over the edge of the foxhole this time. We got the body sliding up the incline and its head and shoulders disappeared over the top. We had the hips just about there when we heard a "pop" sound somewhere in back of me. Goodling said, "Grenade!" We let the corpse go and both fell to the floor of the pit and hugged the ground. The grenade exploded near the head of the corpse and literally blew the body back down into the hole where it came to rest on top of me again. This time it lay on its back, its right hip and buttocks covering my left shoulder and its lower legs balanced on my raised knees.

I suspected that as the corpse came back down the back side of the hole that Goodling was pushing it over onto me, but I never said anything about that to him. After that we just sat there and waited. I could smell the blood and the urine of the dead Marine and soon the two smells blended into one. Even today when I smell one I think of the other. Goodling thought that perhaps the grenade was thrown by one of our comrades from a nearby hole when they heard the noise we made.

Until morning came, whenever a flare was thrown into the air I would turn and look at the corpse's face. It was turned slightly toward me and its pale yellow skin really bothered me. The flare's light would give movement to his features and after a while I began to watch closely to see if he really wasn't making faces at me. Later I began to get the impression that the corpse was accusing me, "How come I got killed and not you?" At times I felt compelled to answer him that I didn't know why, but I never did. I did think of one thing again and again, I wondered what his mother and father were doing right then.

Whenever a flare would ignite overhead the first thing I would see was the dead man's boots as they were positioned directly in front of me. He had rolled his pants legs up a few inches higher than the usual. His body was twisted so that his boot toes were pointed downward toward my right side. The rainwater would fall on his body, legs and boots and run down to the toes where it collected and formed into large drops that would drip off onto my trouser legs and my shoes. I could hear and feel the water drops hitting me and after a while even when it wasn't raining, I found that I was listening and waiting expectantly for the sound of those drops to fall.

I asked the sergeant if he really thought that the Marine had been killed by a bayonet. He said that he thought so. He tried to reconstruct what had happened during the last attack. He described how he had heard the running footsteps and had swung his rifle toward me, striking my shoulder and said, "Here they come, throw it." He heard the grenade's firing pin strike the cap so he knew that I did throw it. Then in the darkness he saw several dark forms of the enemy in front of our foxhole. He saw their rifles and the glint of metal. He believed that they charged us while holding their rifles and bayonets out in front of their bodies at arms length. He was under the impression that a bayonet entered the Marine rifleman's chest as the Jap holding it lunged forward into the hole. Luckily the other Japanese bayonets missed the two of us. Apparently, I was struck with a rifle butt in the melee. I realized that if the young rifleman had not forced himself into the hole between the sergeant and me; that the bayonet might have struck me instead.

The sergeant went on to say that after some punching and kicking, the Japs had scrambled out of the hole. After waiting in the darkness for a while and not getting a response from either the rifleman or me, he decided that we were both dead and he braced himself for another attack or for dawn to arrive. When the next flare arrived to illuminate the scene, he saw the huge wound in the Marine's chest and, after shaking my shoulder and looking at the blood on my face, he decided I was dead too.

Sergeant Goodling and I sat there the rest of the night, with the corpse between us, but mostly with it sitting on me. There were no more attacks on our position but, we could hear fighting along the line. The rain was very chilling and after a while it got pretty cold before dawn came. Suddenly I felt a slight movement in the corpse's legs as they rested on my knees. It was very dark and I thought I might be imagining things about then. When a flare lit up, I looked up over my left shoulder and at the face of the cadaver. The eyes seemed to stare at me. As I studied its face I thought I detected a slight smirk of an expression that no doubt was further exaggerated by the flickering of the flare light.

After a while I felt the legs move again. This time I was sure it must be rigor mortis setting in, brought on a little early because of the cold wet night. I tried to rationalize it that way anyhow. Then there was more movement and then more. I could hardly wait for the next flare to light up so that I could see what the corpse was up to. When the flare ignited, I was already looking at the dead man's face. The head had risen from the ground a few inches, its mouth had opened wider and I swear the face was grinning at me. Both arms and hands that had been lying at its sides were now up off the sand and the legs had twisted in my lap. I could see that the knees were beginning to rise also.

Each time after the yellow and amber flares lighted the area and then died, I became more and more tense and frightened. The scene became unreal. The Hollywood movie industry could not have staged a more macabre production.

I couldn't stand it any longer, I pleaded with Goodling to help me get the corpse off me. We got onto our knees and lifted the body and then with one big effort we pushed it up and over edge of the hole with success. What a relief to be rid of it, but it seemed I was colder than before, now that the corpse was gone.

We sat there for the rest of the night and we could hear the Japanese moving around, trying to mark our positions for an artillery bombardment the next day. The Japs would call out to us. "Dirty Marine Bastards" or "Marine Son-of-a-bitch," hoping to get an answer so that they could throw a grenade at us. After one of these very lively sessions of insults, I couldn't resist whispering to the sergeant, "They don't mean me; I'm a U.S. Navy hospital corpsman!" In the darkness, I just had to imagine that he grinned at me.

CHAPTER TWENTY-NINE

A Painful Sunrise

THE DULL GRAY light of the early dawn poured into our rifle pit. I watched as it illuminated Sgt. Goodling's face. He was not grinning at me this morning. He looked exhausted and dirty. We huddled against the front wall of our rifle pit, keeping our heads down as we listened to the battle noises as they increased. Finally, it was he who got the courage first to raise his head high enough so that he could take a quick look around. He quickly lowered it again, "No Japs... but I can't see any Marines either!"

I looked out and was startled to see a number of dead Japanese soldiers lying on the northern side of our foxhole. Looking again, I quickly counted nine of them. I was puzzled and whispered to Goodling, "There's a lot of dead Japs out there, how come? They weren't there when we dug in last night!"

For the first time ever he glared at me and said, "What do mean, how come! How the hell do you think, how come?" Confused because of his reaction, I didn't respond.

For a while I huddled against the front wall of the rifle pit thinking. "What happened last night? What did I do, or not do? I don't remember very well after being struck unconscious and the only thing I know now is what Goodling told me." I decided I had better not to ask him any more questions though while he was in his present state of mind.

We were careful not to raise our heads above the rim of the foxhole for fear of being fired upon. Sgt. Goodling began calling out loudly to any of his squad members who might hear him. On the third try he received an answer from two who were dug in about twenty feet away in back of us, across that old dirt road.

Relief showed quickly on his face as he exclaimed, "I'll go check on them," and he left the pit with one leap and was gone, leaving me alone. I sat in the hole thinking about what may have become of the wounded and helpless men lying in that large crater in back of us. I wondered if perhaps I should run up there to see what I could do to help them, after all I was a medical corpsman, and it was my primary job to help the wounded.

Then I heard Goodling's voice, "C 'mon Doc... C 'mon..., over here!" The sergeant's call made the decision for me and without further hesitation. I leaped from the rifle pit and ran in the direction of his voice. I saw three Marine helmets at ground level in front of me and I dove for them, hit the edge of a crater and tumbled into the hole with the sergeant and two of his squad men. That was a very joyful reunion after spending such a horrible night. And even though I was in much agony I felt, "it is great to be alive this morning!"

A moment later I was asking Sgt. Goodling what he thought about me going back and trying to help the wounded as some may still be alive? He insisted that I not go there and that my first duty was to the 2nd platoon members. After all, what would happen if while I was away and the Lieutenant moved the platoon suddenly to a new location and I was left behind? "And remember something else," he grunted, "I heard what the Lieutenant said to you back there on the beach. You are to stay up with the platoon when we move forward and do *not* drop behind to help anyone!"

This directive, one of not being able to help a wounded man while we were moving forward was to plague me the rest of my days on Iwo Jima and much longer. I knew the reason for the directive, but I did wish that the officer would tell the entire platoon that he had given me such an order. I have always wondered since then what a man injured in battle might think of me as I ignored him while on the advance like that. Would he think badly of me the rest of his life? During the battle I was quick to learn that an officer didn't want to hear details of a man's death or extent of injuries as he couldn't afford to be drawn into such an emotional experience. I wondered how I could escape emotional involvement too.

The continuing battle for Mt. Suribachi started anew at dawn with the 28th Marine Regiment involved in close combat with the Japanese who tenaciously resisted their advance up the steep slopes. Peeping over the edge of our foxhole I could see a dozen or more *General Sherman* tanks in a battle line slowly advancing through the rubble at the base of the mountain. All had their machine guns chattering away and then one, then another would fire their turret gun to tear a target into pieces.

Two or three hundred yards to our rear, and in back of our tanks, were a number of pack howitzers. These small cannons had been entrenched in shell holes and their crews would methodically shove 75 mm shells into the breeches firing the weapon, eject the shell casing, reload and fire again.

Most of the north side of the mountain was covered by these exploding shells as well the ones from the tanks and from ships firing from far out to sea. The island was again becoming enveloped by rolling, choking clouds of smoke from burning explosive powder. It burned the inside of my throat, my nostrils and sinuses. It irritated and burned the inside of my lungs and it was agony to try to suck in such contaminated air.

Lt. Horvath came running along the line and once safe in our hole began briefing us on what faced us. I watched him talk. I was very much surprised to see him alive. He didn't ask any of us how we fared over the night hours. He said that the 2nd battalion would stay on reserve status and that we would reinforce the 3rd battalion on the western beach. I thought the "reserve status" remark was a bit humorous as, if we were considered in reserve last night, what must it be like up on the front line?

When the call came, we moved out of our holes going north onto the saddle back, the lowest part of the island. Up ahead I could see Captain Tom Fields crouched on the sand giving hand signals to the platoon leaders. The artillery shell fire increased sharply and we dropped to the sand, crawling forward on hands and knees. Some men chose to bend at the waist and run forward, but I saw a few struck down who fell forward on their faces, so I decided that it was better for me stay down on my knees and stomach.

An awesome explosion occurred in the center of the gathering formation before we reached the Captain. In some way the Japs had detonated a buried fifty-five gallon metal drum of gasoline and oil. No one was injured, but most of us were flattened by the explosion. The flames and black smoke shot straight up into the air and on top was the lid from the barrel which after reaching its peak in flight came back down spinning to the ground not far from where I lay. A few Marines near me began shouting, "Whoopee, do it again," until quieted by officers. I thought it remarkable that men under all that stress and facing that danger could retain such a sense of humor.

Quickly the company formed a single column and I found myself jogging on a footpath toward the western beach. The terrain was very rough as big chunks of volcanic rock and many bomb craters obstructed our progress. Even though I felt much pain in the back of my neck and head I felt better because of being able to run upright on my feet again.

The company was moving well when suddenly a machine gun began its chattering off to our right where I thought the base of Airfield #1 began. That was puzzling to me as according to our plans the 27th Marine

226

Regiment was supposed to be occupying that ground. The men in front of me moved faster and bent over lower trying to make themselves smaller targets. I heard that "tzing, tzing, tzing" as the bullets passed in front and in back of me. I came to the body of a Marine lying on the path. He had fallen on his stomach and his mouth was open as if he had been biting at the sand. The Marine in front of me leaped over the prostrated form and I followed him.

Further on I came to another Marine sitting on the path. He held his hands together on his left leg below the knee. I hesitated long enough to see that blood was gushing from a wound there. "Hey, use your battle dressing to stop the bleeding and crawl back toward the beach!" I yelled at him and I continued on. That "tzing, tzing, tzing" of bullet noise continued and I increased my speed to catch up with the platoon. I looked back at the downed man just once and saw him fumbling with the battle dressing kit that hung from his belt.

On the way to the western beach we began passing bodies of Japanese

Two dead Japanese soldiers along path towards Western beach. Note "tabi" style boots.

227

soldiers. They had fallen to the ground and lay in every such way, some crumpled, others lying as if taking a nap, but many of them had parts of their bodies missing causing me to think it could happen to me too. The soldiers were clad in khaki shirts and trousers, their legs wrapped with khaki colored leg wrappings. Most wore steel helmets; others wore a cloth khaki cap that had a red star fixed on front just above the visor. On their feet they had ankle high shoes with unfinished leather, not unlike the ones we wore. A few wore those odd looking rubber and canvas split toed sneakers they called 'tabis.'

Earlier in our training we had been told that during a night fighting situation we might feel for a man's feet to tell if he were a Japanese or not. If he was wearing a tabi, split toed shoe then we should kill him. After the last night's experience of rough and tumble combat I wondered 'how the hell' I was supposed to get someone in the dark to remain still long enough so that I could feel his feet.

As we approached the beach our platoon broke away from the rest of the company and we tumbled into craters, behind broken pieces of concrete or other cover, as we approached the edge of the wet sand at the water's edge. I found myself running along with Sgt. Brock's 1st squad as we sought cover behind a five foot high mound of sand. Heavy machine gun fire was coming from high ground north of our position and from down at the water's edge, so we all clambered for the south side of the sand pile, and we quickly discovered a concealed concrete bunker. I was one of those who happened to fall to the ground right in front of the bunker's crawl hole and when I did look up I was looking directly into the opening. The thought of bullets coming out of there caused me to scramble over other men in my haste to escape that danger. Lord, I hoped there weren't Japs in there! Sgt. Brock was yelling for one us to throw grenade in the opening. One of us did and the explosion jolted those of us who were lying near the opening and it also caused a lot of sand, dust and smoke to come flying out the doorway.

Having had enough of that spot I crawled away and toward the back of the bunker where I was confronted by some eighteen to twenty inch high, odd looking, cast iron jars that had large ear type handles on them. I crawled close to them thinking they might stop a bullet coming my way. Sgt. Renner who was at my side yelled, "Those things are anti-tank mines and if a bullet strikes them just right, we are done for!"

Since the Jap's machine gun bullets were hitting the sand covering the bunker, scattering it all over us I thought, "Well, to hell with that!" and crawled back around the bunker again to the doorway. I saw that Sgt. Brock was inside and was beginning to crawl out. I said, "What the hell are you doing in there?"

"There are a couple of dead Japs inside," He answered, "They sure are a mess, but I don't know if the grenade killed them or they were dead already!" Brock had some Japanese canned food and some crackers with him, the small kind of cracker that is often served with chowder at a restaurant in the States. It was unbelievable to me that he took the time to gather food from what must have been a mess inside the bunker. He stuck the tip of his bayonet into one tin and a purple liquid oozed out. It looked and smelled terrible so no one would taste it. I thought it was probably squid. I did eat a few of the crackers, but quit as my hands were filthy, being covered with dried blood and black sand and besides, I did not have an appetite anyway. It was now over twenty-four hours since I had breakfast the day before and I still was not hungry.

After a while the company formed up into a skirmish line and began to move forward. Our left flank was in contact with the open beach and surf. The Japanese artillery spotters saw our movement and sent over a barrage of mortar and artillery shells. The

On Iwo Jima, most of the enemy had to be blasted in their caves. This gruesome scene recorded by a combat photographer found this Japanese soldier's body thrown up and stuck against the roof of the cave, while his legs remained on the ground.

bombardment was devastating to our unit. Men and equipment went flying through the air and our advance was stopped immediately. Most of the injured suffered from shell splinters that tore through clothing and stuck in flesh.

These pieces of razor sharp metal were very hot and carried burning cloth inside the wound. Some of the smaller pieces of metal could be pulled out by thumb forceps, tweezers or a hemostat. We corpsman left a lot of the cloth material from an injured man's dungarees in the wound, because once it was blood soaked it wasn't easily seen. After sprinkling sulfanilamide we applied a sterile compress over the wound. Morphine was injected into the patient to prevent pain which would leads to shock. A medical tag, according to proper procedure should have been attached to the patient recording what medication had been given, but the pressures of battle were too great to take the time to do that very often.

After the barrage of exploding shells diminished enough for us to move the word was passed for us to straighten our line and to dig in again. The intent was to form a defensive position against a counter attack. The enemy fire eased up on us and shifted elsewhere. I peeked over the rim of the shell hole I was in and saw lying on the ground nearby a Japanese officer's cap. Reaching out, I almost touched it only to hear Lt. Lewis yell out for me to "leave it lay" as it might be booby trapped, and also I might be seen and draw enemy fire. He was right, I was determined after that not to try to collect another souvenir, but still I did at least once again.

We were told that the 3rd battalion was moving in front of us and were in direct contact with the Japanese forward lines. We would stay in reserve and back up G Company while they carried out a frontal assault. For the first time since we had landed we felt we could relax a little, rest and eat something. I tried to eat, but couldn't swallow any of the K ration food, for reasons I didn't understand. I did feel some nausea, and my neck and head pain were constant. I dug out a bottle of codeine tablets from my kit, took a half grain and almost immediately the pain lessened.

The remainder of the day was spent huddled in our rifle pits. I was gratified that during that time not one of our platoon members were seriously injured although many others in the company were. The Japs continued shelling G Company who were involved in assaulting the defensive forces directly in front of us. G Company was situated on top of a small hill, probably fifty to sixty feet higher than we were. They tried to advance against great odds against the Japanese, who were well protected by camouflaged concrete bunkers.

The defenders were calling for artillery fire to smash down Company G's assault. These shells probably 75 mm from their field pieces were hitting the target very well and stopped the attack by the Marines. But, many of these shells missed the primary target and went over our heads to explode in back of us. Unfortunately, some of those overhead shells struck the tops of trees surrounding us and exploded sending down steel fragments onto us. These pine trees had been stripped of all limbs and foliage by the action, leaving only the ragged and bare tree trunks standing.

Dusk approached. Even though G Company was greatly mauled they were committed to holding their position that night and were destined to resume their attack the next dawn. I was relieved. My thought was that I could get some rest and even sleep knowing that there were friendly troops between the Japs and us. The Japanese artillery assault subsided greatly with night fall.

Lt. Horvath crawled along the defensive line to tell us that even though G Company was in front of us we should stay alert to intercept any infiltrating Japanese. My Marine partner, PFC Paul Pugh and I continued to relax by huddling in the rifle pit. About nine o'clock, we heard scuffling noises directly ahead of us. Even though it was dark I could see dark forms rushing us. Before I could react properly the infiltrators passed me running by my right side. On the left side of us I could hear metal strike metal, grunts, groans and cursing as men fought men.

Rain began falling and the area surrounding our position became quiet. Leaning forward and on my knees, I held my rifle high, waiting in fear of what was to happen next. My partner, Pugh and I remained quiet, not daring to speak lest there be an enemy lying nearby ready to throw a hand grenade. We lay there against the forward edge of our pit thinking the worst scenario's of our plight. Were our comrades still alive? Were we all alone? Who would be lying close to us when the dawn showed light?

We attempted taking turns sleeping. I could not sleep, my neck hurt, the back of my head hurt, my eyes would not even close even though I felt drowsy at times. I took one quarter grain codeine to subdue the pain. For the drowsiness I took Benzedrine tablets provided us to keep awake. When I heard a noise nearby a rush of adrenaline would enter my blood stream. I desperately wanted to sleep, but did not want to be asleep when some Japanese soldier tried to stick a bayonet in me.

When dawn broke on February 21, the third day, it wasn't only the light that came, but a terrific barrage of shells. It probably was directed at G Company in front of us but those shells landed on us too. They forced us to cringe in the bottom of our holes while we suffered from the concussion and the shells splinters that cut down any living thing above ground surface. I found myself grasping at loose sand in an attempt to prevent being bounced about. The one thought I always had during these bombardments was to be on the alert once the shelling stopped to face a possible counter attack of the Japanese.

After an hour, maybe it was two, of this heavy bombardment, the number of shells arriving diminished and heavy machine gun fire began to come our way. But, that was all right as long as we could stay in our holes.

G Company began their assault. Word was passed that the enemy was well dug in several hundred yards away and our Marines were trying to get at them but, were suffering heavy casualties in doing so. Apparently this was true as there began a steady stream of wounded men coming off the battle line. Those men needed a lot of help, but our officers gave me the impression that they were not about to help. They were concentrating on their own goal, which is getting at the enemy. I wanted to help, but didn't leave my hole as I knew I would told to stay where I was. Instead, I slumped down in my rifle pit and refused to look out.

Two members of the 26th Marines support casualty in from the front.

The Japanese, well entrenched could easily see the men of Company G as they tried to attack across an open plain. The enemy's machine guns cut their ranks decimating them. Heavy mortar fire accompanied by cannon fire greeted them and caused their advance to falter. Some of the cannon fire passed over their heads and again landed among us causing injuries.

D Company was ordered to advance into the line with G Company. We filtered into the rifle pits left by the casualties of that unit. G Company continued to attempt their advance while we stayed in our holes. Again we took an unbelievable pounding by Jap artillery and it continued on until dusk. By then the attack by G Company had not succeeded and those Marines fell back into their previous position with us.

We prepared for another night as dusk approached. I dug in this time with a young Marine named Glen Brown from Springfield, Illinois. Lt. Horvath and a rifleman took a position to our immediate right. Things got bad right away. Gray slanting rain fell, machine gun fire continued sweeping across the ground and mortar shell explosions were constantly falling among us.

Lt. Horvath crawled the line again warning about Japanese attempting to infiltrate and that we should kill anything moving above ground and that we should use hand grenades more freely. I did not see him leave his foxhole again so I suspected that Sgt. Goodling may have given him some advice of the merits of staying put during darkness. That night the Japs ran through our lines again and Glen and I tossed grenades out front as soon as we heard a suspicious noise.

The Japanese infiltrators often carried packages of explosives apparently in an attempt to blow up our supply dumps or the command posts in an attempt to kill our officers. When they tried doing that they might stumble into a Marine's foxhole.

Several Japanese got past me running between Lt. Horvath's position and ours. My failure in allowing this to happen bothered me immensely and I tried harder to think of a way I could become more efficient. Luckily no Japs came into our foxhole as they did the first night on the island.

Again I got no sleep as I was just afraid what might happen if I were not awake. I kept taking those Benzedrine tablets to stay awake and I was under the belief that the drug would give me more energy. My older and more experienced corpsman friend Nyle Weiler had previously told me that some people took these pills to give them more pep. I probably should have never taken them at all.

Relieving Company G

IN THE DARK, PFC Glen Brown and I lay huddled against the forward edge of the rifle pit that we had fashioned from a shell crater the day before. We waited anxiously for the dawn to come although there was some dread of what the light might bring with it. Would we be all alone? Would our comrades be gone, wounded, or dead? Perhaps we would be surrounded by Japanese infantrymen who had moved forward in the darkness. We had listened all night to clashes of metal, grunts, groans, and curses as men fought each other in hand to hand combat. We were unsure of our situation.

With a mixture of relief and anxiety I saw a dim glow showing in the eastern sky. Now Brown and I could tell the approximate time. Not that it mattered really! I raised my head so that just my eyes could see above the edge of the foxhole rim and took a quick look around in all directions. I was relieved to see the dark green helmet of Lt. Horvath elevated slightly above the ground level to our right. We stared at each other momentarily before exchanging quick nods then lowering our heads. I told Brown about what I had seen and he was relieved. It wasn't long before we heard other men talking on either side of us as they called back and forth to each other. Then the sergeants came out of their foxholes and crawled along the ground from hole to hole counting the men assigned them and checking on their condition.

Suddenly the area on the rise in front of us erupted in multiple explosions causing a horrendous noise. I lost sight of the ground because of the gray dust, smoke and debris blown into the air around and above us. The troops up in front were taking a terrible beating from artillery, mortar and machine gun fire, all at the same time. I frantically hugged the ground more tightly, even trying to dig into it with my toes.

A stream of wounded men began to filter down the hill past us. Some were being carried by litter bearers, others dragged along by other wounded men and some crawled on their hands and knees. I could not stay huddled in my hole and ignore the sight one of one of the injured Marines as he crawled along the path on his stomach, trying desperately to reach safety. He was calling out for someone to help him, and I could see the wound bleeding profusely. I leaped up onto the rim of my rifle pit and was confronted immediately by Lt. Horvath who stared at me from his foxhole and slightly moved his head side to side. The message was obvious as the look in his eyes told me, "No, you are not going anywhere. Stay where you are!"

I slipped back into my hole dismayed and confused and I refused to watch the wounded any longer as they came down the hill. I was sick with the feeling that my Marine buddies might be wondering why I didn't jump up to help the wounded.

Brown and I tried to ignore the sight as we huddled in our hole and talked about how we got through the night without much violence and agreed that as soon as we got the word that we were to hold our position for a while, we would try to get some sleep. Then we heard the Lieutenant's shout!

He was yelling for the platoon to hurry and follow him and to take up a platoon formation, and that we were going up to relieve Company G. Brown and I were dismayed upon hearing that. I felt I had a large hard object in my stomach that was growing rapidly. We reluctantly climbed over the edge of the hole and began crawling forward on our knees with the other members of the platoon and up the incline toward where Company G was dug in. We fell in line with men from other platoons of our company who were crawling along in a single file. I was relieved to find so many other Marines preceding me in line.

Then, suddenly, with a prolonged crashing of noise, it seemed as though the entire earth's surface had erupted again. I fell flat to the ground and buried my face in the sand. I shut my eyes and grasped the volcanic ash with my hands in some useless attempt to hang on to something solid. The ground under me was violently jerking, shaking and smashing at my body as hundreds of mortar shells tore open and smashed into the earth around where we lay. There were so many explosions that there was no time interval between them and it seemed that there was only one continuous roar. I could hear the screaming and shrieking of hot steel splinters as they passed around me and those men near me.

The larger fragments made that "fluff, fluff, fluff" sound as they whirled and ripped through the air. These larger pieces, I had already found, could cut a man's body in half or remove one's arms, legs, or head very quickly. The Japanese had our movement under observation and were desperately determined to break up our advance. I looked back over my right shoulder at Mt. Suribachi and cursed that mountain as it was from there that the enemy observers were directing their fire.

The entire column of men, who now lay flat on their stomachs, inched its way into, and then along, a very shallow dry wash that began somewhere around the area where we had spent the night and ran forward up toward the Japanese lines. The right side of the small wash was a low embankment that rose up only as high as two feet in some places, but it gave some protection from flying steel shell splinters that came from that side of us.

The Japanese artillery had pulled back slightly from our position and was furiously targeting the area into which we were intending to move. That area was still being occupied by G Company. Those mortar shells would make a "whoosh" sound immediately before they impacted and exploded. When hearing that noise, we learned to drop our faces down to the sand to avoid getting a piece of steel in them.

We were about half way up the incline when the word was passed back, "Drop your packs!" That meant to me that we were to pull our packs off and lay them aside as we went on. "Damn, there goes the rest of my Van Camp pork and beans and the candy bars," I thought.

If I had been a combat veteran like sergeants Renner and Goodling, I'd have known what it meant to 'drop packs' like that. It meant that we were going to close with the Japanese, and it was going to be hand to hand fighting. I became aware that off to the right of our column and up in front of where I lay there was a large amount of black smoke boiling up into the sky. I assumed that the smoke was from oil and gasoline that was burning in a wrecked Japanese or Marine vehicle. I didn't dare raise my head high enough to look though!

I heard someone yell out, "Doc, Doc!" and so I peeked out from under the visor of my helmet and saw one of the mortar platoon sergeants up in front of me waving his hand trying to get my attention. He pointed toward the black smoke and red orange flames off to our right. I assumed there was someone wounded over there and after taking a few hard swallows and a deep breath I gathered nerve enough to crawl up and over the two foot embankment at my right side. Once up there I could see a General Sherman tank that was burning, and it was from there that the flames and black smoke were raising into the air. The turret had been blasted off and lay upside down a few feet away from the left front side of the rest of the vehicle.

Between me and the tank, I saw the back side of a Marine down on his knees, apparently watching the tank burn. He was only about thirty feet away from the inferno and definitely exposed to the flames and smoke as well as enemy fire. I crawled to the man, and found that it was one of my corpsman buddies, Ph. M. 3/c Burke Pace who was serving with the mortar platoon. He was staring at the side of the flaming tank and what I could identify as the remains of one of the tank crew. What was left of the crew member's body was hanging downward, on the outside of the tank, the legs were still inside. The body had been incinerated and only smudge was left of what had been a fighting man a short time before.

The imprint, made by the man's burning flesh and clothing, outlined the body as if it had been painted there with an artist's brush. On the ground below I was shocked at the sight of a small round object covered with short flickering blue, orange, and yellow flames and smoke. I stared at it before recognizing it as a tanker's leather tank helmet that contained what was left of his head.

I forced myself to tear my attention away from that scene and I turned

I couldn't imagine that a human body could be fried like a piece of bacon, like that against the side of a tank. My buddy corpsman Burke Pace suffered more at the sight.

toward Pace, yelling at him to get down onto the ground to escape the Japanese machine gunner that was now coming at both of us. Obviously the gunner had us in view and his intentions were clear, to kill us. Pace appeared not to hear me, but kept staring at the burning helmet. I slapped him hard on the back of his left shoulder and he still didn't react so I reached up and grabbed his left blouse shoulder and pulled, toppling him over onto the ground. He looked at me, but there was no sign of recognition in his eyes. His look was very strange, one that I'd never seen on anyone's face before. I demanded of him, "Keep up with your platoon!" He answered weakly with only with a slight nod of his head.

Waiting until he had made a move to go forward, I scrambled across the ground and back into the small dry wash where in front of me the last few men of the 2nd platoon were now disappearing over the edge of the rise that had been confronting us. I never saw Pace again after that.

One of the mortar platoon sergeants months later described what befell the corpsman. He said that he had seen me approach Pace and after I left, the medic turned and followed his platoon forward in the advance. Three men of that platoon, carrying their mortar equipment, rose to their feet and ran forward toward a shell crater which they hurled themselves into to escape the bullets and exploding mortar shells. As they disappeared into the hole, Pace ran forward to join them. When he reached a point a few feet from the lip of the crater he leaped forward. A shell landed inside the crater and exploded on the three mortar men, tearing them apart. Pace, who was airborne at that moment, landed on the torn and bloody remains of his comrades.

The sergeant in describing this incident said he ran forward and upon reaching the crater found Pace sitting there among all that gore and viscera at the bottom of the hole. He couldn't speak or respond to the sergeant's attention to him and later he was led back to a safer area and evacuated to one of the ships standing off shore. Months later, in attempting to establish contact with him, I wrote a letter to his home address, but never received an answer from him or his family. He was the first of many men I would observe collapse under the strain of battle.

The 2nd platoon following Lt. Horvath crawled over the edge of the plateau on our stomachs and in single file. We lay there, head to foot, stretched out on a narrow footpath that ran straight forward across that wide plateau in front of us, and disappeared into the Jap lines among the bunkers that confronted us, probably three hundred yards away. We inched our way forward and cringed at the screaming hot steel fragments tearing through flesh, air, and sand around us. We wouldn't raise our heads to look around for fear of it being struck down. I slid my body forward constantly keeping the top of my helmet in contact against the feet of the marine ahead of me. When he moved his feet, I moved. The tip of the visor of my helmet dragged in the sand as I held my face close to the ground. I could feel the metal buckle of my web belt dig into the earth, and I could imagine it leaving a furrow in the sand behind me as I moved forward.

We were in plain view of the Jap artillery observers who were behind us on Mt. Suribachi and those in front of us who were on higher ground toward the north. It was obvious that they were watching our advance and were very determined to stop it as we began. They were doing a good job of it, as the falling and exploding shells were as heavy as we had experienced on the beach during D-day. I could see men being tossed about like rag dolls as the sand under them erupted. I tried not to look to the right or left of me. I knew there were many men being injured or killed then, but I was determined to give my attention only to the men of my platoon. The problem was that I couldn't tell if they needed me because it was impossible to raise my head to look.

The ground to our left, or the beach side, rose and formed a small knob of sand and rock and then fell off sharply to the beach on the other side. On our right, the terrain sloped gently upward for several hundred yards to the base of what was the south end of Airfield #2. There on that gentle slope First Lt. John Noe was leading his remaining mortar men toward the Japanese bunkers that were confronting us. He had already passed by the burning tank and was attempting to place his men in a position to support our assault with their mortars. His platoon was caught crossing an open area by a sudden heavy barrage of artillery and mortar fire coming from a Japanese defensive position directly in front of us. He was struck down by a jagged piece of steel shell splinter that tore into his right jaw, knocking him to the ground. Bleeding heavily he frantically struggled with a compression bandage taken from his belt to place it over the wound to stop the bleeding. Unbelievably, he managed to stop the flow of blood somewhat, and was able to stagger back to the battalion aid station, even assisting another injured Marine on the way to the aid station.

While lying still with the right side of my face pressed into the path's surface, I could see the small hill on my left. It was only about fifty or sixty feet away. I saw a helmet pop up above the surface of the ground near the top of the little hill and I realized the man wearing it was Ph. M 3/c James Carmen of Madison, Wisconsin. He looked my way and in the midst of all those explosions, he grinned and waved his hand at me. As he did that a shell landed a few feet away in front of him at the edge of the depression he was in. He disappeared from my view because of the sand and smoke of the explosion. I was sure that he died right then as that shell landed no more than ten feet from him. I stared at the spot where I had last seen him and watched smoke from the exploding shell whirl and blow away from the point of impact. Then to my surprise and relief, Jim's head came back up into view. He was grinning and he shook his head a couple of times, then waving again he ducked out of sight.

The artillery and mortar shells were exploding among us three or four at the same time, they seem to come in clusters. They dug holes in the ground about two feet deep and four feet in diameter all through the area of Company D's advance. As they impacted and exploded, the shock that ran through the ground smashed against my body and seemed to be about the same as if a giant had picked me up and had slammed me onto the ground. I could feel my senses begin to dull and even the desire to escape began to leave me.

The feet of the Marine ahead of me began to move forward and I managed to scrape along the ground after him keeping the top of my helmet in contact with the bottom of his shoe soles. I came to a copper wire that lay stretched across the path in front of me and started to crawl over it when the Marine in front began to scream at me that the wire was probably a trip wire leading to explosives and that it would get us all killed if it was activated. Hell! I thought it was just a communications wire and so I motioned him on. I got all entangled in the wire and it didn't cause anything to explode.

I saw the helmets of two Marines who were huddling in a shell hole. Thinking that they were two of my platoon's members, I crawled into the hole with them. They were strangers to me and it turned out they were Marines of G Company who looked and acted a mess. With their facial muscles loose and jaws hanging slack, they stared at me with a dull, absent look that men get when subjected to exhaustion, and it appeared to be the symptoms of battle fatigue. Their eyes seemed to fail to register what they were seeing. I could see fear, confusion, and exhaustion in their eyes and their grime covered faces were void of any expression.

I yelled to be heard above the din of the battle, that I was from D Company and that we were there to relieve them! Slowly, as my words got through to them, their faces showed a little emotion, a little relief perhaps. One turned his head slowly to the other and said, "Let's get the hell out of here."

Before they left the crater they told me of the last two day's fighting. They arrived at this location and were told that they would charge across the open area and attack the row of bunkers on the other side. Each time they rose to move forward the Japanese had laid down an impenetrable barrage of shell, machine gun, rifle, and rocket fire, forcing them to return and take refuge in the same holes they had advanced from. After that the artillery and mortar fire continued to fall incessantly upon them causing a very high number of casualties. As the two Marines left, crawling out on their stomachs, one paused to look back and say to me, "Don't raise your head to look around. You'll get it taken off!"

Well, I didn't intend staying there by myself so I crawled out and back on the path. If I were to get hit and die, I didn't want it to happen while all by myself. I saw a nearby shell crater and crawled to the rim of it to escape the steel splinters that were tearing into the ground all around me ,and sending up showers of sand and dirt. The metal fragments made various noises as they went by me. Some made a whirring noises, others went "zinnnng" and the larger pieces "fluf, fluf, fluf, fluf".

I found two of the 2nd platoon's members already in the shell crater. PFC's Raymond "Abie" Hower and Donald Giles who were lying side by side on their stomachs on the sloping side of the crater facing the Jap lines. I crawled forward and squeezed myself in between the two and the three of us lay there with shoulders touching and our faces pressed into the sand. As the shells hit around the hole we were bounced up and down together and if we hadn't been so frightened, I suppose we might have seen some humor in the situation. A shell exploded on the back rim of the crater. The larger fragments missed us but some smaller hot ones penetrated our clothing covering our backs. Hower, who was to my right, yelled out, "I'm hit!" I turned and reached over and pulled up his blouse covering his back and found several small hot steel pieces still steaming sticking into his skin. Reaching into my medical kit I found my thumb forceps and pulled out the splinters. The rubbery like texture of the skin had closed around the metal and resisted my efforts though. I dabbed iodine on the wounds and covered them with some band aids.

When I was through with him, I heard Giles say very calmly, "Me too, Doc!" I found two pieces of steel sticking in his back and treated him the same way as I had Hower. When I was through, I felt a stinging sensation on my back that I hadn't noticed before. Giles pulled out a splinter of steel that had been embedded there between my shoulder blades. We escaped serious injury and possibly death this time, but I was already beginning to think that we would never leave this island alive.

The word was passed back along the line of men huddling in these shell holes to fire at the bunkers that lay in front of us. Peeping over the edge of the shell holes, I could easily see the long hump of sand that stretched from the area of the sand beach on our left to where it ended at the base of the airfield. We had no idea where our bullets were striking the sand covered bunkers at that distance as there was no way we could leave our heads up high enough long enough to study the conformation of the fortifications. We found this to be the problem facing us for the rest of the battle. The Japs, on the other hand, had the opportunity to watch us advance from a protected fortification and sight their weapons in a much more advantageous manner.

There was a call for "Corpsman!" I had listened to many in the past two hours, coming from either side of our platoon's position but this one came from directly ahead of where Giles, Hower, and I lay while being bounced around by the shell concussions. I was sure it was one of our platoon's members and the call wouldn't cease. I told the other two, "Well, here I go!"

Giles grabbed my arm and held me and said, "Don't go out there Doc. That's sure suicide!"

Hower too, was pulling at my blouse on the other side. I paused, deeply touched by their concern, but I said, "I don't want to go, but what if that was one of you out there calling for help?"

I crawled over the rim of the hole and forward. On my right side there was that two or so foot high embankment that offered some protection. It ran forward about one hundred feet and at its base lay a large number of the men of Company D head to foot and in some places two and three men were laying side by side. The call for a corpsman came from somewhere up in front of this line and was being passed back.

I began crawling forward over the prone bodies of the Marines in the ditch. I never heard one complain while I was on top of them. I suppose it was because my body offered some protection for theirs. Many of these men had already suffered slight wounds and had treated themselves as had Giles, Hower, and I. Many of these minor injuries had never been reported to the battalion aid station's medical register and therefore never counted in the battalion's casualty statistics.

I crawled along for about twenty feet like that until I saw the feet of a Marine projecting over the embankment, just above my head, I asked the man that I was about to crawl over if that was the wounded man up there and he responded by nodding his head without looking at me and mumbling something like, "Yeah, I think so!"

I gathered my legs and feet under me and leaped up the embankment to the fallen man. I recognized the Marine immediately. He was a corporal assigned to the machine gun platoon. He lay on his back and I straddled his body between my knees and bent forward to examine him. Serum and yellow gray brain tissue was oozing down his temple. A burst of fire from a machine gun scattered around me. The Jap gunner had missed me on the first try. Moving quickly, I grabbed at the corporal's blouse with the intention of to pulling him to a sitting position, then hurl both of us over backward and down the embankment which was in back of me. While pulling his body like that he made an odd sound that came from his throat. A second burst of bullets missed me again, scattering along both sides of me. But I saw what looked like a small explosion appear on the front side of his neck as a bullet emerged spraying me with blood and flesh and passing by my right shoulder. I threw myself backward pulling the dead corporal with me over the side of the short bank and fell onto the Marines laying there. I struggled to free myself from the corpse and demanded of the Marine I had spoken to before, "Did you know that he was dead? You almost got me killed!" The riflemen nodded, I supposed he meant yes.

"And you let me go up there to be killed!" I yelled at him.

He turned his face away. I could see he was frightened and confused. Someone up ahead of me continued yelling, "corpsman!" The call was being passed from man to man right down the line to me so I began crawling forward again. It was about then that I wished Lt. Horvath could see me and order me back again. I crawled along on the backs of the men laying up against the short bank that was to our right.

The front of the column ended where the short bank disappeared and only a flat piece of land lay ahead. I crawled onto the back of one of two men who lay side by side. A sergeant, I recognized him from the 1st platoon, looked up and me and said, "This is it; this is as far as you go. You go on farther and you're dead!"

I suddenly realized then the man I was lying on top of was Lt. Aloysius S. Fennel the 1st platoon leader and I said, "Oh, sorry sir." He sneered and growled something at me.

"We can't go any farther because of a Jap bunker sitting right out there in the open and the Japs inside it are giving us hell with their machine guns!" the sergeant explained, shaking his head.

CHAPTER THIRTY-ONE

February 22nd: Unbearable Agony

THE FLAT AREA that confronted us was about one hundred fifty feet across. The area on the other side was scattered with shell craters and smashed trees, the roots of which had been torn from the ground and ripped apart. It was just one 'hell of a mess'. I could hear the yell, "Corpsman!" coming from over across there somewhere.

To the left of where we lay a Sherman tank was sitting in the open flat area firing its turret machine guns toward the bunker on our right. The Jap gunners inside the bunker were firing back at the tank with machine guns. I could see the bullets striking the tank in a grayish blur as they ricocheted off the armor. The bunker was covered with sand, piled perhaps six or seven feet high. The tank gunner's bullets were kicking up a lot of sand that interfered with our view in locating the exact position of the gun ports.

The bunker stood overall about fifteen feet high and it reminded me of a large beehive. I would describe it in the future as being the 'Beehive bunker.' In back of this lone bunker, about two hundred yards was a line of sand covered concrete bunkers that stretched from the western beach on our left for about a mile to our right and to the base of a north and south running cliff that edged the western side of Air Field #2. We had to destroy this bunker first in order to attack the bunkers it guarded to its rear. This was difficult because the rear bunkers had a commanding view and their guns protected the Beehive bunker's position.

Our gunner inside the tank was firing its machine guns in bursts of three to five bullets. When he thought he was on target, he fired his large gun hitting the same spot where his machine gun bullets had struck.

The call for a corpsman continued and I could see two Marines huddled together with another one lying on the ground. I made a move to cross the plain. The sergeant spoke again, warning, "Don't go out there. Those Japs will kill you!"

I paused long enough to think about what the rest of the Marines would think and say about me if I didn't go forward to help one their wounded. I crawled onto the open flat and sure felt all alone and very vulnerable but kept my eyes on the tank. Its machine guns were firing over my body and I told myself, "What the hell, we had practiced doing this type of thing back at Camp Pendleton." I was more afraid that the driver might not see me and if he suddenly sent the tank charging forward I would be in real danger! I thought of the larger 75 mm gun and what might happen when it was fired toward me. I had just passed the center front of the tank, which was about twenty five or thirty feet away when the gun was fired. Fortunately I was looking forward toward my goal when it happened as the blast tore up the sand and rock between us sending it with hurricane force, stinging my face and body. My helmet was almost torn from my head and was pushed down over my face. I bounced and rolled along the ground for a few feet before crawling forward again, shaking my head trying to clear it. I assumed that the gunner in the tank could see me and allowed me to pass by a little before firing.

I went on to where the three Marines were hugging the ground up against a large tree root that had been torn from the ground. I found PFC Dennis Love lying there with a big piece of flesh missing from his right thigh. A splinter from a mortar shell had done the damage. It was a bad looking wound. I gave him a morphine injection, sprinkled some sulfa power on the wound, and bound it with a sterile battle compress.

Love was a member of the machine gun squad. His two comrades who assisted him with the gun could have done what I did but instead they chose to kneel nearby and yell for a corpsman. And one could have continued firing the machine gun at the bunker. I told them that and they nodded in agreement.

I was beginning to learn what authority was about. Even though I was a medic I had more training in the Marines than a lot of those kids who had just come from Boot Camp. Some had to be prodded into acting responsibly. Informing them that I would not attempt to get Love back to the aid station, I told them to stay there, fire their weapon at the bunker, and try to flag forward a litter team.

"Yeah, we'll do that!" One said and gave me an odd, silly looking grin that I didn't understand the meaning of.

There was more yelling for help going on near there so I turned in the direction of the sound. Moving toward a shell hole I found a Marine inside the impression down on his knees. He had his hands over his eyes and was screaming that he was blind. I pulled his hands away from his face and told him I was corpsman. Oh Lord! He had his helmet on and a piece of hot sharp steel had penetrated it just above the visor and had stuck there. A closer look revealed that the splinter had entered his helmet, gone through the metal and inner fiber liner, entered his forehead and was stuck in his skull. I tried to pull the metal out with my fingers, then a forceps, but I couldn't. Perplexed I finally decided to push on his face with one hand, put my other hand cupped in the back of his helmet and pulled. The steel helmet came forward and down pulling the hunk of shrapnel from the wound.

The Marine was screaming out that he was blind while I struggled with him to keep his hands out of my way. I could see right into his skull and that frightened me. Blood was pouring out of the wound and running into his eyes. He continued to scream out in pain while I sprinkled sulfa powder in the wound and placed a battle compression bandage over it and tied the ends behind his head. I gave him a syrette of morphine and told him that he was not blind but that blood was in his eyes and he wouldn't see for a while because I had them covered with a dressing. He calmed down after that, probably the result of the morphine injection. Another man jumped into the crater with us. I could see he was a corpsman, but didn't recognize him. I said, "Who are you?"

He said that he was with the 3rd battalion and this was one of his men, and that he would take him as the battalion was withdrawing. Off the two went crawling along on their knees; the corpsman was tugging and pulling on the blind Marine's blouse as he led the way.

After they left I realized that I was alone. Afraid, but curious as what was in front of us, I crawled through a mass of roots and peeked out at a wide plain. It was at least two hundred yards across, and a row of sand covered the bunkers that confronted us. The Japanese inside were just waiting for us to come to them! There were no Marines between the Japs and me, so I thought it best to crawl back toward our lines and find some one more friendly.

Most of the shells being fired us were landing in jumbled roots and up-turned earth in back of me. Steel splinters were flying about cutting into tree stumps and roots that lay about on the ground. I hesitated a while thinking that although I was in a lot of danger now, it would be more dangerous crawling through the open and back to the 2nd platoon. I huddled a moment under a tangle of roots. Then I thought again. This wasn't proper. I should attempt to get back to my buddies, so I began sliding along on my stomach in that direction.

Crawling past tree roots and a stump I heard a calm voice nearby say, "I'm hit too!"

I felt my skin jump at his voice. Damn it! I wasn't three feet away from him and had not seen him huddled there among the debris. He saw I was a corpsman and had propped himself up on one elbow to reveal himself. He was smiling, calm and seemed not to be in pain. A bullet had passed through the muscle of his left leg just above the knee. I placed a battle dressing over the holes which were hardly bleeding and gave him two sulfadiazine tablets and a drink of water. I asked him if needed morphine and he shook his head. "No! I don't need that, it doesn't hurt much." I took him to be a Marine officer because of the numbers shown on his blouse. They also indicated he was from the 3rd Battalion.

I helped him back to where PFC Love laid awaiting litter bearers. The two machine gunners assisting Love were sitting by their gun but still not operating it. I lost my temper. "God Damn it, you are supposed to be shooting at that bunker. Do it!"

This time they both moved toward the machine gun and I turned away from them to rejoin my platoon. I glanced back at the wounded marine officer I had just helped and he was smiling at me as if he had found some humor in my remark to them. I hoped that he would encourage the two young Marines to fire their weapon.

The tank that I had crawled in front of previously was now about two hundred feet forward of where I had previously seen it. It was moving slowly and the gunner inside was still firing the turret machine guns at the bunker. There were Marines at the back and far side of the tank scrambling over the sand, keeping pace with it. I recognized Lt. Horvath by his odd colored green helmet. I set a course to intercept him and just as I came along side the left side of the tank a shell came from my left, passed by the front of the tank and exploded on the far side among some of our men. I dove for the ground and hugged it. There were three more shells that came, all passing barely over of the tank and exploding against a bank of sand on the far side. If an artillery shell did strike the tank, the explosion could possibly wipe out one half of the platoon and me for sure.

I crawled into a small crater to await Lt. Horvath, as I could see he was coming my way. I thought he resembled a big sand flea jumping up and down as he came over the sand. Moments later he tumbled into my hole and when he realized someone was already there he swung his carbine to face me. He demanded, "What are you doing up here?"

I gave him my explanation and couldn't help but grin as I thought that I, a medic would be often found up front of the platoon helping someone and he should know that. The Lieutenant ignored my grin and said that the platoon was going to attack the bunker in front of us. "This is our tank!" and he pointed at it even though it was the only one in our sight.

The shelling continued, but I wasn't about to stick my head up and watch the tank get smashed. I was amazed that the Japanese artillery men could not hit the tank by firing all those shells at it. I expected it to be blown up by each one fired. The machine gun fire coming from the beehive bunker was increasing in an alarming rate now that we were within a hundred yards of it. I suspected that the Japanese defenders inside were frenzied as they watched the tank draw closer to annihilate them.

The Lieutenant and I lay side by side for a while. I watched him as he turned to face one way and then another apparently trying to think something out. I peeked over the rim of the hole for a look at the bunker. The Lieutenant yelled to me, "The men are not firing enough at the bunker!"

Well. I had not been at all, so taking his remark as a command I pushed my carbine barrel over the rim to fire. The Lieutenant apparently intended doing the same. The sand immediately in front of his head was engulfed in multiple blasts of sand that smashed into his face and shoulders. I flung myself back and down twisting my body until I reached the bottom of the crater. I was sure we had just lost our platoon leader. I intended crawling back up the slope to where he lay dead, but before I got on my knees he was already moving backward wiping frantically at his face, trying to clear his eyes. I thought it was a miracle that he escaped that burst of bullets alive. I recovered his carbine and shook the sand from it and stared at him in disbelief.

A moment later I peeked over the rim again. No bullets came, but I did see some light blue smoke on the side of the bunker and I fired at a mark that indicated a gun port from where the Jap gunner was firing. After firing, I quickly ducked down to a more secure place. I didn't think my little carbine was equal to a heavy machine gun in battle and didn't intend to become involved in a duel with that enemy gunner.

As the tank inched its way closer to the bunker, those of us in back of it advanced also. The platoon spread out behind, and on each side of the vehicle. We crawled from one hole to the next, or leaped forward and hurled ourselves into the next. The machine gun fire at us became more intense, but I preferred it to the mortar shells that exploded among us.

Lt. Horvath and I once leaped from one hole and ran forward to jump in another when several mortar shells exploded around us. We both landed with our faces forced into the sand. We were two very shook up men. I fought to recover my senses and struggled to raise my face from the sand, but it didn't seem to feel like sand that the right side of my face rested on. My face was numb and I had trouble focusing my eyes. My vision began to clear gradually and my eyes began to focus in on an object that my face had pressed upon. I saw it was a human hand. It was severed at the wrist, bloodless and paper-white with its palm upward. "No, I thought I'm seeing things I shouldn't." Then the thought jumped into my mind that the hand was mine. I pulled my arms loose from under my body and looked. I had two hands. The hand on the sand was a human's right hand. So I looked at my right hand, opening and closing it to make sure it was there.

Then another dreadful thought came to me, I looked at the Lieutenant and watched as he shook his head to free it from the sand. "Lieutenant," I called to him. He either couldn't respond or he had not heard me. Fearfully, I called again and was about to ask him if he had lost his hand! But, before I could finish he busied himself brushing the sand from his face with his right hand. He turned to look at me with a questioning expression. I said to him, "You all right?"

He nodded, "yes!"

Then he saw the hand lying on the sand under my chin and a questioning looked appeared on his face. He looked at my two hands and then turned to look about us for signs of another victim.

I looked at the hand on the sand again and wondered whose hand it was. There was no one else in sight. I pushed some sand to cover it and moved a few feet away. That hand bothered me and during the remainder of the day I would frequently pick up a handful of wet sand and try to rub the feeling away from my cheek that had rested on the hand. I did it so many times my skin became raw and stinging.

The Lieutenant scrambled away toward the tank and I followed closely. The tank gunner was firing his turret machine guns continuously at a gun port on the side of the bunker. In turn a machine gun in the bunker was firing back at the tank. Ricocheting steel scattered all about the Lieutenant and me. We managed to crawl up under the rear of the tank and huddled there for shelter.

I thought this whole experience was insane and that I was going to be killed any second. The machine gun fire from the tank and the rifle fire from my comrades did drive the Jap gunners away from the firing port, this gave the platoon some relief and we crept closer to the bunker to finish if off. To get close to the bunker, the tank had maneuvered its way through a maze of tank traps which were there to protect the bunker from just that kind of attack. The traps were rectangular pits dug in the earth, about eight feet deep, eight feet across and usually about twenty feet long. The Lieutenant tried peeking around the rear of the tank's tracks and drew fire from the bunker no more than thirty feet away.

He grabbed at the field telephone that hung from the back of the tank and began yelling into it, desperately trying to be heard over the noise of the tank's engine and exploding shells. I suppose he was trying to tell the tank's commander where he saw a gun port and machine gun located on the bunker. I wished that he'd quit yelling as I was sure he couldn't be heard above all that noise. Besides that, the telephone hookup was a one way connection and he could not receive a message on it.

He gave up all right, because the driver put the tank in reverse and began moving backward over us. I was on the seat of my pants propelling my self backward trying desperately to escape the tank's metal cleats from running over me. The Lieutenant and I were forced backward to the point where we fell into a large trap. I tumbled over backward into it and landed on my head and shoulders. Even so, I could think of only one thing, that tank could fall and crush me!

Once I recovered myself at the bottom of the hole I looked up and was horrified to see the rear end of the tank slowly appear overhead, then the bottom of the tracks came into view. They crushed the sand and sent a lot of it down on us. Lt. Horvath and I scrambled to the right on our hands and knees, where I climbed half way up the side of the trap, crouched and waited for the tank to tumble backward into the hole. The driver stopped that tank just at the right moment as it teetered on the edge of the trap, its tracks extending perhaps three feet out over the hole.

The tank lurched forward slowly again and the Lieutenant climbed out of the pit and went along with the tank back up to the bunker. The Japanese machine gunner inside the bunker was frantically firing his gun, spreading bullets all around, but most hitting the tank and ricocheting all over the area. I told myself that this was not right, why should I go back behind the tank with the officer, and what could either of us do in that position?

A series of mortar shells landed right around us and we went through the bouncing bit again, but were not struck by fragments. By then I was hoping that if I might get hit it would be on the top of my head so I wouldn't feel it. I didn't want to be left alive, torn up the way I had seen some of the men. I only waited for about five minutes before I heard another noise, a man's loud voice. I dared peek over the rim of the pit and saw a marine standing alongside of the tank's left side. He held a Thompson sub-machine gun in his right hand and was reaching up to bang the butt of it against a port on the side of the tank. The tanker opened the port and I heard him say above the noise, "What the hell do you want!"

The Marine answered, "I want some ammo for this!" and he waved his Thompson machine gun. The tanker, after a moment handed out several boxes of 45 cal. ammunition to the marine and slammed the port shut. The Marine filled a magazine and began firing the weapon point blank at the bunker; I supposed he saw the gun port I couldn't see.

The Lieutenant was crouched again under the rear of the tank futilely trying to use the telephone, and at the same time was looking at the marine standing there. The Lieutenant had a look of awe on his face. More shells fell. The first one struck to the right of the tank. It flattened the Lieutenant; the second was along side the standing marine and two more landed in back of me. I was looking at the marine as the second shell exploded along his right side.

He was no more than twenty feet from me. I saw a flash of red, orange and gray and the sand exploding. I was bounced up and slammed down again, became stunned and fought my way out of it. I tried to lower my head when I heard the "swoosh" of the shell coming and I suppose I did or I would have had a face full of shrapnel. I waited several seconds then looked up to see the Marine lying on the ground, his uniform smoking as it burned from the explosive powder.

I crawled toward the fallen man, and as I did I saw Lt. Horvath rise again to his knees and crouch under the rear over-hang of the tank. He was shaking his head to clear it while he tried again to use the telephone. I straightened out the Marine's body expecting to find him dead. To my surprise he was conscious, looking up at me and even smiling. His right hip was torn open, broken bones protruding from the flesh. He had more small wounds on his right side. He waved his right hand toward me, it was horrible. There was not one bit of skin left on it, just bones, veins and tendons so I gave him an injection of morphine quickly. Afterward, I spread sulfanilamide crystals over the ruined hand and bound it between two battle compresses.

The marine kept talking to me, "Well, that's the end of my hunting with my uncle. He will be disappointed!"

"Naw." I answered, gulping down whatever it was that was building up in my throat and at the same time trying to smile. "You can use your left hand to hunt with,"

He just grinned at me. I really didn't expect him to live but a few minutes longer. Since he was talking, I asked him who he was as he was a stranger to me. He told me that he was a 4th Division Marine. I said, "What are you doing here, this is 5th Division Marine territory?"

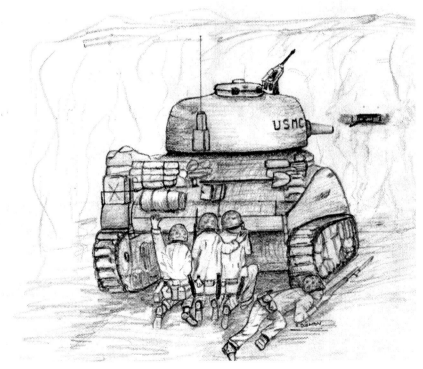

Richard Overton, Sgt. Nick Abromovich, Lt. C. Horvath and an unidentified Marine taking cover behind a tank.

"Yeah, I know, but I was up on airfield number two and a shell blew me off the cliff down here, so I just joined up with you guys!"

I looked at the cliff about one hundred yards away at the edge of the airfield and could see it was about fifty feet above from the plain we were on. I thought that this was one tough marine.

The gunner inside the tank found what he was looking for and he fired the large gun in the turret at the bunker's gun port at blank point range. I really don't know how the injured marine and I survived because the exploding shell knocked me over and I skidded away lying on my back. I sat up stunned that I wasn't full of steel fragments. After examining myself for wounds, I crawled back to the injured Marine. He was no worse shape than before, at least that I could see. I saw Lieutenant Horvath struggling to get back on his knees for about the fourth time and wondered if there would be a fifth time as he couldn't possibly continue taking this kind of punishment much longer.

The bunker was destroyed, at least the men inside were, they must be dead as the tank gunner put the shell right in the opening of the gun port. The concussion, steel splinters, and flames should have destroyed every living thing inside. Soon one of our flame thrower operators would come forward and finish the job.

CHAPTER THIRTY-TWO

The Death of Powers , Kastan and Hower

AN ARTILLERY AND mortar barrage fell furiously upon us. I formed the impression that each and every shell had its own extreme hatred and was out to kill me personally. Obviously we were in clear view of the Japanese gunners who had seen us destroy their bunker and were now swarming over and round it and preparing to assault the next one. It was a very costly experience for us to take these bunkers. I was not aware of it at the time, but many of my comrades were already dead or wounded in the taking of this one. The dead lay where they fell, the lesser wounded were treated by their comrades or had crawled off making their own way to the rear the best they could.

PFC Paul J. Rush of Texas was killed here instantly by mortar fire. Pvt. Tony Lozano, the big American Indian fell wounded. Corporals, Robert G. Riebling and Howard N. Corbett were knocked down by steel fragments. Both, Bush and Lozano were men who had been handling their Browning automatic rifles in a very effective way. They were mainly responsible for destroying the Japanese machine gunner operating his weapon from inside the bunker which allowed the tank crew to move forward to make use of its large gun.

I saw a Marine fall and writhe about on the ground in agony, and I fell beside him to help. He was 1st. Lieutenant Jack Jones, the company executive officer. His right ankle had been smashed by a steel splinter and was turning a deep purple. I cut his boot off, bound the wound and offered to carry him back to the aid station. I shouldn't have made that offer which he rejected immediately. I think he thought that being carried back to the aid station over the shoulder of a corpsman would be a humiliating experience and ruin the image of him being 'one tough marine'. It was OK with me as he was a very large man, well over two hundred pounds. He was a very good marine too.

PFC Paul Pugh, of Salt Lake City leaped to his feet then dropped his rifle. I grabbed at him, pulled him to the ground and into a shell hole. He had a horrible looking jagged piece of steel embedded in the back of his right shoulder. The fragment had taken some of the dungaree cloth into the wound and it was still smoldering after being set on fire by the hot steel fragment. I tried to pull the steel out with my fingers, but only succeeded in burning them. I used a thumb forceps and failed with that too. The rubber-like skin surrounding the wound closed on a portion of the steel and held it in place. I couldn't spend any more time with Pugh but took the time to squeeze a one half grain of morphine into his arm.

After placing a compress over the wound, I told Paul the best chance for him to get out of there was to crawl, "like hell" for the aid station somewhere in back of us. He started out and he did make it. We had a joyful reunion on Guam a few weeks later.

To our right side, 1st Lt. John Noe was leading his mortar platoon forward and ran into the barrage of mortar and artillery shells that the Japanese were sending at us. He had already lost several of his men including his

Marine lies wounded in a shell crater, holding the shrapnel piece that wounded his neck. After receiving first-aid and a shot of morphine from a corpsman, he now awaits stretcher bearers to take him to an aid station.

corpsman, Burke Pace, and now, he was struck down by a flying mortar fragment that smashed into his right jaw. Terribly disabled and bleeding he was attempting to stop the hemorrhage when corpsman George Hall of the 1st platoon appeared to assist him. Still, severely damaged, the Lieutenant was able to make it back to the battalion aid station and even assisted another wounded Marine on the way.

So many of Company D men fell at that time and yet I didn't know what had happened until months later when I read the casualty reports back at Camp Tarawa. It was very disturbing to me to have lived so closely with men for over a year and then to have them disappear suddenly like that without hope of ever seeing them again. Even today I feel that there never was closure regarding that part of the battle experience.

After Pugh left me, I crawled to the nearest shell hole and I found a sergeant assigned to the first platoon talking to a few men of his squad, one of which was wounded. It was then I learned that the first platoon had been advancing abreast of the second platoon on our right side. They filled in a two hundred-yard-wide space that extended from us to the base of a cliff. Up on that cliff was the west boundary of the Airfield Number Two. The sergeant told me the third platoon was spread out behind us in reserve to back us up.

The sergeant went on to say that the first platoon was hit 'bad' and he didn't think that we could advance any farther. He said that he saw corpsman George Hall who was assigned to his platoon over at the base of the cliff and that he was acting very strange and wouldn't speak to him.

I crawled in the direction he indicated and found George in a shell crater. He was alone, down on his hands and knees, looking at the sand before him. He didn't give any response to my questions and didn't seem to be aware of anything happening around him. He showed no fear or alarm over our situation. I compared his behavior with that of corpsman Pace's about two hours before. I filled out a casualty tag and wrote on it, "Battle Fatigue," and pinned it to his blouse. I told him to begin crawling back to the aid station and talk to the surgeon. He didn't respond so I pushed and shouted for him to go. He began crawling away, but after about fifty feet and to my dismay, he slowly got to his feet and began walking casually on. He seemed to ignore my shouting for him to "get back down on the ground." I watched him go and thought that he would never make it to the aid station.

When he was about one hundred yards away a shell exploded ahead of him and off to his left side, but he kept on walking slowly along, obviously not struck by shell splinters and seemed oblivious to the danger. Three more shells landed in front of him and still he remained on his feet. I thought how odd it all was. The Japanese, no doubt saw him and directed one of their mortars to fire at him thinking that he was in among other Marines gathered there. And now, he was drawing that gun's fire away from those Marines advancing on the line of bunkers they hoped to defend.

Hall did make it to the battalion aid station. As I understand it, the doctor gave him a sedative and told him to lie down and rest. Nyle Weiler told me later what happened to him after that. He said that Hall was half sitting, half lying on the side of the large shell crater that served as the battalion aid station. He leaned back to rest on his left elbow near a piece of tree root sticking up from the ground. A shot was fired near the edge of the crater causing the corpsman and doctors to flinch and fall flat on the ground. Hall, was heard to cry out, "Oh, no. Not now!" and then he collapsed. A bullet had entered his right upper arm and after passing through the muscle had gone on into his chest. Weiler said that he died immediately afterward.

The Japanese, who had been hiding in a spider trap near the aid station had risen up and fired the shot that killed Hall. He was found by other corpsmen and Marines who looked for and killed him. When his body was searched, it was found that the Japanese had been carrying a student body card with his picture on it, issued by a junior college in Texas. I was very sorry for Hall and his family. He left a pretty wife and a three year old blonde daughter in San Francisco. He had been very proud of them and had regularly shown us, their photographs.

After Hall left me I crawled forward toward the base of the cliff and found two more Marines from the 1st Platoon huddled in a crater. They cautioned me about going farther, pointed toward the cliff and said there were 'Japs' up there on top and inside the cliff. I said, "What do you mean, inside the cliff?"

One answered, "See that little hole over there at the base of cliff? A little while ago Lieutenant Lewis came up and ran toward it. A Jap crawled out of there and shot him in the stomach then went back inside."

I saw the entrance to the cave that I hadn't seen before the Marine pointed it out. I asked the two men what they were going to do about the cave. One answered, "I don't know except that I'm not going over there and get shot in the stomach like the Lieutenant did!"

Chapter Thirty-Two

"What ever happened to the Lieutenant?" I asked.

"I dunno," one answered, "I think Hall (corpsman) went up and dragged him out of there!"

"Where's your Lieutenant Fennell now?"

"He's up front of us, but I'm sure as hell not going up there to be with him!" One answered.

Up in front of us I could see two other Marines run forward at the base of the cliff and I watched as they leaped into a crater. I told the two Marines that my orders were to stay up with the platoon commander, and since I was separated from my platoon I would go forward to be with Lt. Fennell. I asked the two Marines to watch the cave entrance as I passed by it on my way forward. They nodded, and pointed their weapons at the cave entrance. I began crawling forward.

Lieutenant Fennell wasn't there, but two eighteen year old Marines were. PFC William Powers and PFC Robert Kastan, lay-side-by side on their stomachs, their faces and helmets pressed into the sand. I forced my way in between them and the three of us lay there, shoulder to shoulder, while barrage after barrage of mortar shells landed in the soft earth showering us with sand. I felt that I was responsible for that as the Japanese gunners had seen me run forward. The barrages consisted of four shells, one after another, and then a moment's pause, then four more shells. I had it figured out that they were all coming from one mortar that was assigned to exterminate us specifically, or at least to keep us from moving forward toward their bunker line, which was only about two hundred yards in front of us. Between the four-shell barrages I could hear bullets coming from a machine gun directly forward of our position, no doubt from one of the bunkers confronting us. The bullets were 'zinging' as they passed over our hole and some of them hit the sand a few inches above our heads and threw sand onto our faces, helmets and backs. The Jap gunner evidently had seen the three of us go into this hole and he wasn't about to let us out.

In between the barrages of shell bursts, I began to feel sand striking the back of my neck and shoulders. I turned my head to the right to see who had jumped into the crater with us, or to see what it was causing that sand to jump. I saw a small black object fall onto the sand at the back edge of the crater only a couple of yards from our feet. I turned my face away quickly as the grenade exploded and sent sand to strike our back side.

About three quarters of the way up the cliff I saw a Jap soldier partially concealed in the cliff's rock rubble, lobbing hand grenades down on us. The grenades were sinking into the soft sand at the edge of the crater as they landed, and the sand was containing those fragments that would ordinarily fly out horizontally and strike us. I yelled out a warning to my two comrades, raised my carbine with my right hand and pointed it up toward the side of the cliff above us.

I saw a Japanese soldier's head and arm come into view, and then a small black grenade fell down toward us. I fired once then maybe twice, then turned my face away from where I thought the grenade would land. I'm sure I missed hitting the grenade thrower as he had pulled quickly out of my sight. Powers and Kastan both turned to fire. I believe that they too missed the intended target

The three of us lay side by side afraid either to move or to stay where we were. We were caught in a situation where we could not see a way out to safety. Then we heard a voice calling out from far out in front of us. Some one was calling for Powers and Kastan to "Come on up, C'mon up!"

I nudged Powers with my elbow and called out, "Someone's calling you!"

"That's Lt. Fennell," Powers nodded, "I'm scared and I don't want to go. I know I will get killed Doc!"

"Me either, I don't want to go any farther!" Kastan answered. I told them that I was afraid also, but maybe it was safer up there with the Lieutenant than where we were now. I urged powers to get up and run forward as soon as we heard the next burst of bullets go by, and then take three steps like Sgt. Goodling had taught me, then dive into the nearest crater. He looked at me. I could see tears in forming in the corners of his eyes and run down his cheeks. I tried to smile as I slapped his shoulder and said, "Go!" He leaped to his feet and stepped over the edge of crater. Raising my head slightly I watched him take more than the three steps he had agreed upon then he disappeared from my view beyond a light ridge of sand.

Kastan was still lying by my right side, our shoulders touching. His face and helmet, visor were buried in the sand, cradled between his outstretched arms. I used my right elbow to nudge his left shoulder and said, "It's your turn." A small noise came from his throat that made be believe he might be sobbing. I grabbed at his shoulder and shook it and that caused his head to wobble. Then I saw some yellowish-brown looking stuff oozing from out under his helmet and run down his left temple and cheek. Almost frantically I reached up and grabbed the top of his helmet, pulled it toward me and saw that a bullet had struck the right side of his head and exited the left temple. The bullet had hit him as we lay there side by side and I wasn't aware of it.

Something was happening that I didn't understand. I wondered why it was that I was being spared. I lay there along side of the dead Kastan thinking of all the close encounters with death that I had had until now. I had even found bullet holes in my blouse sleeve and yet I had spilled no blood. A sudden thought flashed into my mind, Maybe the Japs couldn't hit me! Then fear engulfed me as a sudden surge of adrenalin entered my blood stream causing me to move again.

When the next bullets passed over me I leaped to my feet and ran forward. Immediately, I could see why Powers had not followed my advice to take only three steps before falling to the ground. The surface of the ground was solid rock and there were no craters to dive into but, ahead of me I could see the edge of a large one. Taking three steps and then angling off to the right, I dived for the edge of the crater. The expected burst of machine gun fire passed me on my left side. After that I was falling into the crater. I rolled over a couple of times and ended up partially lying on the prostrate form of PFC Powers.

He lay there on his back unmoving, his was face very pale. There were four other Marines there lying there side by side on the far side of the crater with their heads elevated just enough to peer over the rim toward the Japanese lines. The Marine on the far right was Lt. Aloysius Fennel, the platoon leader. He recognized me immediately and blurted out, "Powers is hit!"

The other Marines still faced the Japanese positions. The sergeant was lying to the left of the officer and to his left was two young Marines engage in a amazing deadly duel with the nearest enemy machine gunner less than two hundred yards away. Each Marine would fire his M1 rifle then lower their heads immediately to escape the returning enemy fire that would slam into the sand where the two faces had been only a second before. Because of the downward angle of fire from the Machine gun, we could determine that that gunner was elevated slightly above us and he had a good view of us, better than we had of him.

I turned to Powers and asked, "Where are you hit?"

"I don't know, but it hurts a lot, and I can't move my legs." His face was very pale and without expression.

The sergeant behind me yelled loudly for Kastan to "come up!"

"No..., he can't, Kastan is dead!" I said. Both the sergeant and Lieutenant stared at me. I was down on my knees and leaning forward over Powers when a bullet, apparently sent from somewhere in back of me passed over my left shoulder and smacked into the sand just above and a little to the left of his head. The bullet came from the direction of that portion of the cliff back where the body of Kastan lay. I shouted at the sergeant, "Get that guy, he's trying to shoot me in the back!" I gave Powers a quick examination and couldn't find a sign of injury, not even blood. I began all over again, more thoroughly this time and beginning with his head. I ripped open his blouse, his green undershirt showed no blood or holes. I loosened his cartridge belt buckle, pulled open the fly of his trousers and examined his groin area. There I found a small blue hole with a red tinge around it in his left hip, under his belt. Fearfully, I leaned over more and examined his right hip and found a jagged hole there with serum oozing from it. I drew an imaginary line from one point of entry to the point of exit and realized that the bullet had passed through his lower intestine and perhaps bladder then exited from his right hip. He had to be hemorrhaging immensely inside his abdomen.

Powers was still able to talk and was saying that "it hurts." And then he began to weep. I quickly injected a one half grain of morphine into him. He began calling for his mother. I told him his mother wasn't here but, I would get him home and he would see her then. I knew that he was bleeding to death and there was little I could do for him but stop the pain and perhaps use one of my bottles of serum albumin to replace the lost of blood. Then, all I could hope for was that the hemorrhaging to stop on its own.

The Japanese rifleman fired again and the bullet hit the sand just above Power's head again after passing by the left side of my shoulder. I looked back at the sergeant and he screamed out in reaction, "I can't see the bastard!" I became angry as I saw that the sergeant had not moved to a more favorable position where he could see the enemy soldier and fire his rifle at him, but instead remained in the better position of safety.

I jammed the barrel and bayonet of Power's rifle into the sand at his right waist and then proceeded to tie the bottle of serum to the wooden stock with the light canvas straps intended for that purpose. I pulled the coiled rubber tube fastened to the bottle down and removed the protected glass cover from the needle. Of some concern it had begun to rain lightly.

To my relief I found the vein on my first try. I inserted the needle through the rainwater and dirt covering his skin, while all the time a voice was saying in my head, "Cleanse the skin first with alcohol and use a rubber hose to tie off the arm in order to enlarge the vein." The lectured words I had heard in field medical school at Camp Elliot came back to me very clearly. I forced the thought from my mind considering the situation and milked the blood in the tube back away from the needle until I saw some appear in the glass inspection tube at the base of the needle. I knew then that I had entered the vein. I released the hose clamp that would allow the serum to flow down the tube into the vein. When bubbles appeared in the glass bottle, I knew the fluid was moving correctly.

Powers quit crying out for his mother and became quiet even as I watched the color of his skin become more pale. Then he began calling out for a priest, "I want a priest," over and over again until I said, "There is no priest, only me," I was feeling very helpless by then. I knew that he was going to die and nothing, not even a team of surgeons could stop it now.

Again, a bullet passed by my head and struck the sand in the same place the others had landed, just above Powers head. This time I turned quickly to look at the sergeant who turned his face away from me and didn't attempt to respond to my cursing at him. I said, Goddamit, get that son-of-bitch up on that cliff that's shooting at me!"

"I can't see the bastard," he replied again.

I turned my face back toward the serum bottle again to inspect the flow. I reached for it with my left hand when the rifle stock exploded right in my face. It had been struck by a bullet and shattered. The impact of the slug threw the rifle stock forward and with that movement the bottle of serum was abruptly forced forward with it. It was then brought up short when the rifle stopped and the glass container of serum rebounded as it was jerked back toward the rifle. It struck the trigger assembly broke into many pieces allowing the remaining serum to fall and escape into the black sand.

Powers could plainly see what had happened but, he didn't seem to be very alarmed. I knew for sure that he was lost, and the only thing I could think of doing was lean over him to protect him from the rainwater falling on his face and into his eyes. He was even calmer now and his eyes showed very little expression. I knew he was dying. I could feel tears as they ran from my eyes and down my cheeks. Powers saw them too as he said "Its all right 'Doc,' don't worry I can feel myself going!"

"No you are not, I'll get you out." I blurted out.

"No, I can feel it coming. It's OK now. Don't worry, I can feel myself going. Doc..., please hug me until I go?"

I could feel the tears as they coursed down my face and I was weeping unashamedly. Here he was dying and at the same time, he was trying to console me! I reached forward and placed the crook of my left arm around the back of his neck and pulled us together hugging him cheek to cheek. Our helmets clanged as they met. My left ear was toward his mouth and I could easily hear his labored breath. After a few moments his breathing changed to a rattling sound for a while and then he sucked in a big breath of air and failed to expel it. He lay very still and I was sure he was dead. I raised my head and looked at his face. Rain water was collecting in the depressions around his eyes which were directed upward at the sky, but seeing nothing. I closed his eyelids, brushed the water from them and pulled his helmet visor down to cover his face. The Jap riflemen fired again and as before hit that same portion of sand just above Power's head.

I got to my knees ignoring the Jap who I now figured as a poor marksman. I turned to and looked at the four Marines who seemed motionless except for watching me. Both the Lieutenant and the sergeant had tears running down their cheeks. It was the Lieutenant who brought us back to reality when he snapped "All right, cover him up." I needed to hear those words just then.

I pulled Power's poncho from under him and wrapped it about his head and shoulders. Then I reached over to his rifle still stuck in the sand and pulled the trigger housing loose, so that the Japs couldn't retrieve it and use it against us. I saw that the Lieutenant was still staring at Power's body. I crawled toward him and lay along side, primarily to escape from the view of that enemy rifleman.

I could see that the officer was under a lot of stress and was trying to determine our options concerning our immediate future. His eyes were darting here and there. He'd look at me, then at the sergeant, at the two riflemen and at the body of Power's over and again. One possibility, as I saw it was to dig in and hold the ground until the company's commander could come up with relief. Or then, maybe we should continue the attack and try to move forward to overcome the Japanese positions that were holding us up. However, I didn't think that was possible. Or, again, maybe we should withdraw. I was against attempting this because I knew that when a soldier sees his enemy turn and withdraw he becomes more confident and assured and is able to aim and use his weapons more effectively. I watched the Lieutenant's face as he made his decision. "We are in a tough spot, and will withdraw!" He said it very clear, loud and with authority. I felt a knot grow in the pit of my stomach.

While I had attended to Powers, one of the two Marines that were contesting the enemy machine gunner had fouled his rifle with sand and had slid down the incline and asked for my carbine. I was too busy to object and he regained his former spot to continue his duel with that enemy. Lt. Fennel selected him to withdraw first, the other rifleman was to go second, then nodding at the sergeant said, "And then you go after him. He turned to me and said, "You go next and then I'll follow."

The officer turned and pointed at the first Marine and said "go!" The rifleman leaped to his feet, ran down the incline, jumped over Power's body, ran up the incline in back of me, over the crater's lip and disappeared from my view in the direction of Kastan's body. He had taken my carbine with him leaving me without a weapon. I turned quickly to object about the route of withdrawal to the Lieutenant. I wanted to tell him that this was not the best was out of there as it afforded no concealment on the way. But, he was already assigning the second rifleman to "Go!"

That young Marine followed his companion out of the crater causing me to wince, but I hesitated as it was too late to protest further. The bullets came as I knew they would. They passed right above our heads on the way directed to strike the two young Marines. I looked at the Lieutenant just as he turned his head toward the sergeant and nodded. The sergeant rose quickly to his feet, ran and leaped over Power's body but, did not follow the other two. Instead he ran straight up the back of the crater wall, the highest part of the crater sides and as he reached the top he threw himself forward over the edge. There was a flurry of sand amongst his feet and I wondered if some of it was caused by bullets from the machine gunner.

I turned back to the Lieutenant expecting to hear that word 'Go," again, But instead I found that the Lieutenant was looking at me He had a smile on his face, That was a surprise as I had never seen Lt. Fennell smile before. He said, "Good luck!" and nodded his head at me.

I was taken aback by this and said, "You too Lieutenant!" Then with some sense of compassion or comradeship I reached out and slapped the toe of his shoe with my hand then took hold of it and squeezed it. Then letting go of it I was off running. I could not bear to leap over the body of Power's but ran around his feet and followed the sergeant up the incline in the back of the crater. My feet bogged half way up the incline and I paused, waiting for the impact of bullets I was sure to come. However, I lunged forward and with my hands I was able to pull myself over the lip and into what I assumed a depression beyond.

As I was beginning to fall I could see that there was a depression in front of me all right, but not the crater I had expected, it was a tank trap instead. As I fell forward I became involved with a heavy copper wire stretched across in front of me, it caught me under my chin and I pulled along on it with me. Down below me I saw the sergeant that had preceded me kneeling and he screamed up at me, "Don't touch that copper wire it's a trip wire to set off these shells!" It was too late as I was already falling with the wire caught above my outstretched upper arms and my chin. I landed on top of him smashing him to the ground. It wasn't ground really as he had been kneeling on top of two large fifteen inch naval artillery shells that lay side by side. A third was there also here, but slightly aft of the others.

I found myself being pummeled and kicked as the sergeant broke loose of me and then cursing me loudly he made his way up the back side of the sand trap and disappeared. Instantly, I thought that if the shells did explode the sergeant couldn't be so far away from me that he could escape being blown into vapor either. I did wonder if I would hear anything during the explosion. I shouted after him, "You are one bastard I never want to serve with again!"

Chapter Thirty-Three

Without A Platoon Sergeant

I SAT ON one of the huge fifteen inch naval shells. I was too exhausted to care whether they exploded or not. I wouldn't know it if they did. I pulled the copper wire taunt across the smooth shell casing and whacked it with he sharp blade of my Kay-Bar knife, cutting it in two. Then realizing that the blow might set off some of delaying action timing device in the detonator of the shell, I leaned down to listen for a 'tick, tick, tick' noise that might indicate that. There was so much other noise I couldn't hear much of anything else. While my head was in that lowered position I saw some printing in English, it read *U.S. Navy Ordinance*, followed by a series of numbers.

We had seen many of these huge shells land, fired from our large warships far offshore. They would come 'whooshing' in to burst on the Japanese defenses in front of us, after having been directed there by our naval gunnery observers accompanying us. I watched as missiles struck the sand out in front of our lines, most exploded, but all did not. The ones that failed to do so, either skidded across the sand throwing up a rooster tail effect or would tumble end over end and roll until they were trapped by a depression in the sand. I supposed that these shells were called 'duds' and that they had not exploded because there was not enough heavy impact on the detonators, or because they were faulty.

I sat there ten minutes waiting for Lt. Fennell to arrive. I was certain that he would follow me and not go by the way of the two riflemen. My mind seemed to want to focus on how Powers and Kastan had died. Their deaths bothered me as I felt partially responsible because I had urged them forward. Both of these boys had graduated from high schools only eight months before in June of 1944 and joined the Marine Corps immediately after. They had transferred to our battalion from a replacement unit just after we arrived in Hawaii. I looked upon them as youngsters even though I was only a year older than they. Kastan was barely shaving at the time he was assigned to D Company and was quickly was a subject of Goodling's good natured antics and remarks. He was at first assigned to the Second platoon, then transferred shortly thereafter to the first.

I did not see the other four Marines again. Lt. Fennel left the large crater just after me, but not by the same path. The casualty reports show that he was struck in the head by a bullet that day and in the area I had last seen him. He was found still alive and carried back the aid station where he died the next day. The two young courageous riflemen became casualties, but whether they lived or died I was unable to ascertain. The Marines I interviewed after returning to Camp Tarawa could not help me identify either them or the sergeant who also failed to return.

After ten or so minutes Lt. Fennell still had not arrived; he should have reached me by that time. I considered going back to the crater to see if he were still there, either injured or dead. But then there was the possibility that he followed the path of the two young riflemen. I cringed at that thought: it was a certain death corridor I thought. An enemy machine gunner would be shooting at his back while he ran toward another enemy concealed in the cliff armed with a rifle and hand grenades.

I decided that I could not go on and leave the Lieutenant lying injured in the large crater. I couldn't live with that on my conscious. I stood up on one of the artillery shells and began to claw my way up the sand bank from where I had fallen. When the level of my head reached the rim of the sand trap, I pushed sand high into a mound and raised my head behind it and pushed it out to the right side. I had only a glance of the interior of the large crater, but I could not see Lt. Fennell in there, only the body of Powers.

Deciding to follow the Lieutenant's orders and withdraw, I climbed out of the tank trap by the back side and slid over the sand pulling myself along by my hands and pushing with my toes. But then I found that I had to contend with that one Japanese soldier now over my left side, the one that killed Kastan and had fired several bullets at me while I attended Powers.

That guy fired at me again, and again his bullet went high and left above me. He fired twice again at me with the same failed result, failing to correct his aim. The thought flashed into my mind how he would fare on the company rifle range as the Top Sergeant looked on and saw his poor marksmanship.

Seeing the very top of the 'beehive' bunker over the edge of one crater, I crawled in that direction. When raising my head once I found I was looking into the muzzle of an M-1 rifle and above it the face of PFC "Abie" Hower. His eyes grew big and then a big grin spread across his face and was I happy to see him. He yelled out, "Hi Doc! What are you doing out there? C'mon in here!'

I rose from the ground and leaped over his head and shoulders and landed on his back after which I rolled down to his feet. I turned and quickly crawled up along his left side and we both began to peer over the crater's edge toward the Jap lines. I began to tell him about being with Lt. Fennell.

Almost immediately I heard the 'whoosh' of the first mortar shell arriving. It was followed by the usual three more and they all exploded in a straight line along the right side of the shell hole that we lay in. The smoke swirled about us and settled in the low area of the crater. I coughed as the smoke burned my nostrils and throat but was relieved that I was not hit by those screaming pieces of flying hot steel. Both, Abie and I were covered with sand from the explosions. I looked at him and saw that his face was still pressed onto the sand He was making a horrible sobbing noise. I said, "Come on. You better get ready to shoot. They may come at us!"

He didn't move but kept making those same sounds and that was beginning to unnerve me. I shook his shoulder and his head wobbled, just like Kastan's had. I reached out and placed my hand on top of his helmet and pulled his head toward me. Immediately my finger tips found the small jagged opening in the right side of his helmet where a small fragment from one of the mortar shells had entered. It had gone through his head and come out the left side. I pushed his head away from me and the gray stuff oozed out from under his helmet and down the side of his face.

I jumped to my feet. I felt panic again and I had to get up and away from there. I ran at the crater's side, leaped up and over it and hurled myself into the next one. I found that I was in the midst of Sgt. Goodling's 2nd squad who were all huddled at the bottom of the shell hole. Goodling looked at me with obvious surprise and demanded, "Where the hell you been?"

"Up with the Japs! Where have you been?"

I knew I wasn't right to retort like that, I felt that there was something wrong with me. Then Logel who was there asked me if I had seen Hower?

I remembered later of telling them all of Hower's death and thought that I gave a little laugh as I did. PFC Leonard Logel looked shocked. He asked, "Where is Hower?" I told him and he jumped to his feet and scrambled back the way I had come. I sat still for a moment trying to understand why I should laugh like that when I told of Hower's death. I felt embarrassed. I went on to tell Goodling of what I had been doing and seen and that Lt. Fennel had ordered his platoon to withdraw.

Then suddenly I felt a surge of energy. I felt 'peppy' and invincible, as another surge of adrenaline entered my blood stream. I told Goodling that I had found out that the Japs couldn't hit me! He looked at me in an odd way. Then he said, "I don't know where Lieutenant Horvath is, but since the 1st Platoon is withdrawing I will have my squad dig in a defensive line right here and hold."

Logel returned and sat down alongside of me and began sobbing; he and Hower had been the best of buddies. Two days later he would join his friend in death. He would fall and die the result of being hit by many bullets from a machine gun.

I felt terrible and embarrassed about Hower's death. To get away from my comrades, I told Goodling that I was going to find the Lieutenant. He answered, "You tell the Lieutenant what you told me and say that based on your information I'm going to spread my men out right here in a defensive line until I hear from him."

I left the crater running and crawling toward the lone sand covered bunker where I'd last seen Lt. Horvath some time before. One of the company machine gun squads was working a gun near there, and they were firing their weapon at the long line of bunkers out in front of us. I paused in a shallow crater near them and then suddenly Platoon Sergeant Nick Abromovich appeared and fell to one knee at the edge of the hole. I heard a burst of bullets go overhead and I yelled, "Get down, Nick. Don't you hear those bullets going by? That guy's trying to get you!"

"Yeah, but it's OK. I found that the Japs can't hit me!" He spoke very casually. Staring at him I thought war can rob us of our reasoning power so we think and believe strange things.

He asked me if I knew where the Lieutenant was and I told him that the last I'd seen him was when he was behind the tank which was up close to the line of bunkers now. We both looked toward it and I could see several Marines down on their knees at the rear of the tank. The front of the tank was up against the sand mound. I could see the turret move back and forth as if the gunner was seeking out a target to shoot at with the large gun. The tank was only about one hundred yards west of where the body of Powers lay, and I hadn't seen it before as I was too afraid to raise up and look around when I was up there.

The sergeant said that the Lieutenant must be there with the tank, so he jumped up and ran toward it. I then decided that this shell crater was no place for me and that I should follow the sergeant and go find the Lieutenant too.

When I'd covered half the distance to the tank, I dove head first into a crater and saw a Marine lying at the bottom of it. It was the same 4th Division Marine whose badly damaged hand and injured hip I had treated beside the tank about two hours before. He was now a good one hundred yards forward toward the Jap lines than when I had left him. He grinned up at me and I could see he was in a lot of pain. He said that he wanted to kill Japs and he held a sheath knife in his left hand. I was amazed and couldn't understand how a man injured like he was could crawl along the ground for the distance he had.

I injected some more morphine into his good arm and over his protests put him on my spread out poncho and dragged him at a run for the lone bunker in back of me. There I stretched him out on the sand and shouted to some nearby Marines that I could see nearby peering out of a hole at me to send for litter bearers who could carry this injured man back to the aid station. This injured Marine was probably the toughest one I would ever hope to meet.

The machine gun crew off to my left looked at me, and the gunner grinned and nodded at me. I crawled over to him and said that I was going to run up to the tank near Lt. Horvath, and that I'd run along in the tank's tread marks to avoid land mines. "Don't hit me," I said. The gunner, PFC Lynch, gave me a big smile showing his teeth and nodded again. I ran the two hundred yards to the tank, diving into several shell holes on the way. At times I could hear bursts of bullets coming from Lynch's gun going by my left side. He was firing at a spot in front of the tank as I could see the bullets smashing into the sand there.

When I got to the rear of the tank, I found a rifleman kneeling and peering around the right rear tank treads toward the front of the vehicle. There was sudden burst of sparks and grey metal particles at the rifleman's face. I thought, "He's dead," and moved forward to aid him, But, he rose to his knees where he was partially sheltered behind the right tracks of the tank and brushed furious at his face.

Lt. Horvath was to his immediate left, and he was kneeling under the overhang of the rear end of the tank. To his left, on his knees, was Sgt. Abromovich. The Lieutenant was holding the telephone and yelling into it, trying to be heard over the roar of the engine exhaust. I fell to my knees on the sand along side of them. I leaned forward, my left hand holding onto the trailer hitch and my helmet against a metal plate nest to that.

An explosion shook the tank. I could feel the tank rise from the sand. The force of the explosion threw me backward where I slid about twelve feet away on my back. The smoke and dust swirled on and around me almost suffocating me. Lying there temporarily blinded, I frantically fought to free myself from a heavy weight and came to realize that it was Sgt. Abromovich who was lying on top of me. I kicked loose of him and as he attempted to rise, I put my foot against his back and kicked him back toward the tank. We both struggled to our knees and I followed him back to the tank.

My first organized thought was that the gunner inside had fired the 75mm. gun and that along with the propelling charge of the shell had caused a double explosion, But then realized that didn't happen as the explosion was too great for that. Then a series of smaller explosions occurred in back of me and I fell flat to the ground and looked back. I saw more black Japanese hand grenades land only about twelve or fifteen feet away from us. I turned my face away and yelled, "Grenades," I reached out and slapped the Lieutenant on the back of his left shoulder causing him to fall forward taking the sergeant to ground with him.

The Japanese soldiers had come out of the bunker crawl hole and had taken a crouched position in front of the tank, under its gun muzzle. They were now throwing grenades over the tank to land near us. Fortunately the grenades sank into the soft sand as before and smothered some of the fragments that would probably have struck us in our bodies.

The Lieutenant pushed the rifleman aside, peered around the steel track and yelled, "There's Japs at the front of the tank. Who's got grenades?"

I was already pulling two from my blouse pocket. He grabbed one, pulled the safety pin, and hurled the grenade forward over the tank turret. With the other grenade I did the same thing. There was so much noise being made by explosions in back of us and by the engine of the tank I couldn't recall later hearing the two grenades explode.

Then the tank engine revved and the machine jerked and then the right track came moving back toward us and began to pile up on the ground at our right. The Japs up in front of the tank had blown it off the tank somehow. The Lieutenant yelled for us to cover the sides of the tank and to emphasize his command further he struck me a blow on my shoulder with the flat of his hand knocking me flat on the ground near the left rear part of the tank track. I pulled my sheath knife, got to my knees and waited. I wondered how I would fight off an enemy soldier with only a sheath knife while he had a rifle and bayonet.

After a few moments the tank engine stopped and I heard metallic noises and voices coming from under the vehicle. The tank crew was abandoning their machine. They came crawling out of the escape hatch under the tank, and Sergeant Abromovich and I grabbed at their hands to pull them free from the sand. I didn't see the machine gun they were supposed to bring out. Lieutenant Horvath said to one of them who appeared to be the commander, "What do we do now?"

Apparently he was referring to the lecture on tank abandonment given back at Camp Pendleton by the tough looking Major. The Major had said the tank crew would bring out a light machine gun and set it up and then we would all work together in order to fight off the enemy and save the tank. The tank commander replied, "I don't know what you're going to do, but we're getting the hell out of here!"

With that the three Marines ran for the rear lines. I watched them go part way, as they popped up here and there from a hole and ran to the next in a frenzied attempt to get away from where we knelt in back of their tank. Well, so much for that tough talking Marine Major son-of-a-bitch and his procedures! In the end, it is always the foot soldier that does the dirty work and gets little credit for it.

Now! What was in store for those of us left there at the tank? We were huddled up under the back end, and we had no idea how many Japs were at the front. The Lieutenant and I were without a firearm. A Marine had run off with mine and I don't know what the officer's excuse was.

The two enlisted Marines and I looked to the Lieutenant for guidance. He didn't seem to know what to do. Suddenly Sgt. Abromovich jumped to his feet and looking up yelled, "I'll get the gun!" He apparently meant the fifty caliber machine gun mounted on the tank turret.

Lt. Horvath came back with, "No, don't." It was too late. The sergeant was already up on the motor cowling on the back of the tank and was crawling forward to the backside of the turret. He slowly stood up raising his hands forward and toward the handle grips of the guns. His hands paused just before making contact with them. Then he fell backward into sort of a sitting position on the motor cowling and tumbled over backward in a somersault fashion and down onto me. I scrambled to avoid his falling body but he landed on me anyway, pinning my legs to the ground. As I shoved him off me, I could see the bullet hole in his helmet over his right eye. There was one of those little blue holes in the front of his neck and another larger one at the back side where blood was running out on the ground. Seeing two more holes in his clothing, I pulled his blouse open. There was blood oozing from the two holes in his green undershirt.

The Lieutenant and I stared at each other. I was trying to comprehend what was happening to us. Then, not knowing what else to do, I reached down and pulled the 45 caliber pistol from the sergeant's holster and handed it to the Lieutenant. He took the weapon and placed it inside his right blouse pocket. Since he carried no other weapon I thought that was a strange act, considering our predicament. I still had no weapon, and I looked for the Sergeant's M-1 and discovered he had left it up on the tank's motor cowling. I started to rise to my feet but the Lieutenant anticipating my intended action barked out, "No!"

That brought me back to realty, the Lieutenant seemed to be thinking clearly again. He said to the riflemen and me, "Let's get out of here." He told the Marine, "Run for it!" The rifleman, who I thought might have been PFC Roy Johnson was off in a flash, he needed no further urging. The Lieutenant and I watched him make the first shell hole, then the next, and the next.

The platoon leader then said, "You!" I was up and running very quickly. At about one hundred feet out I heard a bullet pass about waist high on my left and it struck the sand in front of me. I took another three steps and leaped to the right as another bullet whizzed by on my right and hit the sand about twenty feet in front of me. I took another three steps and jumped to the right again as I saw two Marine sergeants, Russ Renner and Bert Faltyn firing away with their M1 rifles at Japanese soldiers who were in front of the tank I had just left.

The two combat veterans were kneeling in a shallow shell hole with their heads and shoulders showing above the ground. Both men were having trouble because of the sand getting into their rifles and interfering with the shell casings being ejected properly. The two had an entrenching tool using it to knock the slides back in order to cause the ejection. I dived into the hole where they were and lay gasping for breath. Renner fired at a target and then banged on the slide with the shovel. "How do you like it?" I supposed he meant combat. "I don't, I'm scared!" Both answered the same way at the same time, "Who the hell isn't!"

I went on to tell them that Sgt. Abromovich was dead and that Lt. Horvath ordered a withdrawal back to the bee hive bunker; that I had just left him back at the tank. I asked for their help in getting him out.

One of them said, "OK, get going. We will get him out!"

I jumped up and ran back to the isolated bee hive bunker again. I could see machine gunner Lynch and his assistants fire their weapon toward the disabled tank. I ran directly at the machine gun in a straight line. It was no time to be zig zagging and chancing being shot by one of our guns. Lynch was firing burst after burst and they were going right by my left shoulder. I could imagine him grinning as he leaned forward over the gun sight. When I reached him, I ran by and threw myself into the hole behind him and gasped again for air.

Moments later, after telling the gun crew what I had learned of the withdrawal, I found Sgts. Charles Goodling and Earl Brock organizing their squads into one defensive line. The men were ordered to dig in and hold that position. No one there knew where Lt. Horvath was and we also were missing the 3rd squad. After waiting for about fifteen minutes or so, we saw a wounded man, shot in his side come crawling in and as I treated him, he described where he had been and where the rest of the squad was now. He said the other men were up ahead of us to the left near the base of a huge concrete bunker and that Cpls. Roy Tinnemeyer and Orville Wilson were both badly wounded and needed help.

I told Sgt. Goodling that I was going up there and help those men. This would be the third time that I had gone forward to the Jap bunkers where the Japs were in control and I couldn't imagine that I'd make it back. As I ran by Lynch and his gun crew I told him where I was going and that I needed cover and please help me. He grinned, nodded yes, and swung his gun to cover my route. I ran and I heard the bullets from his gun go by me and some strike the top of the sand hill in front of me. I scrambled from one hole to another, in and out for two hundred yards until I reached the base of the bunker.

There, I found several men of the 3rd squad and to my surprise Lt. Horvath. I don't know how he reached there alive as he had taken a direct route from the tank to this point and certainly he had run in front of a number of enemy machine gun positions. Cpl. Roy Tinnemeyer was lying on the ground, very pale and in pain, but he manage a smile and said,

"Glad to see you Doc."

He had hand grenade fragments in his right hip and a bullet wound in his side. He was trying to talk and I gave him and injection of morphine. He was talking as I tried to stop the hemorrhaging, He told how it felt to be shot. He didn't seem to know about the fragment in him from the hand grenade. I told him I was going to get him out of there and then he became quiet as the morphine took hold. The Marines helped me construct a litter from two rifles and a poncho and we lifted Tinnemeyer onto that rig.

Lt. Horvath spoke, "Lets get the hell out of here!"

I directed three of the Marines to take a corner of the litter and I would take the fourth, the left rear one. Then I said "Let's run like hell for the rear and if anyone gets knocked down the others should grab Tinnemeyer's blouse at the shoulders and run, dragging him on the ground."

Immediately Lt. Horvath countered those instructions with, "No Doc, You stay, Prunty will take your place."

One of the Marines had just told him that Cpl. Wilson was still on top

Stretcher bearers running to deliver a casualty from the front lines.

of the rise of sand and may be alive. Prunty picked up the left rear corner of the litter and the group began running across the open space toward the rear where Goodling had set up the defense line. Later, I found out that Prunty was shot through the calf of his left leg and knocked down about half way across, but managed to crawl on to safety by his own efforts and was eventually evacuated. I have not seen him since.

When the litter team left, the Lieutenant, two riflemen and I were left at the base of the bunker. One of the riflemen began telling the Lieutenant about what had confronted them up on top of the bunker. He said that when they tried to go over the top of it they came face to face with many Japanese soldiers who fired at them with rifles and threw hand grenades. Cpl. Wilson was hit and fell to the ground wounded or dead and he was still up there.

Cpl. Tinnemeyer went down at the same time and the squad withdrew, dragging the corporal with them. Lt. Horvath looked at me and said, "We can't leave Wilson up there. He may be still alive. You go up and see. I'll follow and protect you" I turned and climbed the sand mound quickly and without hesitation as he had given me a direct order. The small bluff was about twelve to fifteen feet high and I had to climb up it by clawing at it with my hands and knees. The Lieutenant followed me. I peered over the edge at the top and saw that the surface was flat and it was about fifty feet across to where it fell off to the original ground level on the other side. Right in the middle of the flat area was a large crater made, I supposed by a bomb. At the crater's left edge was the exposed top and side of a concrete bunker that had the sand covering blown away from it. I could see a gun port facing toward me.

Across the crater, on its far edge was the still form of a Marine lying face down in the sand. The shortest way to him would be down through the crater and up the other side to where he lay. I ran down into the depression and looked over at the gun port. I didn't see any gun barrel protruding from there. Looking back and up I saw the Lieutenant perched on the crater's edge where I had paused seconds before. I saw he held a hand grenade in his right hand. It was then that I realized that neither of us had a firearm. I felt a flush of anger as I realized that the officer wasn't thinking right. Why hadn't he brought the two riflemen up with him to protect me? After all if I were rushed by Japanese soldiers, what would he do with a grenade, throw it in my direction?

I dashed up the other side of the crater to where Wilson lay. His skin was very pale and he didn't seem to be breathing. I examined him and found a bullet hole in his right side and another jagged hole, probably made by the bullet's exit or a grenade fragment in his back. It looked as though the metal might have smashed through his spinal column. Finding no pulse, I was sure he was dead. Then half rising, I bent over in an attempt to lift him in a fireman's carry to haul him out of there. At that elevation I found I was looking down the other side of the sand mound and saw a line of Japanese infantrymen perhaps only fifty feet from me. They were all poised and down on one knee, their weapons pointed to the sky with the bayonets gleaming in the light and the rifle butts resting on the sand or on their knees. The Japanese soldier and I stared at each other then I ducked quickly away.

I let go of Wilson's body and it slumped back onto the ground. I leaped backward into the crater tumbling over and over before hitting the bottom. Turning, I faced toward Lt. Horvath who was still near the side of the bunker. There, slightly to his left and framed in the gun port opening of the fortification, was the face of a young Japanese soldier. He appeared to me about fourteen years old and was looking out at me. There was no sign of a weapon in his hands. I scooped up a handful of sand and threw it at the gun port as I ran toward the Lieutenant and watched the enemy soldier pull his head back out of view. I reached the Lieutenant's position and shouted to him, "Wilson is dead and there are probably a thousand Japs lined up right over there." (A slight exaggeration no doubt). The Lieutenant was still holding the grenade in his hand, there was no sign of the pistol I had handed him back at the damaged tank a short while before.

Without waiting for the officer to answer I twisted around causing the sand to cave away from under me and I began to fall from the edge of the embankment down to where I landed on the same spot where we had left the two riflemen. Only one, PFC Don Giles, was still there. I didn't know what had become of the other.

Lt. Horvath tumbled down the side of the mound in back of me. He said, "Let's withdraw." I knew the withdrawal scenario by then, the rifleman would go first, and then me, and then he'd follow. When it came my turn, I ran. I heard and counted five bullets that passed by me and hit the sand on either side and in front of me. I could tell that the Jap rifleman was on the rise in back of me and was firing downward at my back. Since he had to have been less than seventy-five feet behind me when I first began my run, I remembered thinking later, "That Jap is a lousy shot, too!" The shots were fired at such regular intervals I was sure there was only one man doing the shooting and that he was using a bolt action rifle.

In front of me I saw a helmet and a BAR rifle barrel projecting above the rim of a small crater. I ran and jumped into the hole in back of PFC Donald Giles. He had interrupted his return to our lines in order to turn his weapon against the Japanese who were now at our backs. His weapon was jammed with sand and he was working furiously to clear it. I told him some Jap was trying to shoot me in the back while I was running, He answered, "Yeah, I see him. He's dug into a little hole on the side of cliff, but I'll get the bastard!" I watched as he fired and saw his bullet kick up sand on a dark spot on the side of the bluff. I saw movement there and a moving object which resembled a stick and which in reality was a rifle.

While he was trying to do that, Lt. Horvath came running by us at an accelerated pace about the speed of a fast moving freight train, and he didn't slow down or speak a word either. Giles yelled to me, "Follow him, I'll cover you!" Giles later followed me back to our lines, I thought him a pretty brave and competent Marine, besides being one hell of a nice guy.

For the third time in a two to three hour period, I collapsed to the sand near Lynch in a fetal position trying to regain my breath trying to repulse the sharp pain in my chest. Lynch was doing an outstanding job of shooting at the Jap position and I told him so. He grinned and said, "Hell, we've burned out three barrels on this gun so far." Scattered about him were also hundreds of empty shell casings and empty ammunition boxes. He gave me the impression that he was enjoying all of this shooting.

When I told him what I had seen on top of the large sand mound and that maybe the Japs were preparing to charge us he retorted, "Great, let them, I hope they do, we'll take care of them!"

I lay there and watched him rake the top of the sand mound with his weapon, the bullets kicking up sand wherever they struck. I'm sure he kept the Japanese thinking that it wasn't wise to charge us. He and his crew were the last to withdraw. I know that they had held to their assigned position well over two hours in plain view of the Japanese defenders who must have been trying to hit them the entire time. I think that there were many of us that day who owed our lives to the efficiency and bravery of those machine gunners.

A defensive line was organized by Lt. Horvath and mostly with the assistance of Sgt. Goodling who warned us to expect a counter charge. We were short of weapons as many of ours were fouled with sand. I still did not have one as I had neglected to pause long enough to take one up from the ground. God knows, there were enough out there after all those men of the company had been wounded or killed.

PFC Glen Brown and I dug out a shell hole together and fashioned a rifle pit. Afterwards I watched two riflemen near us digging a hole. They kept at it until their hole was about six feet deep. The men worked in such a frenzy to construct a shelter that they did not realize their folly. Sgt. Goodling was soon over there, lying on his stomach looking down at them and yelling, "You dumb bastards! How are you going to do any shooting out of something like that?" He ordered them to fill in the hole to about a four foot depth. I felt amused by the incident and made faces at Goodling in an attempt to return some of his ridicule. That added to his chagrin, but it wasn't enough to help my morale much.

I sat in our rifle pit and began thinking that I was lucky to be alive after this day's experiences. I knew that the 2nd platoon had about forty two men in it when we began our attack that morning, and I began to add up in my mind how many men I knew had been wounded or killed. I knew of eight. Actually there were thirteen. There were many more casualties than that in the 1st Platoon. The company was in trouble. I crawled across the ground to where the Lieutenant was sitting in a hole. I told him what I knew of casualties in both platoons and he listened quietly. He looked exhausted, his face blackened by sweat and dirt. He stared at me out of tired bloodshot eyes and all he said afterward was a curt, "Thanks. Keep quiet about it!"

I thought as I left him, "What a story he and I could write about the happenings of this day!"

Before darkness set in that night the company commander arranged for an artillery barrage to land along the entire line of sand covered bunkers out in front of us. That was done to discourage a counter attack. We crouched in our foxholes wet, tired, filthy, very discouraged, and demoralized. Most of the men's firearms were fouled with sand, and there were several of us who didn't even have a rifle. I clutched at the bayonet I carried in my belt.

The Lieutenant crawled along the line and said to show our rifles to the Japanese and if we didn't have one to hold up a stick or anything that would resemble one. Hell! We were out of hand grenades and I had not seen anyone from the supply unit bring anything to us since we had been on the island, including ammunition and food.

The Japanese did not rush our part of the line that night. I always thought later that they made a mistake as I'm sure they could have overrun us if they had. We crouched there until dawn watching and waiting for them to come at us. I watched the tracer bullets from the enemy machine guns come floating out from behind the Japanese lines toward us in the darkness, searching and searching. It was quite a sight to behold.

CHAPTER THIRTY-FOUR

How Can God Let This Happen?

POM, POM, POM, pom went the battalion's 81 millimeter mortars. I judged them to be about two hundred yards in back of us, probably set in at the bottom of a large crater. PFC Glen Brown and I cautiously looked over the top of the edge of our rifle pit toward the Japanese line of bunkers. A few seconds passed before the shells exploded on top of the long sand mound that covered the fortifications which resembled a huge windrow of cut hay in a farmer's field.

Dawn had just broken on the fifth day after our landing. We were far behind the schedule we were given to follow as told to us on board ship. The island was supposed to have been secured in three days and all of the 5th Marine Division members were to have been back on board ship and headed toward Okinawa by now. Instead, we were thankful that the Japanese hadn't been able to throw us back into the ocean.

The 81 mm mortars kept up their barrage and we could hear coming from way in back of us the booming husky voices of the 155 mm. 'Long Tom' cannons as they added their powerful weight to the assault. These shells cruised over our heads and landed up on top of the Japanese fortifications. Passing over, they reminded me of a railroad freight car rolling along the tracks as they made a loud "Whooshshushshush" noise. None of us there in those rifle pits could resist the impulse of looking out as those huge shells exploded among the enemy's positions.

Later on, we could hear a rolling booming noise far out to sea to the west. Huge shells began arriving from our battleships and cruisers as they applied more punishment to the Japs out in front of us. "Good!" I thought. "That'll teach them not to maul us again, as they did yesterday." Together all these shells ripped open the top of the sand mound and we could see chunks of concrete being tossed up above ground and knew that Jap's were dying over there. All the while a little artillery spotter plane circled around over the enemy position, and not very high either. The men inside of it had guts for sure as they were under heavy fire all the time they were out there.

After a while the larger guns were quiet and the smaller "bang" of our regiment's pack howitzers could be heard as they fired away at targets over on the other side of the sand mound. We couldn't see where those shells were landing. But then, artillery shells began landing on our position again and I could hear men scream out that our artillery was firing short and into our lines. That wasn't true though as we could hear the noise of the Japanese field pieces as they fired barrage after barrage at us. Those of us left in the 2nd platoon took the brunt of the barrages, and we huddled on the floor of our rifle pits hoping to escape the shell splinters that were cutting through the air all around us.

To our right was that high plateau on which Airfield #2 was located. At the plateau's nearest point to us, just above where Lt. Richard Lewis had been shot down, there was a sand covered bunker. This bunker provided the defending Japanese inside with a clear field of fire with which to sweep the flat plain of the airfield and to see and fire at us down below to the west. Brown and I watched a few 4th Division Marines near to the south of the bunker raise up and charge it. Making it safely to the base of the sand covered installation, they climbed its steep side, apparently intending to fire their weapons into the gun ports.

But then, a series of mortar shells landed on top of the bunker and knocked down all five Marines who were there. As the dust and smoke cleared we could see one man struggle to his feet and attempt to help one of his fallen comrades. More shells landed and knocked down the lone Marine again. Then from one side several other Marines rose from the ground and charged the bunker and upon reaching it dragged their comrades back to their previous safer position.

As I watched the heroics of the Marines in attempting to save their comrades, I had been giving a verbal commentary of it to Brown. Suddenly he cried out, "How can you look at that!" I turned and found that he was really shaken up. To now he had been praying some and I had been telling him it was better that he shoot at the Japanese instead of praying. After all, the Lieutenant had on several occasions admonished us that we weren't shooting enough.

The bunkers that were confronting us, I found interesting. Usually they were constructed in the fashion of a square concrete box that had for a door a small crawl hole that was inserted low to the ground. On each side of the bunker there were gun slits or ports that had been built into the wall. These slits were about twelve inches high and about twenty-four inches wide and enabled the man inside to fire his weapon out at us. On the floor of the bunker, just under each of the gun ports, there was constructed a hole with a funnel shaped top. That was there to catch a hand grenade thrown through the opening from the outside. The grenade would fall into the hole where it would explode and the fragments would be contained. That prevented the defending soldier from being killed or severely injured. The sand piled high on top of the bunkers, or pill boxes, as some called them, absorbed the force of the shell exploding on them, as well helping to camouflage them from us, the enemy.

Sitting there in the rifle pit I watched the sand covered bunker up on the edge of the airfield for more activity. I made out a small amount of blue smoke coming from a dark spot on the side facing our position. I told Brown about it and said that I thought the smoke indicated an enemy machine gun position firing out toward us. I made out a little bit of blue smoke coming from a dark spot on the side facing our position. I told Glen about it and said I thought that smoke may indicate a machine gun firing out toward us. He couldn't seem to see the spot I indicated, but still was upset. I bor-

Scores of wrecked planes provided cover for Japanese defenders, resulting in hundreds of Marines being killed or wounded in taking Motoyama Airfields.

rowed his M-1 rifle aimed and fired at the dark spot that I figured to be a gun port. The first bullet hit to the left of the target. After correcting my aim, I fired again several times. I did not see where any of the other bullets hit and even though I watched the spot for a while, I didn't see any more blue smoke either.

The Japanese artillery barrages were constant and very damaging to us. If not disabling or killing our men outright, the barrages were affecting our morale greatly because of the constant concussion and fear of death or dismemberment. Each time there was a pause in the shelling, we would scramble to our knees and watch to see whether the Japanese would make one of their banzai charges. Right then I wished that they wouldn't as I still did not have a weapon.

One enemy battery specifically kept up the assault on us. I supposed that's what they were assigned to do, in order to keep us down so that we couldn't initiate an attack on them as we did the day before. The shelling caused many casualties to the company. The Japanese had an interesting weapon. It hurled a missile the size of a large garbage can at us and was launched from a wooden ramp about two hundred yards behind their lines. When launched it was sent up the ramp by a propelling charge and the racket it made was a loud screeching noise. When it reached its maximum height, it would come tumbling end over end and down toward us. When I first heard and saw it, it was frightening. After that it began to be a laughable affair. The first shell landed short of our lines. All subsequent firings of the strange missile brought cheers from our men and they yelled out encouragement for the Japs to try and do better. The situation provided us with some very necessary comedy relief and raised our morale substantially.

At about midmorning on the 23rd of February we became aware that G Company had been returned to the line and established right in back of us to reinforce our position. Those poor guys didn't have even twenty four hours to recuperate after the beating they had taken on the D+1 through D+3. I crawled up close to two young Marines who had dug into a shell hole about twenty feet in back of where Brown and I were positioned. One of the Marines had the first name of Peter, the other I never learned. They were both just kids, about eighteen years old. They told me that G Company had suffered over sixty percent casualties in the past three days fighting when trying to get across the open space that we still hadn't crossed permanently.

I went back to join Brown in our rifle pit. Later we heard the roar of an engine behind us. We looked back and saw a large half-track vehicle with a strange apparatus constructed on its bed. Suddenly the thing belched smoke, flames, and burning particles and with a screeching noise sent out dozens of rockets toward the Japanese lines. When the smoke began to clear, we saw that the Marines operating the half-track were moving off to the rear at a fast speed with the tracks throwing up a spray of sand clear back and over us. No sooner had they disappeared than we heard the "Shushish, sushish, shushish" of Jap artillery shells coming at us. We threw ourselves onto the bottom of the hole and clutched at the sand.

The Japs were right on target and bracketed our area. They inflicted a lot of casualties on the G company men. Brown and I sat there looking at each other and wondering why many of our men weren't killed. It was unbelievable that we survived that barrage. At times I was again entertaining the fantasy that I couldn't be killed. I would feel that way for a while and then I would change and become terrified that I would die.

I did learn one thing here. After heavy artillery shelling as the one described above, the men on the receiving end could be found in a stupor or state of shock. The mind would struggle to regain control; the body is numb and not reacting to command. I attempted to straighten my legs and in doing so inadvertently kicked Brown on one his knees. The pain caused him to grimace and apparently feel some irritation as he quickly recovered from his shocked state of mind. Thereafter, each time I suffered from that state of shock caused by artillery fire concussion, I would try and kick my foxhole partner on the side of his knee, hoping for him to have a speedy recovery and even retaliate in some way. I think that some of my foxhole comrades thought me weird at times.

It wasn't long after this shelling had ceased that we heard a Jap field piece out beyond the line of bunkers fire a round. The gun went "Pom" and the shell came "shushshushing" at us. Brown and I stared at each other and I could see the terror come back into his eyes. We relaxed a bit as we heard the shell pass high overhead. It exploded a long way in back of us, perhaps four hundred yards away. Then the gun was fired again and this time the shell seemed to be a little lower and exploded a little closer to us. I saw the fear rise again in Brown's eyes, and he said, "They're cutting the range after each shell."

The third shell came screaming over head and landed another hundred yards shorter than the last. By that rate the next shell should land right on or very close to us. The gun fired again and the shell had to have been only a couple of feet over our heads as it landed twenty or so feet behind us. As it passed over, Brown and I were hugging the sand at the bottom of the pit. The explosion bounced us up and down and then the sides of the hole caved in on us. We shook loose from the sand and struggled to a sitting position. Again we couldn't understand why we had been spared. I sat there feeling sick all over while trying to shake off the numbness and the fogginess from my brain. As it cleared I began to hear someone calling out, "Corpsman, Corpsman!"

I struggled to my knee, my ears, eyes, and mouth full of sand. Brown said, "Don't go. You'll get killed!" But I had to go. I crawled out of the hole and back toward the voice calling for help. I found the shell hole containing the two young G Company Marines to whom I had spoken earlier. Neither one was capable of yelling for help.

The two had been sitting in the hole facing each other with their knees drawn up to their chests. The last shell had landed between them. The hot steel fragments had mutilated them both, and they now sat there very white in deep shock and dying. The one to the left, named Peter, had fragments in his chest, stomach, arms, and his legs. His right leg was hanging by skin and muscle only. I grabbed a tourniquet from my unit three kit and placed it around the leg and stopped what little blood that was flowing. Peter was mumbling something and I couldn't understand him. I injected morphine into the Marine's body. I knew that he would die and the only thing I could do was to try to make his death less painful.

I couldn't do anything for the other Marine. He sat there very white and looked as though he was on the verge of dozing off. His legs, stomach, and chest were perforated with large fragment holes. I could see that he was still breathing though. I yelled out for litter bearers and to my surprise a team did appear after a few moments. This was the first time that this had happened to me since I had been on the island. I suppose that the litter bearers had been close by, lying low during the shelling. I lifted Peter up and placed him onto the litter. When I did that, his leg hung loose over my arm and the broken jagged femur bone stuck out like a broken branch of a tree limb. The pink colored muscle and tissue surrounding the fracture was exposed and lay over my arm in the same manner as I might hold a bath towel there. I grabbed at my sheath knife and cut through the muscle and the cloth of the dungaree trousers and the leg fell onto the rim of the shell hole. From there it slid onto the lap of the second Marine. I placed a large battle dressing over the end of the leg stump and I was thinking about how useless this all was as the kid was certainly going to die very quickly anyway. I advised the litter bearers to get up and run like hell with the injured man toward the rear because I was sure that the Japs had us under observation and were sighting their gun in on us again. The litter team left on the run.

I checked the other Marine over and decided that he was not going to live very long. It was a hell of a decision for a nineteen year old hospital corpsman, but there wasn't anyone else with more authority to over rule me. I left him sitting there holding that severed leg on his lap, his head looked down as though he were studying it. I scrambled back to Brown and our rifle pit, and no sooner did all hell broke loose again. The Japanese had followed up again with another four shells that lifted up the surface of the ground around us and scattered it all over the place.

When the barrage stopped and we had shaken the sand from us, we peeped over the edge of the hole in front of us. In back of us I heard that dreaded call again: "Corpsman, Corpsman!" Someone was yelling and he sounded as if he were in pain. Every time I heard that call a big knot would form in my stomach and my body would begin to shake.

I was a mess. My hands hadn't been washed for the five days I had been on the island. My arms, chest, and face were covered with layers of blood and dirt, and that loose volcanic black sand was sticking to that. This time I crawled out to look for whoever was calling me, but then he stopped yelling and I couldn't locate him.

I cannot say enough about the courage of the brave men who served on the litter teams. These were Marines who were assigned to gather up the wounded men injured during the fighting. In doing so they exposed themselves to heavy fire as they operated in teams of six men. Four would carry an injured man on a stretcher while one would be a guard in front while another was on guard in the rear. Of course they would change positions when physical relief was necessary. Six men in a group like that were bound to draw not only machine fire, but artillery and mortar fire much more often that a single rifleman would. They were Marines first, however, and they did their share of the fighting too.

When I crawled back to my own foxhole, I passed by the severely injured G Company Marine who remained sitting upright in the shell hole;

his face was very white, and after I examined him I knew that he had died. His head leaned back against the side of the shell crater and he appeared to be looking through half opened eyes at where his friend Peter had been sitting when the shell struck. Peter's leg still lay in his lap. I put a poncho over him and crawled back to where Brown waited.

I told him about the two young Marines and described their condition. I shouldn't have done that; I should have known by then to keep my mouth shut. He was sitting there leaning against the side of the rifle pit and he was lightly sobbing. Thinking that it would be better for him to do something more active than to sit there and think, I told him that he should shoot at the bunkers out in front of us as the Lieutenant wanted him to do.

"Oh, how can God let this all happen?" he suddenly cried out.

"God isn't here!" I quickly replied.

"God isn't here" I quickly replied

CHAPTER THIRTY-FIVE

Losing Our Top

THAT MORNING, FOLLOWING another artillery barrage that had enveloped our position, I heard another call for "Corpsman!" This time I recognized the voice of the Top Sergeant and he was calling out from somewhere in back of me. He was yelling out, "Doc! Doc! Doc!" I crawled out again and saw him huddled in a small shell crater about ten feet away from the hole where I had found the two mortally wounded G Company Marines.

The Top-Sergeant was lying on his back and side with his knees drawn up and he was holding both arms pressed tightly over his abdomen. He seemed to be in a terrible amount of pain. When he saw me he screamed out, "I'm hit bad, Doc. I think I've done it now!"

I slid into the hole alongside him as I was very mindful that the Japs could see me. I had to force his hands away from his stomach. I couldn't see any blood or even holes in the front of his dungarees, so I unfastened his gun belt and opened the front of his blouse expecting to find the worst. I examined his chest and stomach and found no wounds there. He kept on holding his hands lower down over his groin area and the picture came into my mind of horrible wounds I had seen where steel shell fragments had entered and torn open the lower stomach, rupturing, and exposing the intestines. I feared treating that type of injury. I forced his flailing hands away as he involuntary reacted to the pain. I ripped open the fly of his trousers to expose the skin area there. I saw no wound or blood! I was puzzled and said, "Top, I can't find a wound anywhere."

"Well, I know there is one," he blurted out, "because I hurt so goddamn much!" I told him again that I couldn't find any wound. He sat up and began examining himself. When he touched his penis, he let out a yell and said, "There it is!" When we looked further, we found the source of the pain. A small shell fragment, about the size of a pencil eraser, had gone through the double fly cloth of his trousers and struck the end of his penis inflicting a deep purple and blue colored bruise. The skin appeared unbroken and it was not bleeding.

In reacting to the relief of knowing he was not seriously hurt, we began to laugh and we leaned back against the side of the shell hole. We laughed and laughed and got rid of a lot of tension I believe. The Marines who were huddling in their foxhole within hearing distance of us must have thought we had gone berserk. This was the only instance that I remember really laughing while on Iwo Jima. And as I left him to return to my own foxhole I heard him say, "And Doc, you don't have to go telling this around either!"

No matter where a person stands on the island of Iwo Jima, if he looks toward the south, he can see Mt. Suribachi. Of course, anyone positioned up there can see the rest of the island too. As I sat in the rifle pit, resting with my back up against the front side of the hole, I focused my eyes on the top of the hated mountain which was about a mile or so distant to the south. I could see the dust and the smoke float in the air around the mountain, but my attention was drawn toward the fluttering of something white on the very top of the hill itself.

Shortly after the first flag was hoisted, Marines throughout the island took courage at the news that Mt. Suribachi was at long last, secured.

Brown was on his knees peering toward the Japanese line when I asked him to look at the top of the mountain. He agreed that what we were seeing up there was a white cloth fluttering in the wind. Remembering that Lt. Horvath had binoculars, I called over to where he sat in his foxhole and asked him what he thought of the sight of a white cloth being blown about in the wind up on the mountain top. He looked through his field glasses and after a moment he said, "That's an American flag up there. I guess the 28th [regiment] have secured the hill."

The word spread quickly and the morale of the men seemed to rise immensely. Our possession of the mountain meant that the Japanese couldn't use it any longer to view our movements and bring their artillery to bear on us from that advantage. The flag was raised about 1030 hours on February 23, 1945, the fifth day after our landing on the island. According to our battle schedule we were supposed to have taken the mountain by the end of the first day. In reality the battle had just begun.

We still had problems with our rifles, as we couldn't clear the sand from them without the proper cleaning equipment. I crawled back to where the two "G" Company Marines had been struck down by the shell explosion, as I remembered that they had been wearing their combat packs and might have rifle cleaning gear in them. Peter's pack was still lying there; I dragged it back to our hole and looked in it for cleaning gear. There was none but there was a razor that Brown and I used to try to dry shave with. That didn't work as the layers of dirt and grime on our faces made it impossible to slide the razor across the skin.

In the pack we found some pictures of Peter's family, his mother and father, and two sisters. We wondered how long it would be for them to be notified of his death. I hoped that they would never know how he died. I was never officially informed of his death although I knew he was dead as no one could live after being torn apart like he had been. Brown and I put everything back in the combat pack that we had taken out, except for the razor that I still have today.

During the day, the platoon had kept up a constant fire, as best they could, with their M-1 rifles at the sand covered bunkers out in front of us. I had recovered a fouled carbine and banged away with that in rapid fire, but the sand in the action caused the slide to fly off quite often, and the attempt got tiresome so I just sat at the bottom of the hole and felt depressed. The tension and suspense of just sitting there got unbearable after a while. We were under heavy machine gun and mortar fire all of the time and we could hardly raise our heads high enough to look over the edge of our holes. I thought up a plan to escape the heavy pressure. I would use my prerogative as a corpsman to go out looking for medical supplies and find a litter team for some wounded who were lying in holes nearby. At the same time I would find and bring back rifles and cleaning gear for the others to use.

Ignoring the machine guns I crawled away toward the west side of our position making sure that the Lieutenant didn't see me. I thought that our line of men stretched over that way and clear down to the beach. Once away from our platoon's left flank, I couldn't seem to locate any Marines. There should have been another company there, at least. The ground was littered with broken trees and limbs that had been knocked down by shell fire and roots that had been thrown out of the ground. There were huge broken pieces of concrete lying about indicating that the area had been a prime target for naval shelling, air craft bombs, and rocket fire.

I rolled into a large crater and found a dead Marine lying face down on the sand. He wore a combat pack and had his arms and hands stretched out above his head. His rifle lay under his chin and on the sand where he had fallen upon it. I bent over him and pulled a "K" ration from his right rear trousers pocket. I don't think that I'll ever forget the feeling as the waxed paper container resisted the wet cloth as it was pressed against his body. I began unfastening the straps that held the pack flap down too, but then I felt a chill at the back of my neck and I straightened up. On impulse, I turned and ran from the shell crater and went on my way thinking, I would stop on the way back to the platoon and search the dead man's pack for rifle cleaning gear. Suddenly, I was becoming aware of what the feeling of premonition was and that I should not ignore it.

I went on for another two hundred feet and saw several dead Japanese soldiers lying about on the ground. I felt fear tear at me again. This area seemed very eerie and strange to me and I imagined that I was all alone there with Japanese soldiers who must be hiding in the midst of all that rubble. I couldn't understand why there were no Marines, so I turned and ran back the way I had come.

As I approached the large crater where I had left the body of the dead marine I leaped over its rim. While still in the air I saw not just one dead Marine, but now a second one too! He had fallen across the first Marine's body and he was also dead. He had been shot in his back, the bullet entering under his right shoulder blade. I could see that blood had run down the outside of his dungaree blouse from the hole there. Evidently, the Marine had come along right after I had left, and had the same intention that I had of trying to find some rifle cleaning gear or food in the dead man's pack. He had fallen dead across the 1st Marine's body. I realized that could have been me lying there!

I could feel terror build in my chest and knew that there was a Japanese soldier close to me. From looking at the terrain and the location of the bodies, I figured that the sniper had to be within a fifty foot radius of where the crater was. I turned this way and that pointing the M-1 that I had pulled from under the dead marine's body. I jumped this way and that to prevent myself from being a stationary target. Then I ran up the side of the crater and back toward where I had left the 2nd platoon. I crawled into the hole with Lt. Horvath. I told him that I had been over beyond our left flank and

Dead Marine lying on the slope of a shell crater still clutching his bayonet.

couldn't see any Marines. I suggested maybe our flank wasn't covered. He turned his face away from me and said, "Thanks, I'll look into it!"

His attitude of dismissal riled me. Since he had lost his carbine somehow, I held out the M-1 I had recovered and said, "Here's a rifle I recovered for you!" He took the weapon and turned away again without saying anything more. I was becoming more concerned about him.

The presence of Japanese soldiers behind our lines was constant. They infiltrated during the dark hours hoping to destroy our food and ammunition dumps by dropping explosives in among them. Other goals of theirs were to destroy our communication setups and to kill our commanding officers. During the daylight hours it was necessary for them to hide from the Marines and they did this by concealing themselves among the rubble, many in caves.

Some of these Japs were classified as snipers as they waited until they could

Japanese sniper blasted from his Takotubos or octopus pot.

shoot an unsuspecting Marine from the rear. They would conceal themselves in a small hole which they called 'Takotubos', or octopus pots, the Japanese equivalent to our foxhole, and pull a camouflaged cover over the top to hide themselves. Whenever an unsuspecting marine came near them, the Jap would raise up and shoot at him, then return to concealment again.

Strange things can happen during combat. Once Brown and I sat in our foxhole and observed three Marines walk from our rear right by us toward the Japanese lines. The three men wore clean dungarees, were clean shaven, and were carrying on a conversation as though they were on a Sunday stroll. I thought that they all looked pudgy and soft and that perhaps they were rear echelon junior staff officers in the division. The one passing the closest to us looked down at us as he passed by and then away. He ignored us and didn't speak.

"Where do you think they are going?" Brown asked. "They are going to draw Jap cannon fire on us."

"I don't know," I replied. "Maybe to talk things over with the Japs."

Then, once out in front of us, the men split up and the one nearest us stopped at the edge of a large crater about one hundred feet in front of us and fumbled with his trousers belt before going on to descend out of sight into the depression. Puzzled a little, Brown and I stayed on our knees and peered out toward the crater.

Apparently the Japs had been watching too as all hell broke loose. They sent mortar shells screaming at us. I saw the first one land in the hole where we had last seen the pudgy Marine disappear. The shell didn't explode; it must have been a dud. The Marine came running up and out of the hole and back toward us holding his trousers up around his hips. As he ran by he screamed out at us, his face pale and distorted with fear, "You bastards! Why didn't you tell us?"

He ran on and disappeared out of our sight among the rubble of battle to our rear. We didn't see what happened to the others as Brown and I didn't want to raise our heads for fear of getting hit by the flying shell fragments. Brown said, in a serious way, "What do you think he meant by that?"

"I don't know," I replied. I was serious too.

Later, we surmised that the three officers had taken a walk looking for a place to go to the toilet and had strayed away from the safer rear areas of our lines. Inadvertently, they had walked in the wrong direction and into the front lines without knowing it.

For the rest of the day on the 23rd, the men of Company D huddled in their foxholes not daring to reveal themselves to the enemy for fear of inviting those artillery and mortar barrages. It wasn't only the steel fragments that caused injury to us, the body and mind are both injured by these exploding shells, because the shock is terrific. Objects on the ground bounce into the air and then are slammed down hard onto the earth's surface. The air is actually blown away from the center of the explosion creating a vacuum, and the surrounding air being compressed then rushes in toward the center of the vacuum with such force it pounds on any substance within its sphere. The impact can be a destructive power and can enter a person's lungs with such a force that it rips and lacerates the vulnerable tender membranes. The shock to the brain is the same as if a person were slapped across both ears at one time. These constant explosions from shell fire had a terrible psychological effect upon us. There was the always present expectation that the next shell would wound and dismember us.

I observed that men would place various body parts in some kind of protective priority order. Some would consider their face first, others their feet, their groins, or hands. I seemed to think first of my hands which I placed under my chest or up under my face as I lay on my stomach during these explosions. I don't think that death was paramount in our minds. It was fear of serious mutilation instead.

Under the constant and sustained exposure to this threat the mind seems to disengage itself from relationship with the physical body. At first there is excitement as the adrenaline enters the bloodstream and then terror follows. As the exposure to the danger continues, the senses seem to dull. The mind eventually will not perform, and the body cannot act.

There were times during which I could not control or organize my thoughts. My stomach felt like jelly was rolling around inside of it. I could touch my hands to my face and could not feel the contact. I watched my companions go through the same experience. Their jaws would slacken allowing their mouths to open while saliva ran out of the sides and down their chins. Their eyes would lose all sign of emotion and apparently what they were seeing was not registering in their brains.

I recall a mortar barrage once where I tried to count the number of shells that landed on our platoon's position. I counted up to eighty-eight and when I reached that number kept repeating it long after the barrage had ceased. These are the conditions that we found our men in after these barrages.

It would be the job of the NCO's and the corpsman to check on the condition of the men after such a bombardment. The NCO's would report casualties to the Lieutenant and the corpsman would try to help the wounded. Not once after these barrages did I ever see a man crying or sobbing hysterically. Most of the men were not physically capable of this type of emotion. Their eyes would not respond to a stimulus. They would be very slow to react to a verbal command or question. It is for this reason that the enemy will commence an attack immediately after subjecting their opponents to such an artillery barrage. It is the ideal time in which to catch them in a helpless state.

Lt. Horvath was beginning to be of some concern to me, as I thought he wasn't acting right at times. Since the landing he had seemed to respond well when leading or otherwise called upon, probably due to his training. Other than that he didn't act as I thought an average man would act during similar circumstances. He would often say things that were out of context with what was being discussed. He was constantly advising me to watch a certain platoon member as that man might be "cracking up." He seemed to have a hang-up on that word for at one time or another I believe that he covered every man in the platoon. I heard him tell Sgt. Goodling to watch a certain man and after the Sergeant went off the Lieutenant turned to me and said, "Better watch Goodling. I think he is cracking up."

For the rest of the 23rd, we huddled in our foxholes. I knew that I should try to eat something, and I had opened up the K ration that I'd removed from the dead Marine's hip pocket. I ate the dry biscuit and the fruit bar that was in there, but they both tasted like cotton cloth. I offered the small can of American cheese with bacon in it to Brown and he refused it, saying that he was not hungry either. I took the can and threw it out onto the sand in front of our foxhole. It was an act that almost cost me my life the next morning.

This small meal was the first that I could remember since I had been on the island. Some months later I read where we had received hot coffee and hot meals including donuts after the third day of fighting. I never did see anything like that so I supposed it was mainly the boys back on the beach that got it. We didn't even get a proper supply of ammunition and hand grenades, and the water supply was getting to be a serious concern there on the front line. We emptied water from dead men's canteens into our own to replenish our supply, and to keep the Japanese soldiers from using it as they were in very short supply also.

I still hadn't slept up to this point and didn't see anyone else doing it either. All the rest of the night we huddled in our foxholes and waited for the attack that we knew was sure to come. I was beginning to feel like a real veteran now that I had some rest during the day. I was even beginning to want the Japs to come at us during the night so I could kill them in retaliation for what they had done to some of my friends.

About 2030, a flight of Japanese bombers came over from the north and dropped bombs on our position. They flew the length of the island and once they were sure they were clear of their own men, they let go strings of bombs that landed along the water's edge to the west and onto the supply troops in back of us. It seemed like a million guns fired tracers at them at first and the sight was spectacular as the sky was all crisscrossed with tracers of red, yellow and orange. The motors of the bombers "popped" and sputtered as they passed overhead. It was reported later on that they did very little damage on the ground. My company wasn't in any danger until steel fragments from our own bursting anti-aircraft shells began landing on us. Some of the Marines received small cuts and bruises from them. In all, I thought the bombing was a welcome relief compared to what we had been experiencing so far on the island.

Chapter Thirty-Six

Hand to Hand

Oh, what a beautiful morning,
Oh, what a beautiful day.
I've got a terrible feeling
Everything's coming my way!

ABOUT A HALF hour before dawn broke on February 24, PFC Glen Brown and I were on our knees, very tense and peering into the darkness. We listened intently trying to discover some movement near our foxhole that would indicate that the Japanese soldiers had moved in on us during the night. It wasn't an uncommon that the Japanese, while trying to re-establish their positions during the night, would inadvertently encroach on our line of defense. The result would be that Marines and Japanese soldiers would be dug in side-by-side, facing in opposite directions. Somehow the situation was bound be corrected at first light.

The thought entered my mind during the dark hours that since the company had suffered so many casualties in the last three days, perhaps we would be replaced by fresh troops on this sixth day of battle. Instead, we were told to prepare to move out and forward after the cessation of our naval bombardment of the enemy defenses.

While directing the artillery bombardments of enemy positions, one of the Fifth Division's artillery spotters rode in a small plane, a Stinson Sentinel OY-1, which circled over the enemy positions. On this day I thought he was unwisely very close to the ground. As we watched the plane maneuver there was an explosion that took place on top of the left wing causing the plane to collapse and tumble to the ground several hundred yards behind the Japanese lines. My comrades and I were of the impression that perhaps a mortar shell exploded on the wing of the airplane , which had brought it down. Because of the heavy shell and machine gun fire, it was not possible for us to reach the plane, so we had to assume the pilot and spotter were dead.

Soon afterward, Lt. Horvath was on his feet shouting and waving us forward. We knew that the Japs had a good view of us coming at them. I could visualize shells being shoved into the breeches of field pieces and the locks being slammed shut as their artillery spotters called out to the gun crews our range and direction. I sure didn't want to be there when those shells arrived. Instead of running straight forward this time we angled off to the left toward the western beaches.

As I left our hole I saw lying on the sand the partially buried can of cheese I had thrown out the day before. Thinking that I might recover it while on the run, I kicked at it and sent it spinning up into the air in front of me. As it went end over end I could see that it wasn't the can of cheese after all, but an anti-personnel land-mine. It landed in front of my feet and fortunately on its side, or it might have exploded about the time I leaped over it. I shouted a warning to the others that we were in a mine field and I stopped running. Lt. Horvath was right there yelling out to us to keep going and run through the mine field and not to stop for any reason. These terrible small mines took their toll of casualties on Iwo Jima and I treated several men who had been injured by them. I was told that Glen Brown stepped on one several days later and it mangled his foot so badly it had to be amputated.

The platoon covered about two hundred yards on the run and had just cleared the mine field when the first artillery shells landed on the position that we had just vacated. This was to be another terrible and confusing day. Our men became scattered trying to cross the plain that separated us from the Japanese bunker line. We all reached the bunkers though before the Japs recovered from the heavy shelling that had been placed down upon them by our Navy ships and division artillery units. We swarmed over the Japanese bunker positions and fired our weapons into the gun ports and burned the interiors out with flame throwers. The latter resulted in having to cope with the odor of burning human flesh mixed with that of burnt gunpowder. I felt nauseous and horrified when I observed burning Japanese soldiers come screaming from the bunkers and flop about on the black sand until they died.

I worked my way across the plain and assisted wounded Marines who had suffered bullet and fragment wounds. I would not assist any of the injured to get back toward the aid station though, as I didn't want to be separated from the platoon. I gave injections of morphine, sprinkled sulfanilamide powder on wounds and covered them with battle dressings. I would leave a wounded man lying on the ground, telling him to lie still and wait for litter bearers to come up and remove him.

There were times we corpsmen would jam the barrel of the Marine's rifle into the sand to mark his position so that the litter teams might see him better. If the injured marine was capable of protecting himself, we'd prop him up and leave him holding his rifle. There were incidents on Iwo Jima where the Japanese found our wounded lying helplessly on the ground, and killed them. Some corpsmen would stay with the wounded in order to protect them from the Japanese soldiers, and there are recorded incidents where the corpsman died in those attempts. One such incident involved corpsman John Willis of the 27th Regiment who threw several enemy grenades back until one exploded in his hand.

As the day passed, I began to realize that more and more of the men I treated were near death or dying as I worked over them. I became very distressed over this. Of course I wasn't seeing many of the wounded who, after being hit, made their way back to the aid station without waiting for my assistance. As a result of this I lost count of how many men of the pla-

Stretcher bearers return to the front lines.

toon and the company was being lost as casualties. Some of the men just would disappear, and I wouldn't know whether they were killed, wounded, or lost. The officer's of the company didn't seem to be all that concerned about it. If a man wasn't there to fight, he just wasn't there and the attack was pressed onward anyway.

The Japanese continued to lay down artillery and mortar fire and they did so very well. There was no standing, running, or walking out there on that plain, just crawling from one shell hole to another on our hands and knees or sliding along the ground from one shell crater to the next on our stomachs. Along the edge of one crater I found a man's left arm which had been severed at the shoulder. The arm had tattooed on it one of those huge black panthers with the red eyes that I thought once were so pretty. I wondered which one of the two Company D Marines had lost the arm. I looked about the area the best I could under the circumstances, but didn't find the body that the arm belonged to.

I was under the impression that many of the injured on Iwo Jima suffered more than just one wound, especially those who suffered from gunshot wounds. I know from being an eye witness, that many men when hit by machine gun fire, would be hit again and again. After knocking the Marine down the Jap gunner would fire burst after burst at the helpless man on the ground. A bullet would usually leave a neat little hole where it entered, but where it exited, if it did, it would tear out a hunk of flesh leaving a gaping hole. The injured man would suffer immediate shock from pain and loss of blood. Shock was a killer. I imagined it as a predator that waited on the battle ground, ready to pounce on a man as he was struck down.

In advancing once I found Sgt. Brock and his first squad huddled in a shell hole at the base of one of the sand covered Jap block houses. Brock said that he didn't know where the company or the rest of the platoon was. We decided that we should follow what we thought was good battle procedure and dig in right there and hold that ground until we were told to do otherwise by an officer or until some Japs came along and tried to take it away from us.

Eventually Lt. Horvath caught up with us and brought what was left of the platoon. He thought that we were in a good position, and he organized a defensive line position that extended from the beach at our left side and tied in with the rest of D Company which was on our right. Facing us was that long sand mound that ran up to the edge of Airfield #2, and was part of the Japanese Cross Island Defense System. A lot of fighting was going on at the base of the air strip cliff where the Japs concealed themselves in caves and bunkers. Those defenses demanded we use our flame throwers and demolitions before they could be destroyed.

Facing our company to the north was a little canyon. We were entrenched on the south side, on higher ground on the north side were the Japanese, who were concealed in many earth-covered hidden bunkers. Since they had the high ground and were no more than one hundred and fifty yards away, they had the definite advantage. We could only crouch in our shell holes and keep our heads below the level of the rim of the hole as they fired at us.

Lynch and his machine gun crew came crawling up to us and set up their gun near me. Lynch continually amazed me by his tenacity and courage to stay up front and carry on the fight. The Jap gunners on the other side of the canyon sent a lot of bullets at us and kept us down at the bottom of our holes. Sgt. Brock and I dug our shell hole deeper and we just sat there waiting. When Lynch got his gun working he began to duel with the Jap gunners and he did a good job because the Japs quieted down eventually.

Brock and I began to compare what we knew about our casualties. We thought that about half of the platoon was now gone, but weren't sure as there was no way to get a proper count. Actually there were more injured and killed than we thought at the time. We didn't think that we'd last much longer up there as the entire company must be running out of men. We did know at that time that part of the 3rd Marine Division had landed and was now on our right side up on the airfield. I was pretty sure that if we stayed up there much longer, we would certainly be killed.

I tore away a small section of the sand rim from our rifle pit and looked out toward the western beach. I wondered if I could make it to the water through the mine field that was sure to be there, and swim away from there. I said to Brock, "Maybe we'll have to swim for it soon."

"I can't swim," he answered tersely.

I never mentioned it to him again although, I kept thinking about it. There had been three occasions during the battle when I had been with a small group of men and discovered that we had been left out in front while the rest of the company was withdrawn. Each time I made it back to our lines and others had not. I couldn't understand why I was living so long but didn't expect to give up my life easily. If the Japanese were to surround us while this close to this beach, I had it in mind that the surf was one way to escape.

We had been on the island for six days now and I hadn't as yet seen any other Company D corpsmen except Hall and Pace, both of whom had succumbed to combat fatigue. The company commander, Captain Tom Fields had come across me and questioned me as to whether I was the only corpsman "up here." I didn't know, but his question worried me as I though perhaps the rest of them were now casualties. For sure one of the other corpsmen, Cecil Thrower had been shot by one of our own men one night as he left his foxhole. He was evacuated and I did not see him again.

It was about this time that my friend, the mischievous and congenial corpsman, Ivan Munns was killed. Later a sergeant who was near him at the time told what happened:

"We were advancing on one of the bunkers and Munns, a rifleman, and I had just crawled into a shell hole to escape enemy machine-gun fire coming from the fortification. Another rifleman charging at the bunker was knocked down by bullets. Munns rose to go to his aid and I pulled him back down and said, 'No, don't! That Jap is waiting for you! "The wounded Marine kept calling for help and Munns again jumped up and ran toward him. Before reaching the fallen Marine, Munns was hit by bullets and fell to the ground near the man. He tried to get up, but the Jap fired again and hit him. I yelled out to tell him to lie still and to pretend that he was dead. A while later, just before it got dark when we intended to rescue the two injured men, the Jap gunner fired several more bursts of bullets into their bodies." The death of Munns was a disaster to me and I quickly dropped into the deepest of despair.

There was a little clump of rocks off the western shore near us and the Japs referred to this rocky island as Kama Iwa (Sickle Rock). There were Japanese soldiers positioned on the small group of rocks, probably placed there as artillery observers. The Navy discovered the soldiers and a picket boat was sent in to eliminate them. We had a good view of the action. We watched the Japanese scurry back and forth from one side of the rocks to the other trying to keep away from the machine gun fire coming from the little gun-boat as it dashed here and there. One by one the Japs were shot and they would fall splashing into the water. After a while we couldn't see any more of them left on the rock. The little boat then scurried away under a hail of bullets from the main island.

As darkness fell we began preparing for another horrible night. One of the sergeants and I were kneeling at the edge of our rifle pit, waiting for the Japanese to rush at us from the little canyon that faced us. Instead of charging our positions they tried to quietly infiltrate the line to our right side. We heard the usual sounds of metal against metal, cries for help, cursing, and the unmistakable bang of grenades as they exploded.

My eyes were drawn to the tracers again as they floated out toward us searching for a human target. This time they came from the hillside across from us. We could make out the muzzle flash of our machine guns as they fired away at our Company D which as we faced them. I'd watch the tracers sweep our area and as they came near our hole, I'd lower my head until they passed by. Sgt. Goodling had said the Japs were wanting us to shoot back at the their gun's muzzle flash so their soldiers could crawl up to our holes and toss a grenade on us.

Sgt. Brock suggested that we get some sleep. That was a good idea but it was hard to sleep when you know that there are people out there a few feet away who were intent on killing you. Besides, I had taken so many of those Benzedrine tablets by then I couldn't even shut my eyes. I tried to close the lids but the muscles controlling them wouldn't respond. Brock said that I

Waiting in the dark for the next round of Japanese infiltrators.

should try anyway and he would stand guard for two hours and then he'd awaken me to relieve him.

I sat on the bottom of the hole with my knees drawn up and my elbows resting on them. I lowered my head onto my arms and tried to sleep, still my eyes wouldn't close, and I was wide awake. The sergeant, in the meantime, was on his knees and supposedly peering over the edge of the hole. After a while I felt and heard him moving around until he was across from me, his knees touching mine. I raised my head when the next flare went up, and I could see that he was sitting and had his head down on his knees. He was breathing heavy as though he were asleep. I went into a rage and pushed the point of my hand-held bayonet against his chest and demanded "Just what the hell do you think you're doing?"

"I'm going to get a little sleep!" he protested.

That made me more angry still, and I rose to my knees and pushed the muzzle of my rifle up against his chest and said, "You do that again and I'll kill you!"

"No, don't!" he begged and said I was overreacting and told me that of the six men he had left strung out in holes on our left, only one was awake and the others were sleeping and that he'd told them it was OK to do it that way. This was contrary to our instructions on how to act on the battle line where one man in each hole should be awake at all times. The sergeant could not only get us killed doing that, but would it would also weaken the entire defensive line to the point it would fail and allow the Japanese to make a successful counterattack.

I was already angry because, earlier he had urinated in a Jap mortar shell protective case and stupidly had tried to throw it out of our foxhole. The wind brought it back and drenched our heads and shoulders.

I heard a "snap" sound take place in my head, the sound you hear when turning on an electric light switch. The anger toward Brock disappeared immediately, I felt cool and very clear of mind. I felt invincible! I told the Sergeant, "I had taken enough! It is my turn to kill somebody!"

I crawled up on the lip of the crater and waited there holding the bayonet in my left hand and carbine in my right. I spent the rest of the night there and only let myself down inside as the sweeping tracers came my way. I was hoping that a Jap would try infiltrating our line at our position as I wanted to kill one really bad about then. The sergeant demanded that I return to the foxhole. "You're crazy, you will get killed out there!" He said. After a while he became quiet.

I think that the sergeant slept the rest of the night once the Japs settled down. I had time to wonder about my own behavior. Men say and do strange things during battle. In the morning I told the Top sergeant about the sergeant's lack of diligence as a supervisor. I said that if he ever went to sleep like that again when he was supposed to be standing guard that I'd kill him! The Top said very calmly, "No you won't, not before I shoot him myself. I'll take care of him!"

The Japanese had crawled up close to our hole and were within hand grenade throwing distance. Our rifle pit was about thirty to forty feet from the lip of the canyon where the earth fell steeply away and we could hear the Japanese making noises while they moved around. They called out to us, "Dirty American Marine Bastard" and another phrase that they seem to like very much, "Marine Son-of-a-Bitch." Some of the Marines insisted that they heard the Japs would call out, "Corpsman, please help me!" I heard many such calls at night and some were suspect, but I could never prove them as coming from a Marine.

During the night we had a hand grenade battle with the Japs. We always got the best of them in these exchanges as our grenades were more powerful. Five second fuse grenades were sent up to us to replace the seven second ones that we had been using. The Japs had been throwing some of ours back at us and we had to counter that with pulling the pin, letting the handle go and counting off a couple of seconds before throwing them.

Hand grenades are a weird and dangerous weapon. During the dark of night it is very easy to lose control of them and suffer a mishap. Once the handler pulls the safety pin and releases the handle to fly off, the little hammer inside is free to strike the percussion cap, which in turn ignites the short fuse leading to the powder charge. Our fuses were of five and seven second type duration before the powder would explode.

I crouched while waiting for the last shell to land and figured that there must be a battery of four 90 mm. mortars concentrating on us by the number and rapidity of shells landing. To keep control of my mind I began to count the explosions. I got to the number eighty-eight again before I couldn't seem to count any more. I, again, kept repeating that number up and down every time a shell exploded.

I don't know if I remember the shell that hit the edge of the pit just above my head. I do believe I heard a 'whoosh.' I regained consciousness while lying on my back and with my rifle buried in the sand under my hips. I was aware of a loud buzzing and humming noise in my head. I sensed that someone was there with me, but couldn't see except for a little light haze. Someone was shaking my shoulder repeating over and over again, "Doc, Doc." It was Brock. He had returned after the shelling stopped to find me lying on my back and all but my face buried under several inches of sand.

He held my head up while he poured water into my eyes and face to wash away the sand. My eyes were open, I realized, but they were covered with sand. Brock washed most of it away and eventually I was able to sit up. I had been bleeding from my eyes, ears and nostrils as well as my mouth. He told me that he had never seen anyone bleed from their eyes like that before. I felt horribly sick and kept coughing up blood and that also seemed to increase the bleeding.

He explained that when he returned to the pit he found that a shell had exploded on the edge of it and had caved it in on top of me. From what he told me, I assumed that the explosion tossed me into the air and flipped me over so that I landed on my back unconscious. He said he was sure I was dead as I lay there unmoving, with my eyes open and filled with sand. Then the Lieutenant had come along and after looking at me agreed that I was dead and told the sergeant to place a poncho over my head and shoulders. As he was doing that he moved my head and that caused a bloody bubble to rise in one of my nostrils and blood colored froth from my mouth. It was then he believed me still alive. I'm sure that I would have died if Sgt. Brock had not come to my aid.

I was still trying to grasp what was happening when Lt. Horvath appeared again at the side of the hole. He looked at me and raised his eyebrows a little in apparent surprise that I was still alive, but didn't say anything to me.

The Japs had ruined our assault plans so we all remained quiet and sat or huddled in our rifle pits awaiting the word on what we were to do next. Sporadic shell fire landed and it was accompanied by machine gun fire that caused the bullets to 'tzing, tzing, tzing' going by.

Sgt. Brock said that he had to check on his men again and left me alone in the hole. I sat there for a while, felt better and apparently without reason got to my feet. I seemed to have lost all sense of fear or concern and I climbed out of the hole and paused at its edge. A burst of bullets went by my left side. The Top Sergeant who was on my right in a hole about twenty feet away yelled at me, "Goddamn it, Doc, don't you hear those bullets?" I turned toward him and I remember smiling as I answered, just as another group of bullets passed in back of me.

"It's OK, Top," I said, "I found out that they can't hit me." I knelt at the side of his rifle pit and watched as his open right hand come up at me. It caught me on the left side of my face hard and at the same time he had grabbed the front of my blouse and was pulling me upside down into the hole alongside of him. I struggled to sit upright in the hole.

Grinning I said again, "It's OK, Top. What are you afraid of? They can't hit me."

The Top Sergeant was a good wise Marine. He looked at me with compassion and said very calmly, "That might be true; Doc, but when they see and shoot at you they might hit some of us."

All of a sudden my earlier training came rushing into my mind. I turned solemn and was terribly embarrassed and made an apology to the sergeant. I told him that I had forgotten that I'd draw enemy fire if I stood up. Then I crawled back to my rifle pit feeling really remorseful. The lack of sleep, rest, and food was affecting me and I knew it was others as well. I became short tempered and unnecessarily harsh with others as I had with Brock. When Lieutenant Horvath crawled into my rifle pit and asked me if cheese was good for a case of diarrhea, I could only glare at him. With four men being torn apart around us here he was asking me about something as trivial as loose bowels.

Our line was becoming very thin, and it had huge gaps in it. I thought our platoon had lost over fifty percent of its members, but it was many more than that. I supposed the Lieutenant knew but wasn't about to tell the rest of us because of the morale problem it would cause. I saw some clean uniforms on men whom I observed at a distance and surmised that replacements were being brought up to replace some of those men who had been wounded or killed. The 'poor bastards,' they were coming up there not knowing anyone and poorly trained, or so I thought. I didn't want to know any of them either as it would be too painful when they got killed.

At dusk, Lt. Horvath came crawling down the line on the ground in front of our pit while briefing us on what to expect that night. He was telling the sergeant and me that Japanese soldiers were heard moving around in the gully that confronted us. I had raised my rifle so he could crawl under it as he talked. I held a hand grenade in my right hand and rested the barrel of my carbine on the small of the Lieutenant's back while he spoke, but kept my eyes on the canyon rim thirty or so feet away. Suddenly, I saw a Japanese soldier appear. He came walking or trotting very deliberately toward us. He carried his rifle with its bayonet with his right hand and it was positioned to point at me and my two comrades. In his left hand he held a yellow crepe paper wrapped box about a foot long. I suppose the expression that appeared on my face when I saw this soldier caused the Lieutenant to turn and look in the same direction. He saw the enemy soldier and yelled, "Get your M-1s. It's a Jap!"

There was a flurry of activity and I recalled hearing an explosion and shots being fired. As the dust cleared I looked over the rim of our foxhole and saw that the Lieutenant was not to be seen. Further away there was a smoking pile of what looked like debris to me.

Three men of a machine gun crew were dug in over on our right side and one of the men called to me and when he got my attention said, "Good going, Doc, you got him!" I shook my head "No" but all three of the men grinned and nodded back saying, "Yes, you did too!"

I couldn't remember throwing the grenade although I remembered that I had held one while listening to the Lieutenant. Brock said I threw the one I held, but he ducked down as I did and didn't see where it landed. Later I couldn't resist the temptation to look and I crawled out to examine the dead Japanese soldier.

He was lying on his back with some of his clothing still smoking and his entire chest was blown away revealing what was left of some white smashed rib bones and horrible looking reddish-black jelly like stuff that half filled the chest cavity. I turned to crawl back when I stopped to glance at the soldier's face. The man was young, I'd guess that he was about eighteen years old, and I felt a jolt hit me in my chest. He looked very much like a Japanese-American friend of mine back home. I wondered what this young soldier's mother was doing right now in their home in Japan and how she would react when informed of her son's death. I looked over at the one Marine I could see of the machine gun crew. He was still grinning. He held up a hand and formed a circle with his right index finder and thumb that indicated "OK." I didn't feel good about it at all.

I examined the crepe paper covered box that Jap had been carrying. It had a fuse with a fuse lighter attached to its end. Why the thing didn't explode when the grenade went off, I have no idea.

The next day the machine gun crew explained to me that there were at least six Japanese soldiers in a line that had suddenly appeared. They said their attention had been drawn away from the rim of the canyon when they saw Lieutenant Horvath stop crawling to pause in front of Brock and me. They saw me throw the grenade and they watched it strike the leading soldier in the chest as it exploded. They ducked away from the explosion and immediately afterward opened fire on the enemy column. The lead soldier had fallen with the blast, but the other five threw themselves backward to escape the blast and their machine gun fire. They didn't know how many of the enemy they had hit.

That night was a repetition of most of the other nights. We would just sit or kneel and listen. We'd just strain our eyes peering in the darkness in an attempt to see an approaching Jap before he saw us. One Marine off to our left side and not in the 2nd platoon received a bayonet through the upper part of his left leg when a Jap came into the hole while holding his rifle out in front of him. The Jap scrambled out of the hole and ran away leaving his rifle behind. The Marine's foxhole companion pulled the bayonet out and the man lay there in agony until about six hours later when I reached him and gave him morphine.

I believe that it was this night that the Japs blew up an ammunition dump. The flames went shooting high into the night air and seemed to light up the entire island. Shells burned and exploded, others were tossed into the sky but failed to explode when they struck the ground. The earth under us jumped and shuddered and caused the sand to come sliding down into our rifle pits. As tired as I was the sight and experience of it gave me quite a thrill.

Explosions continuously fascinated me, whether caused by an ammunition dump blowing up, artillery, naval gunfire, mortar or whatever. A man could be standing and be knocked over by a distant explosion, or he might be close to an exploding shell with all its flying steel splinters and turn and walk away suffering only with a little confusion. If during an artillery or mortar barrage, I was lying flat on the ground, it seemed that the earth would raise and smash into me.

If I were on my knees, the ground would raise up and hit me. There were times when a close explosion would blow me away from the point of impact and other times I seemed to be drawn toward the impact point. In any event, it was enough to cause mental confusion or cause a man to stumble about aimlessly and eventually be killed or at least tagged as a "combat fatigue case."

For a corpsman, it was difficult to determine from a distance if a man was injured when he fell to the ground or if he was only taking evasive action to escape bullets or fragments? A corpsman would have to make a judgment based on what he saw or knew. A misjudgment could result in death when going to aid a man already dead.

I observed that when a running man is struck in the head or body by a bullet, his knees buckled and his hands and arms would come down. He would let go of his rifle, and then his knees, hands and face would make contact with the ground first. His mouth opened and sometimes he would appear to be biting the ground. If he was mortally injured, he would often roll slowly over on his back and in doing so would invariably leave one leg crossed over the other at the ankle. I learned that this position of one leg crossed over the other was an indication that the man could be dead or near death.

The same condition applied to the Japanese dead. If the corpse lay on his back with his legs crossed, we could assume he was probably dead. Our attention then could be given to other of the enemy supposed dead who might be only pretending and waited for an opportunity to shoot or to explode a hand grenade as we drew close. In that situation it was better to fire a round into the enemy soldier's body first before going on, rather than increasing the risk of death to ourselves.

CHAPTER THIRTY-SEVEN

Violent Death is the Only Death

L ATER I FOUND that from this point on I was unable to maintain the proper chronological order of events that I remember having taken place during the battle. Some of the nights aren't very clear to me as they lose themselves in each other. Although, I could recall very vividly many incidents during the fight, I lost the ability to sort them out as they related to each other. My memory failed completely to recall certain incidents that were described to me by others who were with me in the battle for Iwo Jima. This condition I found to be common among other combat veterans I discussed it with. I place the probable cause for it on the confusion and the physical and emotional stress of battle. Contributing to that was the lack of sleep, rest, and food. I will record some of those incidents that I do recall here.

In the 2nd platoon we had a thirty eight year old Marine PFC Arthur T. Roseler. Most of the members called him "Pop" undoubtedly because of his age. He was very friendly and quick to smile when approached. He carried photographs with him of his wife and children and showed them to us regularly whenever an occasion would present itself and even shared portions of his wife's letters with us. His explanation for being in the Marine Corps was that he had been drafted and had nothing to say as to which branch of the service he was to be in. However, he did his job very well and uncomplaining even though his age and slight body build was something of a hindrance in meeting the physical demands placed upon him. I liked him very much and during the long hikes away from camp I often swapped my smaller carbine for his heavier M-1 while we walked.

One day on Iwo Jima, after about a week, he received a slight head wound. The bullet had entered above his helmet visor scraped along the right side of his skull tearing out some skin and leaving him bloody but conscious. He was able to speak to me and was grinning when he commented, that he hoped I'd get wounded slightly too! That way, he reasoned, I would be able to leave the island alive also. I joked with him, squeezed his arm and said that I'd see him back in the United States. A team of six litter bearers arrived. We rolled him onto a stretcher and the team left the same way they had come, going toward a low dry wash that began to the rear of our position and ran close by the aid station several hundred yards to our rear.

An hour passed by and the word was passed for our company to "dig in and hold." Leaving my partner to dig out a rifle pit I took advantage of the time to crawl back to the aid station to replenish my medical supplies. I went on my hands and knees along the dry wash passing by a destroyed Japanese ammunition dump. It appeared to have suffered a direct artillery shell hit and blown up leaving a number of live mortar shells lying upon the surface of the ground, which caused me to pick my steps carefully to avoid them.

On the other side of the mess I found the trail, but also found "Pop," still lying on the stretcher that obviously had been dropped to the ground by the bearers. His left arm and leg were hanging over the side of the

Stunned Marine explains how he survived after a 40 mm.
shell hit his helmet but failed to explode.

315

stretcher and resting on the sand. He was dead, killed after being struck by several bullets as he was being carried along the way. Three of the six litter bearer team were lying dead on the path, their rifles still slung over their shoulders. The fact that they had their rifles slung told me that the group had probably been ambushed by a Japanese soldier using an automatic weapon. The fourth bearer and the two Marines serving as the front and rear guard were nowhere to be seen and I assumed that they had escaped. Alarmed, I swung my rifle to point this way and that looking for evidence as to where the enemy was hiding. I backed away along the trail in the direction I thought the aid station was in.

A short distance farther I came upon the body of a forth Marine that was also lying on the path. I recognized him as another member of the litter team and supposed that he had been shot at the same time as his buddies, but had made it this far before collapsing. Frightened, I turned and ran along the path until I found the battalion headquarters command center and nearby the aid station that was concealed in a large bomb or shell crater.

A wounded Marine receives treatment from a corpsman.

I sat inside it on the sand and talked to my friend Nyle Weiler. I asked him about how the other battalion corpsmen were getting along. He told me that Don Green, Ph M. 3/c and Thomas A. Cribbs, Ph M. 1/c had both been struck in the head by bullets and had died instantly. Then he told me about Ivan Munns being killed. I again became depressed, it was as though the world had come to the end. I could only sit there with tears running down my cheeks and not able to talk.

Weiler left me alone for a few moments and after I regained my composure I wanted to talk with him again. I told him about finding Pace and Hall both in a bad mental state and that now I wondered what had become of them. He told me that Pace had been evacuated, but that Hall was dead. I said, "Oh, no. I sent Hall back days ago because he was acting strange and he wasn't wounded then." Weiler told me about how the Jap sniper had shot and killed Hall as he lay on the side of the shell hole that served as an aid station.

I got up and filled my Unit 3 medical kits with supplies. That aid station was very depressing to me, more than when I was on the front lines. There were many men lying and waiting for transportation from there all pale, bandaged, and bloody, some with an arm, hand, foot or a leg missing. I saw the row of poncho covered bodies off to one side of the crater. I expected them to be there, but there were so many that I wished that I hadn't looked. The bodies were covered by ponchos and each one had an identification tag tied to one shoe.

Close by the crater was an LVT (Landing Craft Amphibious Tractor) that stood in the open. I told Weiler that I thought that it should be moved as it would invite a Jap artillery barrage. He answered that the armored gun carrier was broken down and that it contained stacks of Marine dead and since it had been sitting there for two days the odor was getting pretty bad. Suddenly, I'd had enough of that sick place and wanted to return up front to where my buddies were dug in on the line.

I worked my way toward the foot path that would lead me back the way I had come and found that an amphibious tractor had just dumped a supply of machine gun ammunition on the ground and was now roaring away back towards the rear. A four man work party was there picking up boxes of ammunition and as they prepared to move out I fell in at the back of them. Seeing one box left behind I picked it up on the run thinking that I might as well take it along and deliver it to the machine gunners assigned to our platoon.

We'd only covered a few yards when I heard the sound of a Japanese machine gun, a Nambu automatic rifle I think it was, and the Marine leading the detail fell dead to the path's surface his face and open mouth digging into the sand. At the sound of the firing I leaped sideways to the right and dove head first toward the lip of a shell crater and fell rolling over and over to the bottom which was covered with a foot or two of rainwater.

When the splashing water subsided, I found myself sitting upright face to face with a dead Japanese soldier who also sat upright in the warm water, his back supported by the twisted remains of a tree root. My shoe soles were resting on his feet. His eyes were half open and I had the immediate impression that he was staring at me as if waiting for me to make the next move. His hands were at his side mostly submerged and hidden from view. It appeared to me that his right hand was close to the stock of a rifle that seemed to have the barrel lying under his knees. I raised my carbine and pointed the muzzle at his chest intending to shoot. I hesitated. A voice seemed to boom in my head, "Shoot! Shoot! What's the matter with you, shoot him!"

I began squeezing the trigger, but I didn't fire. Something stopped me perhaps it was because I thought he was dead. "Shoot! Shoot! You fool! He's pretending to be dead." I heard the voice say.

"No, he's dead, I think!"

Again the voice, "You're a fool!"

I dug my heels into the mud lying under the water and began to back away pushing my way up and out of the water. I watched the Jap's eyes for the slightest change in expression. Once out of the water I turned to crawl away, but that was only a ruse and I turned back quickly to point my rifle at him. I found that he had not moved. His gaze appeared to be on the spot where I had been sitting.

My desire to leave the hole because of the presence of the other occupant became greater than the fear of leaving its safety. I decided to get out of there. I carefully peeked over the rim of the hole and saw the body of the dead Marine still lying where it had fallen. His mouth was open and full of sand gathered while suffering his death throes.

No one else was in sight. I knew that I had to leave there, so I charged up the side of the crater and out into the open holding my carbine in my right hand and pointing it outward in front of me. I picked up the box of machine gun ammunition I had dropped and held it close to my chest as if thinking it might protect me from the bullets of the Nambu. Running along the path I came to the body of PFC Roseler and his dead companions who still lay as I had left them. I had a strong suspicion that the Jap who shot them was the same who had killed the lead Marine a little while before as an automatic weapon was used in both situations.

Once back on the line I crawled up to Cpl. Melvin Lynch and his machine gun crew and left the box of ammunition on the ground beside the gunner. He stopped firing long enough to give me that big grin he was noted for and said, "Hey, thanks a lot 'Doc', we can sure use that." I didn't stay there long enough to tell him what bringing it up entailed. I crawled away and passed close to Sgt. Goodling who was sitting in a hole watching me curiously. He asked, "How is it back there, Doc?"

"It's better up here, Charley," I replied. A puzzled look replaced his grin. I crawled away to my hole. I didn't feel like explaining it any further.

Once, when I bent over a wounded man my trouser seam that ran from the crotch area up the rear to my belt line gave way and ripped open. The thread was rotten, I supposed, because of being wet from the rain for a week or more. The only thing that I had to secure it was a piece of Japanese

Dead Japanese soldier held upright by tree roots,
thought at first to be feigning death.

barbed wire. I unraveled it so that I could use the strand with no barbs on it and threaded it along the open seam and until I closed the seam. It was most uncomfortable but made me feel more secure knowing that my rear end wasn't hanging out. The sole of my right shoe came loose and that allowed it to flop around and double back under my foot when I ran and so I took more of the barbed wire, left the barbs on, and wrapped it around the shoe top and sole in order to hold them together. My foot was able to dry out because it was exposed to the outside air a little. Both feet had been wet since the first day we had landed on the island and I was in danger of getting a condition that was called 'immersion foot' which could be very disabling. All along I had been encouraging the men of the platoon to remove their shoes and dry their feet whenever the time and conditions permitted it.

The Top Sergeant saw me with my pants and shoe repaired like that and he said, "You don't have to go around like that. Go and get yourself a pair of new pants." Since we were on the front line and under heavy fire all this time there was no place to go where I could get me a new pair of pants except out on board a ship somewhere. I had it figured that the Top was beginning to break down like some of the rest of us were doing.

Usually a corpsman was a popular guy in a combat Marine Corps outfit. Most Marines appreciate a corpsman's presence in battle if they think that they may be wounded. One evening before it became very dark, I crawled by a rifle pit that had been dug out by three men of the 2nd platoon. The men were PFC's Leo E. Oster, John Warden and Donald D. Rausch. Oster was a stocky, heavy set marine who carried a BAR and the other two worked with him as a fire team and carried M-1 rifles. Their rifle pit was barely large enough to contain them, but they insisted that I come in with them for the night.

I squeezed myself down into the hole and in the darkness sat leaning back against the back side of the pit. The three Marines knelt on their knees and leaned forward over the edge of the hole with their weapons pointed outward ready to fire at any Japanese who might charge at us from out of the ravine directly in front of us. As the night began to pass and the battle raged along the line on either side, we could hear Japanese soldiers moving about in the ravine in front of our position. They called out to us and made insulting remarks hoping that we would answer and reveal our positions.

We could hear sounds of battle that indicated hand to hand fighting was taking place on the right of us somewhere and a cry for a corpsman. I made a move to go, but the three Marines were quick to tell me not to go as I'd get killed for sure, either by our own men or by Japanese soldiers who were crawling around out there. Oster grabbed at my blouse and said that it could be a Jap calling out "corpsman" in an attempt to trick one of us to reveal ourselves, and besides the call was too far forward of our line for it to be one of our platoon's men injured and needing help.

After a few more moments I couldn't stand to hear the continual pleading for help any longer and whispered to the three Marines that I had to go. I rose up in the hole, turned to the right, and lay on my stomach on the edge of the rifle pit and was in the process of bringing up my right knee to place it up on the edge of the hole. I heard a 'pop' sound. It came from out in front of us near the edge of the ravine and I recognized it as the sound of a Jap percussion cap that would ignite a short fuse within the grenade. I heard the 'thud' sound the grenade made as it landed on the sand where I had been sitting. I brought my other knee up and let my head drop to the sand. The grenade exploded not over three feet from my raised buttocks. I felt some of the fragments hit the folded poncho that hung down from the back of my Webb belt. Other fragments entered the exposed backs of all three Marines, but they still went into action. They began throwing grenades out in front of us over the edge of the ravine trying to drive back the Japanese soldiers who had crawled up to us.

Oster threw an incendiary grenade that landed in some brush and set it on fire and that exposed our position by the light. Then Oster began to fire wildly in the direction of the ravine with his automatic weapon. We had to restrain him as he was using all his ammunition. I jumped up and ran out and beat the flames out with my poncho before coming to my senses, realizing how stupid and dangerous that was and returning to the comparative safety of the rifle pit.

The three Marines stood their positions for a while and then the pain from the fragment wounds began to get to them. I covered their backs with a Poncho and with the light of a single celled flashlight I had swiped from a landing craft, tried to either cut out or dig out the little chunks of steel that had been embedded in the flesh on their backs. I couldn't get any of the bits of metal out and I didn't give them any morphine until morning for fear it would dull their senses and prevent them from defending themselves. When the morning light came, the three crawled off to the aid station and from there they were evacuated out to ships waiting off shore. Two months later all three rejoined the company in the Hawaiian Islands and we had a very happy reunion.

One of the most fearsome sights that I could never become accustomed to was when a flame thrower was used on the Japanese troops who refused to surrender and come out of the bunkers or caves. The riflemen who accompanied the Marine carrying the flame thrower would fire at the gun ports or openings to drive back the defender so that the marine carrying the flame thrower could run forward up to the opening and shoot the flame inside. The Jap in there would get hit with the flaming jelly and begin to burn. If he didn't fall to the ground and writhe about until he died there, he might run outside trying escape the flame that covered his body. In the frenzy, the Marines waiting outside would shoot at him and often many more times than necessary in an attempt to put the wretched creature out of his misery. The sight and sound of a human burning alive is revolting.

PFC Luther C. Crabtree was the Marine who usually carried the flame-thrower and worked with our platoon when we assaulted these pill boxes and caves. How he escaped death was beyond me as he would charge at the enemy fortifications oblivious to the bullets being sent at him by the defenders. He must have developed a hatred for the Japanese as his brother Cpl. Harold "Tiny" Crabtree, who led the 3rd squad of the 2nd platoon, was killed a week into the fighting. Cpl. Crabtree was shot through the head and died instantly. Later when his brother heard of it, he came up and retrieved the body and carried it to the rear for burial.

One of the worst of all horror nights occurred after we had been on the island for over a week. I had sought refuge in a shell hole with a young rifleman during the day, and later we were told that the platoon would spend the night at that location and we were to dig a rifle pit.

Surrounding us were the bodies of many dead Japanese lying on the ground in every sort of crumpled position. On the right side of the pit where I knelt there was a young looking dead Japanese soldier who was lying on his back, his hands at his sides and his left foot and leg crossed over his right near the ankle. He lay with the head portion of his body nearest the Jap lines. He wore a steel helmet. His eyes were open and appeared to be looking up at the sky. From where I knelt my right shoulder was about two feet from his waist.

Before darkness fell I looked at the dead Japanese face and each time was bothered by flies that landed there and crawled into his eyes, nostrils, and mouth and I became even more upset when those same flies would try to land on me afterward. To chase them away I'd throw handfuls of sand at them when they landed on the corpse and after a while I took handfuls of the black volcanic ash and poured it on the dead soldier's face to cover it and to keep the flies away. The young Marine and I sat there after it got dark, listening to the sounds of fighting around us and hoping that no enemy would try to infiltrate our portion of the line. Each time the amber illumination flares lit up the area, we'd both peek over the edge of our rifle pit hoping that we wouldn't see any movement.

It was at such a time long after midnight that I noticed that the corpse lying to my right had moved. His face had turned a little toward us and that movement had accounted for the slight sound of falling sand that I'd heard in the darkness. I had wondered then if I had been imagining hearing such a sound, or was it the enemy crawling up toward us.

As each succeeding flare lit up the area I looked at the corpse to see if it had moved again and each time I found that it had. The light from the descending and swinging flares would animate the corpse's boyish face as the shadows around his eyes, nose, and mouth moved. The face appeared to be grinning at me as the light reflected from a few of his teeth which were exposed by his partially opened mouth. Because of corpse's movement, the sand I had placed on the face was still slowly sliding across the skin and falling to the ground.

"It's moving!" cried out the young Marine looking at the corpse.

"No, it's all right. It's rigor mortis setting in," I answered and I felt that my heart was clear up in my throat because of the horror of it all. Each time that the scene was illuminated by a flare we could see that the corpse's head had risen further from the ground and had turned to face us even more as if it were looking at us. Later, its hands, arms, and knees rose from the sand until the body appeared to be off balance and was in danger of falling over toward us. If it fell, it would tumble into our hole, probably on or against me.

The young Marine began to sob lightly at first and then more loudly as the time passed until he sounded as though he was in danger of losing control of himself. I tried to calm him and at the same time keep watch on the corpse to see that it wouldn't fall over on me. Then the Marine began to insist that I shoot the corpse and make sure it was dead. "No," I said. "It's already dead. The corpse is moving because that's what rigor mortis is doing to it."

"Is that what we are going to look like after we are dead?" he blurted out.

That statement was more than I could bear. Frantically, I put the muzzle of my carbine against the chest of the corpse and fired twice. Of course nothing happened, so I pushed the muzzle of the rifle barrel against the dead soldiers chest, threw my maximum weight against the rifle's butt and toppled the corpse over on its left side and away from our hole. Then I sat back down and felt sick and shaken.

A little while passed and while trying to regain my composure, I became aware of a slight but repetitive fluttering sound near my feet and a tapping feeling against my trouser leg. Frightened, I listened intently and looked at my companion to see if he was causing the sound. A few minutes passed before I discovered the cause. A Japanese illumination flare opened over-

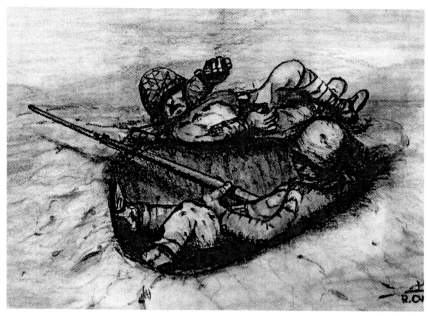

The overhead illumination of parachute flares swinging back and forth, would throw shadows over a dead Japanese soldier, where rigor mortis had set it. The shadows surrounding the mouth, eyes and nose would move, giving the impression that the corpse was struggling to regain life.

head and I saw a movement between my legs that showed that my right hand was shaking so badly it had caused a rhythm to be set flapping against my pants legs below my knees. I had not realized that my right hand had fallen from my rifle to hang there like that. Grasping my right hand with my left I placed it between my knees to keep it still, then, whispering to my companion what I had discovered, I tried to make a joke of it. But he only stared at me as though he didn't understand.

As the light of the dawn came we looked about us and saw that other Japanese corpses were still lying there in that same 'equestrian position.' That description which indicates the head, hands, and knees are raised slightly to resemble the position of a rider sitting upon a horse.

The military historians have reported that the Japanese fought a well organized defensive battle all the way on Iwo Jima. I would agree from my personal involvement. Actually, I never saw many of them moving about in the open though. Once, I did watch as five of them tried to move from one position to another across a hillside in front of us going from the left to the right while on the run. Lynch was working his light machine gun when the group was spotted about two hundred yards away. He fired several long bursts just in front of the running men, and while we watched they ran into the hail of bullets and tumbled to the ground. The machine gunner used up the rest of the ammunition in the belt as he fired at the prone men making sure they wouldn't get up again.

While all that was going on I was lying alongside Lynch and had joined in with some riflemen who were banging away with their rifles at the gun port of a partially uncovered pill box out in front of us. I have to admit while lying there I had taken partial refuge behind the number two gunner who was feeding the ammunition belt into the machine gun. After all I had learned something from Sgt. Goodling who, I figured, must know something as he had survived a few battles in his time.

A Japanese bullet creased the skin under the right eye of one of the gun crew members. It continued through the base of his nose and after exiting creased the skin under his left eye. The Marine jumped to his feet, his face bathed in blood. I heard the impact of the bullet going through his nose and when I realized what had happened, I pulled him down on the ground in an attempt to stop the bleeding placed two battle dressings over the wounds, one under each eye. The impact of the bullet to his face must have been the same as being hit by a heavy weight boxer.

At first, because of the bandages over his eyes, the Marine began to yell loudly as he thought that he was blind. He calmed down after I convinced him otherwise and as the morphine I administered took effect.

Through all of this Lynch kept firing his gun at the Japanese machine gunner who fired right back at him. Lynch seemed oblivious to all those bullets that came at him missed and passed over the top of the wounded man and me as we lay in back of him.

Even wounded and blinded like that, this Marine was able to crawl back to the aid station on his hands and knees with me guiding him. We were on our knees the entire way, about two hundred yards through gullies, over rocks, and through brush. I never saw him again after that. He was one tough Marine!

One other time we watched with jubilation as our artillery shells smashed into a rise in front of us. The hill was heavily defended by concealed machine gun and mortar installations. After a while it seemed that no Japanese soldiers could survive so heavy a bombardment.

When the barrage stopped, we were ordered forward to overrun the enemy positions. We had to cross a small gully first and go up the other side to accomplish our goal. As we descended into the gully, the Japanese came to life on the other side and opened fire with their machine guns and mortars again.

Moving forward with the platoon, I approached the smashed engine of a wrecked Japanese plane that was lying on the ground. I heard a burst of machine gun fire go by me on my left so I fell to the ground alongside the motor. Another burst of bullets hit the opposite side of the engine. It sounded as though someone was over there pounding on the metal with a metal hammer. More bursts were fired and then even more, and I got the impression that the Jap gunner was furious the way he kept it up in order to get at me. After a while I lost some of the fear as I felt confident that while I stayed where I was safe. I even thought that there was some humor to it all because of the frustration the gunner must have been feeling.

I peeked around the engine trying to see what had become of the rest of the platoon. I saw most were downhill from me in a little wash and digging in the sand trying to make rifle pits into which they could escape these bullets.

I watched Sgt. Goodling as he attempted to scoop out a hole while lying on his stomach. A Japanese gunner who was up on the slope above him about a hundred yards away could evidently see the sergeant's helmet and was firing burst after burst at him. The bullets were scattering around Goodling's head in an alarmingly close pattern, and I wondered if he knew that he was under that kind of fire.

His head would appear at the same time he threw out handfuls of sand. As he lowered his head to gather more sand a burst of bullets would strike the ground where his head had been a second before. I began to yell and wave at him; he was only about fifty or sixty feet away. Finally he looked up and saw me. He stopped digging long enough to answer with a wave of his hand and a big grin. Another burst from the Jap gun kicked the sand up from around his head and threw a lot of it right into his face. He disappeared into the hole he had been digging. Certain that he had been killed caused me to feel terrible and a lump formed in my throat as I thought it was my actions that caused him to be hit. Then, after a moment, the sergeant's helmet appeared just for an instant. His face had that big grin on it still, and I knew he was OK. He ducked down again and again the burst of bullets came at him and knocked the sand off the surrounding edge of his foxhole.

I lay in back of that engine for many minutes afraid to show myself as I knew that Jap gunner was waiting for me to do so. I became impatient and nervous and could feel myself beginning to tense up. To my right about three feet from the engine lay a small white parachute of the kind that allows an illumination flare to float to the ground. It had Japanese writing on it, and it was made of silk. I thought that it might make an interesting souvenir to give to my mother. I moved my right hand out cautiously and grasped the silk. As I began to draw it toward me, a number of bullets came and smashed into the sand near my hand. The first bullet hit the sand about two inches under my wrist throwing sand into my face. The second, third, and fourth went up over my hand and into the sand on the incline in back of me. Startled, I jerked back my hand and was very thankful that I hadn't lost it. I did not try again for a souvenir!

After that I decided to behave myself and lay flat upon the ground behind that big chunk of metal that had once been a Japanese aircraft engine. Down in front on either side of it I could see that some of my other buddies were getting worked over by at least two other machine gunners who were shooting the sand off the edges of their foxholes. It wasn't really hard for the enemy to see a new foxhole or rifle pit as the wet fresh dug sand was very black as compared to the sand that had been exposed to the air and sun for a while.

I peered out on either side of the engine and saw Sgt. Brock rise suddenly to his feet, throw his rifle down onto the sand, then turn and run in my direction. I thought, he's as good as dead right now! The Jap gunner's first burst of bullets spread out around the sergeant as he ran and struck the ground in back of him on the hill side. When he was only five or ten feet away from where I lay, the second burst came at him and those bullets missed too. This time the bullets went by and slammed into the hillside again in back of both of us.

I reached out and grabbed Brock by a leg and pulled him down behind the aircraft engine. At the same time I saw that his left foot was all bloody and blood was spurting out each time his heart beat. A bullet had struck his foot and grazed the top of the shoe and had ripped into the bones of his foot just making a mess of them. I cut the shoe off and placed my hand over the wound to stop the bleeding and was rewarded by a warm, sticky jet of blood that struck me in the face and went into my eyes blinding me for a moment while I fumbled to get a battle dressing out of my kit to place it over the wound.

Brock had lost a lot of blood from the severed artery in his foot and I could see he was going into shock so I injected some morphine into him and forced him to the ground to lie beside of me. I had no serum albumin left and I knew I must get him back to the aid station quickly so he could get some blood plasma pumped into him. What could I do? I couldn't expose myself to that Jap machine gunner who I figured to be around one hundred yards away and positioned slightly above me. I thought that both Brock and I had been pretty lucky up to now and it wasn't time to push it much further.

The wounded sergeant and I lay there side by side for quite a few minutes, with me trying to figure out what do before it got dark. He remained unconscious. Eventually, I heard someone yelling in back of me higher up the slope. I looked over my shoulder and saw Lynch and his machine gun crew looking at me from over the rim of the gully. They were waving at me to come up to where they were and at the same time making motions to the effect that they were firing at the opposite side of the gully where I supposed the enemy machine gun was located. Apparently, they had seen what had happened to Brock and how I had treated him. They realized what a predicament we were in and wanted me to pick up the sergeant and come up the hill toward them.

I didn't like the idea at all since I knew that the Jap gunner was intent on shooting me for sure and was waiting for such a move. Besides that, I was exhausted and didn't think that I could even pick Brock up let alone carry him up the incline. The yelling and motioning continued and since it was going to be dark soon, I reluctantly decided to place myself in the hands of the machine gun crew. Squatting behind the wrecked engine, I managed to get Brock up onto my right shoulder.

I glanced up at the machine gunners and could see them firing at the opposing machine gun position. Their light Browning machine gun was jumping up and down, a spray of empty shell casing were thrown into the air as continuing burst after burst was fired from it. I rose to my feet and ran taking about three steps before the first of the Jap machine gun's burst of bullets passed me on both sides and slammed into the sand in front of me. After three more steps I stepped off to the left and the second group of bullets passed high over my right shoulder and again slammed into the

A battlefield helmet was a common sight, left behind when it's owner was wounded or killed. Often the interior would reveal a personal history in the way of a family photograph, wife or fiancé, and an all too common bullet or fragment hole.

incline in front of me. Another several more steps and I saw before me just under the rim of the little canyon, a small shell crater. I thought that this was my last chance before the Jap gunner fired a third time and got me for sure. I threw Brock off my shoulder and into the small depression. I took a breath and dove at the crater myself. I was on my knees falling forward when the next group of bullets came smashing into the sand between my face and Brock's body. I could actually feel the breeze caused by the bullets as they passed. I rolled him onto his back at the bottom of the hole, fell beside him and lay there struggling for breath.

Lying on my back beside Brock, I watched as the Jap gunner's bullets hit the near edge of the shell hole, cross over our stomachs missing us by inches and then strike the far side. From where I lay I could see Lynch's machine gun jump up and down while spent copper colored cartridges were sent spinning away from it.

Later on, two of the machine gun crew jumped down to the shell hole where we lay and lifted the sergeant and literally threw him over the rim to safety. I crawled up a few moments later and was too exhausted to care whether I got shot or not. When I crawled over the top into a hole, Lt. Horvath and corpsman Gene Olson were in there watching me. I sat alongside of them for a few moments without anyone saying anything. I felt completely spent and I supposed looked it too. I suppose that I expected the Lieutenant to say something about a job well done, but he didn't. Instead, he spoke to Olson, "I think that there is something wrong with Overton. You had better watch him."

When he said that, I was so taken aback and shocked I could only look at him and stare for a moment. My shock turned to dismay and I felt I was going to collapse. I buried my head in my arms in complete exhaustion and to hide whatever tears I felt coming from my eyes.

The Lieutenant appeared to be detached from the present situation. He showed no remorse, no fear, nothing that would indicate his concern for the welfare of others. I thought that this is not the same man I have been training with for the past year. Men do and say strange things during periods of heavy stress.

CHAPTER THIRTY-EIGHT

Combat Fatigue: Our Constant Companion

A DETAIL OF men from our company was sent back to the battalion command post for supplies of food and ammunition. I went with them as I needed medical supplies. I fell in at the tail end of the line. We moved quickly in single file spaced well apart over the flat shell torn ground, but a Jap artillery spotter called in an artillery barrage upon us.

We fell to the ground when we heard that first "Pom" sound and buried our faces in the sand, hugging it as the first three shells passed over us and exploded about a hundred yards beyond. I heard the Japanese field piece fire the fourth time and the shell arrived, but instead of the expected explosion, I heard a 'thud' sound in front of me as if someone had thrown a full barrack's bag to the ground.

Hugging the ground and crawling along on my stomach I could only see the Marine directly ahead of me. I stopped when I was confronted by something strange stretched across my path. It was several yards long, grayish in color and about the size of one of my fingers in diameter. It was sprinkled with a layer of black sand and I stared at it for a long moment before disregarding my first thought that it was some kind of Japanese trick. But, when I saw flies land on it, I knew that it had to be a man's intestines that were stretched taut. I looked around for the rest of the body, but because I couldn't raise my head I couldn't get a view of the surrounding terrain.

Frightened, but still cautious, I rapidly crawled over the viscera and followed after the Marine ahead of me. I caught up with him in a shell crater. He was down on both knees using both hands to cover his face. When I spoke to him, he looked at me and I could see he was very pale and seemed to be in shock as he had difficulty in responding to my questions.

He did tell me that he had been crawling along the ground when the four shells were fired at us, and he remained flat on the ground when he heard the first one. As he heard the fourth shell fire, another Marine rose from the ground off to his right side and attempted to run across in front of him. The artillery shell struck the running man's body head on. The shell didn't explode for some reason, but literally tore the Marine apart with a "swoosh" and in a spray of pink liquid vapor. The impact spread what was left of the Marine all around him.

I urged the shocked Marine to move on and I accompanied him to the battalion aid station. He seemed to be in very poor emotional condition. I fastened a casualty tag on him indicating he suffered from battle fatigue and left him there to be seen by the battalion surgeon. He never returned to the company.

His type of behavior caused by emotional stress combined with physical fatigue was very common to see during this battle. For many years after this experience I thought, "Is it any wonder that men who fought in such intense combat could not recall what had happened to them. For acquaintances to say of a combat veteran, "He saw such horrible things during the war, he doesn't want to talk about it!" is often an erroneous statement I believe.

Exhaustion and fear of the unknown can bring about combat fatigue. Fear of dying was not much concern after a few days, we expected to die, we just didn't know when and how it would happen. When the mind can no longer handle the load, it shuts down both the mind and body.

Usually men can't remember all the details involving a horrible event. The type of intense combat experienced on Iwo Jima blocked the mind's memory function, leaving men frustrated because of the inability to fill in all those little details needed to complete the story of what occurred. It is easier to "not want to speak of it." It is a very complex, confusing and frustrating thing to face, believe me! I speak from personal experience!

During one afternoon when our advance was stalled, we heard what we thought was a gasoline engines operating from behind the Japanese lines. Fearing that the enemy was activating some of their small, but highly mobile tanks that we had so far found entrenched only as gun emplacements, apparently the company commander apparently requested the presence of an anti-tank gun. A gun crew came dragging up a 37 mm mobile gun and installed it in back of us. They sighted it in on an opening in the seven foot high berm directly in front of us, thinking that this opening was the most likely spot a tank would come charging at us. The gun crew then settled down to wait.

Feeling a little more secure by the gun's presence, my foxhole companion and I settled down and tried to rest. But we were startled by the sound of the gun firing. We rose to our knees, ready to fight, but all that we could see was some smoke and dust swirling around in the opening. We waited a while wondering why the gun had fired, if not at a Jap tank. Later I crawled back to the gun emplacement and spoke with one of the gun crew.

He said that he had been crouched beside his gun while on watch while rest of the gun crew relaxed. He casually leaned forward and looked through the gun sight to make sure it was clear. He saw a Japanese soldier walking through the opening in the berm toward us. He pushed the mechanism firing the gun, and saw the shell hit the soldier in the body and explode. He thought the explosion was larger than one usually caused by the shell and suspected the enemy soldier was carrying explosives with him which was detonated. Later, we advanced passed the spot where the Jap soldier had died, and saw the remains of him lying about on the ground. It was a classic example of a case of overkill where cannon fire was used to kill only one soldier.

A useful weapon of ours was the 'satchel charge'. It resembled a canvas suit case and contained any number of one-quarter pound blocks of TNT, a powerful explosive. In an attack on an enemy fortification a Marine carrying this package of explosive would run forward to the side of the installation and place it at the most vulnerable place, then escape before the explosion occurred. His comrades would try to protect him by firing at the gun ports in order to drive the defenders away from the opening.

I think it was a time that I had strayed over into the 27th Marine's territory. I had sought refuge up against a dry stream embankment and found myself huddling next to an officer while I waited for the opportunity of asking him directions.

Over to our right, at the base of a smashed tree, its trunk and bare limbs all scarred by shell fire, a satchel carrier prepared to run forward toward a cave entrance. While being supported by other Marine riflemen he climbed over the edge of the embankment, and ran toward the cave entrance. On his approach he pulled the fuse lighter, made an underhanded swing and threw the charge into the cave opening. Then turning back, he returned running safely to our position. But, for some reason the charge didn't explode.

After a period of waiting and a discussion among the other Marines, one of the men there volunteered go up and burn the cave out with his flame thrower. I could hear the officer next to me as he directed others to commence firing at the cave entrance to drive the other Japanese away from the cave entrance. As his comrades fired into the opening, the Marine carrying the bulky flame thrower was helped up over the edge of the bank where he lumbered on toward his target. When he reached his target he stopped planted his feet and fired his flame into the cave. The officer and I, watching with our eyes at just above ground level saw a brilliant flash of orange light and watched the sand around the cave entrance rise. Instantly we tipped our helmet visors down to protect our faces.

A terrific explosion had occurred which demolished the cave entrance and scattered debris over the entire surrounding area. It also resulted in blowing the Marine who carried the flame thrower high into the air where his body was caught on a naked tree limb. Hanging there it appeared to be an old soiled discarded uniform with one shoe hanging from it. The sight was sickening to me when I first realized what it was I was seeing. At first I turned my head away and pulled down my helmet visor to cover my eyes and huddled against the bank. Then recovering a bit, I mustered a little courage, I pushed myself away from the bank and stammered, "I'll go get him down!" intending to crawl around the officer and toward the tree.

"No" he commanded sharply, "you will only draw enemy fire!"

I don't think any one else attempted to go up there and retrieve the body.

To the dead Marines buddies it must have a horrible shock to deal with. It probably was in view of other Japanese soldiers that were concealed in nearby fortifications. I left the area a short time later and as I did I looked back at the Marine's body I could still see it draped over the ragged and leafless broken tree limb. I crawled away, only about fifty feet and sought shelter in a shell hole occupied by two Marines. After looking me over one said, "What was the big explosion over there Doc?"

I tried to tell them but the words wouldn't come out right and I realized that they, only fifty feet away when it happened were not aware of the horrible incident.

Chance or luck has always been a puzzle to me. I don't understand it very well. On Iwo Jima, beginning on the first day, I was lucky by 'chance?' During that first night's fight I was kneeling in front of the 28th Regiment Marine and yet he was the one bayoneted in the chest by charging Japanese soldiers. At other times shells had landed in foxholes I had just left, killing comrades who remained behind me. On other times I had been shoulder to shoulder with men when they died. To this day I still don't understand.

A young Marine and I shared one foxhole, we sat side by side. He was to my left. Being constantly reminded to do so by the sergeant in the next shell crater he leaned forward every fifteen seconds or so to look over the rim to watch for the enemy. He made me very nervous and I became annoyed as his timing was much, much too regular. I thought that routine was dangerous as a Japanese rifleman might see him and wait for the next time he stuck his head up. When I thought I couldn't stand it any longer, I told him that he should take a rest and I'd watch for a while. He relaxed against the back side of the crater and shut his eyes. I moved forward and to the right and peeped out from the corner of the pit several times and for several minutes before sitting back along side my partner. After a while I felt his head and helmet lean to rest on my left shoulder. "Let him sleep!" I thought and didn't move.

A few moments passed before I decided I had better look out again, and I reached across my chest and pushed on my companion's head and shoulder until he was sitting upright again. When I removed my hand and to my dismay, I saw blood, serum and that horrible yellow gray liquid ooze out from behind his right ear. He was dead, the bullet passing through the cloth covered helmet and through his head while I was leaning forward. I stared first in shock and then moved frantically forward as I realized that the bullet that hit him should have struck me first if I had been sitting there. Later, I couldn't escape the thought that I had caused the Marine to die because of my insistence to lean forward in place of him. My 'bucket' that was filled with 'guilt' was beginning to overflow.

I huddled there in shocked silence and eventually I heard voices nearby, and I waited a few moments until the platoon leader's head and shoulders appeared over the rim. He lay prone up there on the sand and told us that we were to move out in about fifteen minutes. He kept moving his eyes from the dead marine to me and then back to the dead man as he talked. Perhaps he thought the Marine was dozing at first. Then finally he stopped talking, paused, looked at the Marine for a moment, then back at me, this time there was a question a question in his eyes.

"He is dead." I said, anticipating his question.

"Oh," the Lieutenant replied with startling casualness. Then he crawled away.

I huddled in the forward corner of the foxhole feeling very depressed, until we moved out. I kept thinking about why the Lieutenant didn't ask who the dead Marine was, as he couldn't possibly have seen his face. "Didn't he care?" As I crawled forward on toward the next position I paused and thought, "I didn't know the name of the dead Marine either." That was going to bother me for a long time too.

Once, a comrade and I waited for the order to move out against a heavily defended bunker directly in front of us. When it came we leaped to our feet and side by side placed our right feet on the edge of the crater to step up. The sand gave way under my foot causing me to stumble. Recovering quickly I stepped up again and was only a half step behind my partner when a mortar shell landed in front and to the left of him. His body took the full brunt of the blast mangling him horribly.

I was thrown back into the hole where I landed on the back of my head and shoulders. Dazed, but trying to clear my mind, the thought came to me that I was mortally wounded and would soon die. But, after a moment I felt pain only at the back of my neck, I sat up and examined myself and found no blood or open wound.

Then suddenly remembering my partner, I found him lying in front of the hole where he had fallen, his clothes were still smoldering. I reached out, grabbed his shoulders and pulled him back into the hole and onto my lap. His clothing was perforated with fragment holes, some still smoking from burning cloth pushed inside his body. I gave him morphine and later another one-half grain when he cried out in pain. He had a large wound in his abdomen and his intestines were protruding even though I attempted to restrain them with a large compress. He looked down and saw what was happening to him and began to scream.

A sergeant crawled over from the next foxhole and told me to "shut him up" as he was attracting the enemy to our location and that they were throwing hand grenades into our positions. I gave the injured man another half-grain of morphine thinking that since he was dying anyway, what did it matter if he were overdosed? He quieted down again. Darkness set in and after a few moments passed the wounded man began screaming again.

The sergeant called out threatening, "You better shut him up! I'll throw a grenade in there, that will shut him up for sure!"

I was appalled! There was no way I could save the wounded man, I was sure of that. No litter bearers had come up, I couldn't blame them either as the machine gunners facing us seemed to be almost frantic in attempting to keep us down. As it grew darker, I thought about carrying the Marine out over my shoulder but discarded that idea because of the type of wounds he suffered. He'd bleed to death long before I got to the aid station and besides, I would probably be shot down by our men in the dark.

I searched my kit and found I only had one morphine syrette left. I felt for the dying man's carotid artery with my fingers and attempted to inject the morphine directly into the bloodstream. Evidently, I missed doing that because his screaming continued. I placed the palm of my right hand over the injured man's mouth each time he sucked in air to scream out. When an illuminating flare lit up his face, I saw his eyes. The look there was one of agony and puzzlement, pleading for me to help him. Still, when he attempted to scream I placed my hand over his mouth and I could feel his teeth. Then, after he had just sucked in air I placed my hand over his mouth, but he gave no response. I kept my hand there a moment longer thinking that he might be trying to deceive me. But, it was over, he was dead.

I spent the rest of the night alone in that crater with my dead comrade wondering what life was all about. I thought that I'd probably never know as I expected to die soon.

The hatred that developed in our troops toward the Japanese showed itself clearly beginning immediately after our landing on the island. The feeling intensified as each day came and passed and that hatred interfered with the military tactic of capturing the enemy for interrogation.

Once I saw a white flag tied to the end of a rifle barrel being waved from the interior of a shell crater. All shooting in that immediate area stopped and then slowly and cautiously a Japanese soldier emerged and stood hesitantly at the crater's edge waiting for our next move. I heard a shot fired and then it seemed that every Marine's rifle in view of the Jap spoke and he crumpled to the ground very dead for certain. I felt no remorse over his death.

I sat in a shell hole once and listened to a sergeant tell how he and another Marine had come across a wounded enemy soldier partially covered by sand and suffering from body and leg wounds. According to instructions on how to handle a captive they half carried and half dragged the fellow back to our battalion aid station where they placed him on a stretcher. The sergeant told me that he caught the attention of one of the doctors and said to him, "Here is a wounded Jap who needs medical attention."

The doctor pulled his pistol from its holster and pointed it at the Jap's head, fired a bullet into it and said, "Not any more, he doesn't!"

The sergeant was peeved and complained about having carried the Jap all that way back for treatment and interrogation only to have the surgeon shoot him. He said that from now on, he'd do his own shooting! This incident was later confirmed by a statement made by Nyle Weiler who said that he was there when it happened. I don't care to identify the doctor involved.

I understand how that doctor felt when he shot the Japanese soldier. I recalled the bloody and disfigured Marines who lay in the filth surrounding the aid station, crying out in pain, their eyes wide open and bulging; faces white with shock, their expectation and fear when facing death. I recalled the continually growing rows of poncho covered bodies that lay upon the edge of the crater that served as the aid station. I knew how that doctor felt!

There were many incidents reported of Japanese soldiers who, after getting behind our lines, would attack our wounded who lay unprotected on the ground or on litters in aid stations. Several reported incident happened when a Marine, who fell wounded and was dragged among the Japanese soldiers, and was later found to have tortured by his captors.

I was told by Marines and by corpsman Gene Olson who had recovered the bodies of the two young Marines, Kastan and Powers, that those bodies had been mutilated by numerous bayonet wounds by the Japanese after I had left them dead on the battlefield.

These incidents serve to show the emotional intensity of feeling of both sides of the combatants during the battle for Iwo Jima. Scattered about the island were documents issued by the Japanese commander, Lt. General Tadamichi Kuribayashi. One such directive encouraged the Japanese defenders to die fighting for their Homeland and Emperor and asked that each one of them kill at least ten American invaders before they perished.

It didn't work out that way in the end because of over the approximate 22,000 Japanese who defended the island only 1,083 were captured alive. On the American side 6,821 died and 21,965 were wounded including those suffering from combat fatigue.

The hatred developed and displayed during this type of battle environment is called "being callous" I suppose. The combat participant must develop an unfeeling or hardened attitude to survive the ordeal. If the comrade along side of him is killed or wounded, he must ignore it and continue toward his objective. If he can't ignore it, he may be killed or disabled as he hesitates. Battles are not won by soldiers who in time of combat stop their charge to cradle the head of an injured fellow soldier. It's won by those who keep going on to the end.

It took me several days of fierce combat to understand why our officers didn't want to hear about who was killed or wounded. Emotionally, they couldn't afford to know. The Marines, in attacking the enemy, concentrated on killing an enemy and may be required to pass by a fallen comrade. The corpsman, on the other hand, whose primary duty it was to attend to the fallen, had to endure the pleading and screams of the injured and dying and all the while trying to give emergency treatment under the most adverse conditions. I got to the point that if a man died while I tended him, I suffered horribly from guilt. If, on the other hand he was already dead when I got to him, it bothered me little.

Dead Japanese soldiers became fly spots to us, they mattered not at all except for the annoyance of having them lying to close to us when we lay prone or crawled by. I noticed that we passed by a number of the dead, who suffered severe damage to their lower jaws and hands. I wondered what kind of weapon we had that did that to them. Eventually, we came to learn the injury was caused by them holding a live grenade to their throats and exploding it in order to die quickly. It was said they were afraid of being tortured if taken alive. I don't believe there were tortures. Americans don't like to torture, kill maybe, but not torture.

We shot their dead because some of them only wounded, but pretending to be dead, would hold out a live grenade ready to explode as we crawled by.

It was better to shoot a corpse as we approached rather than be subjected to that possibility.

Once I watched one of our officers order a rifleman and "runner," PFC Roy Johnson, run across an open area in order to carry a message to Sgt. Goodling. Five of us were lying flat on the ground partially concealed by low brush and rock and receiving heavy fire from a Jap machine gunner concealed in a concrete bunker. Johnson, who was my age and one of my close buddies, was immediately machine gunned down to my dismay.

Without hesitation the officer ordered a second Marine across. This Marine didn't hesitate either, but jumped up and ran. He was shot down too and fell over the body of Johnson. We watched as the Jap gunner fired several bursts of bullets into both bodies. I was shocked as I listened to the bullets make that, 'thud, thud' thud' sound as they hit the bodies again and again.

I heard the officer order a third man to cross over. This Marine, PFC Don Giles and another one of my close friends refused, saying he would be

The Japanese would sometimes feign death in order to detonate a grenade when a Marine passed by. This Japanese soldier still clings to a grenade, and would likely have been repeatedly shot by approaching Marines to insure he was dead.

killed also! The officer said, "Are you refusing an order while in combat?" and swung his body and rifle to face the young Marine. The Lieutenant had a very odd look in his eyes, as though he wasn't seeing any thing.

My immediate thought was, "This officer has gone crazy. I'll kill him first if he intends to shoot my buddy." Instinctively, I moved my carbine only a little to point at the officer's left armpit. But first I said, "He's right Lieutenant, that's a 'machine gun lane' out there, he will be killed!"

The officer paused, he seemed very composed. Then he calmly said, "Oh, OK then, let's withdraw.'

We crawled away leaving our two dead comrades lying where they died. I felt myself shuddering, thinking about what I had almost done. What bothered me most was that I had actually considered shooting the officer, who I had always respected very much. How did I ever get into such a frame of mind? Under the pressure of battle, men think and do strange things.

Chapter Thirty-Nine

Leaving Iwo

A T DAWN I sat alone in my rifle pit, wondering if this would be the day I died or was torn apart by an exploding shell. I had no hopes of living at all. Why should I? I knew that I was in pretty bad shape and did not expect things to get better. I didn't even know what day it was or how many days before we had landed on this damn island. I couldn't even remember if I had shared the rifle pit last night with any one else. There wasn't any more 2nd Platoon, or 1st, or 3rd either. The men who had been assigned to those platoons and who still survived were now gathered together in some loosely organized group that gave very little semblance of the original finely trained and well organized fighting machine that had been called Company D.

Lt. Col. Joseph Sayers, the battalion commander, was injured by steel splinters from an exploding shell and was replaced by Major Amedeo Rea who was the battalion's executive officer. Rea in turn was replaced by Captain Thomas Fields who had been the commander of Company D. With Captain Fields detached from the company, First Lt. Charles Horvath remained as the only officer of the original seven officers who had begun the battle. He would be injured soon by a bullet that smashed into the binoculars hanging from his neck that sent metal fragments into his chest.

I sat in that hole thinking that I was just too tired to care any longer whether I lived or died. Suddenly I heard voices and the sound of running footsteps on sand, then two Marine riflemen came crashing into the crater and landed on top of me. Once the two men regained their balance and got off me, I realized that they were not of company D. I could only stare at them. They identified themselves as members of the 27th Regiment and said that they had been told that they were replacing us.

I could hardly believe this unexpected turn of events. It took a few moments for me to comprehend what the two Marines were saying before one slapped me hard across my shoulder knocking me backward and said, "Get the hell out of here while you can, go on... get out!"

Apparently I didn't move quickly as I found myself being shoved from the hole and back toward our rear lines. I left the crater crawling on my hands and knees, then joined others moving in single file toward the rear. As I crawled, I heard other Marines say that D Company had been ordered back to a position several hundred yards from the front line. We crawled into a large bomb crater and, for the first time since D day, I sat down to rest without fear that the next man coming into the hole would be a Jap soldier. I lay on my back and tried to shut my eyes and found that they wouldn't close. I tried to eat cheese and crackers from a K ration and found it tasteless and then discovered that I couldn't swallow the food as it just kept falling out of my mouth and spilling down the front of my blouse. Even the water I tried to wash it down with refused to enter my throat and ran out either sides of my mouth.

I lay back on the sand and tried to shut my eyes. They wouldn't close and that frightened me as I couldn't understand what was happening. After a while I gave up trying to eat or sleep, crawled out of the crater and went in search of the battalion aid station thinking I should replenish my medical supplies. I also thought it necessary to let someone there know that I was still alive and on the job. I crawled into a large crater being used as an aid station and found some wounded Marines I recognized who were from Company D, lying on litters awaiting evacuation. I sat among them on the sand and tried to carry on a conversation with several of the corpsmen working on the wounded. I guess I didn't do too well as the battalion surgeon came over and began to speak to me.

From what I remembered later of the conversation the doctor seemed appalled by my clothing and how filthy I was. My hands and arms and face had coatings of dried blood on them layered with dirt and scum. The knees of my trouser legs had long since given way and the barbed wire holding the shoe sole on and the wire holding my pants together was becoming rusty.

The doctor gave me some tablets and said that I was to go down to the beach and go on board a ship standing off shore where I was to eat, sleep and bathe and then to get into a clean uniform and return to the battalion the next day. As I later recalled this incident, I believed that I had carried on a lucid conversation with the surgeon. Corpsmen who were there assured me later that I had not spoken to anyone or answered any of the doctor's questions, but had just sat there looking at him.

Once at the beach I joined a long line of wounded who were wading out to a waiting LST. We were transported to one of the many APA's anchored offshore, awaiting its complement of wounded men. After climbing the ladder to the deck of the ship, I stood there in some disbelief that I could actually stand up straight and motionless without the fear of being struck by bullets or flying shell splinters.

A young Navy doctor was on deck and directed me below to a compartment where I was confronted by another young physician who began to question me. He seemed pleasant and respectful. I liked him immediately. He made jokes about my appearance such as, "How did you get so filthy? I know what happened. The Japs took one look at you and sent you back to be cleaned up?" I thought he was very funny as he spoke.

The doctor kept asking me questions and repeated them time and again. He would snap his fingers in front of my eyes in an attempt to make them

These dead Marines are being sprayed with disinfecting solution as they lay on the beach, waiting to be buried. In the background can be seen a few ships of the invasion fleet.

react and commanded me to shut my eyes which apparently I could not do. He'd say. "Talk to me... talk to me!" when at the time I thought I was speaking to him. He eventually 'pulled rank.' on me by saying, "Listen, I'm a US naval officer and you are an enlisted man. When I speak to you I demand an answer. Do you understand that?"

I thought I had answered him. But suddenly, it seemed to me that I must have taken a giant step and was now standing to his left, facing the left side of his face. I felt no pain. It wasn't a good feeling; it wasn't a bad feeling either. The doctor kept talking to the spot where I thought I had been standing. I looked there and was amazed that he was speaking to an odd looking figure. I was dumbfounded when I realized that the figure was me. I was looking at my "old self" still standing before the doctor as he questioned me. I was appalled at what I saw. I looked terrible. I was dirty, my face blackened with dried blood, sand and scum. My clothing was in rags. Physically, I felt nothing. I spoke to my old self, "Come on now, the doctor is trying to help you. Now answer him!" Neither, the doctor or his two aids seem to take notice of my remark or of me.

Standing there at his left side I was totally impressed the doctor's appearance. He was clean shaven and dressed in a clean pressed a khaki uniform. "How does he keep clean like that in combat I wondered?"

The doctor ordered my old self to lie down on the bunk and close my eyes. Apparently I didn't move because he turned and spoke to his assistants. They stepped forward, picked my 'old self' up and placed 'it' on the bunk. "Shut your eyes," the surgeon commanded, "go to sleep!"

As soon as he spoke, my "new self" joined with my "old self" on the bunk and I became 'one' again. I lay there with my eyes wide open and feeling all the misery and pain again. It seemed only a few moments passed before the doctor placed his hand over my eyes and closed my eyelids. When he removed his hand my eyes would open. He tried again and my eyes would open again.

I suppose he gave up trying because he said, "Oh, OK you're not ready to sleep yet, huh. I'll fix that!" He went away for a moment and came back with a syringe and needle. A corpsman began fumbling with my trousers belt buckle and the doctor said, "Don't fool with it, cut it off!" The corpsman pulled out a sheath knife and leaned forward. I wondered what it was he was going to cut off, but wasn't very alarmed about it. The next day I found that the medic had cut my trousers belt in two and slit the cloth of my trousers at the hip so that the doctor could inject me with a drug. I didn't remember anything after that but darkness until midmorning the next day. Well, I thought it was one night but there is still a strong suspicion, because of what the doctor said later that I actually slept through that night, the next day and that night too. But that first night, after dark, the ship pulled anchor and sailed for Guam, where some us would be taken to a U. S. Army field hospital.

When I did awake my head was a solid mass of pain. It hurt so much that my vision seemed dimmed by rolling waves of orange and red that lightened and darkened alternately. I had nausea, but couldn't vomit because nothing was in my stomach. I became aware of the thumping of the engines immediately, because of the vibrations coming through the steel decking. I felt panic as I realized that the ship might have left Iwo Jima and I was being separated from my buddies.

I heard loud metallic banging noises from the weather deck above and wondered if we were under attack and those were our ship's guns. Then I realized that it didn't sound like that after all. It must be a noise made by the ship's deck crew. I was so very weak that I found that I could not sit up on the bunk, but had to roll off it onto the deck. After a few moments I felt strong enough to pull myself upright by grasping the tiers of bunks.

Deciding to find my way to the weather deck I worked my way through the tiers of bunks. I was soon confronted by the doctor who had spoken to me before. He was tending an injured Marine with the help of his two assistants. He saw my approach. "Well, well, you finally woke up did you? You sure slept a long time, how do you feel now?"

At first when I tried to answer only a garbled noise came out of my throat, but trying again I got my speech straightened out. I asked him what the noise on deck was..., gunfire?

"No, no!" It's the deck crew making noise up there and they had better stop soon. These guys can't take much more of it!"

He was referring to the many wounded Marines in the compartment who were lying on bunks. As he spoke a loud noise sounded again and the injured man he was tending gave a startled jerk. Other wounded reacted by crying out. Thinking later about the events that next followed, I suppose I took his comment as a directive to me to do something about stopping the noise. After all, he was a US Navy physician, an officer and I was a Navy corpsman, an enlisted man.

I climbed the ladder to the weather deck and by following the sound of the noise. I came upon a sailor sitting on the steel deck chipping paint with a hammer and chisel. I was dumbfounded. This was a ridiculous situation, him chipping a rusted spot on the deck while we are in combat. I stepped forward and stood before him and said, "Knock it off. Don't you know this ship is full of wounded Marines?"

The young sailor looked up at me and said, "Shove off, Mac. The chief told me to do this." He then went back to chipping paint. He struck the chisel with the hammer again, as if to emphasize his point. I reached down and twisted the hammer from his hand and threw it over the side of the ship and into the ocean. The sailor screamed out at me, "I'm checked out with that hammer. Now I'll get into trouble!" He rose up from the deck with his hands raised, I thought reaching out for my face.

Later, I thought I remembered correctly everything that happened during the next few seconds. There were about a dozen Marines sitting on a nearby hatch cover who watched the incident who confirmed it later. When the sailor reached for my face, I grabbed him by the throat with my left hand and using my right grabbed his trousers just below his belt buckle. I picked him up and put him on my right shoulder and I walked to the port rail of the ship and threw him over the steel cable life line toward the ocean water below.

Fortunately for him the back of his right leg scraped the steel cable and the back of his knee caught and held him momentarily. My next recollection was that the sailor was hanging upside down on the outside of the ship's hull with the back of his knee bent over the steel cable and he was screaming out in agony. I reached under the cable with my right foot and gave him a solid kick with the heel and sole of my shoe in an attempt to break his hold and cause him to fall into the water. If I had succeeded, he would have surely died as we weren't very far forward of the ship's propeller. If that missed chopping him up, he would have drowned as ships don't stop to pick up people from the water while cruising in battle zones during wartime.

The sharp barbed wire wrapped around my shoe slashed into the side of his head and out gushed pretty, bright red blood from deep cuts on his right temple to mask his entire face. As I kicked at him, I became aware that another deck crew member had run up and had grabbed the sailor by his foot and was bending the leg down toward the deck inside the cable, preventing him from falling into the sea. I gave him another kick trying to knock him loose from the rail. The sailor must have been suffering a lot of pain from the steel cable leg and from the blows I gave him.

Suddenly, I realized that three of the ship's crew had jumped on my back and were trying to pull me away from the rail. The dozen or so Marines sitting on a nearby hatch cover, who had observed the incident jumped into the fray and began punching other deck sailors who had come to the scene to help restrain me. The sailors were outnumbered and were getting the worst of it when a very young officer, a very short Ensign became involved. He suddenly appeared between me and a sailor I had just struck in the chest and was preparing to strike again. The officer held his arms and hands stiffly down along the sides of his body and grimaced as if in anticipation of being struck. He yelled out, "Stop it! Stop it!" Surprised, I withheld my punch. I certainly had no intention of striking an officer. He had a lot of guts to do what he did. I respected him very much for that and the common sense he displayed.

Once things were calmed down he called for an explanation of what the commotion was all about. "Who's responsible for this?" he demanded to know.

I told him that I had tried to throw the sailor overboard because he wouldn't quit chipping paint that caused the noise that so terribly affected my wounded comrades below. I added that, "I wasn't going to permit that!"

The Marines who still stood in a group surrounding the officer called out their opinion. "He's right!" they shouted. "We're not going to permit that!"

The Ensign held up his hands and very wisely said, "It's OK. There won't be any more chipping of paint until we reach our anchorage at Guam and all the wounded have been removed from the ship." He ordered the injured sailor, who now lay on the deck whimpering and bleeding profusely be carried below to the sickbay. He then faced the Marines and ordered them to disperse and return to what ever they had been doing before the incident arose

He ordered me to go below to my assigned compartment and stay there. He didn't ask for my name and rate there on the deck. I'm sure he got it that information later from the doctor who had attended me below in the troop compartment; I sat on a bunk down below. I didn't seem to have any concern at all over what I had done. It seemed very logical to me that if someone was hurting one of my Marine buddies that I should try to destroy them, after all that is what I had been trying to do for the past ten days or whatever, on that damn dirty island.

Once below it was only a few moments before the young doctor came rushing up to me. With a grin on his face he said, "Well now, when I told you I wanted that noise stopped, I didn't know that you would act so efficiently. I'm sure glad you stopped it though as I don't know how these wounded men would have stood it much longer!"

He examined me again and said, "Kid, you sure are a mess. You look terrible! Go find the quartermaster (Marine storekeeper) and get a fresh uniform and shoes. Get a shower; get all that blood and dirt off. Find the galley, get something to eat and then come back here and see me." He gave me directions on where to find the quartermaster sergeant's compartment.

I found it up on the weather deck and stepped inside. It was a small room, divided in half by a counter that stretched from one bulkhead to the other. Behind the counter stood a Marine staff sergeant dressed in a clean, pressed khaki uniform. He looked pudgy and soft to me like a 'pogy bait' non-combatant Marine. I knew right away I wouldn't like him. He was sipping coffee from a mug and he eyed me suspiciously over its rim as I approached. I didn't like his looks, and obviously he didn't like mine. Behind him stretched a heavy wire mesh screen that separated the front part of the room from the back. In back of the screen there were stacks of equipment and uniforms and that area was guarded by a steel mesh gate.

"What do you want?" It was almost a sneer instead of a question that he asked.

"I came for a clean uniform and some shoes," I replied.

"I don't have any uniforms for you. What do you think this is, the Red Cross?"

I don't remember saying anything else to him. It did flash into my mind to reach over the counter, grab him, pull him to the outside deck and fling him over the side though. I immediately discarded that idea, remembering what had happened earlier on deck. Perhaps it was the look on my face that caused him to turn and run into the screened off storage area slamming and locking the door behind him. He stood back from the door yelling for me to not to touch him or he'd send for the ship's master-at-arms, the chief petty officer who is responsible for maintaining discipline on board a warship. I stood leaning against the counter there watching and listening to him yelling out for help for a half hour before deciding that he was not about to come out. And besides he had worn his voice hoarse and was only making croaking noises when I left and went back down below where I sat on a bunk until the doctor saw me there.

He seemed very upset and demanded to know why I had not followed his orders. After listening to my explanation as to why I couldn't do as he had directed he said, "Oh yeah, I'll fix that!" Then he told me to follow him. His face was red with anger as he ran up the ladder so quickly I found that I couldn't keep up with him, so I followed at some distance.

I heard some shouting inside the compartment as I approached the quarter master's doorway and then the doctor stepped from the room. He said to me, "Go in, you'll get your clothing now!" Inside, the sergeant was standing behind the counter, this time without his coffee cup and his face was very pale. He looked sick and he appeared worried. He looked me over in order to judge my size and politely offered me a used, but clean, set of Army fatigues, which he apologized for by saying that he had no Marine uniform my size. I got a pair of almost new shoes, but he didn't have any stockings, underwear, towels or soap to give me. I stared at him the entire time he waited on me and maybe that was the reason he didn't get close to the counter.

I left him after saying 'thanks" and found a head (lavatory) just off the weather deck. I could not get my shoe laces untied so I could remove them and my trousers. I turned the salt water shower on and sat on the shower floor with the water pouring down on me; it felt great, even though my feet and scalp began to sting. After a while a sailor walked by the head door, looked in and continued on by. I knew he would come back and look a second time at what he might think was a strange sight. When he did only his head appeared in view as he peeked around the side of the doorway. "Hey, come here I want to use your knife!" I yelled out.

"What for?" He asked with a very suspicious tone.

"To cut the shoe strings off my shoes that's why!"

"Well OK, but stick your feet out toward me, I'll cut them loose." He answered hesitantly. After cutting the laces he hurriedly left the room and I thought, "He's going to have something to tell his buddies at chow time, I bet!"

I showered in the fresh ocean water and took a long time, perhaps an hour to remove the dried blood and grime from my body. Afterward, since I had no towel to dry myself with so I dressed while I was still wet. I threw my old clothing and shoes into a garbage can. The new 'boondockers' hurt my feet because I had no stockings to wear, but at least they were better than my old shoes. The new shoe leather's dye stung my feet something terrible and I found that both of them were covered with small dish like ulcers that were all pink with traces of blood oozing out. I got dressed; found the galley was occupied by only a mess steward who was reading a comic book. He glanced at me and then pretended I was no longer there. I decided that I didn't like him either and glared at him. He deliberately ignored me by holding up his magazine to cover his face avoiding any eye contact.

I did not feel hungry, but realized after all the days of not eating I had better try to get some nourishment. I took a mug of hot coffee, picked up a square of cornbread from a large pan, went to a table where I stood supporting myself with my elbows. There was absolutely no odor or taste to the hot liquid. I took a mouthful and held it for a moment before swallowing it. I tried again and again before finding a bitter taste. I took another swallow and more taste returned. I tried the cornbread and after chewing it for a while detected a small taste there too. At first I only nibbled at it but in a short time I found it was so delicious that I began shoving it into my mouth with both hands. I went back for more coffee and two more pieces of cornbread and stopped just short of gorging myself.

Finding the bunk I had slept on before, I removed my shoes and lay down. I fell asleep quickly and stayed that way for a couple of hours. When I awakened it took a few moments to understand where I was. My feet were still feeling pain, and I managed to raise my head high enough from the bunk in order to see them. I was shocked to find that the ulcers had turned a sickening looking yellow color. The thought of gangrene came first to mind and I pictured myself with no feet. But, while lying there feeling sorry for myself, the thought came to mind that the color gangrene isn't just a yellow color like I just saw. So after examining them again I decided that someone had come by and after observing their condition had doctored the ulcers with a medication, probably a sulfa ointment which was mustard color.

Later on I went back up on deck again and on the afterdeck I found a hatch cover that wasn't being used so I lay down on my back and looked up at the sky. There was a high cloud cover up there blocking off a lot of the sun's rays, but the warmth felt good on my face and body, and I soon fell asleep. Later, something caused me to awake. Sensing that I was no longer alone on the hatch cover, I propped myself up on my elbows and looked to my left. There, beside me were five white canvas wrapped bodies laid out all in a row and ready for burial at sea. In another moment I was watching as ship's carpenters busied themselves constructing a scaffold that would form a platform which, when placed against the rail the bodies would be dumped from and into the sea.

The ship's chaplain and Captain appeared on deck and the burial at sea ceremony commenced. The five corpses were laid on the platform constructed of plywood, their feet pointed toward the ship's rail. Each body was covered with an American flag. The chaplain somberly said all those things necessary to conduct the ceremony and his last words were, "And now we commit their bodies to the sea." The ship's Captain looked up toward the bridge and raised his hand in signal. I could feel the thumping vibration of the ship's engine cease as the huge propeller stopped turning. The ship continued to glide through the water from its momentum.

The inboard ends of the sheets of plywood were raised by members of the crew upon command and the five bodies slid out from under the American flags and over the rail and down toward the water. I could not see them enter the sea, but I could hear the splash as the heavy weights sewn into the canvas bags at the corpse's feet drew them down deep into the water, twisting and turning on toward the ocean bottom.

The Captain raised his arm in signal again for the men on the bridge to see. Through the steel deck under my feet I felt the 'thump, thump, thump' as the propeller's blades turned again to grasp the water and push the ship away from the spot where our five comrades were to stay forever at the bottom of the Pacific Ocean. I went immediately to the taffrail and stared down at our ship's wake. I tried very hard to see the bodies as they disappeared from view twisting and turning under the white foam.

Very quickly the crew, most of who appeared to have a trace of tears in their eyes, gathered up the five flags, dismantled the temporary scaffolding then carried it away. The ship's crew disappeared from that part of the deck and suddenly, I felt very tired and very much alone. I lay back on the hatch cover and quickly fell asleep.

Chapter Forty
Guam Army Field Hospital

T HE DESTINATION OF the ship was the island of Guam in the Mariana Island group. The United States had developed Navy, Air force, and Army bases there in 1944 for use in attacking Japan by air and sea. The rest of the four day trip to Guam was uneventful, except for the several times more that the propellers were stopped momentarily about midmorning. One of the Marines sitting on a forward hatch cover once took notice of it and remarked, "Wonder why they stop the engines like that?" He got no reaction from me, or anyone else. I didn't want to discuss it at all. The sea remained calm during the voyage while overhead the azure sky was clear of clouds and the rays from the sun warmed the deck.

I noticed that whenever I came on deck members of the ship's crew found reasons for not being near me, or it seemed to me it was that way. That didn't bother me though, as they ignored the other Marines lounging on deck too. I supposed that the ship's Captain had ordered the crew not to fraternize with the troops after my attempt to throw one of his sailors overboard.

To spend the daylight hours we, who were referred to as the 'walking wounded,' usually sat on the deck or a hatch cover. There was very little conversation about the battle that we had just left. I suppose it was avoided purposely. We sat there, staring off over the surface of the sea or looking down at our shoes. But, there was something going on here that drew men together as comrades. I suppose it was the common denominator of men who had fought together in close combat and survived.

Once the ship anchored off the beach at Guam, an LST came alongside and removed the lesser wounded men. We were transported to the U.S. Army's 204th Field Hospital in the Yigo area at the northern end of the island. The hospital was one of those large tent affairs that resembled an octopus when viewed from the air. There were examination, surgical, and administrative rooms in the center, and the wards extended out in different directions. The side walls of the wards were rolled up to allow air to circulate among the rows of canvas Army cots. The flooring was made of portable 4' x 8' sheets of plywood, laid flat on reddish-brown earth. Probably the most noticeable thing about the place was the odor of decaying vegetation emanating from the jungle.

I was examined by a young medical corps Army Captain. He repeatedly examined my eyes, ears, lungs and annoyed me by snapping his fingers in front of my eyes. He had me do coordination tests where I touched my fingers together while my eyes were closed, or he had me stand on one foot while trying to maintain my balance. He said that he couldn't do anything about my neck and pains from the back of my skull, and that I should turn in to the next naval hospital I came to.

He was a pleasant, considerate and sensitive man. He said that he thought I suffered from physical exhaustion and no doubt lung damage caused by concussion from the explosions that I had endured. There was also the possibility of brain damage caused by the blow to my head during the first night's brawl with the Japanese on Iwo Jima.

For treatment he ordered bed rest. I was to spend my time in a half sitting-up position, and could only leave the bed for meals or go to lavatory. One of the Army nurses assigned to that ward came by four times a day and put several tablets into my mouth and told me to swallow them. I don't know what the medication was, but it did help to lessen the pain in my head and neck. Each day at various times the doctor called me into his office to question and examine me.

The nurses insisted I go to the mess hall and eat at meal times. I didn't feel like I wanted to eat at all, but I was impressed by the quality of food that was served. For breakfast we had fried eggs and bacon, orange juice, and toast and butter. At night we were given things like steak, pork, or lamb chops, with mashed potatoes and gravy. That was always followed by a serving of ice cream. Apparently the cooks had never heard of Spam as I didn't see it at any time. Apparently the Marines had bought up all the Spam on the market so that we had to eat it every day.

The Army nurses were very pleasant to us, I thought. They insisted that we write home to tell our families what had happened to us. We were given pencils and paper to do that. I wrote two letters home, only to have the nurse in charge tear up both. She insisted that she would write one for me instead. Apparently she decided that I could not write a complete thought about my experiences let alone complete an entire letter. I realized that there must be something wrong with me, but I couldn't figure it out.

One day at noon, after I had been at the hospital for about four days, I watched a mess steward push an insulated food cart down the aisle between rows of bunks in the ward. He brought the food for those men who were not able to walk to the mess hall by themselves.

When the attendant reached the end of the row of bunks, he stopped and began to serve one of the patients. I became aware that the attendant was involved in some sort of altercation in which there was shoving and yelling. One of the men involved, dressed in old U. S. Army fatigue clothing, broke away, ran in my direction, passing by the foot of my bunk. As he passed by he was confronted by the supervising nurse who had been attracted by the sounds of the disturbance.

"All right, what is going on here?" She demanded to know. The figure dressed in Army fatigues raised a dinner knife he held in his right hand and brought it down forcibly at the nurse's chest. She uttered a small scream and fell to the ground clutching her breast with both hands. Her assailant ran to the end of the ward and ducked under the raised tent flaps. He disappeared into the dense jungle in back of the tent. Meanwhile, the mess attendant who was still standing where the disturbance had begun yelled out, "It's a Jap! He's a Jap!"

Apparently the nurse's assailant was a hungry Japanese soldier who had been hiding in the jungle since we seized the island back from the Japanese in July of 1944. When he saw the food being served, he could not control himself any longer. He rushed out to grab a tray of food. He was first challenged by the mess steward and then while trying to escape from him, was confronted by the unsuspecting nurse whom he stabbed.

Medics came and attended the injured nurse, then carried her away. There was a lot blood left behind on the wood flooring at the foot of my cot. I was told later by one of the attendants that she died but I don't know that for sure.

I felt outraged over the incident, and the fact that I was sedated and under the influence of painkillers didn't deter me from going into the doctor's office later and telling him what I thought of the security around the hospital. I recall later telling him that the Marine Corps would never have allowed this to happen, and that the Army should be ashamed of itself!

He seemed to think my statements were amusing and he tried to kid me out of the angry mood I was in. I didn't go along with that and told him I wanted to leave the hospital and go find a Marine Corps unit somewhere to join up with. He said that I wasn't ready to leave just yet and that he wouldn't let me go. He ordered me to stay. I told him that I would just walk away from the hospital then. He seemed like a good guy really, and said, "Well, if you do, you had better take some of this medication because you will need it. But, I'm still ordering you not to leave!"

I went back to my bunk and sat down to think about it all. In a short time the Doctor summoned me back to his office saying, "I don't want you to leave, but if you do I want to give you some medication to take. With that he filled up a bottle with several kinds of medication and told me that I needed to take so many at a time several times a day. He added that he didn't think I'd get very far if I did leave and that I had better turn in at the next naval medical facility I came across!

Later, when I saw him leave the ward I got up from my bunk, picked up my helmet, towel, soap, and razors and walked out to the dirt road that seemed to appear out of the jungle on one side of the hospital compound and disappear into the jungle on the other side. I felt sick, tired, and discouraged and it didn't help to have a long shallow cut running down my face from my right temple to my chin.

The day before the ward nurse, seeing me unshaven, told me to go to a certain tent occupied by a member of the Red Cross and get a razor with which to shave. I still carried the razor that I had taken from the Marine, Peter's pack on Iwo Jima, but had discarded the dull blade as useless some time before. A blonde fleshy looking Red Cross woman at the tent seemed more interested in trimming and caring for her fingernails than dealing with me. Continuing to work with her nails and without looking up at me she said, "Well, what do you want?"

I told her that nurse had sent me for a razor, soap and a hand towel. She handed me towel, a bar of soap and an adjustable razor that was made from plastic. When I told her that I had never seen one like it before, she just uttered "Huh!" and turned her back on me.

Back at the washroom I lathered my face with hand soap and drew the razor down the side of my face and then watched in amazement as crimson blood gushed out through the white foamy soap covering the side of my face. The plastic razor had become warped from the heat of the tropics and allowed the sharp new blade to act as the point of a knife blade as it sliced open the skin on my face. I could not feel any pain and I suppose that was due to all of the pain killers that I had in me. The Army Doctor who attended to my injuries attended me again and with a shake of his head he said, "Kid, you're a mess!"

I answered him by saying, "A Navy doctor already told me that!"

I stood on the dirty, dusty road at the front of the hospital waiting for someone to stop and give me a ride to somewhere else. The Army sentry in front of the tent administration office kept looking at me with suspicious glances and I knew he would come eventually and ask me questions. I kept glaring at him until he turned away. "No guts," I thought. "No wonder Jap stragglers can run free through the hospital without fear of being caught."

I stood in the tropic heat sweating and chased flies away that persisted in swarming around my head and shoulders. They were attracted by the blood on my face. Then suddenly, a noisy, growling dark green truck appeared from out of the jungle, bouncing along on the rutted, dusty road. I immediately felt better when I saw the orange letters, 'U.S.M.C.' painted on the dark green paint of the truck's dusty front bumper. I raised my hand, and the truck stopped. I waited for the heavy dust that rolled over the truck and swirled to engulf me to calm down. I was greeted by the driver, a sergeant who held an M-1 rifle across his lap with the muzzle pointing out his window.

"Hey Doggie, 'whatta ya' doing out in the middle of the road?" He yelled out at me and rightfully so too, because he saw the U.S. Army dungarees I was wearing.

"I'm not a 'doggie' Mac. I'm a Navy corpsman from the 5th Division just off Iwo Jima and I'm trying to find a Marine transient Center to report to."

His eyes grew larger and a huge grin filled his face as he shouted to be heard above the noise of his engine. "Climb in; I'll take you to one. That's where I'm going now to deliver some chow!" He seemed overjoyed at being able to help me. For a mile or two until we arrived at the camp he plied me with questions about the Iwo Jima invasion and said he wished he had made it to that fight.

The camp was several miles farther up the side of the island and it was designated as a Marine transient center, a place where Marine personnel, while in transit from one station to another or en route to rejoin their own units, would stay temporarily until travel arrangements were made for them to continue on.

A staff sergeant was in charge. His attitude and behavior showed signs of boredom and he came slowly from his tent to check the supplies being delivered by the trucker. After the truck had left I approached him and explained that I had walked away from an Army hospital a few miles away and could he accept me there?

He groaned and grimaced as though I was causing him a lot of pain. "Hell, I don't know," he whined. "You are supposed to have papers. I 'gotta' keep records you know!"

"Sure, but I have to go some place. Do you refuse to allow me to stay here?"

He grimaced again as if he felt more pain, but he said, "No..., but I will have to go to the hospital and try to square things away you know? Go find an empty bunk in one of the tents, I'll see you later." If he ever did get to the Army hospital to square things with them I don't know it as I never saw that sergeant again or heard from the hospital either!

This transient center was a horrible mess! The small camp had been constructed after a bulldozer cleared the jungle growth from the ground to make a clearing. All the rubble had been pushed to the perimeter areas and left there piled up. There were about twenty, six man tents in the clearing. One large tent served as a mess shelter. One smaller tent was used by the sergeant in charge of the camp as his office and sleeping quarters. Another was used as some sort of sick bay as there was a table with a box on it standing inside. The box was adorned with a red cross but, there was no corpsman stationed there.

I walked on fine red dirt that turned to dust by my movement and swirled up my legs and over my body. I noticed three Marines who were sitting on their bunks, peering out from under one of the rolled up tent walls, were watching me closely. One yelled, "Hey 'Doggie,' what the hell you doing here, you lost?"

All three of them thought that was a funny remark and guffawed.

"No, I'm not lost and I am not a Doggie either, dammit. I'm a corpsman from the 26th Marines and I just got off Iwo and I want to find a way back to my outfit!" That sure lit a fire under those three as they leaped from their cots and crowded out the doorway.

"Come in..., come in here with us. We got room!" They all agreed. Those three 4th Division Marines made me so welcome I darn near had tears in my eyes. I had found some of my own at last.

There was not much fresh water available at the camp and what water was there was brought to us each day in a large water tank on the back of a truck. The truck was parked out in the sun and that heated the chlorine treated brown water to point where I wondered if it was safe to use at all. Lister bags were kept filled with the water and each morning we were issued one canteen of water for drinking purposes. Each morning and at recall at the end of the day, a helmet full of water was issued from the water truck to wash and shave with.

For bathing we were told by the sergeant that we could depend on rainfall that fell each day about 1500 hours. That was right. It rained every day that I was there and right at that time. All the men would quickly discard their clothing as the first rain cloud drifted over and grasping their bars of soap, would hurriedly lather their bodies and then rinse off as the rain poured from the sky. The rain would stop falling just as suddenly as it began and sometimes we would get caught with our bodies all covered with soap which would dry almost immediately in the hot sun's rays that followed the disappearance of the rain cloud.

Bathing was a necessity there in that camp. The dust and dirt covered the outside and the inside of the sagging tents. The smallest breeze would send clouds of the reddish brown dirt rolling along the ground and it seemed to envelop everything in its path. Field kitchen food was brought in to feed the men in the morning and evening and for lunch we got a peanut butter and jelly sandwiches or sometimes a K ration. For a beverage, lemonade was made from a powdered extract and that was mixed with the chlorine flavored water. The coffee was Luke warm and made from the same water.

It was hot and humid every day until 1500 hours when the rain fell and cooled the area. The rainwater would turn the ground into a morass of mud that was about ankle deep and it stayed that way until about thirty minutes after the sun came out. Then the mud would turn back to the light dust that swirled around our legs as we walked.

The only work assignment we had there was to go out into the jungle and look for Japanese stragglers who roamed the brush looking for food. The Americans had taken the island back from the Japanese several months before and some of the Japanese soldiers feared for their lives and would not surrender to our military. They seemed to be in a pretty confused state and were considered a nuisance more than a danger by the local military authorities, except when one would do something like attacking that Army nurse back at the hospital.

The Army authorities constantly sent out word into the jungle using captured Japanese soldiers as messengers. The stragglers were told that they wouldn't be harmed if they surrendered, but would be treated and fed well. The men who served on the same hunting details as I were most recently from the Iwo Jima battle, and they didn't seem to concur with the Army's idea of how to treat a Jap after catching up with him in the jungle. I wholeheartedly agreed with my Marine comrades.

The two searching patrols that I went on did not locate any live Japanese in the jungle although we came upon many remains of their dead bodies, not only theirs, but others as well. One day we came across the site of a battlefield and found many human bones lying about on the ground. Some of the many wild pigs which roamed the island had been there and had dug around the remains. The sergeant leading the detail said that the bones probably belonged to Japanese soldiers who had been killed there and buried. I picked up some fabric that I pulled loose from the ground in the vicinity of the bones and without speaking I showed the sergeant the bit of dungaree cloth and the U.S. Army button still attached to it. I held the button up against one that was on my blouse for him to compare with. The sergeant turned a bit pale and quickly led us out of there.

Once we crawled into a hole in the jungle growth and found an undamaged Japanese light tank sitting there under the canopy of vines with its turret lid open. A tanker's leather helmet was lying right side up on the ground near the machine. One of the Marines used the toe of one of his boots to turn the helmet over. A dried up Japanese soldiers head was still inside of it and there were thousands of little red ants feeding on the dried flesh still clinging to the skull. I felt sick to my stomach!

Against the warning of some of us, one of the Marines suddenly climbed up on the tank and peered down into the open cockpit. Then, he quickly threw himself off backward from the machine and bent over the ground before vomiting. The tank still contained the decaying corpses of the three tank crew members and after being in that hot humid place for these past months the putrefying bodies were still emitting a horrible stench.

On another day we sat in the shade of some tall coconut palms trying to avoid the midday heat. Suddenly we heard the roar of engines, and the noise was increasing as each second passed. Someone yelled out that maybe the Japs had brought out a couple of their hidden tanks and were intent on attacking us. Then the vibrations from the sound became so large that coconuts began to be shaken from the palms and they fell to the ground around us causing us to run into the open for fear that we might be struck on the head by them.

Over the tree tops came dozens of huge airplanes rising from a lower place on the island. These were the great B-29 bombers that we had heard about, but not many of us had seen. The noise and size of the aircraft was unbelievable to us as we watched the fifty or sixty aircraft rise above us and go in the direction of the Japanese mainland which was about a thousand miles away to the north.

I shared the tent with a Marine named Frank. The next day at dawn we hitch-hiked to the air base where the huge aircraft had taken off from. We spoke to an Air Force Captain who said that he piloted one of the B-29's and the Marine asked him if we could go for a ride when he next went on a bombing mission. The officer said, "Well, OK, but don't tell anyone that I gave you permission to ride along."

The next morning Frank was up at four o'clock and tried to prod me out of my bunk. I told him that I was backing out of the trip; so he went off alone. I didn't think that he'd make the flight as it was a long way to walk to the airfield and besides, how was he going to get past the sentries and all of that sort of thing? The Marine didn't return until late that night and then he was all excited about being on a bombing run over Tokyo, Japan.

It was interesting to listen to his account of the long flight. He said that he was going again the next morning and tried to get another one of us to accompany him. We all refused. When I awakened the next morning, he was already gone. That night he didn't return to our tent, or the next day either. We never saw him again. When someone in our tent left the camp for good, a few days later, his personal belongings still lay where he had left them.

I believe his last name was Frank, and he was from Oakland, California. He was a member of the 4th Marine Division. Perhaps the plane he was on made an emergency landing on another island or in the ocean after being damaged by the Japanese, or perhaps it had been shot down over the Japanese islands. Regardless, I have often wondered how the Marine Corps explained his disappearance to his family if he never returned.

The medication that the Army doctor had given me ran out after four days, but even so I felt pretty good except for the pain that persisted in the back of my head and neck. I still had some soreness in my lungs. I was determined not to give in and return to the hospital. I was wrong though as I soon realized the doctor was right and that I should have never left the hospital as I did.

A special services sergeant came into camp one evening from somewhere and set up a movie projector and screen under a palm tree. He announced that he was told to show us a recreational movie film. I sat with PFC Paul Pugh, one of my Marine buddies I had treated for injuries on Iwo Jima and another Marine from the Forth Division. I commented to Pugh that the sergeant should start the picture now as it was plenty dark enough. He replied, "Why Doc, it's not dark enough at all!" Even so, I couldn't see the back of my hand when I held it in front of my face. Dismayed, I realized that I was completely blind!

My two comrades led me to the sagging tent that supposedly served as an aid station. No doctor or corpsman was located at the camp or even the sergeant who was supposed to be in charge. There wasn't even a jeep or truck available at the camp to transport me to the Army hospital down the road except the one used by the movie projectionist sergeant who objected to us using that. My two comrades took me to my tent and I lay down on my cot wondering what was to become of me. After about thirty to forty minutes my head began to hurt something terrible and it got to the point where I thought I'd never be able to stand the pain. Then my vision began to return slightly and I could see a dim light. I began to get nausea and vomit again and again. There were orange and red colors rolling along in my vision and the pain continued to be excruciating. Finally my vision returned after an hour passed and I felt completely exhausted. This condition was to occur on a daily basis for years after this first episode and even after ten years had passed it was happen periodically.

CHAPTER FORTY-ONE

Escaping Guam

ONE DAY SOME friends and I went into the jungle to search for bananas. We found some after about an hour and returned to camp. When I approached my tent, I was yelled at by my 4th Marine Division friends who were already on board a truck preparing to leave. "C'mon Doc, where the hell you been, we're leaving!"

Not hesitating a moment I ran to the tent, got my helmet, bag of toilet articles, and blanket then climbed aboard the truck as it began to move. We were transported to an isolated beach where we could see a troop ship off shore moving slowly parallel to the beach. A landing craft was leaving its side and coming to where we waited on the beach.

"OK, answer to your names," bawled the sergeant as he dismounted the truck. He called out the name of every man there except mine. I knew I had made a mistake and had to make a quick decision.

"Dammit," I thought. "I'm not staying on this dirty island any longer!" The sergeant called out for the detail to wade out to the waiting boat and climb aboard, I went too! We climbed into the landing craft by way of its downed ramp. The crew backed the boat off the shore, turned and made its way to the ship.

The APA was already underway when we scrambled aboard by way of the lowered gangway. When we reached the deck we were confronted by a Marine Corps staff sergeant who officiously announced himself as the NCO in charge of all Marine Corps troops aboard and that he would assign us to our bunks and issue a 'chit' for meals. I'd never heard of either one of these things being done before, but I knew it meant a problem for me. I had to stand there and listen as he called out the name of every man in the detail except mine.

I had a problem. Without a meal chit I wouldn't be allowed to enter the galley to obtain food. Thinking that was one hell of a way to treat a combat veteran, I spoke to the sergeant and told him that my name had not been mentioned in the orders he held in his hand. He glanced at the list of names, and when he found that I was right, he became very upset and his face became flushed with anger. "Don't tell me you're on board, do you understand? I don't want to know about it or I'll get in trouble!"

I asked him how I was to eat and where would I sleep, but he was already hurrying away and didn't answer me. I walked off in another direction mumbling something about "thick headed jarhead." On deck I spoke to various Marines and found that they were all mostly from the 4th Marine Division and as far as they knew were going to rejoin their division back on the island of Maui in the Hawaiian Islands. I was disappointed as I thought the ship might be headed back to Iwo Jima and where I might rejoin the 26th Marines.

Since I was a member of the 5th Marine Division and that organization was established on the big island of Hawaii, I figured that I was headed in the right direction anyway. I tried to put out of my mind what would happen when I was discovered missing from that transient camp on Guam.

I was on board that ship for over two weeks and didn't have a bunk to sleep on during the entire trip as I could find none empty. The first day I made my way forward to the bow and found a small alcove which was under the forecastle gun tub which would offer me some shelter from any rain. On the backside of the alcove was a high metal tool locker about ten feet wide and that would protect me from the view of personnel on the bridge. Also, there was a large metal life jacket waterproof box that was fastened to the deck and held a number of life preservers, both the belt type and the kapok jackets. Selecting a belt type I put it around my waist as I knew I'd draw the attention of a master at arms if he saw me without one.

I had missed lunch, and by dusk I was getting pretty hungry. I sat by the hatch leading to the mess down below and watched guards marking each man's meal chit as he filed by. I suppose they were assigned to do that to prevent men from going through the mess line twice. I thought that seemed pretty childish thinking on the part of some officer. After all, these men had just survived a pretty horrible battle and now they were being treated like adolescents.

The troops entered one hatchway to descend to the galley and left there by ascending another ladder back to the main deck where they exited from another hatchway. I simply entered the exit hatchway and went below where I got in line with the other men and was served food the same as everyone else. As I exited from the galley after each meal, I glanced at the guards checking the men's passes and wondered at the logic of it all.

The first seven days on board the ship were exciting. A hurricane hit us on the second night out and seemed to travel eastward with us. I had never experienced such 'devil' weather. The ship rocked and rolled in the sea troughs and through the mountains of water that rushed at us. One moment the ship would be perched on the edge of a deep canyon in the sea, its propellers free of the water and spinning wildly, and the next instant it would be sliding down the canyon's side as would a skier on a ski slope. Then with a crash, the ship's momentum would stop as the craft hit the bottom of the valley, and all those men who dared attempt standing on their feet would be brought down, crashing to the deck.

No sooner than the ship hit the bottom of the trough than a huge mountain sized mass of water would again come rushing at us. When we were almost certain it would fall upon the ship and drive it down into the depths of the sea, the little vessel would be picked up as though in the hands of a giant and lifted to the next crest of water.

Up there it would look to those of us still on deck that we were perched on a high mountain peak with a visibility of a hundred miles, and, as we turned this way and that in order to see the most we could, the ship would fall off into the next trough and leave us gasping for breath. Over and over again we would slide down the water and rise again as no giant roller coaster could ever simulate.

The storm became so furious that all personnel were ordered off the deck and all hatches were secured. I concealed myself from sight of the bridge by huddling under the gun tub and grasped the life preserver box expecting to ride out the storm there. The wind from the north, or the port side of the ship, was so fierce that the ship began to heel over on its right side and stay there. I grabbed a stanchion, or steel post that served as one of the four "I" beam legs holding up the gun tub, sat on the deck with it between my thighs, wrapped my arms around it and held on.

The starboard deck railing was under water most of the time. I heard a loud metallic screeching noise once, opened my eyes and watched as a huge piece of machinery that had torn loose from the deck, sliding forward and across the deck and carrying away everything in its path. Fortunately, it veered away from me, smashed through the ship's starboard life rail, and disappeared overboard.

Another time while the ship had rocked back to an almost upright position I glanced to the left and saw a huge wave coming at us and as I prepared for impact, the entire top of the wave was lifted from the surface by the wind and carried our way until it smashed into the ship's forward area where I was huddled. I was certain I was going to die right then, but the gun tub saved me from the direct impact of the water. I was held under water, pinned against the steel pole I grasped between my legs. That pole saved my life as I would have been swept overboard. By then the fear had left me. I was convinced that I would die soon and I might as well enjoy this experience until it happened.

The ship's bow also took the brunt of the high wave's force as it would burrow into the waves and the water would come washing high over me but, each time I managed to hold on. I was not very concerned of being smothered by the water because back at camp a group of us would spend time practicing holding our breath. I was proud to say that I had reached the goal of three minutes time and time again.

The fear I felt was that the ship might turn upside down, trapping me under the deck. And I could imagine what would happen down below. Those sailors and Marines would be caught like rats in a box. There was no way out for them.

Once again, when the ship rolled to an upright position I saw a mountain of water bearing down on our starboard side. I thought, well this it, I'll probably have to let go the post and be washed overboard! I was fascinated by the huge wave as it raced at us. I felt the ship drop into a chasm just before the mountain of water struck. I watched in dismay as the water smashed into the top of the superstructure near the edge of the bridge. I heard the shrieking of metal as something was torn away from the ship. But, the water did something else. The large wave had collected a small wall of water in front of it as it traveled and this small collection hit the side of the ship first, straightening it up just before the larger one struck. It dashed with such force against the side of the superstructure, that it actually helped the ship right itself. I figured that if the main point of wave impact had struck a little higher, at top of the superstructure, it would cause the ship to capsize. I became very concerned as I had almost let go of my hold on the post. If I had done so, I would have ended up swimming out there alone in mid-ocean.

The storm began to diminish after midnight on the second day. I went below to find the sickbay, as I needed to repair some damage done to my arms, hands and legs done by the metal pole I had held onto. I couldn't get near the aid station as there were probably well over a hundred men waiting down there in line for assistance also so I abandoned that idea.

Back on deck I stood in the chow line. The guards were no longer there; some one had come to their senses I thought. I stood in back of two Marines who were telling of the horror of being locked in below decks during the storm and how they were tossed from one bulkhead to the other while 'getting the hell beat out of them.' I listened for a while until one made the remark, that he was glad they were not caught on deck during all that action.

Unwisely I spoke, "I was. I stayed on the deck for the entire storm."

They both looked at me sourly and one said, "Don't be stupid. You werc not!"

The sea continued to calm and by the time we neared the Marshall Islands it had become very placid, with a blue-sky overhead. The scuttlebutt went around the deck that we had passed through the edge of a hurricane that had been responsible for the sinking of several small Navy ships north of our position.

I was very depressed on most of this voyage. I missed my comrades of the 2nd Platoon and longed to be back with them. I still had not accepted the fact that the platoon had been decimated during the battle on Iwo Jima and that I would only see eight of the original forty-three men ever again. There were times when I was under the impression that the platoon had gone off and left me behind. I mentioned that once to Paul Pugh while on Guam after the battle. He looked at me in surprise and said, "Doc, what are you saying? You know that the rest of the guys are all dead or wounded!"

During the night I slept under my one blanket that had been issued to me while at the transient center and which was usually wet from spray splashing over the bow on the deck up forward. I passed the hours of the day, when not eating, by sleeping on the deck and staying out of the way of the crew. It's a wonder how a military man can exist in the service and stay out of the way of higher authority. I became a master of it by experience and necessity. The small convoy reached the Island of Kwajalein, which is located in the Marshall Island group late one afternoon. The island was similar to that of Eniwetok which we had stopped at on the way to Iwo Jima. Again, our ship entered the small channel of the lagoon at fast speed, slowed, then headed for a designated anchorage on the far side.

It was announced over the loudspeaker that once we were anchored along side of a tanker and refueling was under way, a movie would be shown on deck. It would be the first movie that most of us troops had seen in four months and we looked forward to it even though we knew it would be an old tired one. Before darkness fell many of the Marines on deck began finding a place to sit and watch the film while the ship was still under way. Some of them climbed onto deck booms, hatch covers, and other deck equipment for a view advantage. I climbed up onto a metal encased deck winch and settled down to wait.

My attention was drawn to a smaller ship approaching from off our port or left side that might have intentions of crossing our path. It seemed to me that it was on a collision course with our ship and that we would collide if neither vessel changed course. The smaller ship continued on and so did our ship remain on course. Then from the bridge of our APA a horn sounded in warning, but to my surprise the smaller ship ignored or didn't hear the warning and it continued to try and cross in front of our bow.

The small ship, one that I thought was about 100 feet long was struck on its starboard side just at the wheelhouse. Leaning over our ship's port rail I watched as it pushed the smaller vessel down farther into the water. Then the smaller craft turned over on its left side and its stern rose from the water. The smaller ship continued to roll over until it was upside down. Our ship continued on, scraping its way over the forward half of the small craft's hull and keel.

At the moment of impact I could see several of the small ship's crew members run to the stern and dive into the water where they swam frantically to get away from the stricken craft. I don't think that any crew members caught below in that vessel had an opportunity to escape the sudden disaster and went down with it.

When our larger ship struck the smaller one there was a slight hesitation and then a horrible metal scraping of metal sound. Then, as the ship freed its self from the smaller one, it surged ahead and continued on. Over the public address system the command came to release the ship's port side number three life raft.

Several Marines and I ran toward our stern, all with the same intention of jumping overboard and attempting to rescue the sailors in the water. But, a chief petty officer arrived there before us and by holding up his hands signaled us to halt, "Stop… it's of no use, our propellers are still turning," he exclaimed!

Looking back at the smaller ship I could see the lagoon waters breaking over its exposed keel and that it was on the verge of sinking. Darkness was coming on fast and I could barely see through the gloom the small figures splashing in the water along side the stricken little craft. I felt so helpless, as probably the others did who watched.

Our ship did not stop or reduce speed until we reached our destination, the tanker that awaited us about a half mile away. Of course there was much excitement on the deck of our ship as the troops asked questions about why our ship had not stopped so that some of us could have gone into the water to save the sailors. The crew members did not have an answer to that and appeared as dumbfounded as well. The bewilderment continued until another incident happened about twenty minutes after the first.

We approached the tanker. It was low in the water indicating that it was full of oil as it waited for us to come alongside. Our ship's engines were reduced appreciably as it glided in toward the other ship, at about a thirty-degree angle. According to proper procedure, our ship would soon reverse its engines so that the stern of the vessel would be brought alongside of the anchored ship in one smooth movement. I had seen it done dozens of times and appreciated the skill used. Once the two ships were secured to each other the refueling operation would commence.

This time, it became obvious that the movement wasn't carried out properly. Our ship continued its angle approach much too long and eventually rammed into the starboard side of the tanker's well deck at amidships. Most of us saw the imminent collision coming and grabbed for something to hang onto. On board the tanker, we could see the deck crew frantically 'shutting down' large valves to close off the oil lines and then running to the opposite side of the ship where they dove into the water and began swimming away.

As the bow of our ship struck the side of the tanker, there was an abrupt cessation of speed, our bow went upward as it climbed up onto the tanker's well deck, hesitated there a moment and then began to slide back down. As it slid back, it slashed a wide gash in the tanker's hull at the water level. The black oil gushed out in a heavy stream to mix with the beautiful lagoon waters.

Most all of the troops were thrown from their perches in the rigging and deck apparatus. I hung onto the winch box cover with both hands. Little good that did, I was hurled forward as my grasp was torn loose. I hit the deck and slid across its rough surface tearing holes in my skin and clothing. That was enough for me; I got up quickly from where I lay on the deck and ran all the way to the stern where I stood on the taffrail, preparing to jump over the side at the first indication of fire. I listened to the public address system on board the tanker come to life. An angry sounding voice came blaring over it. "What dumb son-of-a-bitch is in charge of running that ship? Whoever it is, he won't be for very long."

Eventually things did quiet down and the refueling process began and completed. We even got to watch a terrible "B" rated, western movie starring the old western movie star, Hoot Gibson, which we had already seen several times.

Seven more days were required to reach the island of Maui. The troops were happy to have the trip end. During the two weeks on board this ship we had survived a terrible hurricane force storm and two shipwrecks. We were informed that President Franklin D. Roosevelt died. But an interesting and pleasant thing happened too. We crossed the International Date Line on Easter Sunday and so we got to celebrate two Easter Sundays, one on either side of the line. The ships Captain ordered that we should have turkey dinner on both days.

I did not leave the ship at Maui. As the Fourth Division Marines left the ship, I decided not to report to the authorities ashore that I was a straggler. The ship's crew was informed that the ship was going on to Pearl Harbor. I decided to go there thinking I'd have a better chance there to get back to the 'Big Island' of Hawaii and Camp Tarawa.

When we docked at Pearl Harbor no one questioned me as I left the ship. I thought that was odd as I was wearing an Army uniform. I was feeling pretty ill by then, as I had constant head and neck pains that were accompanied by nausea that would come and go. I found my way to a Marine transient center by tagging along with some Marines who had been sent out on a work detail from there. I wandered about inside the compound until I found an unoccupied bunk in a hut and settled down on it.

That night I became very ill and a nearby Marine guided me to the medical dispensary for help. There was a corpsman on duty and I told him that I lost my vision, was very ill and needed help. He wanted to call an ambulance and send me to a hospital. I told him no I wanted to see the medical officer who was on duty. He told me that the duty doctor had left instructions that he was not to be called out at night unless it was for a great emergency. The doctor had then added that if the emergency was of a serious nature to send the patient to the naval hospital instead of calling him. The Marine assisting me lead me back to my bunk where I suffered horribly all night long.

In the morning I was still ill, but was determined to return quickly to the 'Big Island' in some manner. After having a cup of coffee at the mess, I happened to pass by a few Marines who were standing by a truck and overheard one of them say something about going to Hawaii. I stopped and asked how he intended getting there. He said that they were all waiting for a ship that will carry them to the island. I ran to my bunk and got my helmet and cloth bag containing toilet articles and returned to the truck just as a sergeant ordered the men to climb on board. Once the sergeant climbed into the cab of the truck with the driver, I climbed into the back with the Marines.

To my surprise the truck took us out of the Pearl Harbor Navy Base and into the city of Honolulu where it stopped at the yacht harbor. The sergeant told us to get out and form a single line, then follow him out onto a wharf where a small inter-island steamer was tied. The sergeant didn't notice that there was extra man in his group. We followed behind him as he led us up the gangway where he stopped in front of the officer of the deck who stood there and handed him the list of men in his detail.

I thought to myself that this was where my luck was going to run out and I'd have to surrender myself to the authorities. Each man in front of me gave his name to the officer who checked it on his list and the man would step past him onto the deck of the ship. He had just checked off the name of the Marine in front of me and had motioned him to step onto the deck when a sailor came up alongside of the officer and said, "Sir!" The officer turned toward the crewman who had addressed him and I took advantage of the situation by stepping past him onto the deck. He seemed not to notice my movement and instead turned his attention to the man who waited in back of me.

That night after dark the little ship left the dock during a wild storm. The vessel rolled and bucked; it shook and staggered as it tried to free itself from the clutches of the raging sea. It wasn't safe to stay on deck so all personnel were ordered below where most of us became violently ill. We could not stay on a bunk as the lurching rolling ship kept throwing us out onto the deck. Most of us sat or lay on the deck for our own safety with our arms wrapped around stanchions, our hands grasping at any stationary part of the ship we could reach. Most of us vomited at one time or another and soon the deck became a slippery and slimy mess. By the light of the next dawn the ship was entering the little harbor at Hilo and the sea was very calm there. I went directly into the compartment shower room and with my clothes still on washed the filth off me.

I was very relieved when the ship was secured to the wharf at Hilo and the passengers were allowed to disembark. But, then another problem presented itself. The wharf area was heavily guarded and all who entered or left were examined for travel orders and since I had none I wondered how I was to leave there and travel the sixty miles up to where I hoped the 5th Marine Division was still based. I walked around for a while before noticing a Marine Corps truck loaded with supplies that was about to leave.

I spoke to the sergeant in charge of the detail and I learned from him that the supplies on his truck were assigned to Camp Tarawa and he was about to leave for there. After explaining my problem to him, I found him very willing to help. He said, "Naw, that's no problem! Take your shirt off and climb up on the truck and pretend you're one of my 'helpers' when we go out the gate."

I did as he suggested and sat down on a box on top of the load. At the gate the military police stopped the truck and questioned the driver. Then one climbed onto the truck bed to inspect the cargo. He gruffly told me to move from the box I sat on so he could make his inspection more complete, after which he climbed down and told the driver to continue on.

Two hours later we arrived at Camp Tarawa. It was just about four months after we left it to go to Iwo Jima. I was wearing a U. S. Army fatigue uniform, helmet, fairly new 'boondockers,' but no stockings or underwear. In my pockets I had a small Japanese body flag, a packet of Japanese bandages, two safety razors, a photograph of my sister Margie and another one of my father milking a cow.

I walked to the battalion dispensary and went inside where I was greeted by Pharmacist's Mate first class Lloyd Beckfield who had stayed behind to maintain the premises and records when we had left for battle. He said, "Where have you been? You have been reported as missing for the last two weeks!"

The 2nd battalion and the rest of the 26th Marine Regiment was ordered off Iwo Jima on March 15, 1945, about a week after I had left there. The battalion or what was left of it boarded ships and sailed to Hawaii. Even though Iwo Jima was officially secured on that date there were many Japanese soldiers left alive and in hiding. They refused to surrender and fanatically fought the U. S. Army and Air Force personnel left behind to garrison the island.

Chapter Forty-Two

The Atom Bombs Force Surrender

W HAT WAS LEFT of the 2nd Battalion arrived within a few days after I returned to Camp Tarawa. I was surprised and dismayed how few trucks stopped on the company street and very few men dismounted. There wasn't many men left of Company D. I didn't recognize many of them as they were replacements to those men wounded or killed.

Of the forty-three men of the second platoon who had landed on Iwo Jima, only two had gone the length of the battle and returned. They were PFC's Billy Eller and Marshall E. Bailey. The rest were listed as battle casualties.

The Marine Corps released the casualty list for the division. It revealed that the 2nd Battalion had landed on Iwo Jima with 37 officers and 917 enlisted men. Of these 26 Officers and 728 enlisted men were considered battle casualties. These figures were obtained for this writing from an official U.S. Marine Corps publication, The Spearhead, The World War Two History of the 5th Marine Division, by Howard M. Conner, Infantry Journal Press, Washington D.C. 1950. The publication also states that during the battle 14 officers, and 251 enlisted men were sent in as replacements to the battalion. Of those 10 of the officers and 141 enlisted men became battle casualties

After recovering from his injuries, Lt. Horvath rejoined the company as the Executive Officer. Captain Fields returned to take over the duties of company commander again and five fresh young 2nd Lieutenants arrived to replace the six who had been killed or wounded.

Top Sergeant Neef was given a promotion to warrant officer, a most prestigious rank in the Corps and one that was held in high esteem by officers and enlisted men alike. He was then assigned to the payroll unit of the regiment. I thought he certainly deserved the promotion and the recognition.

Sergeants Renner and Goodling rejoined the company. Both had suffered from concussion and exhaustion on Iwo Jima and had been evacuated.

On June 25, 1945, Major General Keller Rockey was relieved from duty and appointed to replace him was Major General Thomas E. Bourke, one of Rockey's assistants.

I continued to suffer from the effects of the beating I took on Iwo Jima. The pains in the back of my neck and lower part of my skull did not lessen. I complained to Dr. Popkess about it as I lost weight and often lost my eyesight and was still vomiting. He said he could do nothing for me, as the battalion aid station wasn't equipped for that kind of examination. He suggested that I might be sent to the naval hospital in Honolulu for further examination and medical tests and went off to discuss the matter further with the battalion surgeon. When he came back he said that the surgeon stated that he would not send me to the hospital as the division commander had become irate because of the number of men turning into sickbay for treatment and he wanted it stopped.

Well, that was what I was told anyway. This was the same battalion surgeon I had told earlier that he was 'drunk' and that he should pull up his pants and take his Red Cross girl friend out of the dispensary. Since that incident had occurred we had avoided each other. I couldn't forget his last remarks to me though. "I'll, I'll fix you!"

Other replacements joined us until the battalion reached full strength again and transfers were made to balance out the ratio between combat veterans and newcomers. Those of us who had recently seen combat were given five days leave in Honolulu after which we began training for the next battle. We were not told that we would invade the Japanese home islands, but that was a foregone conclusion.

We were given lectures on the Japanese way of life, taught to use phrases in Japanese which included the asking of directions and the giving of commands. We were told not to expect the Japanese to surrender easily, but to count on the Japanese civilians to fight alongside their military in the defense of their homeland.

Camp life at Tarawa was different than before the battle. I missed my friends, especially Edward Monjaras and Ivan Munns. Eddie and I had spent many days on liberty together. Now he was dead, after having several steel splinters from an exploding shell crush his chest. One of his surviving Marine comrades told me that Eddie rose from the comparative safety of a rifle pit and was running forward to help a fallen Marine when a 90 mm Jap mortar shell fell and exploded on the ground in front of him. He had been struck down within four hundred yards of me on the island and yet I wasn't to hear about his death until a month later.

Two others I would miss were the two young Hebrews of the 2nd Platoon who had been often referred to as the "Katzanjammer Kids," because of their continuous capers and amusing dialogue. PFC's Logel and Howard would often come up with some comment or act at just the right moment which would help make time pass by and be a little bit more enjoyable. While we took long hikes we would be given a break every hour during which we would often stretch out on the ground to rest. At the end of the ten-minute break period neared, Lt. Horvath would make some small move indicating that he was about to order us up on our feet. Logel would anticipate the officer's move, leap to his feet yelling out in his best Jewish accent, "C'mon Abie, take down the 'vallpaper,' we're moving." Laughing, we would rise from the ground. Eventually the Lieutenant came to expect the statement to be made each time and when he was ready to give the order to resume the hike, he would glance at Logel as if to give the signal. Then he'd turn his head, showing the slightest suggestion of a smile as the young Marine carried out his routine. Hower and Logel were very brave young men during the fight for Iwo Jima. I have missed them very much.

The Marines and corpsmen who had now returned to camp after the battle joined other Marines who had been in battle before, in other campaigns. We combat veterans had our own exclusive club. The requirement for membership was to have suffered the pain of losing comrades. I became a member of that club. It wasn't as I thought it would be. We never mentioned the battle or those comrades who had died or were seriously injured. We wanted only to be left alone and didn't want to join in the enthusiasm or the discussions of the newer and younger men coming fresh into the outfit. I didn't want even to speak to or make friends with the new men. I didn't want to read their letters from home or hear about their mothers, fathers, sisters, and brothers or even their dogs, let alone see the pictures of their family sent them from home.

I didn't care to get mail from home anymore either. The letters I got from my family were full of the same old family problems and subject matter that I could hardly consider of importance after having had my recent experiences. I took exception to remarks my mother made in her letters as she complained how much all were suffering at home because of such shortages as steak, sugar, and gasoline that were rationed. A lot she knew about deprivation and despair.

The battalion went back to rigorous training in June 1945. Since the unit had been so badly depleted of its well-trained men, and we had so many youngsters coming in from boot camp, we had to hurry to get them trained before we were ordered into battle. Every day, time was spent getting us into good physical shape. To accomplish this we took many long forced hikes out into the boondocks where we were often not given a ten-minute rest on the hour.

Our clothing and equipment underwent an extensive inspection and study and replacements were made. We were given vaccinations to guard against yellow fever and other diseases, some of which I had never heard of before, but were said to thrive in Asia.

One day the entire division was ordered into the field for a three day firing problem. We walked the seven miles to a place where the exercise was to begin on a road, and then we were spread out in battle formation as if we had just left our assault landing craft. We preceded inland firing at silhouette targets and blowing up mock enemy positions while Marine Corps Hellcat fighter planes flew support overhead. These planes would come screaming up from behind us and fire their 50 cal. machine guns at targets less than one hundred yards on the ground in front of us. The empty shell casings from the plane's guns would shower down on us and bounce off our helmets and shoulders

One aircraft's guns were fired too soon by a careless pilot, and a long burst of slugs tore up the ground a few feet off to my right and narrowly missed hitting one of the men, a PFC. The plane went off and made a circle in order to come around again. As it passed over the second time, to my surprise the PFC raised the muzzle of his BAR and fired upward into the plane's path. Apparently some of the slugs struck the plane as the battalion was called out the next day and we men were threatened that when the man responsible for the shooting was found, he would spend a term in Portsmouth Naval Prison.

The pilot wasn't injured and the man responsible was not identified. I don't think the Marine cared much about the threat. I think his attitude reflected the thinking of many of the men at the time. The men seemed to be getting more and more irritable as time went on and display of short tempers was a common occurrence. I know I was so afflicted as many of my friends so informed me.

In August, the division went out on another three-day exercise, and on the first day everything seemed to come to a halt. We were told to relax a while and wait for further orders. For about two hours we did nothing but sit in the hot sun and wait. Suddenly we were told to fall into formation. We began the long hike back to camp without any further explanation as to why the exercise had been called off.

Once in my tent, I stored my gear and walked over to the aid station where I met Nyle Weiler. He was very excited and said that we (Americans) had just dropped a large bomb that was the equivalent of twenty thousand pounds of TNT on Japan and that the war might be over very soon. The date was August 6, 1945.

About two hours later the men were told by the Top Sergeant of the company that the United States had dropped an atom bomb on the city of Hiroshima, Japan, and it was very possible that the end of the war was near. The camp was very quiet for the next two days and then it was announced that a second bomb had been dropped on August 9 on another city named Nagasaki. On August 14, we were told that the Japanese were going to surrender unconditionally.

The men of the 5th Division went wild as all training was suspended. The men went on a party for several days and consumed all the beer and hard liquor there was available. Men began to write home to loved ones saying that they would see them soon. Some of the men began to pack up their belongings in preparation to leaving Camp Tarawa for the trip back to the States. They were to be disappointed however, to find that the United States Government had further use for their services.

On August 27 we were ordered to pack up and then were rushed to the dock area in Hilo where we were combat loaded onto attack transports. We sailed on September 2 for Japan where we were to make an assault type landing on the southernmost island of Kyushu. It wasn't known whether the Japanese would fight or not when we landed, so we prepared to follow the plans laid out several months before for an assault landing on Kyushu Island.

On the same day we sailed, representatives from the Japanese government and the Allied powers met on board the Battleship Missouri in Tokyo Bay to sign the instrument of surrender, ending World War II.

CHAPTER FORTY-THREE

Sasebo

WHEN DAWN ARRIVED on 22 September 1945, the 5th Marine Division on board attack transports was within view of Kyushu Island, the southernmost island of the Japanese mainland. Above us the sky was heavily overcast, and the land in the distance was a dismal looking gray. The second battalion was on board the U.S.S. Karnes, an attack transport.

The ships in the convoy fell into a single column following several battle cruisers and destroyers. They didn't reduce speed as they ran in from the open sea through the narrow channels leading into the bay and toward the Sasebo Japanese Naval Base.

About two-dozen Japanese civilians standing on the end of one breakwater watched silently as we passed by. Some of the women wore kimonos and some wore other unfamiliar dress. None of them waved at us, none of us waved at them. Most of us still considered them the enemy.

As our ships cleared a point of land, the Sasebo Navy Base came into view, and we could see various large Japanese warships in near the water's edge. There were three aircraft carriers, two of which had their decks tilted sharply to starboard. Both ships had been torpedoed. Large holes had been torn in their sides and they had been run aground purposely and lay with their hulls resting on the mud bottom of the bay. The third carrier still was afloat but appeared so badly damaged by bombs and shellfire that it looked as if it were in danger of sinking. Farther away rested several submarines that seemed to have been damaged and now appeared abandoned.

We troops took our debarkation stations at the ship's rail and waited for the signal to go over the side into the landing craft that now cruised alongside. We were told that we would be the first American troops ashore on Kyushu Island and that we should be prepared to overcome any resistance the Japanese might offer.

As we got closer to the Navy base we could see row after row of Japanese aircraft parked on the concrete seaplane ramp that led from the hanger buildings down into the water of the bay. D Company was going to land on that sea plane ramp.

The U.S.S. Karnes was still underway when we received the word to go over the side of the ship and into the boats waiting below. Down the cargo nets we went and entered the LCVP's even while the ship was traveling along at five or six knots. Without delay we pulled away from the ship's side and turned toward the concrete landing ramp about a quarter of a mile away. I think that the transfer of troops into the small boats was one of the smoothest and quickest debarkation's our company had ever made. And I had been on every one of them.

`There was no talk among the men as we approached the shore but, I could feel the underlying excitement and tension that spread through the platoon. I did think that the curiosity of the strange land and its people replaced most of the fear that normally would have been there.

The platoon leader gave the hand sign for us to kneel on the deck of the boat. We waited a moment or two for the bump that would signal the boat's bow hitting the surface of the concrete ramp. When it did come, it was a surprise as it was just a gentle nudge. The ramp fell forward and down onto the float plane ramp that led up to the hangars. Running from the LCVP the 2nd platoon ran forward and spread out into a skirmish line formation. We paused as the Lieutenant commanded, "Fix bayonets!" We were on Japanese soil again, the first since Iwo Jima. The landing was so easy that my feet did not get wet in the small surf.

If there was ever to be Japanese resistance it would have started at this point in our landing and that bit of knowledge caused us to run quickly up the slight incline toward the hangers, which were about one hundred and fifty yards away. We ran past aircraft that had their propellers removed. This was good sign to us as this was what the Japanese had been directed to do prior to our arrival. Two of the aircraft had huge green crosses painted on their fuselage. These were the two planes that carried the Japanese surrender emissaries to Saipan earlier to discuss surrender plans with our military representatives there.

When our platoon reached the first hanger I saw the first Japanese soldier I had seen since Iwo Jima. He didn't look any different either, and I felt the anger rise throughout my body. Other men felt the same way apparently as they began to verbally abuse him. Some of the Marines wanted to stick him with his own bayonet. This was broken off sharply by an officer who commanded, "Knock it off. Take his rifle and send him home." The resentful but obviously frightened soldier didn't hesitate, but quickly left the area.

We searched through the buildings and found no other Japanese. The rain began to fall heavily, so we broke out our ponchos and wore them, carefully leaving our weapons exposed and at the ready in case we had to use them. Captain Fields organized the company into two columns and off we went slogging through the mud of the road leading toward the city of Sasebo about a mile away.

We climbed to the crest of a hill and then looked down at the city sprawled out below us. It had concrete streets lined by houses and stores. That somehow surprised me, because it was such a contrast to the mud roads I'd seen so far. While our officers made necessary decisions, we men squatted in the mud under our ponchos, which worked well enough to keep the water off of us.

The members of the platoon were positioned on the edge of a bluff that rose one hundred or more feet above the city streets. A dirt path, or rather a very muddy one just then, zig-zagged from a city street, up the steep hill to the muddy road we waited upon.

We watched the only person in view as she ascended the path in the pouring rain. She was an old woman, probably in her seventies, and she took one haltering step after another as she laboriously climbed. Her feet were covered with clumps of sticky mud and her old worn looking clothing was soaked through with the rain water. On her head she wore a cloth bandanna that was tied up under her chin and soaked through with rain water. The water then collected on top of her head and shoulders, then the dripping water soaked her dress. Across the back of her neck and shoulders she wore a heavy wood yoke from either end, suspending two full pails of water.

Although, I experienced some curiosity and felt some empathy for the old Jap woman, I could feel no sympathy for her. She was very bent over and struggled up the path to where we knelt. My comrades had ceased making derogatory comments about the old woman and had become silent, giving their full attention to her and her task. She never looked up at us until she took the last step that put her on the even ground of the muddy road. She stopped within arms length of me gasping for breath. She raised her head, and I could see her trying to focus her eyes on my face. A puzzled look came across her countenance as she didn't understand what she made of me. Then she looked at the other two hundred Marines crouched on the ground before her, all dressed in their battle clothing, wearing helmets and carrying their weapons of war and staring back at her.

It took several seconds for her to focus her eyes in on us and for it to register in her mind. Then, reacting with a wild shriek she threw off the yoke supporting the water buckets. They landed upset on the ground, spilling their contents and making a clattering noise as they bounced wildly down the hill. Turning her back on us the woman leaped outward and landed on the muddy path below, falling, slipping, sliding, shrieking, and falling again and again as she descended. She would rise to her feet only to fall again, always sliding downhill through the mud either head first, feet first and sometimes rolling over and over. She continued this wild, violent descent until she reached the street level below and then moaning and obviously exhausted, got to her feet and tottered toward the nearest house. During this entire episode I don't believe I heard one word uttered by my comrades as we watched her descent.

We heard voices down below where she disappeared, shouting and calling out in alarm, windows and doors were slammed shut, we could hear them being bolted, and we watched as curtains were pulled closed.

It wasn't long afterward that we received the order to move forward and descend to the street below. Fifteen minutes later we left the mud road and stepped onto a broad paved street that continued westerly. It was fronted on both sides by small houses and then changed to larger business type buildings as we went toward the center of town.

We could see no signs of life at this point. No Japanese could be seen watching from doors or windows of houses, there was only quiet. The Lieutenant briefed us saying that it was our job to go to the train depot and seize physical control of it. We were to overcome any resistance we met on the way or there. The platoon was split into two columns, each taking a side to the wide street with instructions to stay close to the walls of the buildings for cover.

I was the third man in the left hand column and we began walking slowly and cautiously along the sidewalk, close to the walls of the buildings. A young woman, wearing black pantaloons, blouse and sandals came out of a house door and stepped onto the sidewalk in front of the squad sergeant without seeing him or us. She walked along in front of him for a few yards, then suddenly stepped off the curb with one foot onto the pavement, stopped, spread her legs apart and urinated. The urine ran down her left leg and into the open gutter of the street. The young Marine in front of me couldn't control himself and yelled out in disgust at what he saw. Hearing him the woman turned, looked at us, gave out a scream and then shrieking loudly, ran wildly down the street away from us. We watched her until she disappeared into a side alley. Other citizens appeared in the street, craning their heads to look at us, and then they too ran and vanished from the street.

The Lieutenant ordered us to double time march and within three blocks farther on we found ourselves across the street from the entrance of the train depot's main entrance. In squad formation we ran across the street, up the front steps and pushed open the wide wood doors where we entered the large lobby. It was filled with Japanese civilians who only at first stood to stare at us in obvious fright. They gave me the impression that they did not understand what they saw.

The Lieutenant motioned a Marine and me toward a closed door. I pushed the door open with my foot and with our rifles held at the ready stepped into the doorway. We saw a room that was obviously a large common toilet area. There were about two dozen people inside squatting over small rectangular holes in the floor. Men, women and children were there side-by-side answering nature's call and the stench was terrible, so much it gagged me and I had to back away.

When the people inside realized that we were foreign soldiers displaying our weapons they seemed to go crazy like chickens in a pen being molested by coyotes. They screamed and ran here and there, clothing in disarray in a frantic attempt to escape, but my partner and I blocked the only doorway. On the opposite wall there were a series of windows all about five feet from the floor and they were open, for ventilation I suppose. They became jammed with the bodies of people trying to climb out . Several men and women had their trousers hanging from their ankles showing their bare rear ends as they scratched and kicked away at the smooth stucco wall with fingers and toes trying frantically to find a hold in order to pull themselves up to climb out the window.

The two of us backed away and I closed the door and gasped for a breath of fresh air. We turned to watch as most of the Japanese in the lobby backed quietly away from the other Marines, then turned and hurried through the doors leading into the street.

The civilians were ordered to leave the depot, to go outside in the street. One Japanese man, well dressed, in his late forties I would say remained. He glared at us with his fists clenched. A young Marine replacement faced him and hesitated, not knowing what to do. The Japanese obviously saw that weakness and raised his fists. I stepped forward and said to the Marine, "Don't let him get away with that. Stick him in the chest!" The man quickly looked at me; I could see a lot of hatred in his eyes. I believe that he understood English well enough to know what I had said. He planted his feet even more firmly, clenched his fists and glared at me.

I held my carbine at the ready and stepped forward to smash him in the face with my rifle butt, but before I could he 'wilted' and stepped backward holding his arms and elbows across his face to protect himself. Then he backed into a corner. Because of the way he had reacted I suspected that he had military training and I said to him, "You Jap son-of-a-bitch, I'm looking for an opportunity to kill one like you!" He quickly lowered his eyes, turned and hurried out the lobby door and went into the street. I turned toward the young Marine and said, "You let them get away with that 'crap' and they will begin doing it all over you!"

The Marine looked confused, embarrassed and didn't respond to my remark. I turned and became aware that the Lieutenant was close by and had watched the incident. His eyes and mouth were wide open and he appeared astounded at what he had seen. He too, was a replacement and I thought him a little unsure of himself, even if he was a nice guy.

From off to one side and back of me I heard some one laugh and I heard Sgt. Goodling yell out, "Atta boy, Doc, you're learning!"

The Lieutenant turned away to carry on with his duties. After a few moments only we 2nd Platoon members remained in the station house. The officer directed us to search the rest of the depot and parked trains for armed soldiers, but we found none. Much to the disappointment of some of us.

Once the initial landing force had come ashore and spread out across the naval base and immediate area, the rest of the division was landed in the dock area. From there units were sent hastily into the surrounding towns to seize control of transportation, water, and power facilities. Other units located coastal defense guns and arms and ammunition storage emplacements. The Sasebo area had many arms including huge coastal guns that were strategically placed on the higher elevations of the city, which could be used to fire on ships at sea, aircraft, or approaching foot soldiers. Our engineers quickly used their torches and put these guns out of commission.

Captain Fields brought the entire Company D back to the naval base where it had been reported that seventy-five Japanese soldiers carrying rifles had been seen. These soldiers as it turned out had been assigned to search for and destroy mines along the waterfront. One of our units intercepted the soldiers in the dock area and had them stack their weapons without incident. When that happened, we were fairly certain there wasn't going to be any organized resistance to our occupation.

Just as it became dark, the rain fell heavily. We still remained out in it and moved about in ankle deep mud as not many walk or street areas of the Navy base were paved. According to the terms of surrender, we troops were not permitted to occupy any building without the consent of the Japanese authorities. We thought that this was one 'hell of a way' for victors to be treated, and a lot of us made that complaint to any officers who would stand still long enough to hear us out. I think that the men's demands had some effect as we were told eventually to escape the rain and cold by entering a barracks building.

Inside the building we found things pretty dirty and dark too as there were no electric lights. We had brought ashore three K rations each and in the darkness we attempted to eat the last one of those. Then we settled down to await the morning. There were no bunks in the barrack; just some fiber sleeping mats that the Japs had used called *tatamis*. We had no rest by sleeping on those as during the night we found, to our dismay, that we were all infected with body lice that came from the mats.

The next day a supply of K-rations and some DDT insecticide were delivered to us and that helped our morale some. The 2nd Platoon was assigned to guard a portion of the dock area. That became a very boring job as we were restricted to the area and told not to leave it. Our headquarters became a Japanese naval base office. Since it rained most of the time, we were forced to stay inside except when on guard post.

After a few days we were allowed the freedom to go into the city and look about. At first when we walked into a shop to look around, the Japanese would all run out the back doors and hide. Others would step into the street and walk far around us to avoid a confrontation. About a week of this went on before the civilians began to trust us not to hurt them. Soon they began to act friendly toward us, especially the children who enjoyed Marines who gave them American candy and food from their rations.

We veterans of the Iwo Jima campaign did not fraternize as much with the Japanese civilians as did the newer men. I don't know why the Japanese treated us as well as they did for certainly many of them must have had relatives and friends killed by our troops in the Pacific Island battles.

Several of us walked along a side street which had been abandoned by the civilians who saw our approach, we heard a hissing noise that kept us looking for its source for minutes. One of the Marines saw a Japanese man peeking at us from around a building corner. Once the man got our attention, he smiled and signaled us to follow him. He led us to the gate of a small cottage that had a beautiful little flower garden in front and vegetables growing along the side and back. The man quickly ushered us into the house apparently not wanting his neighbors to see us there. Seeing him take off his shoes at the door we removed our boots, too, but I felt a little hesitant in doing so.

Inside he introduced himself, speaking perfect English. He brought his wife in and introduced her. He said that he had been an English teacher in one of the Japanese schools until the war started and then he was forbidden to teach that subject any longer. His speech was interesting to me as it was without any suggestion of slang and I was reminded of the Jap who, the first night on Iwo Jima, had approached Sgt. Goodling and me in the darkness and who had spoken the same kind of English.

This civilian and his wife asked us to sit and have tea and cookies. They were both very polite; even so, I wasn't very trusting. I sat down on the floor mat in front of a little table that was about a foot from the wooden floor, and I kept my carbine lying across my lap. The woman kept smiling the entire time we sipped the tea, but she also kept glancing nervously at the weapon.

The tea was served in cups with saucers. The saucers were hand painted and portrayed men and women in all forms of sexual activity. My two Marine comrades got all excited about this as they had never seen or heard of such a custom as painting such scenes on eating and drinking utensils. I was a little bit ahead of them there as I had grown up in an area that had many Japanese families in California and had visited in their homes and seen this type of decoration before. I explained to them that this was not considered pornography in Japan, but only art design. One of the Marines got so carried away that he insisted on trading several packs of cigarettes for one of the saucers and the Japanese couple went along with that, but were rather puzzled by the Marine's behavior.

The Japanese man didn't want us to leave but, apparently wanted to practice his speech on us. We had to leave though and thanked them for their kindness and left them what little food we carried with us.

Once, a barber motioned for us to come into his shop where he would shave us. One of the Marines accepted his invitation and sat down in the chair and the Jap barber began lathering him up with soap. Instead of putting the lather only on the cheeks and chin of the Marine he spread it all over his face including eyebrows, nose, ears, and forehead. Then the barber whipped out a straight razor and began stroking it on his leather-sharpening strap, and I could see that the Marine was becoming worried.

The other Marine and I began speculating on whether or not this barber had lost a close relative on Iwo Jima and was about to take revenge by cutting the first marine's throat. We told him though that if he did get his throat cut, we would get the Jap with our rifles. We could see that the Marine's throat and neck muscles were tightening up as he waited. Then the barber began working on him and after doing a clean shave of his face, went on and shaved around his ears, nose, and eyebrows. I declined the Jap barber's offer to be shaved. The Marine dug out of his pockets some Japanese money and gave it to the barber.

Incidentally, we were forbidden to take U.S. currency into Japan and had to surrender it on board ship. I kept a paper silver certificate dollar though and carried it while there, then brought it home with me. While sitting at a desk in the Japanese Navy office, I used a rubber stamp I found and marked this bill with it. I still have that bill today and keep it as a memento of the occupation. Once in Japan, we were issued Japanese yen with which to purchase needed items. As I remember it, one U.S. dollar was worth forty-four yen at the time.

The downtown area of Sasebo was a mess. Entire sections of the business and residential districts had been bombed. Many of the bombings had resulted because our B-29 bombers, having been turned away from industrial and military targets, had dumped their bomb loads on the city on their way back to the Marianas. The wreckage of the buildings still lay there and covered many dead bodies as was indicated by the horrible stench. I didn't like to go into those areas and stayed away especially after seeing a lot of rats running through the wreckage.

Two buildings that I saw interested me. One was an auto dealer's garage with a huge sign over the door that read, "Chevrolet." The other was a Catholic church which was in service and had been in use throughout the war.

There were many English street signs in the city and other signs in English that warned foreigners to stay away from certain areas which were of some military concern. One street sign that I read admonished the automobile driver to, "Please to toodle your horn when approaching," I wished that I had carried a camera over there to record such things.

While assigned to the wharf area of the base, we had some time to explore the many caves and warehouses. We soon had a lot of loot that we picked up and expected to take home. Captain Fields heard about it and made us turn it all in so we had to give up a lot of pistols, cameras, and binoculars among other good things.

We did uncover a large supply of Jap beer that they called 'beeru,' and I found it very tasty and not very alcoholic. We seemed to have an unlimited supply of that. We had sake too, that's Japanese wine. But, I didn't care for it.

We found a new motorcycle that was no doubt a copy of one of our Harley Davidson models in the U.S. We never could start the darned thing and that spoiled our idea of hauling the Lieutenant around camp while on his inspection tours. The men resorted to pushing it up a fairly steep street that led down a short distance and out onto a concrete pier. Some of the men began competing to see who could ride it the fastest as they coasted down the hill and onto the wharf. That suddenly came to a stop though when one of the corporals came down the hill and missed using the brakes properly; he and the motorcycle went flying off the end of the wharf into the cold waters of the bay. He surfaced and swam ashore somewhat battered and sore for his experience. The cycle is no doubt still at the bottom of the bay..

A wooden structure that served the company as its latrine, was built at the end of this concrete pier. The structure extended over the end so that the holes provided for the men were out over the water of the bay. Ten holes were cut in the wood platform to allow the men to sit side-by-side to perform their natural body functions. The entire structural affair was prevented from falling into the bay by several heavy wooded planks that extended from it onto the concrete slab of the pier for a distance. The inboard end was weighted down by heavy bags of sand that acted as a counterbalance and kept the structure from falling into the water.

There were times after dark when the holes were occupied by men doing their business when jokers would run out onto the pier and pull aside the bags of sand, in an attempt to allow the entire structure with its occupants to fall into the bay. The intended victims seeing their proposed fate would curse and shout as they tumbled off the structure and onto the flat surface of the pier while attempting to pull their trousers up. I thought the scene always hilarious except for the one time I was one of those proposed victims. I recall using this latrine on a cold and stormy day when the wind came whipping up through the holes. Some of the men would say that it was a 'hellava' thrill when it happened to them. I didn't think so when it happened to me.

CHAPTER FORTY-FOUR

Stateside

O NE DAY A British ship came into the harbor and anchored off the end of our wharf, about a half-mile away. A small boat was put into the water and it began to move toward us. To us the little craft looked ridiculous as it wasn't over twelve feet long but had a tall skinny cabin that resembled an outhouse. Only one person was on board, a naval officer dressed in whites who stood upright in the boat and maneuvered it by using a steering wheel.

The tide was out at the time so the water level was about seven or eight feet below the top level of the wharf. There were no steps or ladders for the British naval officer to climb up He began to plead to us for help in securing his boat and climb up onto the wharf. None of the Marines loafing on the wharf wanted to assist him and mostly ignored him. I felt sorry for the poor guy. I couldn't help but notice that his white uniform was very soiled and wrinkled.

My embarrassment got so great that I eventually got up from where I had been sitting and went over and caught the boat's painter that he had thrown up toward me. I tied the boat fast and then reached down and grabbed his hand and helped him up onto the wharf.

I led him to where the Lieutenant was quartered. I did not learn what the Englishman wanted and when I got back to the wharf, I asked the men of the platoon why they hadn't wanted to help the British officer. One answered "To hell with him, all we want is to go home!"

The food situation was pretty bad and the steady diet of K rations only helped to erode the battalion's morale further. We tried to supplement our food by using vegetables that were grown in the area by the Japanese, but that was dangerous as they used human excrement for fertilizer and that could cause some real intestinal problems.

The Division's medical officers denied us permission to eat anything other than that provided by the military. We did anyway as we thought that the food we were getting was insufficient in quality and quantity. There was a tomato patch next to our office building and the men couldn't ignore the red ripe fruit just lying there going to waste. I insisted that I alone would prepare the tomatoes before they were eaten and so I washed them first in my steel helmet with soapy water using a hand scrub brush that I carried in my pack. No one ever got sick fortunately. My platoon stayed in one location on guard duty for twenty-six days, and the only food we had to eat were K and C rations that were delivered to us each morning. It was as though the higher command had forgotten all about us.

Then one day the U.S. Army arrived. The 32nd Infantry division landed and came ashore to relieve us of our duties and the first equipment they brought was a field kitchen. They also brought in some engineers to make a mess hall. The building was constructed the same day the Army arrived, and that night the soldiers arrived on trucks. After they dismounted, they went into their mess, sat down, and had a hot meal. We sat not far away griping and eating our K rations.

Later that evening when it became dark and our guards continued their duty to monitor traffic, the Lieutenant and I pulled off a sealed five gallon can that was labeled food from one of the trucks. While we were doing that the truck driver was complaining to the guard up front about being stopped, saying, "You know, we fought on the same side of the war."

Once back inside of the building where we stayed, I opened the can and found that we had a five gallon can of dehydrated cabbage. I had never seen dehydrated food before. Some of the men said they thought it would be okay to eat, just put it in a helmet with water and hold it over a slow fire. One of the men scrubbed out his helmet and gave it to me to use. I built a fire in the kitchen area, put some clean water in the helmet and put in a handful of the cabbage. As the water simmered the cabbage began to swell, it finally got to the point where it overflowed the brim of the helmet. I'd take some of the cabbage out and throw it away and kept doing that until all I had in the helmet was just a smelly gooey mess and it stunk up the entire building.

No one wanted to even taste what was left, so with the help of one of the guys I pulled up some floorboards in the building and put the remainder of the cabbage, left in the five gallon can under the floor and replaced the floor boards. The Marine whose helmet I borrowed insisted that I clean out his helmet, and that ended my short disastrous career as platoon cook.

The next day it was announced that we were under the jurisdiction of the U.S. 6th Army and its commanding officer Lieutenant General Walter

Krueger. That night we were invited to eat in the soldier's mess and I had almost forgotten how real food tasted. Regardless of this new turn of events, irreparable damage had been done to the men's morale and dissension was still in the wind.

On October 19 we were told to pack up, and that since the Army had relieved us of our duties, we were going to be sent to the Palau Islands, which are near the Philippines where we were to guard Japanese prisoners of war. Many of the men of the 2nd Battalion became very upset when they heard this information and it was obvious that some sort of a rebellion was forthcoming.

Once on board ship a few angry men began to toss various items of deck equipment overboard and made statements aloud such as, "If we are going to have to guard Japs, there won't be many Japs to guard for very long." I was certainly in sympathy with the men's attitude and listened to their discussions on how we could work out our frustrations of the present situation and get revenge against the Japanese for our buddies who had been killed on Iwo Jima.

Alarmed, the battalion commander sent several smiling junior officers onto the deck where they mingled with the enlisted men. Speaking in low tones they tried to calm the men down. That didn't work at all as several ugly scenes between officers and enlisted men took place. The officers quickly retired from the deck.

It wasn't long before two trucks full of military police arrived on the wharf. Once off the trucks they formed a line up by the gangway. They were only made fun of and were taunted by the shipboard Marines. The officer in charge of the detail was "invited" to come on board first as it would be he who would be the first to be thrown overboard. He did not accept the invitation and the MP's stood on the pier for a short time going through a period of snapping to attention, at ease, and whatever the officer thought might impress the men on board with their strength.

That attempt was ridiculous as we had about a thousand fighting men on board and they numbered only about fifty. The military police officer began using a radio and after talking on it for while ordered his men back into the trucks. The contingent then left the wharf.

About another two hours passed before the troops were told by way of the ship' public address system to prepare to disembark as we were not going south or anywhere else to guard prisoners of war.

Trucks arrived on the wharf and we were all transported back to the Navy base where we were quartered in the Ainoura Japanese Naval Officers Training Academy. The only aftermath of the disturbance on board ship was that we were informed that the 2nd battalion would be disbanded and we were to be sent home.

Our living quarters at the Navy base were terrible. We were billeted in a three-story concrete barracks building that had very few windows left unbroken. Even though it was about the middle of November, there was no heat and we slept on the concrete floor with only one blanket wrapped around us. When it rained, the water splashed in through the broken windows and got us wet along with the floor.

The Japanese had latrines established on each floor level, but they were of the Asian kind where one would squat over a rectangular hole in the floor. After some time passed the excrement would be dipped out and carried away to be used as garden fertilizer. In the meantime the place would stink terribly. Our engineers came in and built temporary structures out in the street that had wooden seats in them and a pit under the ground to collect the waste. Periodically a Japanese using a horse pulling a large barrel type wagon would arrive, collect the excrement for use as fertilizer in their gardens.

The men, after hearing that they would in all probability be sent home, began to celebrate. We were given time to sight see in the area and take care of our personal needs such as washing our clothes to get rid of lice and other vermin.

One morning at roll call it was announced that a working detail of about forty men were to be dispatched to the area of Nagasaki. Seeing that there was no corpsman assigned and since I seemed to be on my own I volunteered to go. I volunteered again but it was worth doing because our trip included seeing the beautiful Japanese countryside. Arriving at our destination we were billeted in an office building outside of the city where we were told to 'stand by' and await further orders. It appeared the next day that the work detail had been canceled. Since it was a Sunday, several of us caught a ride in an Army truck, to the very edge of the city of Nagasaki where the second atom bomb had exploded.

We stood on a low hill and looked down into what was left of the city which was all gray and black rubble. We walked about a mile into the city before a U.S. Army Captain came along in a jeep and warned us that the city was still "hot" and that we shouldn't be there! We didn't know what he meant by "hot," but we turned around and left the area anyway. We were returned to Sasebo the next day without explanation.

While the battalion lay in limbo, all duties were held to a minimum and that gave us time to move about while we waited to see what was to happen next. Some of my buddies and I walked along the waterfront and inspected some damaged ships. I remember best the old battleship, the 15,000 ton Shikishima, that was tied up to a pier. It had been used to fight the Russians in the Russo-Japanese war of 1906.

The hull of the ship was made of steel, but the interior fittings and the deck were of wood. We clamored down into the ship's interior inspecting the various sections and officers quarters seeing only by the light of day that filtered in through port holes. We descended six or seven levels to the bottom deck where we found a metal safe and several of the men spent several hours breaking into it only to find some Japanese books inside. After inspecting them they tossed them aside. I wish I had kept them.

Near the old battleship was tied a modern warship, a destroyer. It seemed eerie to roam about its decks and interior and be the only persons on board. When we left some other Marines had come on board and were trying to figure out how to scuttle the ship just for the hell of it. Our group left hurriedly.

My friend, Nyle Weiler became very ill. He had a mental condition where he didn't seem to know what was happening around him. He would just stand and stare at walls, things and persons as if he didn't see them. The battalion surgeon refused to send Nyle away to the division hospital for examination, saying the division's commanding general was still 'raising hell' because of the number of men turning in to attend sick call. The doctor said for us to take turns walking Nyle around the grounds and try to get him interested in what was going on.

After a week of doing that Nyle's condition developed into a complete catatonic state. Only then did the battalion surgeon send him away for specialized attention. He was sent back to the United States to the U.S. Navy Hospital at San Leandro, California. He was there only two days before he hanged himself in one of the shower rooms. Nyle was a very sensitive person and had showed a lot of concern for those needing help. I know that he suffered a lot from his battle experiences on Iwo Jima, and I was very angered with how the battalion surgeon handled the matter.

More unrest grew among the men as they wondered why they weren't being sent home. The food was still pretty bad as it was mostly dehydrated potatoes and frozen pork chops or chicken. The chicken was bad as it was often spoiled around the bone areas, but still it was served to us.

When the day before Thanksgiving came, I heard a loud ruckus outside of our barracks and went out to see what was happening. At the rear of the building stood several large refrigerated trailers that were used to store food for the officer's mess. Some enlisted men had gathered and had opened the door of a trailer. One Marine sergeant was standing in the opening and was telling a gathering crowd of Marines that the trailer was full of frozen turkeys that were going to be served the next day to the officers while we, the enlisted men were going to get the usual spoiled chicken for our Thanksgiving Dinner. I could see that there was going to be trouble soon if the crowd of angry men didn't calm down.

A few higher NCO's came up and began talking in low tones to the men attempting to quiet things. I saw no officers or military policemen though. After a while the men did calm down a bit, but most just stood around and muttered complaints against what they considered to be an unfair situation. Thanksgiving dinner turned out to be better than we had expected. We got a piece of the frozen turkey along with some chicken. I suspected that the officers got the same fare.

About the first of December some of the older men who had been in the war from the beginning were detached and sent back to the States. Then as days passed, more and more men left. Things became much more disorganized, and I didn't like it. Every day men would pack up and disappear. Some left that I didn't know were leaving, as they were given only a few minutes notice. Apparently as ships prepared to leave Sasebo for the States, our men were being shoved on board to fill up any passenger space found before sailing.

The entire company had disintegrated and one morning I found that Captain Fields, Lt. Horvath, and even the "Old Top" had left Japan. Corpsman J.J. Vanere found me one day and told me to report to the division hospital to help out with the sick men there. The hospital was located in an old building that the Japs had used for a hospital too, and it was in a poor and dirty state.

Vanere assigned me to work in a skin disease ward with a Pharmacist Mate named Bean. I spent a week in that ward and on the first day the doctor who was assigned there came in about 0830. He obviously had been drinking. He looked around and told Bean and me to apply boric acid soaks to any affected skin areas of the sick men. When Bean asked him about a specific case where the patient had a bad skin infection, the doctor snapped at him, "Use penicillin. That's what it's for."

The doctor never returned to the ward. Each morning, after being certain he wouldn't come in, Bean and I would apply boric acid soaks to the men's affected skin areas. We even gave some of the men dosages of penicillin without proper authorization. I only saw the doctor one more time and that was near the end of the week. I was asked to come down to the front door of the little clapboard hospital and help carry a man upstairs to the surgery. The man was intoxicated and had fallen down the front stairs while in a drunken stupor and had broken his leg. The injured man was our ward doctor a Lt. Commander. I never saw him again.

The last day I worked at the hospital, corpsman J.J. Vanere assigned me to the venereal disease ward. There were only about four or five men in there being treated for gonorrhea. Mostly all they needed was an injection of penicillin three times a day. One man, for some reason, needed an intravenous injection of saline solution that the ward doctor had ordered in writing.

Who, the ward doctor was I didn't know. I had been there since early morning, and I hadn't seen him. I hung up the bottle of saline from a stand provided for that and had just gotten the needle into the man's arm vein when Vanere came into the room and said, "Hey are you doing that right? You're supposed to milk the tube back and draw blood into the tube to make sure you're in the vein."

Vanere grabbed the hose while I had hold of the needle. With his right thumb and forefinger he stretched the rubber hose and at the same time I let the needle go. The needle was jerked from the patient's arm and propelled through the air and up against a wall where it stuck in the wood. The Marine yelled, "Ouch!" and sat up in bed. I told Vanere that I had enough and that I was quitting and then I headed for the door.

The Marine said, "Me, too. I'm getting out of here!" and then he got out of bed and reached for his clothing. I went back to the old concrete barracks that I had been staying in and sat on the floor for most the rest of the day without seeing anyone from the hospital.

The next morning Vanere came into the building looking for me and said, "Hey, forget all that stuff that happened yesterday. Come over and help throw out all the drugs we have left into that little lake out in front. We're closing the hospital and we're going home."

I followed him hesitantly and found that the hospital had been ordered closed all right. Some of the equipment was being packed for shipment but most of the medicines and drugs were to be destroyed. We carried the hundreds of bottles of medicines and drugs out to a small clear lake that stood out in front of the hospital. After loosening the caps on the containers, we threw it all into the clear water from one side of a little bridge that spanned a narrow part of the lake. The water was cold and crystal clear and I had often walked out onto the bridge and watched fish swim about in the deep water.

One of the corpsmen, standing on the other side of the footbridge looking down into the water said, "Hey, you guys, there's some guy down there on the bottom who is just lying there and looking up at me!"

Sure enough there was a man down there, but he wasn't really looking at anything as we were pretty sure he was dead. He appeared to be a Negro and lay on the bottom of the lake on his back with his face pointed up toward us. I could see that his eyes were wide open. Not one of us wanted to go into the cold water to retrieve the body, so we all stood there, leaning on the rail and speculating on who would eventually pull the body out. Finally one of the Negro stewards from the officer's mess happened along and looked down into the water to see what it was that we were interested in. He exclaimed, "Why that's Ol' Charlie down there. He got himself drunk last night on the officer's whiskey and went off by himself".

After a while a young "Gung Ho" Marine came along and announced that he had been a lifeguard back in the States and that pulling the dead man out of the water would be easy. The rest of us quickly convinced him that he must be very courageous and that he should be the one to dive in and bring the dead man to the surface. He stripped down to his shorts and dove into the very cold water and dragged the body up to the shore. I guess we forced him into doing what he did as he did not want to lose face. Regardless, he did a very courageous thing and received the admiration of us all that stood there.

Two curious junior officers, attracted by the activity came to look and got involved and so took charge of the situation. They had the body carried off to wherever it was that they took dead bodies. Those of us who were there surmised that the dead man had gotten drunk on whiskey that he had taken from officer's mess and had walked out onto the little foot bridge and had fallen off a portion of it where there was no handrail. Regardless of what happened to him, no formal investigation was ever carried out in the matter that I knew of.

Two days later those of us remaining at the division headquarters were ordered to pack up and we were taken to the dock area where we boarded ships for the return trip to the United States. The weather was getting cold, and some snow had already fallen, and I was ready to leave that country. I had enough of uncertainty, confusion, disease, and boredom.

The boredom factor did create one positive thing though. While spending the long days sitting about the Japanese naval base office in September and October, I sat at one of the office desks and wrote notes on what I remembered happening during the battle of Iwo Jima. I kept those notes I had made, some written on Japanese stationery through the years and used them in the formulation of this chronicle of my wartime experiences.

Our ships left Japan before the middle of December, 1945, and while in the middle of a snowstorm; we traveled the long miles of the northern pacific route. On the way I celebrated my twentieth birthday. We arrived at San Diego during the last few days of December. It was raining very hard when we docked at a concrete pier at the foot of Broadway Street. The area was almost deserted except for some civilians who stood in the rain to greet a few of the men as they disembarked.

If we expected bands to be playing and speeches to being made, we were to be disappointed. There was only quiet cold winter rain to greet us as we left the ship and climbed into waiting trucks to be carried to Camp Pendleton.

The truck I rode in stopped at the intersection with the Great Pacific Highway to wait for a traffic signal light to change. The rain water flooded street near us, and a sailor wearing a white uniform was caught in the drenching rain and he paused to wait for us to move out of his way. His uniform was soaking and he was standing in water that rose above his shoe tops. One of my Marine companions, sitting next to me called out to him, "Hey Swabbie, where's your boat?"

None of us laughed at the remark... not even the Marine who uttered it. It didn't seem a bit humorous anymore. I suppose it didn't really matter that we were not greeted when we arrived in port. We had gone to war and we won. Now, we were going home.

Richard E. Overton

O, now that the battles are over,
I'll tell you what we won:
A chance to fight in some other war,
And the pride in a job well done.

The heroes who died aren't remembered.
The wounded we try to forget,
And we poor damn sinners who came out as winners
Are blamed for the national debt.

The Krauts soon got richer than we are,
The Japs found gold in their sun,
But this we can say to our last dying day:
They sent us to war and we won.

So bless 'em all, bless 'em all, bless 'em all,
The long and the short and the tall,
There will be no promotion this side of the ocean,
I still say, my lads bless 'em all!

Sloan Wilson
"Pacific Interlude"

Iwo Jima: The Second Time

O<small>N</small> 14 M<small>ARCH</small> 2000 I returned to the island of Iwo Jima. This time there was no death, no anguish, no deafening noises of battle, nor the acrid odor of burnt gunpowder. Joan and I were included in a group of veterans and other persons interested in seeing the island of such historical fame.

The tour was organized and led by Retired Marine Colonel Warren Weidhan. On 9 March we stayed overnight at the Airport Hilton Hotel in Los Angeles.

At a meeting there the Colonel informed us what we should expect to experience on our trip. Also present was Retired Lieutenant General William Snowden, formerly of the 4th Marine Division who traveled with us. He told us of the political problems encountered in arranging this visit to Iwo Jima and admonished us to avoid any conflict with the Japanese on this trip as they are not very enthusiastic about our coming back, if only to visit.

We departed the Los Angeles airport on 10 March on board a Continental Airways DC 10 and stopped at Honolulu, where we transferred to a similar jetliner for a six-hour flight to Guam. There we registered at the Outrigger Hotel, which is located on the beach at Tumon Bay, on the west side of the island. It was of special interest to me that this is the same beach I went ashore on in March 1945 while being sent to a U. S. Army Field Hospital. There were no buildings standing there then as there are now. The beach today is lined with multi-story hotel buildings and other businesses which cater mostly to Japanese tourists.

An interesting incident happened during a social hour at the hotel. A veteran of the Iwo Jima battle approached me. He claimed that I had saved his life during the combat 55 years before, saying that as he and other members of his squad charged forward, he had been struck down by bullets from a Japanese machine gun. Wounded and helpless he lay on the ground where he was exposed to further enemy fire. He described how I had run forward, picked him up and carried him to safety. He identified himself as Jay Kerr of Dallas, Texas. I could not recall that specific incident or him. Wounds caused by fragments and bullets were common on Iwo and I had treated very many similar cases under circumstances he described.

Jay mentioned that he had been a friend of PFC Paul Rush who was killed on Iwo Jima and asked if I had known him. He said that during the years since the war, Paul's sister, Bonnie had wondered about the circumstances surrounding her brother's death. I knew Paul Rush, and described to him the events leading up to his death. A week after the tour's end I received a letter from Bonnie Rush Moulton thanking me for filling in the missing details of her brother's death. We traded correspondence again after that initial letter.

On the second day of the tour our group explored the island of Guam. The first stop was the 3rd Marine Division's landing site, located at Asan Beach where that Marine unit landed in June 1944, to liberate the island from the Japanese who had taken it from us forcibly in 1942. We listened to a battlefield commentary and memorial ceremony and watched as General Snowden placed a wreath on the monument decorating the site. We also visited the War in the Pacific Museum located on that same beach.

On 14 March with approximately 24 veterans of the Iwo Jima Campaign on board a Continental-Micronesia chartered flight we left Guam bound for Iwo Jima. The other 100 passengers consisted of spouses, widows, sons, daughters, and grandchildren of Iwo Jima Marines, along with a few historians and history buffs. We landed on Iwo Jima at mid morning. Before landing our passports were collected for Japanese Immigration inspection. They were returned later stamped "Iuo Jima" (Iwo Jima) Japan.

The United States returned the island of Iwo Jima to Japan in April, 1968 with the provision that the U. S. would have access to it for limited use as a weather station and be able to commemorate there the 1945 assault landing. It is still equipped with an airstrip, a U.S. Navy built hangar and living quarters for the personnel who service the airfield.

When we disembarked I shook hands with the first woman U. S. Marine Corps General I ever met. She was the first person to welcome us and was one of about one hundred U.S. Marines who had been flown to Iwo Jima three days previously from Okinawa to greet us and take care of our needs for the day.

After the initial greeting we were directed toward the hangar building and were astonished when we saw the rest of the command formed up into two welcoming lines facing the other and standing at attention in salute to us. We all filed through this impressive formation without a dry eye among us as we were unprepared for the unexpected emotional experience of the greeting.

We entered the hangar building where we were joined a moment later by those same Marines and enjoyed engaging in a pleasant social hour with them. These young service people were respectful, attentive and I was very impressed and proud of them.

Eventually, we were taken by Marine Corps transports to the landing beach site, on the eastern side of the island. An American and Japanese joint monument stands there today commemorating the battle. A very impressive memorial program was held. It was referred to as the, '55th Anniversary of Iwo Jima Reunion of Honor.'

The U. S. Marine Corps Band from Okinawa was flown to the island for the day. A color guard consisting of both American and Japanese service men walking side-by-side, shoulder to shoulder carrying their respective country's flags seemed very strange to me.

Once the colors were posted, speeches were made by General Snowden, a Mr. Saisu, representing the Japanese Government and a Japanese priest as well as a few other Japanese dignitaries. Three wreaths were laid on the monument, two Japanese and one American.

After the ceremony we were invited to meet with a small number of Japanese war veterans of the Iwo Jima battle who had traveled from Japan to attend the ceremony. General Snowden earlier had made a suggestion that it might be proper to shake hands with them as it was time to heal the wounds of the battle and of the war. Listening to his remarks it entered my mind that perhaps I should do that, it may very well be the right thing to do!

I approached one of these men, but a U.S. Marine veteran inadvertently stepped in front of me, took the Japanese veteran by the hand, and shook it. The Japanese allowed the handshake, but refused to make eye contact with the ex-Marine, looking away for the entire few seconds. I saw, or imagined I saw bitterness show in the Japanese's eyes. I stopped, turned away from him and thought, "The hell with this nonsense, I haven't forgotten either!"

We saw only one Japanese military duty person on the island. He was an enlisted man stationed near the hangar. We did see several Japanese officers and enlisted men who were involved in the ceremony; however they disappeared as soon as the program concluded. The Japanese military maintained a very low profile while we were there, I suspect to avoid any unpleasant incident.

In the water off Mt. Suribachi's eastern slope, about where I watched the

U.S.S. Tennessee lay fifty-five years ago, blasting away at concrete bunkers, a modern looking U. S. warship circled in the water. Accompanying that was another sleek looking, but smaller landing craft.

It was a ship to shore boat very capable of ferrying trucks and other heavy equipment onto the beach. The larger ship had delivered six, five-ton transport trucks to Iwo Jima from Okinawa for our use. The secondary purpose of the craft that day was to perform a burial at sea ceremony for an American veteran of the battle of years ago.

After the ceremony we were taken by truck to the top of Mt. Suribachi. There are two monuments up there. One is American, where the American flag was raised on 23 February 1945 and is memorialized in history by the famous photograph taken at that time. The other monument is Japanese, commemorating that country's defense of the island

From this mountaintop can be seen our assault landing beach below as one looks northward. Standing near our memorial on this day, I know now how our assault troops appeared to the Japanese defenders fifty-five years ago, as they directed their machine guns and mortars to fire at us. The view from there is what I had imagined it to be all these years.

After spending an hour on the top of Mt. Suribachi, Joan and I walked down the mountain road looking for familiar sites from those many years ago. However, the island is covered now with high thick green brush making this difficult to do. I could recall certain areas and especially the slightly elevated piece of ground where Sgt. Goodling and I survived the several bayonet attacks during the first night. The small dirt road that was at our back is still there and maintained. I located one of the small concrete bunkers that had confronted the 2nd platoon during our advance in 1945. We had bypassed it then leaving it to be destroyed by one of our demolition teams later. Only a single crumbling wall remains now among a heavy thicket of brush. I stood on a piece of broken concrete to view the area and placed my hand on the concrete wall to steady myself. I felt an object under my fingers and found it to be a corroded expended rifle cartridge and magazine clip, caught in a small crack. Both pieces of metal were affixed to the concrete by crystallization. I'm certain it has been there the entire fifty-five years.

From there we walked to the beach where the 2nd Battalion, 26th Marines had landed during the assault. We were on the exact location where I had treated so many of the injured and saw so many men die. Of interest yet is the wreckage of the amphibious landing craft I saw burning off to my right during our landing in 1945. It is half buried in the sand now, but even so, easily identified by the rusting sprockets that guided the tracks. Its position made identification of our landing location a positive.

We spent an hour on the beach, collecting sand and talking with other veterans who had also been in on the assault landing those many years ago. We all agreed that the beach was wider now and that the sand bluffs that had confronted us were not as high now as then. That isn't surprising because when I passed over the beach when leaving the island in 1945, I saw our heavy equipment being used to rearrange the earth, in order to bring ashore thousands of tons of supplies.

A Marine Corps truck arrived and picked up Joan, me and a dozen others who wanted to travel the island's western side. From that small narrow road I could look down at the beach where Sgt. Goodling and I had taken shelter from the machine gunner by taking cover in back of the overturned Japanese Army truck. The beach is safe now. There is no truck, no smashed galvanized roofed building, no machine guns... only clean black shiny sand which is washed constantly by the incessant wave action.

We rode north, up the slight grade to higher ground and although the brush is six to eight feet high I could still identify the areas where Company D spent the second, third and fourth days and nights of the battle.

As we continued on, the road leveled off, we passed over ground where the 2nd battalion had suffered many casualties on 22 February 1945 during the assault on the numerous bunkers of the 'Cross Island Defense' system.

PFC's Paul Pugh, Paul Rush, Tony Lozano and Cpl's Robert Reibling and Howard Corbett, along with Lt. Jack Jon. Lt John Noe and others, were struck down here in one sudden barrage of artillery and mortar shells. Today, the island's brush growth is very dense and high making it difficult to locate our exact positions during the battle.

I remember well the area west of Airfield #2 where in 1945 I looked back at Mt. Suribachi and saw what I thought was a white cloth fluttering up on top. I called it to Lt. Horvath's attention and commented that perhaps the Japanese had surrendered! He examined the mountain top through his binoculars, then replied that, "That is an American flag flying up there!" A pronouncement that bolstered our morale immensely.

On our far right the bluffs lining Airfield #2 began. Pharmacist Mates George Hall and Burke Pace collapsed there, Lt. Richard Lewis was shot in the stomach, Lt John Noe fell when his jaw was shattered by shrapnel.

PFC Robert Kastan was shot through the head while lying shoulder to shoulder with me, PFC Bill Powers died after being shot through the body. And after giving us the order to withdraw, Lt. Aloysius Fennel fell shot in the head. He died the next day. It was the same area and day that PFC Raymond Hower was struck in the head by shrapnel and died immediately while lying beside me. Cpl. Wilson and Sgt. Abromavich died on the little ridge in front of us while Cpl. Roy Tinnemeyer suffered hand grenade and bullet wounds. This is the same area that Jay Kerr says fifty-five years later that he was shot down by machine gun fire and that I picked him up and carried him to safety

I did have one desire, that is to remember and locate an exact spot, one where I have a faint recollection of burying the body of a Marine. I did so at the time with the help of another Marine. We had been told to do so by directive earlier if we were forced to withdraw. Apparently, the Japanese had been mutilating the bodies of our dead after we withdrew. My memory is too frail, the brush too thick and the ground still very mutilated from those days of war to accomplish finding the exact location. That dead Marine is no doubt one of the men reported missing during the action. He will have to spend eternity with the many other unknown dead who remain on the island.

We were told, with good authority that there are still some 12,000 Japanese soldiers unaccounted for on the island. It is thought that most of them are underground, buried in tunnels and caves. The Japanese still have teams of workers attempting to locate and identify these bodies, even after fifty-five years. We were told that they have objected to our heavy aircraft landing on the airstrip as many of the undiscovered tunnels and caves are under the runway and are in danger of collapsing.

My first impression of the island during this trip was that it is smaller than I remembered. Its surface is covered at present with a dark green cover of brush that reaches to eight feet in height. Close scrutiny of the ground beneath the brush reveals that its surface is still marred by the action of the battle. Still visible are the outlines of foxholes, tank traps, shell craters and the broken remnants of concrete bunkers. Time, helped by wind and rain has worn down the jagged edges of such things, but then they are only the scars of what once was.

If I were to pause, close my eyes and listen, as General Snowden suggested we might, and I dared not do, I might hear again the sounds of the battle and smell the odor of burning gunpowder. As I viewed the island it came to my mind the similarity between what I viewed there and the state of my own mind. The damage to both is still there, but is now hidden by scars or by a facade, which only give the impression of being healed.

Before coming back to Iwo Jima I wanted to see all those locations where the heavy action I had been involved in had taken place. After spending a few hours on the island I found I did not want to do that any longer, I hoped the affair was over and done with. Now, I'm willing to allow the ghosts still present there, to occupy the island for themselves... to the end of time.

Richard E. Overton
Mar 31, 2000

Epilogue

THE 5TH MARINE Division arrived at Camp Pendleton, California in late December 1945 and was disbanded. Many service men and women who served during the war years did so at the convenience of the government. Now it was time for the government to return them back to civilian status; a monumental task and one that was not to be done overnight. The Marines were sent off to separation centers near their homes. We Navy corpsmen were sent to Camp Elliott near San Diego for processing back to the Navy. On December 31, 1945, I was released at Camp Elliott, to begin a thirty day "overseas leave."

On February 1, 1946, as ordered, I reported for out-processing to the U.S. Navy Separation Center at Camp Shoemaker, in Pleasanton, California. On April 10, 1946, I was given an Honorable Discharge from the United States Navy. I was twenty years and four months old.

In retrospect I don't believe a man can ever forget the time he spent serving with the United States Marines. Even today when I hear the Marine Corps Hymn, I close my eyes, but I do not envision Marines dressed in their beautiful blue uniforms standing at parade. Instead, I see a band of hardy young men in field formation, their faces firmly set as they trudge their way across the dusty expanse, dressed in loose, worn, green battle fatigues with baggy, dirt stained knees, collars and sleeve cuffs lined with grime and sweat, pants legs flapping round the tops of their rough dusty field shoes. I see the helmets proudly fixed straight on their heads, the chinstraps striking softly the sides of their faces. Their rifles are slung and I listen to the metallic muffled rhythmical sound as the stocks beat gently against a canvas covered canteen, and the creaking and rustle of canvas rubbing against canvas.

Writing this manuscript caused me to reflect again on the wonderful Marine comrades I served with in the Fleet Marine Force during 1943, 1944, 1945. I feel very humbled and honored to have been associated with them. Combat veterans such as Tom Fields, Charles Horvath, Frank Caldwell, Charles Goodling, Russ Renner, Robert Neef, Earl Brock, Bert Faltyn, Paul Pugh, Billy Eller, Jay Kerr, Don Giles, and Roy Johnson come to mind quickly. There are very many more.

For those men the descriptive words, brave, valorous, loyal, resolute, daring, are all appropriate. But to a World War II Marine, the highest compliment I could pay them is taken in part from a Marine song of those days, "Edson's Raiders,"

"A finer band of real Marines,
There never has been seen,
Oh, the 'Raggedy Assed Marines' are on Parade!"

They are all certain to pass on to the world of the legendry one day!

Richard Eugene Overton

Photograph / Illustration Credits

Pave v: Iwo Jima map courtesy National Archive
Pave x: Photo Courtesy Richard E. Overton
Page 62: Illustration by Richard E. Overton
Page 95: Illustration by Richard E. Overton
Page 112: Illustration by Richard E. Overton
Page 145: Illustration by Richard E. Overton
Page 152: National Archive photo - 127-GW-316-111730
Page 154: National Archive photo - 124-GW-341-109135
Page 159: Illustration by Richard E. Overton
Page 170: National Archive photo - 127-GW-350-110955
Page 171: National Archive photo - 127-GW-350-110130
Page 173: National Archive photo - NA
Page 179: National Archive photo - 127-GW-294-110919
Page 185: National Archive photo - 127-GW-294-11xxx
Page 189: National Archive photo -127-GW-306-111245
Page 191: National Archive photo -127-GW-313-1196X
Page 203: National Archive photo - 127-GW-316-1426
Page 212 National Archive photo - 127-GW-335-110606
Page 214: Illustration By Richard E. Overton
Page 218: Illustration By Richard E. Overton
Page 227: National Archive photo -127-GW-313-142161
Page 229: National Archive photo -127-GW-313- 114785
Page 232: National Archive photo -124-GW-331-110156
Page 237: Illustration By Richard E. Overton
Page 253: Illustration By Richard E. Overton
Page 256: National Archive photo -124-GW-331-110159
Page 276: National Archive photo -124-GW-331-113648
Page 284: National Archive photo -127-GW-304-110374
Page 289: Illustration By Richard E. Overton
Page 291: National Archive photo - 127-GW-317-111379
Page 294: National Archive photo - 127-GW-312-113737
Page 295: National Archive photo - 127-GW-313-109777
Page 302: National Archive photo - 127-GW-306-112855
Page 306: Illustration By Richard E. Overton
Page 315: National Archive photo - 127-GW-323-110333
Page 316: National Archive photo - 124-GW-331-113332
Page 319: Illustration By Richard E. Overton
Page 324: Illustration By Richard E. Overton
Page 329: Illustration By Richard E. Overton
Page 332: National Archive photo - 127-GW-314-142674
Page 340: National Archive photo - 127-GW-313-111798
Page 344: National Archive photo - 127-GW-312-111528

Index

Printed in the United States
122375LV00004B/463-465/A